HOME OR AWAY

The Great War and the Irish Revolution

HOME OR AWAY

The Great War and the Irish Revolution

KEVIN JOHNSTON ∿

Gill & Macmillan

Gill & Macmillan Ltd
Hume Avenue, Park West, Dublin 12
with associated companies throughout the world
www.gillmacmillan.ie

© Kevin Johnston 2010
978 07171 4732 8

Index compiled by Helen Litton
Typography design by Make Communication
Print origination by Carole Lynch
Printed in the UK by MPG Books Ltd, Cornwall

This book is typeset in Linotype Minion and
Neue Helvetica.

A CIP catalogue record for this book is available
from the British Library.

5 4 3 2 1

To my daughter Helen

ARMISTICE DAY, 2009

Today we are revising history in stone,
Remembering our young dead, left unmarked before.
In grey Glasnevin cemetery, we now atone.

Let us their lives recall, their dignity restore,
No more their deaths disown, lives sacrificed; no shame
Remembering our young dead, left unmarked before.

Once hidden graves now visibly preserve their name,
Great War men, honoured, like our patriots revered
No more their deaths disown, lives sacrificed; no shame

If for a different cause their lives they volunteered.
Attending silently, these dumb headstones acclaim
Great War men, honoured, like our patriots revered

They gave their lives for what some thought just cause, not
    fame.
We mark our common wealth of wasted lives, mute men
Attending silently, these dumb headstones acclaim

The cost of war; that what was lost is lost again.
Today we are revising history in stone,
We mark our common wealth of wasted lives, mute men
In grey Glasnevin cemetery, we now atone.

ORLA PARKINSON

CONTENTS

Chapter 1 ∽

TO ARMS

It is much easier to make a declaration of war than it is to get ready to fight one. This is particularly true if your nation does not maintain a very large standing army and that army has to maintain a presence in every continent in the world, with the honourable exception of Antarctica. This was the situation confronting Great Britain in August 1914. A few short weeks before, the Cabinet had been concentrating its attention on Ireland, where there was every possibility of a civil war breaking out. Now it found itself sucked into a continental war—by virtue of an eighty-year-old treaty, under which it guaranteed the neutrality of Belgium—that looked as if it would involve every major power in Europe. This was completely unexplored territory. The last European war of this scale had ended almost one hundred years earlier, at the Battle of Waterloo. Britain had, of course, fought wars throughout the nineteenth century, but even the bloodiest of these had been relatively small-scale and far away from home. The most recent of these had been the Boer War, and it was from the middle-ranking and senior officers who had fought this war that the generals and field marshals of the coming conflict would have to be chosen.

The relatively small size of the army, about 250,000, of whom about 30,000 were Irish, resulted to a large extent from the way the Royal Navy guarded its traditional position as the Senior Service, a technicality which resulted from the fact that Edward the Confessor had established a navy under his direct control at a time when the army was composed of levies brought to the royal standard under the feudal aristocracy. This primacy lasted through the wars of Marlborough and Wellington and can be summed up by the fact that there is a day celebrated as Trafalgar Day and that Trafalgar is also the name of the best-known square in London, while the defining battle of the

Napoleonic Wars, Waterloo, is commemorated in a railway station. The navy took the lion's share of defence spending and saw itself as the guarantor of Britain's safety. The job of the army, as the Admiralty saw it, was to garrison the empire and guard the navy's shore bases.

When Sir Edward Grey, Britain's Foreign Minister, spoke to the House of Commons on 3 August 1914, the day before Britain declared war, he spelt out the immediate war aims of the government: the protection of the north coast of France; the preservation of Belgian neutrality; the maintenance of the balance of power, since a German victory, he maintained, would be detrimental to Britain's interests. In order to fulfil the last condition, Britain would have to ensure that France was not utterly beaten in any war with Germany. How to carry out these aims was a question not fully explored yet. It was the instinct of most Liberal members of Parliament to restrict foreign commitments as much as possible. They would have supported the Admiralty's approach to war: blockade Germany as tightly as possible so as to neutralise her merchant navy, bombard German coastal towns and sell arms only to the French, Belgians and Russians. Even within the Cabinet, this was probably the majority view. Only the Prime Minister, Asquith; the Lord Chancellor, Haldane, who had been Secretary of State for War in 1905; the First Lord of the Admiralty, Churchill; and the Chancellor of the Exchequer, Lloyd George, knew anything different. They were aware that talks had been going on between the staffs of the British and French armies about the possibility of a British Expeditionary Force being sent to support the French army. France had enough troops to face Germany across their common border, but there was always the possibility that the Germans would violate Belgian neutrality and try to get round the French flank. It was here that the British would intervene and, considering how closely matched the combatants were, the six or so divisions of the Expeditionary Force might be just enough to tip the balance in France's favour.

It had been only within the previous ten years that the structures had been put in place that would allow the army to fight a modern war. To understand this, it is necessary to look at the organisation of the British army.

The basic unit in the army is the infantry battalion, consisting of about one thousand soldiers, commanded by a lieutenant colonel. A number of battalions are grouped together to form a brigade, commanded, appropriately enough, by a brigadier. At the beginning of the Great War, there were normally four battalions in a brigade, making a total complement of four thousand, plus brigade staff. Brigades in turn were organised into divisions, three brigades to a division. In addition, the division would have supporting cavalry and artillery. The whole was commanded by a major general. At higher levels, divisions could be organised into army corps, commanded by a lieutenant general, and a group of corps would form an army, commanded by a full general. It was the British army's intention to send six infantry divisions and one cavalry division to France as support for the French in the event of war with Germany.

Another innovation which helped to smooth the transition to war was the War Book. This listed in detail the steps necessary for mobilisation, what to do about counter-espionage and the guarding of key points and what to do about trade with enemy states. Draft Orders-in-Council were typeset, ready for immediate printing when the need arose. There was even a draft of the Parliamentary legislation that would be necessary in the event of war. In 1910, the War Book was modified so that its main emphasis was on creating a force that could be deployed in Europe and setting in place a mobilisation scheme that would get the troops there. The railways in England were central to this and the government had taken steps to ensure the smooth transport of troops to the ports. A Railway Executive Committee had been set up whose function it would be to manage the railways if war broke out. On the French side of the channel detailed planning had also taken place. The French would supply the British force with rations for four days, until they got themselves organised. Transport would be arranged, as would storage for munitions, use of airfields and communications. To minimise the possibility of misunderstandings, there would also be liaison officers provided to each staff down to brigade level.

For all that, the British army was still very different from its continental equivalents. Both France and Germany had taken to heart Napoleon's dictum that victory went to the big battalions. Both countries had universal conscription and both required a long period of service in the reserve. In addition, a great deal of prestige was attached to army service. As a result, both countries could put enormous armies in the field. Britain could not. Her army had been maintained largely as a colonial police force and it was only after the Boer War had shown up glaring deficiencies that the reorganisation mentioned above was put in place. While that was happening, Britain's part-time soldiers—yeomanry, militia and volunteers—were reorganised as the Territorial Force. This totalled fourteen brigades of cavalry and fourteen divisions of infantry. Although the territorials had part-time training, it was recognised that they would not be fully prepared for war until they had had six months of full-time training.

The other source of manpower that could be called on in time of war was the Army Reserve. In August 1914 this numbered 145,000 and was supported by the Special Reserve, which had another 64,000 men. The Army Reserve itself was divided into three sections. Section A Reserve was made up of men who had completed the full-time service within the last two years. These men undertook to re-enlist in an emergency, even if the emergency did not require full mobilisation. They had to attend twelve training days per year. For this they were paid seven shillings per week, a substantial bonus to a labourer's wage. A man could serve on the Section A Reserve for no more than two years. Most soldiers joined the Section B Reserve, typically for a period of five years after they had left the army. Here they could only be called up in the event of a general mobilisation. They still had to do twelve training days per year, but were paid only half of what the others got: three shillings and sixpence a week. This was still enough to cause envy in Sean O'Casey, who laboured on the railways with several reservists, and was jealous of the pints of porter that the extra money could buy.[1] When someone had finished his Section B Reserve, he could enlist in the Section D Reserve for another four years. Since terms and conditions were the same, this was an attractive proposition when times were hard.

There was also a Special Reserve of part-time soldiers. In Ireland, where the Territorial Forces had not been established, this was the only form of part-time soldiering. Reservists undertook six months' full-time training to begin with and then had three or four weeks' training thereafter. A soldier signed on for six years, which could be extended for another four, but service could not be extended beyond the age of forty, or forty-two if the soldier had done time with the regulars. Almost all infantry regiments had a 3rd (Reserve) Battalion as well as their two regular battalions, and there was a core of regular officers and other ranks to administer it. In 1914 there were 101 reserve battalions.

When reservists were mobilised, they were first used to bring the front-line battalions up to strength. Those left over when that was done were assigned to reserve battalions. Roughly thirty thousand Irish reservists reported to the colours.

In the very early morning of 3 August, Asquith gave the authorisation required to mobilise the army. The orders did not reach the War Office till noon. By this time Asquith was aware that Germany had invaded Luxembourg and had sent the Belgians an ultimatum demanding free passage through their country for the German army. This was rejected by King Albert. When Asquith was sure of this, around midday on 4 August, he sent an ultimatum to the German government, demanding that it respect Belgian neutrality.

Germany invaded Belgium on 4 August, led by a cavalry corps which crossed the border about seventy miles east of Brussels. Behind them, the leading elements of three separate German armies, First, Second and Third, were dismounting from trains at frontier stations where the platforms had been specially lengthened and broadened to make this day possible. The first major obstacle was the complex of twelve forts around Liège. These refused to surrender, which gave the German artillery the opportunity to demonstrate the advances that had been made in munitions since the Franco-Prussian War. Krupp-manufactured siege howitzers which fired shells 402 mm in diameter reduced the forts to rubble. The Belgian army was forced to retire towards Antwerp as German units invaded their country. Many civilians were killed; it is probably true that most of this killing was accidental, but it is also true that some shooting was deliberate. Young soldiers, frightened by stories of snipers, shot first and didn't bother about questions. Unit commanders also used terror tactics to try to break a level of resistance that they hadn't expected. There were enough atrocities for Western propaganda to build on and to persuade the populations of Britain and Ireland that the Germans were an enemy worthy of hate.

From 11 p.m. on the day of the invasion, Britain was at war with Germany. The provisions of the War Book ensured that things progressed smoothly. Reservists started filling up barracks. Since most units of the regular army were not up to strength, these reserves were assigned to regular battalions and would comprise 60 per cent of the soldiers sent to France.[2] Railway schedules were scrapped so that special trains would be available for the army. Within the first few days, the Admiralty took control of 250 merchant ships, so that troops could be moved around the globe. Buildings and motor vehicles were requisitioned and up to 150,000 horses seized, without any regard for farmers who needed to save harvests or cabbies whose horses were their sole way of earning a living.

The French were not immediately concerned about the move into Belgium. Their calculations seemed to show that there would not be enough troops available to the Germans to do this unless they weakened their centre in Alsace and Lorraine. This would suit General Joffre very nicely, since it was against this centre that he intended to attack. The French advanced in good order, anxious to retrieve their lost provinces, and forced the German centre to give ground. The town of Sarrebourg was taken on 18 August. The French infantry was suffering terrible casualties, however. They were carrying out frontal assaults on ground that was not suitable. The men wore blue overcoats and bright red trousers, and were an easy target for German machine-guns. The Germans used aircraft to direct artillery fire on the French units, which were torn to pieces. All this while the German First, Second and Third armies were swinging round in a right hook that would encircle the French centre.

On 20 August, Crown Prince Rupprecht switched over to the attack. The future President de Gaulle was a captain at the time. He wrote of the shock of being on the receiving end of a modern offensive. Firstly, fire became more concentrated, then more intense. The crack of bullets and the thunder of shells grew louder by the second. Those who were still intact lay as flat on the ground as possible, as if trying to sink into it, while around them the dead lay twisted and the wounded howled in agony. Because of the French tradition of calm under fire, some officers were killed because they refused to lie down. In other units, soldiers fixed their bayonets and bugles sounded the charge, but to no avail. Before the end of August, Joffre had lost 212,000 men. Especially hard hit were his regular officers, nearly 40 per cent of whom were now casualties. Only General Foch seemed able to hold his ground.

On the left flank of the French line, General Lanrezac was concerned that there were large concentrations of German troops moving to the north of him. He wanted permission to turn his Fifth army round to face the threat, but Joffre told him there was no need. It was no consolation to Lanrezac that he was proved right when on 22 August his left flank was attacked by the German First and Second Armies. His forces took a lot of casualties and on the 23rd he was forced to fall back. His safety now depended on the British Expeditionary Force, which was taking position on his left flank.

As we have seen above, the British Expeditionary Force (BEF) was at the centre of British planning for any war between Germany and France. Units had been assigned, commanders had been designated and a travel plan made out that was so detailed that it even included time set aside for the troops to have coffee while they changed trains. The trouble is that the man who was now in charge of the army had had no input into the preparation of the plan. Kitchener was the most famous soldier that the British had. Although he had made his name in colonial wars, he carried a charisma that would encourage the nation, make it feel safer that he was in the team. He had been on his way back to Egypt on 3 August when he was (more or less) hauled off the Dover train and told that he was needed. Asquith thought that the best post to give him was the War Office, and he found himself overseeing the frantic preparations necessary to move so many men across to France. It did not help that he found many of the most important desks at the War Office empty, since the officers assigned to them had got themselves reassigned to the BEF.

In command of the BEF was Field Marshall Sir John French, a hero of the Boer War. In making his decisions he would be helped by his staff. His Chief of Staff, like most of the generals at this stage of the war, had also served in South Africa, where he had received a stomach wound which continued to give him trouble. He was Sir Archibald Murray, who was considered by most who worked for him as charming, but rather ineffectual. With him was Sir Henry Wilson, who was a much more enthusiastic and more motivating person. He had been responsible for most of the arrangements made with the French before the war, having started talks with the French Staff on his own initiative while he was still only a brigadier. There had been a while during the previous months when it looked as if Wilson, who had been born in Longford, had blotted his copybook by his very obvious support of the Ulster Volunteer Force and the British army 'mutineers' at the Curragh. At the time he had been Director of Military Operations, and had passed Cabinet secrets to the Opposition. He might have had expectations of being French's Chief of Staff, otherwise. As it was, it was felt that he had to be included, since he was the man who was thought to know Joffre's mind. Given Murray's poor health, he did most of the work, anyway. Loyalty to superiors was not one of his qualities and he worked hard at displacing Murray while at the same time feeding Sir John French's resentment of Kitchener. The final general on the staff was Sir William Robinson, known as Wully. He had risen through the ranks, and still affected a cockney accent. He was responsible for supplies.

There were four divisions of fighting troops, divided into two corps. The man who commanded I Corps was the very wealthy Sir Douglas Haig, whose family owned the famous whisky firm. He had served as Sir John's Chief of Staff in the Cavalry Brigade during the Boer War. There was a rumour among the army's senior ranks that Sir John, at a moment of pecuniary crisis, had borrowed money from Haig, his junior. This was not what one was supposed to do. Sir John, who was not a great staff officer himself, thought a lot of Haig; not simply for his money, but for his organisational ability. Haig could translate French's aspirations into good army prose. Haig thought French was completely unfit for the job he had to do. French had been very close to King Edward, and they shared a love for life and a delight in female company. King George v was a much more serious-minded individual, however, and the dour nature of Haig, a lowland Scot, was much more to his taste. To cement matters, Haig's wife was a lady-in-waiting to Queen Mary. He was close enough to the King to be able to express his doubts about French before the campaign even began.

The commander of II Corps was a very different character. Sir James Grierson joked that he had won his medals for his dash with a knife and fork. He was so florid that his closest officers had been shown by a doctor how to bleed him if he suffered an apoplexy. It was actually a heart attack that killed him on the train even before he reached the concentration area, let alone the front. This resulted in the first contretemps between French and his new chief, Kitchener. Sir John wanted Sir Herbert Plumer as a replacement; Kitchener gave him Sir Horace Smith-Dorrien, the most senior general in the army. Kitchener may have felt that Smith-Dorrien was more likely to stand up to French if the necessity arose. The two had already crossed swords, meta-phorically, on the best use of cavalry. The new corps commander had a reputation for indulging himself in fits of rage; and French, undoubtedly, felt that a problem had been foisted on to him.

The written orders which Kitchener gave French before he left England on 14 August were those of a politician. The BEF was to support and cooperate with the French against the common enemy. The greatest care was to be taken in avoiding 'wastage'—casualties. This meant that the field marshal had to think very carefully before committing British troops in an exposed position. Finally, he reminded the field marshal that the BEF was an independent command, not under the orders of any Allied general. Later that day, Sir John dined in Paris, confident of success. He wrote in his diary of silly reports of French reverses. Over the next couple of days he visited forward areas and spoke with General Lanrezac. It was not a happy meeting. Although the English field marshal had lived in Paris, his French was painful, and communication was hampered. He asked Lanrezac, in his halting French, whether he thought that the Germans intended to cross the Meuse at Huy. Lanrezac did not even try to lessen his scorn by speaking English. 'No,' he said to his interpreter. 'Tell the marshal that I think the Germans have gone to the Meuse to fish!'

Although Kitchener was the most famous soldier that the British had, his post as Secretary of State for War put him in an awkward position. He had to act as a civilian and, as such, could only give general instructions on strategy to the BEF. He tried to fudge the issue by wearing his field marshal's uniform every time he went to France, but an issue arose straight away. In the plan which Wilson had put together, the assembly area for the force was to be Maubeuge, near the Belgian border. Kitchener distrusted this for two reasons. The first was that, being so close to the frontier, there was little scope to adjust to the enemy's attack. The second was that, being so far forward, the BEF was likely to be attacked while enemy troops were still relatively fresh and the British would be forced back. A retreat, Kitchener maintained, was a bad way to start a war. For both these reasons, he favoured Amiens as an assembly point. From here there would be time to make an educated guess of the German intentions, and the initial momentum of the German attack would be used up before the British brought them to battle. He passed on this advice, which Field Marshal French duly ignored. Joffre actually sent an emissary to Kitchener saying that he needed the BEF to cover the upper Sambre as soon as possible. Faced with this, the Secretary for War stopped nagging.

What Kitchener could do was alter the size of the BEF. Both he and

Haig were concerned about putting all their eggs in one basket. There needed to be adequate troops for home defence as well as a cadre of experienced officers and NCOs to train the new armies that they had in mind. Kitchener cut the size of the force from six infantry divisions to four. There would also be a single cavalry division. The movement of this force was a triumph of logistics. The advance troops were embarking at Southampton by Sunday 9 August. Almost a thousand special trains came into the city's railway station on a single day. In eight days 81,000 men and 30,000 horses had been moved to France, though not all through Southampton; Folkestone, Newhaven and, further away, Bristol, Liverpool and Dublin were also used. On Sunday the 16th alone there was a record of 137,000 crossings, with naval patrols guarding the flanks against interference from German warships.

The 1st Battalion of the Irish Guards completed their mobilisation on 8 August. The next day, Sunday, church parade was to Westminster Cathedral, where they heard Cardinal Bourne preach. On Wednesday they made their way to Nine Elms Station, where two trains were waiting to take them to Southampton. It was hot and still at the harbour, where they embarked on ss *Novara*. It took until 4 p.m. to complete the work and another three hours before *Novara* was clear of the harbour. They landed in Le Havre at 6 a.m. on Thursday morning and had to wait in a shed with a tin roof, enduring the heat, before they were marched to Rest Camp No. 2, on a hill above the town. They were welcomed by pretty girls and offered bowls of drink against the heat of the day. Friday was a free morning and many took advantage to bathe in the sea. The battalion later paraded to the railway station where, at 11 a.m., they began an odyssey that continued its slow progress until they dismounted in the hot darkness of Saturday night and bivouacked on a farm near the railway. On Sunday morning they went into billets in the whitewashed houses of the village of Vadencourt. Here the primary task was to see that all had received their inoculations. This operation lasted three days, and its after-effects some days more, so the men were grateful that they did not have to begin their march towards the front till Thursday the 20th. By Saturday the 22nd they had reached La Longueville, near Maubeuge. That evening they heard the sound of gunfire for the first time.

2nd Battalion Royal Irish Rifles was based in Tidworth, near Salisbury, when the order to mobilise had come. There had been some tension within the battalion during the Ulster Crisis of that summer. The Regimental Depot was in Belfast and, when the commanding officer, Lieutenant Colonel Bird, ordered his officers to be prepared to fight the UVF, one of his captains, Bowen-Colthurst, attacked him verbally and told him that he, Bowen-Colthurst, would not obey the order. The matter was reported to the War Office, but there was no court martial and the order was withdrawn.[3] There was a severe strain between the two men which was not resolved in the strains of battle.

Their order to mobilise was given in the early evening of 4 August and was completed by the 9th. Within this time they managed to get all their inoculations completed. Reserves flocked into the barracks, from all walks of life, some in the garb of tramps while others wore suits and bowler hats. Soon they all wore uniform and had collected their field kits and looked not at all out of place. On the 13th they began their transfer to France, moving in two parties. The first travelled by train to Southampton, where they boarded the hastily converted cattle boat, ss *Ennisfallen*, lately from Cork. The ship sailed at 8 p.m. and arrived in Rouen at 7:30 the following morning. The second party had started an hour after the first and sailed straight to Rouen, arriving in Rouen at 6 p.m. Both parties met at the Rest Camp at Mont St Aignan, where they stayed till the 15th, enduring a terrible thunderstorm that reduced the camp to a quagmire. On the 16th the battalion was moved forward by train and spent the night bivouacked in a large foundry. The next day they concentrated with the other units of 7th Infantry Brigade in the village of Marbaix. It was decided that discipline had slackened, perhaps by the combination of travel and the number of 'old soldiers' who had rejoined. Kit and iron rations had to be paraded at reveille, and this was followed by washing and water-filling parades.

The final move forward began on the morning of 19 August. That night was spent in an orchard, before a short march took them to Avesnes. At 1:30 a.m. on Friday the 21st they received orders to join up with the rest of the brigade and march via Maubeuge to Feignies, where they would be assigned fresh billets. They were on the road at 4:45 a.m. and had reached Feignies by 3:30 p.m., having marched about 17 miles. Even then they had to wait till 8 p.m. before their dinner was ready.[4]

Other battalions came from Ireland itself. 2nd Leinsters were in barracks in Fermoy when the despatch came. Some thought at first that it was notification of a move against the UVF, but were not disturbed to think they were fighting Germany, even given the huge disparity in the two armies. They were confident that, as a fully professional, regular army, they were a match for any bunch of conscripts. There was great enthusiasm among the local populations. Though they left in the early morning, there was a good crowd in Cork City to see them off and cheer them on their way. A draft of the Royal Irish Regiment in Clonmel was escorted to the station by the local unit of the National Volunteers. It was not only the Irish battalions that were given a rousing send-off. The East Surreys had been in Dublin for two years. Given the unpleasant duty of enforcing the lock-out of 1913, they had brought with them from London a sympathy for the urban poor, and there were complaints on at least one occasion that they had not been rigorous enough in guarding a coal convoy, with the result that some women had been able to 'scatter the coals'. They got a rousing send-off.

Trains brought the troops as far forward as possible. Some were luckier than others; their trains stopped further east. All, however, when they had gathered themselves together after descending from the train, had a long way to march. It would have been interesting to watch each infantry battalion as it marched forward. At its head rode its commanding officer, in smart khaki tunic, cord breeches and high, brown field-boots. Since there had been no wars since South Africa, and promotion in a peace-time army depended on dead men's shoes, he was probably well into middle age. He had proved himself in the veldt, but perhaps he worried whether he would be up to this new challenge. For now, his headquarters rode with him, and he depended on its support. His adjutant, a captain, was beside him. Theoretically, his second in command, a major, was supposed to ride in the dusty rear of the column, discouraging stragglers, but, when the battalion was not in contact with an enemy, he was usually at his colonel's side, clearing his lungs with a pipe and having a chat.

Immediately behind this little group came the pioneers, ready to clear any obstruction that threatened to block the way. The Corps of Drums and Fifes came next, ready to strike up a tune to put heart into the men. Also here were the buglers, whose calls acted as a Tannoy system, conveying the co's orders to his men.

After this came the rifle companies. At the head of the leading company was the regimental sergeant major, a figure of real power within the battalion. In some regiments it was a tradition that junior subalterns addressed him as Sir. Each of the four rifles companies had an establishment of six officers and 221 men, though not all were up to strength. Each company had a major in command, with a captain as his deputy. The company was divided into four platoons, each with a sergeant and forty-six men. A subaltern—a lieutenant or second lieutenant—commanded each platoon. The platoon in turn was divided into sections of ten men, each led by a corporal. The remaining men formed a small headquarters section.

The organisation of companies was a recent innovation, new to many of the reservists, who had served at a time when the battalion was divided into eight smaller companies. It is probable that many of them discussed the changes as they marched along in their four ranks. There were soon other things that caught their attention, like breathing. More than half of the men marching east that August were reservists. No matter how well they had kept themselves in shape—and not all had— they were nowhere near the level of fitness of the regulars, who had completed their summer manoeuvres the previous month. Most battalions permitted the men to march at ease, with their collars undone and their rifles slung. They were allowed to smoke pipes but not, theoretically, cigarettes; this prohibition did not last beyond the first day. The roads were paved with four-inch-square granite blocks, set half an inch apart. It was a recipe for blisters and even some of the regulars found the going difficult. By the end of the fifteen miles or so of a day's march, many of the reservists were straggling far behind, even behind the odds and sods who came at the rear of the column: the medical officer and his stretcher-bearer/bandsmen; signallers trans- porting semaphore flags, heliographs, field telephones and miles of cables; the battalion's two Maxim machine-guns on their two-wheeled wagons; five ammunition carts carrying about 100,000 rounds; and, finally, the quartermaster, with wagons of supplies and cookers and water carts.

A large part of the soldiers' problem was the weight that they had to carry. Hanging from their shoulders they had ten ammunition pouches, each with ten rounds of ammunition. Another twenty rounds were carried in a knapsack on the left hip, while an enamel water bottle was carried on the right hip. A trenching tool hung from the bottom of the spine. In the middle of the back was the pack, carrying the soldier's spare clothes as well as the odd treat. So far, this totalled about

80 pounds. It was no wonder that many developed sores on their shoulders. Then there was the rifle which weighed nearly nine more pounds, and the bayonet which went with it.

The rifle was the *raison d'être* of the infantryman. Rather than the mass volley of the continental army, the British believed in the effectiveness of rapid, aimed fire. The rifleman was expected to be able to fire fifteen aimed shots per minute. His pay depended on his accuracy. This was tested annually, when he fired a course of 250 rounds. Part of this was the mad minute when he had to put fifteen shots into a two-foot circle at a range of 300 yards. He got a bonus if he was classified first class or marksman.

By 20 August all preparations were complete. To the east of the main body were the cavalry, patrolling the ground in front of the BEF, searching for contact with the enemy. The headquarters of I Corps was at Wassigny, just south of the Belgian border, on the west bank of the l'Oise. The II Corps headquarters was at Landrecies, almost due north, on the southern tip of the great Forest of Mormal. The infantry was ready to move east against the Germans. Now they marched towards the town of Mons. Often they sang as they marched; the song most of the survivors remembered was 'Tipperary'. It took three days before they made contact with the enemy.

Before that there was some excitement. Major Tom Bridges of C Squadron 4th (Royal Irish) Dragoon Guards had been in Belgium a couple of years previously, one of a group trying to persuade the Belgians to agree to a secret alliance. The mission had not ended well. The Belgian Chief of Staff had told the party that he would fire on British forces if they came to Belgium's aid without being invited. Bridges himself had no interest in politics, so he did not take it personally. The morning of 22 August found him on the main road between Mons and Brussels, on outpost duty. He had two of his troops in ambush positions beside the road. The other two were placed behind the crest on a ridge overlooking the road. At about 7 a.m. a small patrol of German cavalry appeared, led by an officer who was calmly smoking a cigar. Something must have made them suspicious, because they turned around some distance from the ambush. Bridges shouted to his second in command, Captain Hornby, to chase them. The troops on the hill needed no urging and 1st Troop galloped down the road, with 4th Troop following on their hooves. The Irish caught up at the village of Casteau and there was a brief skirmish, with one German wounded and others captured. The surviving Germans fell back on the rest of their troop, who were dismounted at the other end of the village. As 4th Troop arrived Hornby sent them into action on foot. A German officer who was trying to regroup his men was shot down and, after a brief fire-fight, the rest took to their horses and fled. The dragoons followed and, mounted on good Irish stock, soon caught up. The Germans were at a severe disadvantage, since their lances were useless at close quarters against the specially designed British cavalry sword. In the running fight, several Germans were killed and five captured. The rest managed to reach their own lines. Hornby, since his horses were blown, decided to call it a day and retired with his trophies.

2nd Royal Irish Regiment was part of 8 Brigade, which in turn was part of 3rd Division and ii Corps. The division was defending a salient formed by an angle of the Canal du Centre to the north of Mons and its suburb of Nimy. The 8 Brigade was on the right of the salient, with 9 Brigade on the left and 7 Brigade in reserve. Brigadier Doran, GOC of 8 Brigade, deployed his line facing east, 2nd Royal Scots and 1st Gordons on the right, while on the left, guarding a bridge which led to the village of Oburg, was 4th Middlesex. Just south of the bridge was the large wood of Bois d'Havre. 2nd Royal Irish was in brigade reserve. When, on the morning of 23 August, two divisions of German infantry began to attack this line, Irish hopes for a quiet breakfast were interrupted and they were ordered forward to support the Middlesex. Unfortunately, there was a gap in the line between 4th Middlesex and 9 Brigade, on their left. Just when 2nd Royal Irish had settled down to dinner they were ordered back to their original positions to cover this. German artillery observers spotted them and called in shell fire, so the move was a dangerous one, across ground that offered no real cover. It was completed by 1:30 p.m. The Irish deployed in companies and dug rifle pits where there was no other cover.

The Germans crossed the canal from Oburg and attacked the two battalions head on. At first they attacked in mass formation, but the momentum of each attack was blunted by accurate rifle fire. The Germans then came forward in open order, the full weight of ix Corps against this small, exposed section of the line. At one time, German cavalry appeared out of the wood, 600 yards away. The two Irish machine-guns brought devastation to man and horse. The Irish also began to take serious casualties, as accurate shell fire burst among them. Both machine-guns were hit but the gunners were able to salvage enough parts to make one working gun. The lull in firing had allowed the Germans to move forward, however, and by 3:15 p.m. they had worked round both sides of the Irishmen, threatening to cut them off. Casualties were mounting up: A Company had lost several of its officers and was being commanded by the sergeant major and the senior NCOs. The battalion's adjutant was wounded as he tried to organise a fall-back line, but was able to carry on. Wounded were being evacuated to a civilian hospital in Mons. When it came under shell fire, the wounded were moved down into the cellar. The medical officer remained with them until the Germans overran the position.

Another company which had got into trouble was D Company. In the thick of the action it had got separated from the rest of the battalion. Its commander moved it towards the Gordons, on his right, trying to keep a concentration of forces. At this stage a section of field guns from the Royal Artillery tried to support the hard-pressed infantry. All the fury of the German guns was turned on it and it was forced to retire. By this time, threatened with encirclement, the survivors of the Royal Irish and the Middlesex were also retiring towards the wood of Bois la Haut. On the edge of the trees, the Irish held the line, while the Middlesex passed through and retired to the second position. By the time the Irish were ready to follow, the Germans had blocked the road. The field gun section was also caught here and was dug in at a crossroads. For a while it looked as if it was going to be an early end of the war for the battalion. There was someone there to help them, however.

Reveille for the 2nd Battalion of the Royal Irish Rifles had been at 2 a.m. that day. They had expected to move out at 4 a.m., but this was delayed till 7 a.m. They were constantly on the move, deploying on the road from time to time. A squadron of the 15th Hussars and some riderless horses passed along the road, the first solemn sights of war. The battalion was moved forward to reinforce the Royal Scots on high ground near Harmignies station. They started digging trenches on the very right of the British line. C and D Companies were in the firing line, with A and B Companies in reserve along the Givry to Mons road. After a while these companies were moved to trenches along the road, extending the defensive line. D Company had to fill a gap between two companies of the Royal Scots and was separated from the others. The rest of 3rd Division was withdrawing to a defensive line south of Mons, and the Rifles had lost touch with the rest of their own brigade. At 3:45 p.m. they came under fire from German artillery.

They could see German infantry coming forward under cover of the shelling. When the German bugles sounded the charge, British officers blew their whistles and the men stood ready to fire. Each man had the rifle sling taut around his left arm. There was a bullet in the chamber and a magazine holding ten more. The mad minute begins. The index finger squeezes the trigger, then moves to pull back the bolt. As the spent cartridge is ejected from the chamber, the hand starts to move forward again. This time the ball of the thumb catches the bolt, pushes it forward and closes it. The index finger is already on the trigger and, because the tight grip on the sling keeps the rifle on target, the next shot is on its way. He keeps a count of each bullet and knows when his magazine is empty. He opens the bolt and, without taking his eye off the target, reloads with two clips of five rounds each. He pushes the bolt forward and, as the clip is thrown out, the next round is pushed into the chamber. Firing like this into a massed target, no bullet could miss, and many bullets claimed multiple victims. The Germans they were killing were the ones who had originally been attacking the Royal Irish from the east and this eased the pressure enough to allow the other battalion to withdraw.

By 9 p.m., Brigadier Doran ordered his brigade to withdraw to Nouvelles. At about 10 p.m. he met the Royal Irish and told them that it was imperative that they link up with the Gordons. He led two companies to try to make the link, but wasn't able to do so, though they did meet when the battalion started to withdraw in a south-westerly direction. D Company of the Royal Irish also rejoined with the Gordons. By 11 p.m., the brigadier had moved his brigade back to Nouvelles, where they were not so exposed. The Royal Irish had suffered 300 casualties.

Meanwhile, the Germans were attacking all along the line. Once again they started in perfect formation, hoping to break the British line by sheer weight of numbers. The German shelling stopped, allowing the British line to use rapid fire once more. Under the weight of bullets the line of advancing grey staggered, wilted and began to wither away. As it was growing dark, the survivors retreated into the gloom. Cease-fire was called along the British line to allow the Germans to attend their wounded. Late into the night the Irishmen watched lanterns move around the battlefield. Most of the watchers were exhausted not simply from the movement over the battlefield, but from the sheer intensity of the fight. Their ears rang from the metallic crack of the rifle fire and their shoulders were bruised by the recoil of their rifles. They had held their line, ii Corps had held the line, and they were quietly confident as they awaited the morning.

Things were not going so well elsewhere, however. The French 5th Army had been forced to retreat—General Lanrezac neglected to tell Sir John French of this—and now the BEF were left without anyone to guard their right flank. It was not till late in the evening that the field marshal became aware of this and decided that his only option was to retire. He ordered the two forward brigades of 3rd Division to withdraw through 7 Brigade's position. When that was completed, 7 Brigade retired through 4 Guards Brigade.

The 2nd Connaught Rangers, part of Haig's 1 Corps, had watched the action of 23 August from their trenches on a ridge about one and a half miles south of Mons and had enjoyed the spectacle. The different German shells exploded in different ways. The shells of the howitzers, filled with high explosive, produced huge columns of black smoke. The German field guns were firing shrapnel. These shells burst in the air, in a puff of white smoke, belying the deadliness of the scraps of metal cutting into any unprotected soldiers within range. They were delighted when the grey masses of German infantry were driven back by a thin line of British soldiers.

In the morning the Rangers were told that there was going to be a general retirement and that they were to act as rear guard. From their vantage point they watched the other units move to the rear. Some of the officers noticed that the two battalions that had been most seriously engaged the previous day, the Middlesex and the Royal Irish, marched away 'as if they were on parade'. At about 11 in the morning, shells began falling on the ridge, and the Rangers had to endure them for an hour before it was their turn to retire, one of the last units to leave the field. As they fell back, company by company, German shrapnel followed their progress. Fortunately, the fuses were set wrongly and the shells exploded too high in the air to do serious damage. A couple of heavy shells fell among the battalion's transport, destroying some water carriers and mess-wagons. The position of rear guard was now taken up by 4 Guards Brigade, part of which was 1st Irish Guards.

The 4th Royal Irish Dragoon Guards were in action again that day. A battalion each of the Cheshire Regiment and the Norfolk Regiment were holding a line near the hamlet of Elouges. They were on a low ridge, Norfolks to the right, Cheshires to the left, facing north-west, with a clear field of fire over cornfields. 119th Battery of the Royal Artillery and L Battery of the Royal Horse Artillery took up position just behind them. Two German divisions were approaching. The one facing the Cheshires came on, while some of its units started to work round the flank. The other division detached some of its artillery, which took up position to the front of the British line. This second division then started to advance on Elouges, on the right flank of the Norfolks. General Fergusson had originally told the two commanding officers that they must hold the line. He then told Lieutenant Colonel Ballard of the Norfolks that he was to act as a flank guard, and gave him instructions on how to withdraw. Unfortunately, the message did not reach Lieutenant Colonel Bolger of the Cheshires. He told his men that they were to hang on till the end. The two British battalions now faced annihilation, protected only by their artillery. General Fergusson sent to the Cavalry Division, under General Allenby, for help. Allenby in turn gathered the Dragoons and told them that they were to attack the Germans with the 9th Lancers on their right. The two cavalry battalions now advanced with drawn sword, the Dragoons to the west of a lane which ran towards the Germans, the Lancers. Going at a hard canter to begin with, the horses began to feel the excitement and started to gallop. The squadrons began to lose shape as the horses went faster, so fast that the German gunners could not fit their fuses quickly enough and the shrapnel burst high and behind the horsemen. The German infantry were in poor positions to fire, and the cavalry suffered fewer casualties than might be expected. They lost heavily, all the same, and never gained contact with the enemy, did not bloody a sword except for a few German scouts who got caught up in the mêlée. It was wire that stopped them, rather than fire, a twelve foot high barbed wire fence between them and the Germans. They were forced to their right and the slaughter intensified as they crossed in front of the guns like driven rabbits. Many horses were brought down and some soldiers were captured. The survivors rallied near some trees beside a light railway that ran to the east of the field before withdrawing. On the way they passed 119th Battery, where the men were taking their guns out of action; there was no hope of getting them away without the cavalry's help, since it was impossible to bring the artillery horses forward.

This 1914 version of the Charge of the Light Brigade had made little impression on the enemy, but at least it delayed the attack on the two infantry battalions on the ridge. Ballard calculated the 5th Division should have had adequate time to get clear and prepared his Norfolks to retire. He sent two different messengers to the Cheshires to let them know his intention. He got no confirmation that Bolger of the Cheshires had got the message, but heard from stragglers that the Cheshires had retired with the cavalry. This was not true. When, at about 4 p.m., Bolger set out to find his opposite number, he found his way blocked by German infantry who had taken over the Norfolks' position. His right flank was also under attack so he decided to order a general withdrawal. Unfortunately he was seriously wounded and his adjutant was killed before the order could be passed along. Two companies of the Cheshires and a platoon of Norfolks who had got themselves lost tried to retire in an orderly manner, but they were soon overwhelmed and most of the men killed or captured. A and B Companies mounted a bayonet charge to try to relieve the pressure, but most of the charging men were shot down. The Cheshires fought on till 6:30, when their officer commanding gave the order to cease fire and surrendered. As far as the Cheshires were concerned, the charge of the Dragoons had been gallant, but in vain.

It was Sir John French's intention to fall back far enough to be able to regroup his Expeditionary Force. In his path was the great waste of the Forest of Mormal. He decided that the two corps would split, with one each side of the forest. Haig took his I Corps to the east, while Smith-Dorrien went to the west of the forest. This was potentially the more dangerous side, since II Corps was moving with an exposed flank. To protect II Corps from a surprise attack, most of the cavalry division was used to provide a screen. In the event, it was to be I Corps that had to endure a number of surprise attacks during the retreat from Mons— it was no longer being thought of as a retirement.

On 26 August, the Rangers were acting as 5 Brigade rearguard. One company was escorting the brigade's transport. Once clear of the village of Grand-Fayt, and having rested for a while, the officer commanding ordered a retirement, intending to continue covering the transport. A second company of the Rangers went into Grand-Fayt to arrange with brigade headquarters, thought to be there, the allocation of billets; they were also to prepare the defence of the village. They found no head-quarters and, after enduring some shelling in the afternoon, this officer commanding also gave the order to retire. The other two companies of the battalion, under Lieutenant Colonel Abercrombie, had taken up station on a ridge to the north of the village. From here he sent a message to brigade headquarters, giving his location and stating that he would retire from his position at 3 p.m. unless he heard orders to the contrary. For some reason, he was still there at 3:15, when a passing patrol of French cavalry told him that there was a strong enemy force, equipped with machine-guns, quite close. Abercrombie took two platoons with him and went to investigate the report. When he came under fire from artillery and machine-guns, he ordered his men to take up defensive positions. This was a mistake because the Germans were attacking in enough strength to get round the Rangers' flanks and to cut them off.

By 6 p.m. Abercrombie decided that his force was doing no good, so he ordered it to retire. He was undoubtedly shocked to find that his way through Grand-Fayt was blocked as he came under fire from the village itself. The Rangers were forced to fight their way through the streets. They lost one officer and fourteen rangers dead, and well over 50 wounded. About as many again were taken prisoner. Almost as bad was that the survivors got split up in the fighting. The second in command, Major Sarsfield, led a small group south. Colonel Abercrombie, with about fifty men, escaped to the west. They took up a defensive position where they remained till dark before retiring further west. They met up with Colonel Thompson, deputy director of medical services. Realising that they were in bad shape, he took them to Maroilles, where a considerable supply of rations had been dumped. It is hardly surprising that they were taken by surprise the following morning and captured. Altogether one officer and fourteen other ranks had been killed, while five officers and 180 other ranks were taken prisoner, many of them wounded. Colonel Abercrombie died whilst a prisoner in Germany. The remnants of the battalion had reunited by 28 August, and Major Sarsfield took command. At 7 a.m. that day the Rangers were ready to continue their retreat.

II Corps ran into even more serious trouble on 26 August. The Field Marshal had ordered both corps to continue with the retreat, but Smith-Dorrien's II Corps had been through hell at Mons and his men were exhausted, whereas 1 Corps had hardly got involved. On the night of 25/26 August, the last unit to reach Le Cateau, where 11 Corps were rallying, was 2nd Royal Irish Rifles, the rearguard, who reached the town at 4 a.m. It was obvious that they could not march out that morning. Some of the men had marched and fought for seventy-five miles in only five days. Even if he could withdraw, there was no cavalry available to cover him. It was necessary to stand and fight in the hope that a strong blow would stop the Germans at least temporarily. That morning his force was facing three infantry and three cavalry divisions. In addition, the Germans were bringing forward two more infantry divisions, so that their numerical superiority was about two to one.

Smith-Dorrien placed the three brigades of 3rd Division in the centre of his line. On the left of the division was 7 Brigade, with 2nd Irish in support near Caudry, while 2nd Royal Irish was near Audencourt. To the left of 3rd Division was part of the newly arrived 4th Division, which included 2nd Inniskillings, 1st Irish Fusiliers and 2nd Dublins. Field Marshal French had been reluctant to give his permission for reinforcement, because his instinct was to continue the withdrawal if at all possible. The artillery of 3rd and 5th Divisions was brought forward to give close support to the infantry. Because there was not time to dig gun pits, the 18-pounders had to fight in the open, seeking dead ground to keep them out of sight of the enemy. As the Germans came into the attack, all the field guns opened fire with shrapnel. Larger guns, howitzers and 60-pounders, shelled German artillery. Witnesses said that they might have been looking at the artillery exchange at Waterloo, that it was a nineteenth-century battle fought with twentieth-century guns.

Smith-Dorrien's centre was holding, since the Germans were not attacking it directly with infantry, but there was tremendous pressure being put on his left flank. Worse, 1 Corps was still following the order to retreat and soon 11 Corps was left with an open flank and men in the 5th Division began to receive fire from their rear. On 3rd Division's left, B Company of the Royal Irish, under Major Daniell, was supporting the 3rd Worcesters in the village of Caudry. Between Caudry and the main line of 3rd Division were C and D Companies. A Company was near Audencourt, digging support trenches. The Germans were maintaining a barrage of high explosives on Caudry. It eased about 2 p.m. and Daniell discovered that the north-west of the town had been evacuated.

He took his company back to rejoin A Company at Audencourt. By the time he got there an order for a general withdrawal had been given.

Meanwhile General Fergusson, whose 5th Division was holding the right end of the line, was becoming concerned about the number of German troops who were streaming past his open flank. Soon after 1 p.m. he asked permission of Smith-Dorrien to withdraw, since it was beginning to look as if he might be surrounded. The corps commander asked him to hold on as long as possible till the other divisions were informed, but by 2:40 p.m. Fergusson had given the order to retire. This was not easy to do, since most of his units were closely engaged with the enemy. Getting his guns away over ground that was raked with shell fire and machine-guns was fraught with danger, and three Victoria Crosses were earned in the removal of one single howitzer. In the general mêlée, some battalions were completely overrun.

The order to withdraw did not always get through to the fighting men. When 3rd Division started its withdrawal, two companies of the Royal Irish, most of the 1st Gordon Highlanders and a company of the Royal Scots had been left behind. The Royal Irish had been under attack since 1:30. A heavy bombardment was falling on Audencourt, to their right. Shortly afterwards they could see 7 Brigade being forced out of Caudry. About 3:30 p.m., horses and men could be seen retiring from Audencourt. St Leger, the officer commanding, decided that in the absence of orders he was forced to remain in position. Within a few minutes a bombardment of high explosives began along the line between Audencourt and Caudry which lasted until 5 p.m. While this was going on, the men began to come under fire from their right rear, from behind the trenches that the Gordons were supposed to be holding. A scout sent to investigate said there was no movement in the Gordon trenches. The noise of rapid firing came from the left, where part of D Company had been guarding against a flank attack. St Leger decided to move towards the firing. When he got there he discovered that the commander of the detachment, Major Panter-Downes, had been mortally wounded. He was still conscious, however, and reported that the Germans had been able to work their way round to a wood to his rear and he had lost sixteen dead and many wounded. Those who were mobile had been told to make their own way to the British line. St Leger went to Caudry, now held by Germans, and arranged for the wounded to be brought into a private hospital in the morning. It was no comfort to the wounded or the captive, even less to the friends of the dead, but the hard fight put up by these trapped remnants was sufficient to convince German Intelligence that the entire corps was standing its ground. To a certain extent, Smith-Dorrien's aims had been achieved.

The remnants of the Royal Irish had assembled at Beaurevoir. They did not have much time to rest, however, since they were on the road again by 2 a.m. on 27 August. Their medical officer had remained behind at Mons and the brigade field ambulance had gone astray, so the wounded had no more treatment than the application of personal dressings. The wounded could not even take a lift on the battalion transport, since this was trapped in the mayhem of the roads. The men breakfasted on biscuit that they found abandoned at an old bivouac, saving the tins in case they proved useful. After a day marching along dusty, hot roads, they arrived in Vermand to discover that no rations had been provided. Undaunted, they climbed into the adjoining field and dug up whatever root crops they could find. The biscuit tins were soon in use, cooking supper. This kept everyone going till the official rations arrived late in the evening.

If the march had been bad up till then, it now became a nightmare. The retreat started again before midnight, and they walked till they reached the town of Ham at 9 a.m. There was a rest of two hours here and they started again. This time many marched as if they were asleep, continuing through the heat till 6:30 p.m., when they reached Genvry. Here they had reached the Oise, where it was considered safe to allow the men their first full night's rest in a week.

There had been a lot of confusion on the march, with platoons and even companies, as we have seen, being separated from their units. Some of the Dublins got as far as Boulogne, while a platoon of Irish Fusiliers reached Rouen. This led German High Command to believe that BEF was intent on reaching the Channel ports, a misunderstanding which was to cause serious problems for the Germans only a few days later.

1 Corps had a much less strenuous experience on the retreat. The initial retirement was covered by 1 Guards Brigade, which was dug in at Etreux. 2nd Munsters deployed three miles north of Etreux. They were reinforced by two troops of 1st Hussars and an 18-pounder section borrowed from 118 Battery Royal Field Artillery (RFA). They held a line facing north-east, some 2½ miles east of the Sambre l'Oise canal.

C Company was in reserve at battalion HQ in Fesmy. After stand-to, which began at 4 a.m. on the 27th, the cooks prepared breakfast. The thunder they heard was a natural phenomenon, not gunfire, and it looked as if it was going to be a sultry day. To their right, there were signs that the French were retiring. At about 9 a.m., a patrol of German cavalry appeared. They stayed at a range of 600 yards and, for a while, the sides watched one another warily. An order came from brigade HQ that the Munsters should hold until they were forced back, unless they were ordered to withdraw before that. It became obvious that action was near when German infantry appeared.

At first the Germans sent skirmishers forward, but soon followed up with larger groups, with some in company strength coming forward and probing for weaknesses. The Munsters held their fire, even when fired on, and waited for the real attack. When the companies did attack, they were easily beaten back. What the Munsters' CO, Major Charrier, did not know was that these Germans were the leading elements of a German division, and that he was in the way of an entire corps which intended to attack Etreux. The proper attack began about 11 a.m. and Charrier soon became aware of the weight of troops facing him. They swarmed round both flanks and he ordered the companies he had placed there to fall back on his HQ in Fesmy. Half of A Company had formed the extreme right flank and Charrier lost contact with this group. He sent out a platoon to try to relieve them but the rescue party was beaten back. Common sense had prevailed, however, and the lost men had actually extricated themselves from the attack and had fallen back on Oisy, where a platoon of C Company was guarding the bridge.

Back in Fesmy, the cooks started to serve dinner in the middle of the attack. The fact that D Company had deployed on both sides of the road meant that the cooks had to scamper back and forward all the time carrying dixies of hot food and tea. The jeering of the fusiliers was not altogether sympathetic.

Shortly after midday the Germans attacked again, in the middle of a cloudburst. They were supported by artillery, but once again they were beaten back by a combination of rapid rifle fire and the shrapnel of the 18-pounders. They tried again, driving cattle in front of them as cover. This time they got within 150 yards of the Irish position, but Captain Rawlinson led C Company in a charge that cleared the field. Weight of numbers was beginning to tell and German cavalry, attacking with the infantry, managed to get among the transport animals and shot two wagon teams before being killed or captured themselves. During the lulls, the Munster stretcher-bearers brought in German prisoners as well as their own wounded.

In spite of the good show that his men were giving, Charrier knew that he could not remain in Fesmy. Behind him was the canal, and there was a real danger of being trapped against this and destroyed. At 2:30 p.m. he ordered his men to fall back towards the bridge at Oisy. The retreat was slow and thick hedgerows impeded the cross-country travel of the flank guards. The line of the country threw B Company off line and it was not till 5:30 p.m. that all companies had reached the rendez-vous at a crossroads near Oisy. A cyclist arrived with an order from the brigadier telling all units to retire. It had been sent at 1 p.m. and the cyclist had found the Coldstreams long before. They were gone and, once again, the Munsters were on their own. Worse, they didn't know where anyone was.

Charrier took his men over the bridge, but left two platoons to guard it. This rearguard occupied two houses on the west side of the bridge and held fire till the Germans were almost ready to cross. At point-blank range they inflicted terrible casualties. The enemy still came on, regardless of risk, and more and more fire was directed at the two houses. In the end the Munsters were forced to withdraw, but they did so in a disciplined manner, each platoon covering the moves of the others. When the platoons caught up with the rest, the Germans were right on their heels. To discourage them, and to give himself a breathing space, Charrier had machine-guns set up to fire along the road, while the Munsters squashed themselves into the side. The Germans were halted and not a fusilier was hurt.

It was Charrier's intention to make for the Guard Brigade HQ at Etreux. He did not know that the Germans had occupied the town in the early afternoon. As the Munsters came near the town they began to take fire from their left flank. It was obvious that their retreat was blocked. The two field-guns were brought forward but came under heavy fire from artillery on the other side of the canal and one of the horses was killed and others wounded in the first gunfire. Charrier had seen a house to one side of the road which had been converted into a blockhouse and he urged the second gun to fire at it. The entire gun crew was killed before it could do so. If the Munsters remained where they were they would simply be wiped out. In desperation Charrier ordered the leading companies to clear the enemy out of Etreux. The soldiers formed line and charged but, concealed by a hedgerow, the Germans had taken up position in a trench which had been dug by the Black Watch the previous day. The Irish were beaten back. Other attacks were made on the fortified house, while the support company tried to reach the railway cutting and outflank the Germans, but they too were cut down.

With so many officers killed or wounded, and the battalion aid post almost overwhelmed, the Germans counter-attacked. The Munsters concentrated in an orchard and fought while ammunition held out. The senior surviving officer was Lieutenant Gower and, when his machine-guns fell silent, out of ammunition, he knew it was time to surrender what few men he had left. At 9:15 p.m., four officers and 240 fusiliers stood up, hands in the air. For twelve hours they had held out against six battalions and because the German advance had been held up for this time, Haig and 1 Corps had been able to fall back to Guise with only trifling casualties. The Munster prisoners were allowed to collect their dead, who were buried in the orchard. Because most of the Irish dead were Catholics, the Germans sent to headquarters for a Catholic chaplain to conduct the burial service. The Germans also collected some Irish dead with their own, all of whom were buried in two communal graves over which they erected a cross which was inscribed, 'Friend and Foe united in Death'.

The army's retreat continued, but without the same pressure as before. The sun blazed down; there was little sleep, little food, not enough water, yet the pride in regiment that was the cement of the British army held the exhausted groups of men together. Pride kept the men in the ranks, or gave them the energy to lift comatose bodies on to wagons, or to half-carry men who hadn't quite reached the end of their tether. It was more difficult for the horses. A soldier of 4th (Royal Irish) Dragoons remembered later that his unit walked beside the horses to spare their backs. The cavalry had been active from before dawn each day for a full week. Horses fell asleep as they walked, legs buckling under them. Sometimes they lost balance completely and fell forward on their knees, scraping the skin. The men were little better and sometimes they fell off their horses with fatigue. On they went, till 5 September, near the town of Melun. The next day the army turned, and started back towards Germans who had written them off as a fighting force. It was a short advance, before they halted and rested for the night, but it was enough to cheer up the men. The Connaught Rangers had thoughts of revenge, and the Germans were just about to give them the opportunity.

The original German plan had been to sweep to the west of Paris and wrap the French capital in a Teutonic embrace. This had proved somewhat more painful than had been expected and the field commanders had already modified it by striking at the BEF and the French Fifth Army. They thought that the British were a spent force and so they decided to concentrate on the French, coming south in a right hook that they were confident would separate Paris from the French armies. Joffre was delighted. He was like an old rattlesnake waiting in ambush and suddenly the Germans were passing Paris, their right flank completely unprotected. The British leadership was the only thing that worried him. He had visited Sir John French on 3 September and found the field marshal in a very despondent state of mind, wanting to give the British troops some days of rest before they re-entered the fray. Joffre worried that the British might retreat all the way to their base at Le Havre. When Kitchener heard of this, he lost no time in coming to France to instruct Sir John that he was required to cooperate with his allies, no matter what danger to the BEF.

Because the French government had moved to Bordeaux, Joffre was free to incorporate Paris into the Zone of the Armies, which gave him absolute control in the capital. At that time Paris still had its walls and was surrounded by forts with a total of almost three thousand guns. Gallieni, its military governor, made it into a fortified camp, stretching improvised defences far out into the countryside. By 3 September, the German First Army had passed Paris by, and was facing south. Kluck, its commander, did not realise that the Paris garrison had been joined by the newly formed French Sixth Army and that both these forces were in his rear. The 'Contemptible' BEF was on his flank and facing him were the French Fifth and Ninth Armies, threatening a gap that was opening between Kluck and Bulow's Second Army. Even the BEF had been reinforced by four fresh brigades. Joffre now had thirty-six divisions at his disposal while the Germans had at the very most got thirty, most of them out of position for the battle that was about to be engaged.

On 5 September orders came from German Headquarters for First and Second Armies to take up defensive positions outside Paris. Third Army was to attack towards the upper Seine. Fourth and Fifth Armies were to attack to the south-east. The possibility of reinforcing the two vulnerable armies was being made more difficult. There is a good chance that the Germans would have been annihilated but for the preparedness of the corps commander on their extreme right flank, General von Gronau. His corps had been severely depleted by transfers and was in the most vulnerable position, jutting west like a spare thumb, yet the safety of the rest of the army depended on his alertness and wits. On 5 September his cavalry screen began to report that French troops (they were part of the French Sixth Army) were advancing all along his front. Since he had aligned his corps at right angles to the rest of the army he quickly realised that these troops were manoeuvring to take the German First Army in the flank and roll it up. As it was, the French advance guard found itself under attack in country that its leaders had thought was empty. The fight lasted all day, with von Gronau only disengaging after nightfall, when he calculated that he had bought enough time to save the rest of the army from surprise attack. When the French attacked on the morning of 6 September, they found that the Germans had already abandoned their defensive positions.

Kluck moved quickly to save his army, transferring first II Corps on 6 September, and another corps on each of the following three days. As a result he had a firm defence at the French point of attack. He had weakened his centre, however, and was no longer in a position to knock the French out of the war. As well as that, he had greatly increased the distance between his army and the German Second Army, leaving a lot of ground that a cavalry force could exploit. Unfortunately, the cavalry did not take advantage of this situation. Although a few relatively junior officers pressed attacks home, most squadrons were halted by the rattle of distant machine-guns, and the gap between the German forces remained just that—a gap. To be honest, the BEF was too slow to advance and Sir John himself seemed to have lost his nerve. The dash he had shown in South Africa had gone. Even though he knew that the success of the French counter-attack depended on the BEF engaging with the Germans as soon as possible, he held back. While waiting, he reorganised his infantry into three corps, while at the same time creating a second cavalry division. It was not until he had a personal visit from Joffre, who begged for help in the name of France, that he agreed to match the efforts of his allies. As it was, the French armies came into action first and the resulting manoeuvres enlarged the gap between the German armies. It was into this gap that the BEF advanced. Sir John had the force move in line of corps; I Corps was on the right, II Corps in the centre, and the newly formed III Corps on the left. In front was the cavalry screen, which included the Royal Irish Dragoon Guards, the Royal Irish Lancers and the Irish Horse. These units had learned their skirmishing tactics from the Boers, and the German cavalry were no match for them in this sort of hit and run warfare.

The French, meanwhile, were being held up by the Germans, who were defending solidly and counter-attacking when the opportunity arose. A shattering attack upon Foch's Ninth Army led to the imperturbable Frenchman reputedly drafting the following signal on 8 September: *My centre is giving way, my right is in retreat; situation excellent. I attack!* Unfortunately there is no evidence that the message was ever sent. Foch did, however, attack at every point where the Germans showed any sign of breaking through the line. On the French left things were not looking so good. Kluck still had enough troops to outflank the French left and pour into the unprotected country behind. Some of the German divisional generals were still eyeing Paris, only thirty miles away. Then, at 2 p.m. on the afternoon of 9 September, the Germans received the order to disengage. German headquarters had decided that the position of their First, Second and Third Armies was untenable, since each army was fighting as a separate entity, separated from the others and facing the possibility of being surrounded and destroyed. In a mood of caution that we do not often associate with German officers, it was decided that they should reconnect and reorganise, using the River Aisne as a defensive line. This was the last command that Graf Helmuth von Moltke gave as commander of the Western Front. He was replaced soon afterwards.

His replacement was Falkenhayn, who had been Minister of War. His first task was to hold his defensive line and in this he had no worries. The German army had a higher proportion of field engineering units than any other contemporary force. Not only that, but digging defensive positions was a major part of each year's exercises since 1904. The French rejected the very idea of defensive trenches as not being in keeping with their offensive spirit and the British cavalry, although they had seen the effectiveness of trenches during the Boer War, took an equal pride in ignoring the trenching tool. When the British and French troops finally caught up with the Germans, they found the enemy dug in on the high ground on the far side of the River Aisne. The trench line ran north and south for miles. This area was the focus of the Western Front for the next few weeks, as both sides tried to wrestle for supremacy.

It is important to understand the physical layout of the battlefield. The river itself was deep and swift, impossible to ford. Some bridges had survived the fighting, while others had had makeshift repairs done to them. They were overlooked by a massif about five hundred feet high which stretched some twenty-five miles from north to south, and it was a serious undertaking to cross the river while it was open to fire from German artillery. The slopes from the river to the ridge were covered in woods and broken ground, up which it would be difficult to advance. The great number of re-entrants would also cause difficulties for an attacking force, tending to split it up into smaller groups. The defenders, on the other hand, had a road, Le Chemin des Dames, which ran the full length of the massif, making it easy for the Germans to move reserves up or down the lines.

The Connaught Rangers came on a ruined bridge, the Pont d'Arcy. The girders still remained above the water and a company scrambled across these to form a bridgehead on the other side. This gave protection to a group of Royal Engineers who constructed a pontoon bridge, allowing all of 5 Brigade to get across before the evening of 13 September. The brigade took up defensive positions, while the Rangers went forward in order to give added protection to 4 Guards Brigade, which was about to cross. The Rangers reached a point just below the ridge where they bivouacked for the night. In the early morning a company advanced to the ridge itself and occupied a strongly built farmhouse on a spur which stretched towards Le Chemin des Dames. The rest of the battalion had joined them by 5 a.m.

Their presence was noticed and the Germans attacked in force about 9 a.m., supported by artillery and machine-guns. They engaged the centre of the Rangers' position while at the same time sending a force on a flanking move through a wood. They were stopped less than two hundred yards from the farm. The attack continued and by sheer weight of numbers the Germans pressed closer on both flanks. The situation was eased when two companies of Coldstream Guards arrived to support the Rangers and the attackers were forced back. This exchange finished in a way that was not often repeated in the following four years. The German attackers simply stopped firing and stood up to surrender. About two hundred and fifty prisoners were taken. This was not the end of the fighting, unfortunately. A hastily formed German force was moving in to plug the gap in the German front and the defenders around the farmhouse soon found themselves under attack by a full division of relatively fresh German troops. If it had not been for the arrival of 4 Guards Brigade the situation would have been hopeless. As it was, the spur was held, but the Rangers had taken serious casualties with well over 200 killed, wounded or missing.

The British hold on the far bank of the Aisne was neither safe nor secure. They were caught in the narrow ground between the river and the ridge, subject to furious counter-attacks by the Germans. When German howitzers, nicknamed Jack Johnsons because of the power of their punch, were brought into action there was nothing the British could do but dig in. They were handicapped by a shortage of entrenching tools, sometimes with only a half dozen to a platoon, and by the fact that the weather had turned cold and wet. The Western Front was beginning to build its reputation.

Chapter 2 ∿
| RALLYING ROUND THE FLAG

To some people, the war in Europe was almost a relief. To a person constitutionally so opposed to making a premature decision as the Prime Minister, Asquith, about whom nationalist Ireland coined the phrase, 'Wait and see like Asquith', it must have seemed to justify the inertia he had shown in the face of a continuing series of crises which had occupied Ireland over the previous twelve months or so. The unrest in Ulster which had risen from the threat of home rule, the raising and the opposing of the Ulster Volunteers and the Irish Volunteers, and the gun-running into Larne of early 1914, had elicited little response from the government other than sabre-rattling, and the decision to reinforce those army barracks in Ulster which held arms and ammunition. Even this was too much for the army establishment and, by a combination of outright lies and innuendo, Sir Arthur Paget, General Officer Commanding the Curragh District, gave his officers to understand that the government had ordered the army to take offensive action against the Ulster Volunteers. He proposed that those officers who found such action offensive might wish to resign their commissions. The vast majority of the officers, the most senior of whom was Brigadier Hubert Gough, later to command the Fifth Army in the final years of the Great War, indicated that this was the course they would take. Having created a crisis, Paget went off to London to report it. The incident itself was easy to deal with, and the officers were reinstated, but the repercussions were to blight Anglo-Irish relations for many years to come. There was a perception, even within the British government, that the army high command was not altogether reliable, while at the same time nationalist Ireland realised that the threat of coercion got results in the present administration.

From a nationalist point of view, things got even worse. In July 1914, a conference was held in Buckingham Palace to try to resolve the problem of unionist opposition to home rule. It ended, on 24 July, in failure. Two days later Erskine Childers landed rifles and ammunition in Howth Harbour. In an operation that was designed to gain as much publicity as possible, the guns were taken to Dublin with only minor disturbances. Later in the day, however, a detachment of the King's Own Scottish Borderers, which had been given the run-around by the Volunteers for most of the day, were greeted by a jeering crowd in Bachelor's Walk. The soldiers appear to have lost control and opened fire on the crowd; four were killed and as many as fifty may have been wounded. When three of the dead were buried, on 29 July, there was what amounted to a national day of mourning. The cortège was a mile long, and 200,000 people lined the route. Volunteers fired a salute over the graves. The spectacle was not limited to Dublin, as the funeral had been recorded on film and was to be shown in cinemas around the country.

The most obvious result of the killings in Dublin was a surge in recruits for the Irish Volunteers. John Redmond, leader of the Home Rule Party, was defiant in Parliament, asserting that 80 per cent of the population of Ireland would not be coerced by force when they were simply doing what the unionists of Ulster were also doing openly.[1] At a time, then, when the British were about to confront a German army which had invaded Belgium on 4 August, it looked as if the British had antagonised nationalist Ireland to the extent that there was unlikely to be a significant number of Irishmen coming forward to volunteer. The British enthusiasm for war, which was so great that the Labour movement and the Suffragettes had both suspended their activities for the duration, was unlikely to be duplicated in Ireland.

As the last Bank Holiday weekend of the era passed, Irish attention was still focused primarily on the deaths on Bachelor's Walk. Even people who had an interest in foreign affairs found the world had changed behind their backs. There was no sense of war fever; rather, there was a vague anxiety about the future. Right until the last moment, the Irish hoped that war could be avoided. When the declaration of war was made, however, there was a sense of relief; war abroad should mean peace at home.[2] Though this relief may have been short-lived, it may go some way to explain a change in attitude towards the army in the following days. Soldiers became much more visible around the country, guarding coastal regions and taking over sports fields. As some of the 40,000 soldiers marched away for their ships and for France, even the King's Own Scottish Borderers were cheered on their way. When, on 6 August, reservists marched to the North Wall, a crowd that was estimated at 50,000 walked along with them and even sang 'God Save the King'.[3] In Dublin, soldiers leaving on 13 August were cheered on their way and given individual packets of fruit, cake and cigarettes. The Royal Field Artillery left Kildare to cheers on 15 August and later that same day ships taking the soldiers to war were saluted by the sirens of other ships in Dublin harbour. Even in Cork vast crowds filled the railway station to see the lads off.[4]

The soldiers were heading for hardship and war, but there were also changes at home. In spite of the fact that it was harvest time, the price of food rose steeply. At this stage there was no accompanying rise in wages, and there was a protest held in the town square of Mallow by labourers protesting at the increased cost of provisions and coal. It is true that there was some stockpiling by those who could afford it, and a number of shopkeepers were prepared to make what profit they could out of the situation. It was not simply labourers who had difficulty making ends meet. There was no tourism to bring money to rural areas and some of the great linen manufacturers, even in Belfast, put their workers on short time to see how matters would develop. Also in Belfast, there was uncertainty about engineering orders that had been placed by continental customers, and workers were laid off. This trend continued well into September, when it peaked. Only after this did the economy begin to stabilise.[5]

It was obvious that unionist Ulster would support the war. Ulster volunteers had portrayed themselves as being prepared to die to preserve the integrity of the United Kingdom of Great Britain and Ireland. The Germans were now threatening this very integrity, and the logic of the situation demanded that Ulstermen of honour stand by King and Country. This was understood by their leaders, and Edward Carson was soon in discussions with Kitchener. For Redmond and nationalists things were not so clear-cut. The Home Rule Bill had yet to be enacted, and the recent Buckingham Palace talks had brought up the spectre of a divided Ireland. If Ireland were to see 'England's difficulty as Ireland's opportunity', then issues like this should be hammered out before any commitments were made. Redmond, however, seems to have felt that he would rather have a moral claim on Britain's gratitude. On 3 August, in the House of Commons, he pledged nationalist Ireland's support for the war effort. He carried this even further after the Home Rule Bill had reached the Statute Book—albeit suspended until the end of hostilities—when he told a crowd of nationalists at Woodenbridge, County Wicklow, that he believed that Irishmen should give active support to the war beyond the shores of Ireland. In this he got the support of the vast majority of the Irish Volunteers. It was a matter now of the leaders of north and south jockeying for position.[6]

Not everyone in the nationalist camp agreed with Redmond's initiative, or felt that he could trust the British. In Ulster, also, many Ulster Volunteers believed that they had to keep their organisation intact in case of British duplicity when the emergency of war was over. The nationalist dissenters, who were centred around but not limited to the Irish Republican Brotherhood, seemed to be in a small minority, but the fact that they still numbered around ten thousand ensured that they were kept under close supervision by Dublin Castle. This minority became known as advanced nationalists, and their stated belief was that only a freely elected Irish government had the right to decide whether Ireland should get involved in a foreign war. They saw it as their duty to frustrate the attempts of Redmond and his followers to encourage recruitment, and they took part in what could only be termed anti-war activity. The Dublin administration followed Redmond's advice not to make martyrs of these people and their activities were tolerated as long as the majority of the Irish population supported war and the government. It was felt that this broad support would lessen the effect of the dissidents' campaign.[7]

Many women now believed that the soldiers were fighting 'for our rights and liberties'.[8] They felt it was their part to assist the fighting troops. This was not an activity that was limited in class or religious denomination. Fund-raising and voluntary work took place round the country. Sometimes it was simply one or two women, knitting socks for soldiers. In other places it was much more organised, and often sponsored by business. The Cork Steam Packet Company, for example, transported Red Cross parcels free of charge. Money was raised for soldiers' dependants by the Prince of Wales National Relief Fund and, when Belgian refugees started to arrive in the country, money was raised to provide them with comforts as well. A concert was held in the Palace Theatre in Cork where Irish and Belgian flags were intertwined—but surmounted by the Union flag.

The key was the fact that Belgium was seen as a Catholic nation which had been attacked by a bully, Germany, a country that was not only seen as Protestant but which had been, under Bismarck, virulently anti-Catholic. Even though some rapprochement had been made within Germany, the country had not yet normalised relationships with the Pope in Rome. A surprising location for anti-German sentiment was St Enda's School, established by Patrick Pearse; one of the boarders spoke to his father of the level of anti-German feeling among the staff and priests. In spite of that, many parents withdrew their boys from the school because they did not trust Pearse's advanced nationalist beliefs.[9] Most Irish believed the stories of German atrocities and vandalism, especially the burning of the University of Louvain, with its close links to Ireland and its treasury of Irish manuscripts. After the Great War, it was common to hear these stories dismissed as propaganda, but subsequent research has indicated that they were substantially true.

Some citizens took matters into their own hands. Led by a soldier who was too impatient to wait for the chance to fight the German army, a mob attacked the shops of two well-known German pork butchers on Wexford Street and in Portobello. The premises were wrecked and meat was tossed into the streets. There was an outbreak of xenophobia in the country which led to attacks on people who were simply doing normal things. A tourist was arrested at Crosshaven for having in his possession photographs and sketches of the harbour. But it was not only foreigners who suffered; a well-known Cork chess-player was arrested for suspicious behaviour while he was contemplating a chess problem on a miniature board.[10]

There were others who took it upon themselves to be concerned for the moral welfare of women left at home while their husbands went off to war. Vigilance committees were set up in ports and barracks towns lest these unfortunates be tempted to stray from the straight path. In Dublin an Irishwomen's League of Honour was established in November 1914 to guard against immorality and intemperance in those of lesser breeding. The members also saw it as their duty to use their influence to uplift spiritually Ireland's manhood.[11]

There was a great deal of distress caused by the lack of official news from the Front. By the end of August rumours were circulating of the destruction of the entire British Expeditionary Force, including the Irish regiments. Other rumours told of strong bodies of Russian troops being landed in Scotland and taken by train to the south of England. The story of the destruction of the BEF had a basis in reality, since the force had suffered heavy casualties in the retreat from Mons; the mortality rates in 1914 were the highest of the war, unsurpassed even by the Battle of the Somme. By the end of the first August of the war some sense of the industrial-strength devastation of modern war was being conveyed by the press. People began to realise that Kitchener's prediction of a war lasting three years or more was a real possibility.[12]

Newspaper reports became a visual reality in October 1914 when a hospital ship docked at Queenstown. The wounded on board were taken to Cork by train, and such a crowd had gathered in the station that the roads around became almost impassable. The crowds cheered as the patients were taken to hospital. In Sligo, there was a more muted reaction when fourteen merchant seamen were killed when their ship struck a German mine. It became obvious that it was not only those in uniform whose welfare was threatened by the war.[13]

The relatives of those who were at the Front suffered most. It became obvious that farmers who, as a class, had benefitted more from government legislation than any other Irish men or women, were reluctant to allow their sons to enlist. It was not simply the inconvenience of losing labour at harvest time; they did not want their sons to return crippled, or not to return at all. They were confirmed in the wisdom of their judgement when the first casualty lists began to appear in newpapers.[14]

As noted above, one of the first things that Kitchener realised when he became Secretary of State for War was that the conflict would last much longer than the average politician realised. If Britain was to have any influence on the outcome, then it would have to build up its tiny army to the size of the huge conscript armies controlled by its continental neighbours. Even though most of his experience had been with small colonial armies, Kitchener understood that this build-up could not be achieved by adding reinforcements to units that were already established. Such reinforcements are the most vulnerable troops in a unit, and are easily killed. What he wanted was a series of entirely new armies which would be fully trained before they were committed to battle.

In the first of Kitchener's new armies, Ireland was to provide the manpower for the 10th (Irish) Division. This was promulgated on 21

August. Its commanding general was to be Sir Bryan Mahon, a veteran of many colonial wars and commander of the force that had relieved Mafeking during the Boer War. His division would consist of three brigades: 29 Brigade, commanded by Brigadier R. J. Cooper, late of the Irish Guards; 30 Brigade, under Brigadier J. L. Nicholl, who had gained much of his experience in India's North-west Frontier; and 31 Brigade, commanded by Brigadier F. F. Hill, who had recently served in Ulster.

Many of the men who enlisted in this division were men with a sense of adventure, who had found it impossible to join a peace-time army because it wasn't considered a very respectable thing to do. John O'Leary from Skerries took a train from his home to Dublin for this very reason. In the city he went into a recruiting office to take the King's shilling. Others joined for more practical reasons. Many of the working-class men in Dublin had been in penury since the previous year, when an attempted strike by many of them had resulted in a lock-out. These Larkinites, named after their union leader, had lost their jobs because they were considered troublemakers. Men as desperate as this were prepared to take any paid employment, and their wives were delighted to have the separation allowance that would be paid to them when their men were overseas.

There were other, less likely, recruits. Enough rugby players enlisted for there to be a special company in the 7th Dublin Fusiliers specially reserved for them. They became known as the Dublin Pals, although many of them had enlisted in other parts of Ireland. Others of a middle-class background were recruited. Charles Frederick Bell was keeper of the Royal Botanical Gardens when he joined up. Cecil Murray and Frank Laird were sons of Protestant clergymen. The sons of prosperous Catholic families also came forward. Charlie and Tommy Martin from Monkstown joined up together and were accepted as trainee officers in the Dublin Fusiliers. Less well off Catholics volunteered as well. The family of John and Philip Willis had come down in the world as a result of their father's drinking. Now they looked to better themselves in the army. Bartholomew Hand, a Catholic gardener on the Powerscourt estate, joined without his parents' knowledge; he was looking for adventure. Francis Ledwidge, a 27-year-old poet whose social world ranged from the unionist big house to nationalist academia, had sided with the dissidents at the break-up of the Irish Volunteers. He enlisted on 24 October, saying that he was trying to forget an unhappy love affair. Later he said that his real reason was that Ireland had to stand up for the rights of small nations, and to face down the tyranny of Germany.

Bryan Cooper, who was to write one of the most interesting accounts of 10th (Irish) Division, was from Sligo. An old Etonian, he was of sound, Protestant, land-owning stock. He had served in the regular army as a gunner and continued his service in the reserves, from which he then resigned during the Ulster crisis. For a short period he had been a Unionist MP for South County Dublin. When the war started he re-enlisted in 5th Connaught Rangers. He noted that most of the subalterns he served with were from Trinity College, while the majority of experienced captains and majors were ex-District Inspectors of the RIC. Most senior officers tended to be old colonial officers returning to the colours. Writing later, when accusations had been made that the Irish Division had needed English recruits to bring it up to strength, he claimed that 90 per cent of the officers and 70 per cent of the men were Irish or of Irish extraction.[15]

There were, of course, Englishmen who served in the division. Since there was no Irish, Welsh or Scottish artillery unit, the divisional artillery had to come from England. Another unit that had a large proportion of Englishmen was the Ambulance Brigade. Often, the men who volunteered for this had a religious—usually evangelical Protestant—or pacifist background. Many of them found Ireland an alien environment; they felt distrusted by the Irish and found comfort in the company of their own. They were glad when the intensive exercises in County Clare left them too busy to worry about their surroundings.[16]

There were concerns about the recruitment levels in Ireland. In fact, however, recruiting got off to a slow start throughout the British Isles, and the films of almost hysterical crowds presenting themselves to recruiting sergeants were almost exclusively taken in London. In the early part of August, London was providing almost half the national daily total of recruits. It was not until civic authorities became involved in recruiting that the numbers began to build up all over the country, and this did not happen until towards the end of August.[17] Within Ireland the various battalions that had been assigned to 10th (Irish) Division were a long way from reaching their establishment. The Royal Irish Rifles, who were recruiting in Belfast, had come close to their target; they had 900. The Connaughts were halfway there. The two battalions of the Royal Irish Fusiliers and the two of the Royal Inniskilling Fusiliers had attracted a total of only 300 among the four of them.[18] When compared with other areas, where most of the new battalions of K1 had attracted between one and two thousand volunteers, it was a dismal total. It looked as if the 10th Division might have to be held over for K2.

There were several possible explanations. Harvest time was the wrong season to get recruits from rural districts. East Anglia was another area where the level of enlistment was disappointing. Ireland had its own problems as well. The home rule crisis was barely over; the army had got involved on 'the other side' and recruiting officers may have been reluctant to go into areas that were still quite volatile. There was also in Ireland a tradition of younger sons, particularly in rural areas, emigrating to America; this left a shortfall of men that might otherwise have joined the army. Some officers decided to do something practical rather than simply bemoan the state of affairs. One, from the Royal Munsters in Tralee, went on his own initiative to Pontefract Barracks in Yorkshire, where he signed up a sizeable number of Yorkshire miners before the local recruiting authorities realised what he was doing. A further six hundred men from the Bristol region were signed up by the Leinster Regiment. Even with these initiatives, the figures remained poor. On 3 September, 30,000 men enlisted in the UK as a whole. More than 2,000 of these came from Manchester alone. From Dublin, a city similar in size to Manchester, no more than 114 enlisted.[19]

One thing that may have caused hesitancy among Irishmen was that they were committed to one or other of the Volunteer movements. They were waiting for their political leaders to tell them which way to jump. This was certainly true in the north-east of the country. Here there was still some distrust of the government's intentions in the matter of home rule. Some farmers, even, were reluctant to allow their horses to be taken by the army. The leaders of the UVF were anxious to keep it as a force in being, ready to refocus its priorities when the threat from Germany was dealt with. They planned to offer the UVF for garrison duties, relieving up to two regular divisions to join the British Expeditionary Force. Although a letter from Carson to the *Times* had made this offer on 1 August, there was unionist chagrin when Redmond beat them to it in Parliament, offering on 3 August his Volunteers to serve with the Ulster Volunteers in the defence of Ireland.[20]

This had some attraction to the rank and file, and there were reports in newspapers of both sets of volunteers parading, often together, to send off regular battalions to the war. This would not do for Carson and Craig, however, since it was eroding the sense of difference between unionist and nationalist. They were receiving reports, as well, that the Irish Volunteers had no intention of enlisting, but were waiting for the UVF to join up en masse before they would rise against England.[21] In the meantime, however, many of the UVF were joining up already, either enlisting in the 10th (Irish) Division, or, if they were reluctant to do this, joining one of the many Scottish regiments that were actively recruiting in Ulster. By early September, Queen's University OTC had sent over one hundred young men as trainee officers with the New Armies. In order to get a grip on the situation, Carson and Craig wanted to meet with Kitchener, which they did for the first time on 7 August. It was a difficult meeting. They had conditions which they wanted fulfilled before they would offer the UVF to the army. They wanted home rule postponed; they wanted the UVF to serve as a single unit; and they wanted the unit to have the designation 'Ulster' as well as its army number. At this stage they were unsure about the numbers that would come forward, whether it would be an Ulster Brigade or an Ulster Division. Kitchener disliked politicians. On the strength of having been born in Ireland and of having commanded Irish troops in many of his frontier adventures, he considered himself an expert on the country. Irish politicians, he believed, needed a stern talking-to, and he proceeded to give Carson the benefit of his insight. It was an inauspicious beginning.

The negotiations continued for most of the month. Kitchener resented being told how to organise his army, but his need for recruits overcame his original misgivings. The Ulstermen were offered the guarantee that home rule would not be brought into effect while the war lasted, and that there would be an amending bill excluding the six counties of north-east Ireland. Their other demands were also met and Carson was able to announce the creation of the 36th (Ulster) Division to a meeting of the Ulster Unionist Council on 3 September. Territorial units would be formed of the local Volunteer regiments and would receive their initial training in Ireland, in camps at Ballykinler, Clandeboye and Newtownards in County Down and at Finner, near

Bundoran in County Donegal. Crucially, 'sufficient' numbers of the UVF would not enlist, but would hold themselves ready to preserve Ulster while their fellows were preserving the British Empire.[22]

Organisationally, the 36th (Ulster) Division was to be like the 10th (Irish) Division in that the regional designation referred primarily to the infantry. A division is a self-contained fighting unit, and has artillery and cavalry attached to it. These are not necessarily recruited in the same area as the infantry, since the artillery, for example, would come from either the Royal Artillery or the Royal Field Artillery. It was normal, therefore, for a division to have artillery, engineers, Royal Army Medical Corps, Royal Army Veterinary Corps and Royal Army Service Corps attached to it from elsewhere and anywhere.

Still, the Ulster Division was something of an anachronism. They were a covenanting army, as sure as any army that fought in the War of the Three Kingdoms. Its men were oath-bound to defend Ulster, since all of them had signed the Ulster Covenant. They were preparing to fight a man whom they had once seen as a potential saviour; in 1911 Craig had said that the Kaiser was preferable to John Redmond, while Fred Crawford, the man behind the gun-running at Larne, claimed that he would rather be ruled by Berlin than Dublin. They were preparing to fight alongside an army with whom they were threatening to do battle only weeks before. It says much for Carson's powers of persuasion that Kitchener was prepared to allow such a volatile mixture to be integrated into the British army.[23]

What Kitchener had agreed to has no equivalent in the modern British army. The UVF had the authority to run their own recruiting centres, the freedom to choose their own officers and the right to recall officers who had been posted to other units in the meantime. Its recruiting was openly partisan. When, in November 1914, Dublin's *Evening Mail* announced that a company was being recruited in Dublin to serve with the Royal Irish Fusiliers, it stated that none but unionists need apply. Recruiting took place in an Orange Hall. By February 1915 only fourteen Catholics were serving with the 36th Division and all of them, it was said, had signed the Ulster Covenant. To many nationalists, it seemed that the Ulster Division was a sect in arms.

Recruiting for the Ulster Division went smoothly from the start and by Monday 7 September the first men of the 36th (Ulster) Division were travelling on the County Down Railway to Ballykinler. Newspaper reports of the men having what must have seemed to be a seaside holiday at Tyrella beach must have done quite a bit to encourage others to enlist. The following Saturday, Clandeboye, outside Bangor, was ready, and the first detachments arrived the following week. Men from the shipyards marched to the UVF offices in Wellington Place to join the colours. They were enrolled in 8th Battalion, Royal Irish Rifles, known to their friends and families as 'Ballymacarrett's Own'. In the Shankill, men seemed more reluctant to join, since few of them trusted British guarantees about home rule. Percy Crozier, who was later to become CO of 9th Battalion, Royal Irish Rifles, blamed this hesitancy on local community leaders who would not encourage the recruitment drive. In the circumstances, he felt justified in inflating the enlistment figures.[24]

Crozier had already been given the rank of major and appointed second in command of 9th Battalion. He felt it necessary to go to London to obtain enough tough and experienced NCOs to be able to take his Shankill boys in hand. This was easier than it might sound since, each day, Army HQ at Horse Guards' Parade was besieged by veteran NCOs who were available for service. Having got his men, many of whom, he guessed, had lied about their age, Crozier took a diversion on his way home. Travelling through Glasgow, he managed to recruit a number of Orangemen who wanted to serve in the 36th Division and felt that they could do no better than to join up with their Shankill brethren. They gave some idea of their enthusiasm on the ship to Belfast, when the ship's captain found it necessary to turn a hose-pipe on them to cool their ardour. There was little martial verve the following morning, when Crozier marched his hung-over recruits to Victoria Barracks.[25]

One group which would have felt that they had little in common with the drunken Scotsmen was the Young Citizen Volunteers. Though these young men were unionists, they were forbidden by their con-stitution from taking part in political demonstrations. In acknowledge-ment of their difference from the UVF units in Belfast, Headquarters organised them in their own battalion, 14th Royal Irish Rifles, and put them in the same brigade as volunteers from the western counties of Tyrone, Derry, Fermanagh and Donegal. Their basic training was to be taken among the sand dunes of Finner Camp, between Bundoran and the mouth of the River Erne at Ballyshannon. Here they were to be joined by other battalions from 109 Brigade.[26]

Leslie Bell was the son of a prosperous farmer in the village of Moneymore, in County Derry. Although underage—he was only sixteen and a half—he was already a member of the UVF and, like most young Protestants from rural Ulster, he had experience in using firearms. He and a group of friends, twenty-two in all, took the train to Ballyshannon on 5 September, even before Carson had made his announcement in Belfast. They marched the last few miles up the road to Finner and put themselves forward for enlistment. As far as the recruiting sergeants were concerned, a man was as old as he looked, and this group of boys had no difficulty in being accepted. They were eventually assigned to D Company of 10th (Londonderry) Battalion of the Royal Inniskilling Fusiliers, known affectionately as 'The Derrys'. The camp consisted of bell tents, with twelve men to a tent. There were as yet no uniforms, not even weapons, and it must have seemed a very amateur affair after the paramilitary splendour of the Ulster Volunteers. Their days were full, however, from reveille at 6 a.m. till tea at 4:45 p.m. After that, there were the delights of Bundoran to indulge in, and the men were free to go there most nights, as long as they were back in camp by 9 p.m. Lights were out by 9:45.[27]

Not all members of the UVF were as eager to join as these boys. In north Antrim, the local UVF company gave a number of reasons for this. If they joined they would lose their jobs and return after the war to unemployment. Others were prejudiced against the army itself, believing that only the work-shy and the worthless enlisted. In County Down, only about seven in every hundred men who lived around Crossgar came forward to join the 36th Division. Equally, rural Armagh seemed to be producing very few troops. Here, it was concern about leaving the farms short-handed that caused the hesitancy. Those who did come forward travelled to Belfast to enlist in the 9th Battalion of the Royal Irish Fusiliers. For many, this was their first time alone in the big city and there was an unreal feeling about it. They were directed to the recruiting hall, not far from the railway station, where they wrapped their civilian clothing in a paper bag, which was sent home, before being taken by lorry to their barracks at Clandeboye.[28]

One of the disadvantages of the way the 36th Division was recruited was that many of the NCOS were not up to the job. Unlike Crozier's old veterans, most of the UVF's NCOS were related to or lived among the men whom they now had to order about. Some were diffident about this and orders were often given in the form of friendly requests. In addition to this, many of the men living uncomfortably under canvas had homes only a few miles away. The temptation to visit families when they were 'doing nothing' on a Sunday led to many men being charged with being absent without leave.

John Redmond had met with Kitchener on the same day as Carson and Craig, 7 August. Since the field marshal looked on the Irish Parliamentary Party and in particular the Irish Volunteers as little short of rebels, the meeting must have been even less amicable than the earlier one. To recognise and arm the Volunteers was to help the King's enemies; even the ambition for home rule was treasonable in Kitchener's staring eyes. Redmond estimated that the passing of the Home Rule Bill would encourage at least 100,000, and possibly 200,000, men to enlist. Kitchener's sarcastic reply was that he would be surprised and pleased if Redmond brought in 10,000 recruits. He then ordered the army commanders in Dublin to have no further communication with nationalist leaders. In the event, Redmond's upper estimate was lower than the figure generally accepted as the Irish contribution to the war, 210,000. Even this figure did not include Irishmen who enlisted in Great Britain, America or the Dominions.[29]

The meeting with Redmond took place when Kitchener was at the height of his prestige in the Cabinet. There was no one, not even the Prime Minister, who was prepared to stand up to him on military matters. Redmond wrote to Asquith the following day saying that he would not help in the recruitment drive if the Irish Volunteers went unrecognised. He was particularly incensed with an idea that Kitchener had come up with: to use the Territorial Army, which did not exist in Ireland, to guard the Irish coastline. This was a direct insult, since Redmond had already offered the Irish Volunteers for that purpose. There was fairly steady pressure on Kitchener at Cabinet meetings during the month of August to come to some accommodation with the Irish, north and south. This pressure he had no difficulty in resisting. It was pressure from the War Office that finally moved him. He was told that the current impasse with both sets of Volunteers was blocking normal recruitment in Ireland. This news was supported by a telegram from Irish Command confirming that there was no possibility of getting a second division from nationalist Ireland unless some concession was made to Redmond.

The man whom Kitchener had appointed as commander of 10th (Irish) Division, Lieutenant General Bryan Mahon, was an old friend, Irish, Protestant and unionist. Kitchener decided to use him as his eyes and ears in Ireland, and wrote to Redmond asking that Mahon might be allowed to inspect the Irish Volunteers. What Mahon found was a body of men who had put their future in Redmond's hands. Asked whether they would be prepared to serve in the army, they invariably replied that they would do what Redmond told them. As they stood, Mahon thought they were of little military value, much too independently minded and totally lacking in discipline. He spoke to Redmond about this, asking the Irish Party leader to use his influence to encourage enlistment. The Home Rule Bill had not been brought before Parliament yet, and Redmond reiterated his position that the Volunteers could only be used in the defence of Ireland.

During all this time, a steady stream of Irishmen, north and south, were enlisting in the army. By February 1915, the total had reached 50,000. Of these, nearly three thousand were members of the Irish Transport and General Workers' Union, which was itself opposed to the war. Pacifists like Hanna Sheehy Skeffington complained that news-agents refused to display anti-recruiting posters, while anti-recruitment rallies were greeted by jeering crowds. When anti-Redmond Volunteers tried to break up recruiting meetings in Galway, they were beaten up by the angry population. In November John Dillon, Redmondite MP for Mayo East, felt confident enough to write that Sinn Féiners were making no headway in Ireland.

It seemed as if Ireland was coming round to England's way of thinking.

Chapter 3 ~

| THE DEADLY PENINSULA

It is often maintained that the Gallipoli fiasco was a product of Winston Churchill's sometimes over-fertile imagination, devised to win back a share of the action from the army, who had monopolised the fighting—and certainly the public imagination—since the war began. If the plan had worked, it might have taken some of the pressure from the Western Front. In truth, the dispute in the Dardanelles went back to the first days of the war, and was caused by the British playing what should have been a good hand of cards very badly. In the years before the war began, the Turkish government had thought well enough of Britain to place orders for two large warships with British companies. As war approached, Churchill, as First Lord of the Admiralty, had simply confiscated these ships, which were ready to be delivered. He did this without consulting the Turkish government and without mentioning compensation. To compound the situation, the Royal Navy intercepted a Turkish torpedo boat, annoying the Turks so much that they decided to close the Dardanelles to shipping.

This was a nightmare that had haunted Britain's ally, Russia, since the Crimean War. Although Russia was becoming one of the largest countries in the world, she had the problem that almost all of her coastline lay in the frigid waters of the far north. Her only warm-water ports were those in the Black Sea and, if these were closed off to the world by a blockade in the Dardanelles, her trade with the rest of the world would be cut off for at least half of each year. With this in mind, the Russians had approached the Greek government in an unsuccessful attempt to encourage them to invade Turkey. The Germans, meanwhile, had established a naval presence in Turkey, and the Turkish navy bombarded the Russian port of Odessa, sank a Russian minelayer and went on to shell Sevastopol, all in late October. Unsurprisingly, Russia declared war on Turkey on 2 November.

The Royal Navy was soon in on the act. As early as 1 September, having heard of the Russian approaches to Greece, Churchill had ordered naval staff to prepare a plan which would allow the Greeks to invade the Gallipoli peninsula while Royal Navy battleships forced their way through the Dardanelles. The professional naval officers did not like the prospect, and were probably relieved when the Greeks decided not to get involved after all. Now, a squadron of battleships shelled the two outermost forts defending the waterway, Kum Kale and Seddulbahir, on the direct orders of Churchill. A fortunate shell hit the magazine in the latter fort, and a total of eighty-six Turks were killed. Continuing the pressure, the British submarine *B11* penetrated the Turkish minefields and torpedoed a Turkish battleship at anchor.

The fact that these were two isolated attacks alerted the Turks to the fact that they were going to be attacked from the sea. This would give them time to improve their coastal defences. It was obvious that the outer forts gave little protection; the guns on modern warships had a far greater range than the antiquated models in these antiquated forts. Further into the Dardanelles, however, were forts that could not be touched by guns firing from the open sea, and it was these that the Turks reinforced. Now the battleships would have to sail right into the straits if they were to shell the defences. To make this a more difficult exercise, the Turks began to lay even more minefields. Battleship guns fire in a relatively low trajectory, so the Turks brought up howitzers, guns which fire in a very high trajectory. These could be used to fire over the tops of hills, knowing that the naval guns could not reach them behind their natural defences.

In early 1915 the Russian army was in such a difficult position in its war on the Eastern Front that the Russian government made a direct appeal to its Western allies. Russia felt that the presence of Turkish troops on her southern borders was tying down soldiers that were needed to fight the Germans. If the Allies would do something that would draw Turkish troops away from Russia's southern borders it would relieve the situation. The request was taken seriously, and serious planning began at once. Kitchener suggested the Dardanelles as a suitable target.[1] Churchill's first step was to order the reinforcements which were being sent from the antipodes to the Western Front, the Australia and New Zealand Army Corps (ANZAC), to remain in Egypt until they were needed. The admiral in charge of the eastern

Mediterranean estimated that, to have a realistic chance of success in forcing its way through the Dardanelles, an attacking naval force would need twelve battleships, four seaplanes, twelve minesweepers and a number of submarines. To show the seriousness of their intent, the Admiralty at once sent HMS *Queen Elizabeth*, the navy's most powerful battleship, although the rest of the fleet was less glamorous and was made up of ships that could be spared from elsewhere.[2]

Churchill raised the plan at a meeting of the War Council on 13 January. It was seized upon as a possible alternative to the bloody attrition that was occurring in Flanders. The extra ships were approved and there was even a squadron of French battleships sent along for good measure. The operation was to begin in February.

Not everybody was happy. The most senior naval professional was Admiral Fisher, who had guided the modernisation of the service and had been the inspiration for the new 'super-dreadnought' class of battleships. No naval officer likes the idea of his ships being sent into a situation where they would have limited room for manoeuvre and would be relatively easy targets for shore-based guns. In Fisher's view the only possibility of success was if the naval operation was backed up by an invasion by the army. At the next meeting of the War Council, on 28 January, he tried to walk out rather than discuss the operation, hoping that this would at least postpone a decision. When he was prevented from leaving, he threatened to resign. It took the combined efforts of Churchill and Kitchener to dissuade him from this course. They eventually managed to persuade him to support the plan. He had made a sufficiently strong case for army support, however, that it was decided that he should get at least some troops, and orders were given to set up a base at Lemnos. The only fully trained and available unit in Britain at the time was 29th Division. This was seen as something of a crack unit, made up mostly of regular army units with a few Territorial reinforcements. It had been made up of soldiers from overseas garrisons, the sunburnt heroes of many of Kipling's poems and short stories.[3] Although the commanding generals in France considered that they had a better claim to its services, the War Council decided in mid-February that 29th Division should be sent to the Greek Island of Lemnos.

The naval campaign began officially on 19 February 1915 with a coastal bombardment. The Allied fleet had a total of 274 heavy and medium guns, compared with a mere nineteen in the outer Turkish forts. In spite of this huge disparity, the day's action was inconclusive. It did have some propaganda effect: Bulgaria had intended allying itself with Germany but now had second thoughts, while the Greeks contacted the Russians with fresh offers of support. The Turks themselves began to feel depressed. They withdrew from the outer forts. When, the following day, three warships entered the straits, the Turks shelled them using howitzers. Although these guns were ineffectual against the armoured hulls of battleships, they were a real threat to the unarmoured minesweepers that were needed to clear the way for the big ships. To counter the threat, Royal Marines started to carry out nighttime raids with the aim of destroying fixed guns, which were easier to locate than the mobile howitzers. In spite of these raids, shells continued to rain down on any minesweepers which entered the straits. At night the tiny ships, most of them ex-trawlers, would even be illuminated by Turkish searchlights.

It was at this stage, when there were grounds for modest optimism, things began to unravel. Kitchener countermanded the order to send 29th Division to the Mediterranean; he now wanted them in France. Something, or someone, had made Kitchener believe the predictions that the navy could force the straits without army support, and that troops would only be required towards the end of the operation, probably for police duties in a conquered Constantinople. He ordered General Sir John Maxwell, Commander-in-Chief in Egypt, to send his ANZAC troops, totalling two divisions, to Lemnos, where the Royal Navy Division had already arrived. He also ordered General Birdwood, the GOC of ANZAC, to visit the scene of the supposed action. The latter's report, saying that the Royal Navy could not do the job on its own, finally made Kitchener decide that there would have to be a proper force set up to invade the Turkish mainland. He reluctantly released 29th Division for the campaign. The spring battles on the Western Front had stabilised, so he had run out of excuses. He also set about looking for a Commander-in-Chief.[4]

General Sir Ian Hamilton had been a soldier for forty-two years, and had campaigned in Africa and Asia. He spoke Hindustani, of course, but also French and German. There were dark mutterings among his peers that he was not ruthless enough to become a great general, but the real reason that other generals thought that he was eccentric was that he had been prepared to say openly that the cavalry had no place in modern warfare. Nevertheless, he was a friend of Churchill's, and was liked by Kitchener. His present post was as General Officer Commanding Land Forces, England. On 12 March he was sent for by Kitchener. He knew that an expedition against the Turks was planned and he had been given to understand that he might have a part to play in it. He also knew that the scheme had been thought up by Churchill, who was loathed by Kitchener, and was supposed to be a naval affair. This put Hamilton in a bit of a quandary, since he got on well with Kitchener, and would feel torn during his assignment between loyalty to his army superior and loyalty to his friend Churchill.

Without beating about the bush, Kitchener told Hamilton that he was to command a force the task of which would be the conquest of European Turkey and the capture and pacification of Constantinople. Although the Greeks had estimated that 150,000 men would be needed for the job, Kitchener felt that 70,000 would be enough. Hamilton was to have 29th Division, the Australian and New Zealand Divisions and the Royal Navy Division. In addition, there would be a French contingent. From what had been seen of the Turkish army to date, Kitchener was confident that they would not fight. He felt there was no need for aircraft in support.

Hamilton and his staff left London the next day, Friday 13 March. By this time he had been given written orders, which included the instruction that he was to report directly to Kitchener, by-passing the General Staff. Hamilton took this to mean that it would be disloyal if he were to contact Churchill, and he explained to his friend that he would not be writing to him for the duration of the campaign. The entourage left by special train from Charing Cross at five in the evening. A destroyer took them across the English Channel to France, where another special train took them to Marseilles. From there the cruiser HMS *Phaeton* took them on to the Eastern Mediterranean.

On the same day that Hamilton left London, six minesweeping trawlers and the cruiser HMS *Amethyst* tried to clear a minefield off Kephez. It was not a success, with the cruiser and four trawlers being damaged by shellfire. The British Admiral Carden decided that the only way forward was to send battleships into safe parts of the straits in order to suppress Turkish fire. This, he reasoned, would allow the minesweepers to do their task unhindered. It was such a high-risk strategy that he suffered a mental collapse almost immediately after he had made the decision and had to be replaced on 16 March by Admiral de Robeck.

One of the problems faced by the battleships as they went into the straits was that their room for manoeuvre was severely restricted. There were only a few places where there was room for them to turn. Their solution was to sail in line, firing as they went, until they came close to the Kephez minefield. They would then turn to starboard, an action that would take the right-hand ship of each line close to the Asian shore. The Turks were not slow to notice this, and they laid an extra line of seventeen mines parallel to the shore. On 18 March, the battleships went into the attack once again; by midday, the weight of their fire was so great that most of the Turkish guns were silenced. Those not already destroyed were afraid to give away their positions. The first row of battleships began to turn. It was now that disaster struck. The rightmost ship of the line, the French *Bouvet*, struck a mine and sank almost immediately with the loss of 600 lives. Soon afterwards, three British battleships, *Ocean, Inflexible* and *Irresistible*, also hit mines. So did the French *Gaulois*. Three battleships sank and another three were crippled. A further three had received hits. Seven hundred sailors had died and there still remained almost four hundred mines, arranged in ten lines, between the navy and its objective. Some of the naval staff wanted to persist with the attack, and the Turks were worried that they had only enough ammunition for two or three hours if a new attack was pressed home the following day. Churchill ordered four battleships to replace those lost or crippled. Nevertheless, no admiral likes to lose battleships, and de Robeck told Churchill, on 23 March, that he now considered it impossible for the navy to carry out its original plan. He needed troops on the ground.

It is interesting that this decision was taken by the admirals in the theatre, without reference to Hamilton or to any decision-making body at home. As a result, Hamilton was given the task of planning a major invasion of a hostile country while several key members of his staff had not yet arrived. His first problem was how to get troops ashore. At that time special barges were being built in Britain that were intended to launch an invasion behind German lines in the shallow waters of the Baltic Sea. They would have been ideal for Hamilton, but they were under Admiralty control. Hamilton felt that his orders prevented him going directly to Churchill, the First Lord of the Admiralty, to ask for the barges. The admirals, like naughty schoolboys who had broken some of the headmaster's favourite ornaments, were terrified of the First Sea Lord, Fisher, and simply refused to make any approach to the great man. In the end, Hamilton had to ask Kitchener if he could negotiate the loan of the barges. He was told he would have to manage without them.[5]

These were not his only problems. In such an arid region, he wondered whether there would be enough fresh water for his troops; the old maps he was working with gave no indication. What would he do with his wounded? Unless the Turks could be driven far enough back to be out of range with their guns, hospitals on the shore would be unsafe and impractical. Until that happy day, there would have to be an adequate fleet of hospital ships to get the seriously wounded to hospitals in Egypt or the Greek islands. An example of how difficult medical matters could be was demonstrated by someone who was serving with the Royal Navy Division. This was Rupert Brooke, one of the most famous young poets of the time, quite a celebrity. Although he had already seen action at Antwerp, his service record had been interrupted by recurring ill-health. Now he was bitten by a mosquito and died of blood poisoning, nowhere near the action. If this was an unhealthy place without enemy action, what would it be like in the mayhem of battle?

Hamilton's main worry was that the Turks knew he was coming and that the longer he waited the more time the Turks had to work on their defences. Because of order and counter-order, his crack troops, 29th Division, were a long time arriving from the United Kingdom. Churchill wanted the navy to renew the attack, but Admiral Fisher did not consider even the most obsolete of his battleships expendable, and he absolutely refused. Meanwhile, control of the Turkish defences around the Dardanelles was given to a German, General von Sanders. He had fewer men than Hamilton, so he knew that it was important not to allow any build-up of British troops. His only hope was to keep the enemy bottled up in narrow beach-heads, where they did not have any room for manoeuvre. Since he could not guard everything, he concentrated his defences at the three most likely sites. One of these was at the tip of the Gallipoli Peninsula, at Cape Hellas, and here he stationed two divisions, 9th Division and 19th Division, under the command of one of his ablest officers, Mustapha Kemal. Even this was a long stretch of coastline, and Kemal decided he would keep only light forces near the beaches, with his divisions concentrated nearby, ready to come into action when the true nature of any threat became clear.

Hamilton now had only a few weeks to finalise his plan. He was ordered not to land on the Asian side of the Dardanelles. The beaches were inviting, but such a small force as was at his disposal would be lost in the vastness of the great plains of Asia Minor. He had to land on the Gallipoli Peninsula. Most of the peninsula's Aegean coast consisted of almost sheer cliffs coming down to the sea. There was one break in the cliffs about ten miles from Cape Hellas, and this he allocated to the ANZAC forces. He wanted 29th Division to land on a total of five beaches around Cape Hellas itself. Earlier encounters had persuaded the army that the Turks were reluctant fighters. Planners believed that the Turks would fight on the beaches but would withdraw when the scale of the invading army became apparent. Hamilton's staff also believed that the naval offensive would resume as soon as the troops had landed. Neither of his divisional generals was particularly happy with the plan. Hunter-Weston of 29th Division felt that there was a real chance of the entire British Expeditionary Force being tied down on the peninsula. Birdwood, with the ANZAC forces, would have preferred to land on the Asian shore, to the south of the Narrows, no matter what Kitchener had ordered. Paris, of the Royal Navy Division, was concerned that the Turks had up to a quarter of a million troops close enough to be able to reinforce the defenders. With hindsight, it is easy to see that Hamilton had chosen the wrong objectives. He was landing at the tip of the peninsula, far from the mines, and was unlikely to have any effect on the guns that threatened the fleet. His only hope of success was that the Turks might hold back their counter-attacks long enough for him to establish an adequate bridgehead.

It was decided that the first troops ashore should be landed from warships. Steam pinnaces would tow a number of ships' cutters until they were close enough to the shore for sailors to row the rest of the way. Some ingenuity was used to solve problems. At one beach, which was restrictively small, it was decided to sink a number of small barges, or lighters. A converted collier, *River Clyde*, would then steam in and ground herself; when this was done the soldiers would disembark through holes specially cut on either side of the ship. They would then run over the lighters and land on the beach dry-shod.[6] It was important to get soldiers ashore as quickly as possible in order to establish as big a bridgehead as possible. It had been discovered that only two hospital ships were available for the landings. The medical services would be completely overwhelmed if the bridgehead was too small for hospitals and aid stations to be set up on the beach. Staff had calculated that there could be as many as three thousand wounded, not counting the dead, yet the hospital ships could only cater for 700. Worse, they would be off station for much of the time, transporting the seriously wounded to Egypt or Malta. A further eight transports were being converted, but they would not arrive at the landing beaches until two days after the original assault.[7] All depended on the depth of the bridgehead, and Hamilton ordered that small boats, after they had disembarked their troops, were not to be used to evacuate even the seriously wounded. Every effort was to be invested in the rapid build-up of troops, no matter what the cost in suffering and lives.

The assault was launched at Cape Hellas on 25 April. 29th Division had varying results. In some beaches the landings were unopposed, while on others the invaders were slaughtered on the beaches. The converted collier, *River Clyde*, landed at Sedd-el-Barr, on the southern tip of the peninsula. In addition to her sally-ports and her specially constructed gangways, her upper decks were sand-bagged and there were armoured cars of the Royal Navy Division also on deck; their machine-guns would give close support to the landing troops. On board were elements of 86th Brigade: four companies of Munsters, two companies of Hampshires and one company of Dublins, as well as a number of odds and sods; 3,000 all told. All troops were issued with cocoa just before dawn. At 5 a.m. the guns of the battleships *Queen Elizabeth* and *Albion* opened fire on the defensive positions of the Turks.

This bombardment continued until just before *Clyde Valley* grounded at 6:25 a.m. This was the signal for a number of naval pinnaces to tow the lighters into position between ship and shore, and to fasten them securely, forming a bridge to the dry land. That was the theory. The beach was only 300 yards long and was surrounded by cliffs fifty feet high. The Turks had dug trenches which were protected by barbed wire so thick that it was impervious to ordinary wire-cutters. As soon as the Munsters started leaving the ship, X Company on the port side and Z Company on the starboard, the Turks opened fire. Z Company in particular was devastated. In the chaos, the lighter closest to shore broke adrift. Captain Geddis, leading the company, jumped into the water. He found it was too deep and had to swim to the shore. Soldiers who followed his example, heavily laden as they were, did not have his options, and sank to the bottom like stones. Very few got ashore.

Men were still coming out of the sally-ports and bunching up against the ones in front, who now had nowhere to go. The lighters began to fill with dead and wounded, before the sailors managed to re-attach the barges to the beach. Those Munsters who got ashore took cover behind a shingle bank only ten yards above the waterline. There was barbed wire twenty-five yards ahead of them. Captain Geddis took his detachment some distance to the right, where they sheltered by the wall of the old castle. They kept taking casualties. The brigade's Catholic chaplain was killed as soon as he landed. Captain Lane of X Company was wounded within five minutes of coming ashore. He complained that he had not seen a single Turk. All attempts to land more troops from *River Clyde* were halted.

The men of 1st Dublins were in an even worse fix. They were being rowed ashore by sailors. Almost all of the three companies were killed or wounded while still in the boats; the co was dead and soldiers had to take the place of naval rowers who were being cut down. Some tried to escape the boats. Of these, many drowned, while others were shot as they waded laboriously ashore. The water around the boats turned a deep red, shading to pink in the sea as a whole. Only fourteen men managed to join the Munsters. Two platoons got ashore relatively un-scathed, to the right of the main landing. They tried to attack the Turkish left flank, but were overwhelmed by Turkish defensive fire; only twenty-five made it back to the beach.

After ninety minutes of pandemonium, the Turks stopped firing, at about 8 a.m. When Y Company of the Munsters tried to take advantage of this to disembark, firing began again. There were so many casualties that no further attempt was made during daylight to put troops ashore. Those Irish already ashore owed their survival to the machine-guns of the Naval Division. These were supported by the guns of the battleships, which started firing when it became obvious that there would be no further advance on that beach that day. Some of the

Turkish machine-guns were very well sited, however, and could not be reached by shell or bullet. These continued to sweep the beach during the hours of daylight. It was through this continuing fire that the remainder of the soldiers disembarked in the dead of night.

W Company of the Munsters was still held up at the shingle bank. At dawn the rest of those ashore, a mixture of Munsters, Dublins and Hampshires, attacked the old castle under whose walls they had been sheltering. In spite of fierce hand-to-hand fighting, the castle was taken by 8 a.m. By now most of the officers and NCOs were dead or wounded, but this did not stop the mixed group of Irish and English from trying to keep the initiative. The remnants of the three battalions now began to attack the town of Sedd-el-Barr. The attack was led by a staff officer, Colonel Doughty-Wylie, who walked forward in the open, carrying only a cane. He had been a British Consul in Turkey before the war and had been appointed to the expedition because of his knowledge of the area. Here he now died; he was awarded the Victoria Cross posthumously.

W Company tried to move forward to support the attack, but was held up at the intact barbed wire. Corporal William Cosgrave ran forward in full view of the enemy. When he found that he could not cut the wire, he actually pulled the wooden stakes holding it up bodily from the ground. The attack went forward, led by Cosgrave himself. The combined assault on the Turkish defences resulted in the capture of Hill 141 at about 2 p.m. This small group of men had advanced the bridgehead by half a mile. The exhausted men dug in for the night. In the morning, they were relieved by elements of the Naval Division and the French Division. Their units, for all practical purposes, had ceased to exist.

Their Divisional General, Hunter-Weston, had not been much help. He was stationed on *Euryalis*, with the Lancashire Fusiliers, who were landing on W Beach. Here the landing had been against stiff opposition and it seemed a case of touch and go whether it would be a success. By a stroke of luck, one company of the Lancashires drifted into a hidden landing site. From here the company attacked the Turkish defenders in the rear. The Lancashires suffered over five hundred casualties, but they were securely ashore. Hunter-Weston seems to have been caught up in the tension of the action, because he ignored what was going on elsewhere. To his north at X Beach, 87 Brigade, which included 1st Inniskillings, had advanced 500 yards inland and had bivouacked for the night. Further north again, at Y Beach, a mixed force of Marines and King's Own Scottish Borderers landed unopposed, then sat about waiting for orders. During the night the Turks attacked and they re-embarked the following day having achieved nothing. Any of these could have been used to relieve the pressure on 86 Brigade at Sedd-el-Barr.

The fighting continued. Another Irish battalion which had landed was 1st Inniskilling Fusiliers, part of 87 Brigade. They met with no opposition on the beach and were able to advance to the cliff line, 500 yards inland, and here they stopped Turkish counter-attacks. The priority now was to link the parties on the separate beaches in order to launch an attack on Krithia, a key town as important for its supplies of water as for anything else. Before 29th Division could advance, however, the Turks launched a heavy attack which put the British forces on the defensive. It was their chance to throw back the invaders, but for some reason the Turks did not follow this up, and the British had two days to dig themselves in and get organised for the next attack.

This happened two nights later. The Turks charged out of the darkness at 10:30 p.m., throwing bombs as they came. The Dublins and the Munsters were seriously depleted and had a hard job simply holding on. There were still 360 men of the Dublins, but the battalion was com-manded by a lieutenant, while platoons were being led by sergeants. In the six hours that the action lasted, these men fired 150,000 rounds. The Munsters were also hard pressed, but the Inniskillings were fresh and ready for battle, and they gave a good account of themselves, using Verey lights to illuminate the attackers. The Dublins and the Munsters were re-formed into an amalgamated battalion—known to the wits of the division as the 'Dubsters'. 29th Division remained on the line until, on 12 May, they were withdrawn for five days of well-earned rest.

Although the two separate landing forces were able to establish themselves on the peninsula, it became obvious as the weeks passed that the British strength was not sufficient to make any further progress. The army's high command began to look round for reinforce-ments which they could organise into a new army corps and send east. All regular units were committed to the Western Front and so it was to some of the volunteer battalions, made up of men who had enlisted early in the war, that they turned. This was Kitchener's first New Army, or K1 as it was known, and one of the divisions chosen was 10th (Irish)

Division, which had more or less completed its training around Basingstoke. They were to form part of IX Corps, whose commander was Lieutenant General Sir Frederick Stopford. Unfortunately, he had the distinction, unusual for a general so soon after the Boer War, of never having commanded troops in battle. He might not have been first choice, since the more experienced generals were needed as the fighting in France once again reached a crucial stage.

There was now the difficulty of moving an entire fighting corps to the eastern Mediterranean. The urgent nature of the task meant that there was less time for planning than was needed. Units were packed in where they could be fitted, and the same was true of their equipment. Men started leaving Basingstoke in early July. Bryan Cooper's Connaught Rangers marched through the town to the station, singing 'God Save Ireland Cried the Heroes' as they went. They were bound for Liverpool, where they boarded *Mauretania*, less luxurious than she had been when crossing the North Atlantic, but still one of the most comfortable ships in the fleet. On board with them were most of the division's medical staff. 5th Inniskillings joined *Novian* at Devonport. The Royal Irish Regiment was split between two ships. The Field Artillery was spread among three. As part of their preparations, veterinary staff had to get fodder enough for a thousand horses and mules.

Most of the men soon adapted to the novelty of the situation and each ship established its own daily routine. The Dublin Fusiliers were on *Alaunia*. Noel Drury was appointed ship's censor, and it was his job to read the letters that the men were sending home. These were collected to be sent home when the ship reached Alexandria. One letter in particular amused him. It described in bloody detail how the writer had fought hand-to-hand with Turks, killing a number of them. When asked by Drury why he had written this, the soldier replied that he had wanted to cheer up his wife!

While they were not exercising their imaginations, the men had other ways of passing the time. There were regular drills, designed to keep them fit, as well as church services. There were lectures on what to do if the ship was torpedoed. They queued for everything: for vaccination against tropical diseases, for the bathroom, for the water tap, for the beer issue. They were wakened at 6 a.m., and had breakfast at 7:30. There was drill for two hours starting at 9 a.m., and this was followed by swimming in large canvas tanks that had been filled with seawater. The time was their own till they got dinner; most would read, but some enjoyed watching the sharks following the ship. In the afternoon there were lifeboat drills and rifle inspections, but nothing too strenuous in the rapidly increasing heat. They were issued with tropical uniforms and with pith helmets, which they were ordered to wear on deck from 8 a.m. until 6 p.m. In the evenings different events were laid on as entertainment: races around the deck, boxing competitions or even choir practice.

Alaunia was a Cunard liner, built for the North Atlantic trade, only two years old and relatively comfortable. ss *Bornu* was very different. She was a West African trader, and everywhere on board stank of palm oil. Some of the Connaught Rangers were on board her and one of them, Ranger Matthew Whyte, had contracted a serious chest infection soon after leaving Britain. He died of pneumonia shortly before *Bornu* reached Malta and was buried at sea. On *Nintonian*, it was the horses which suffered. Part of the Field Artillery had been assigned to this ship, but the accommodation available for their horses was unsatisfactory, with no room for exercise and very poor ventilation. In the heat of the Mediterranean, one of the horses went mad and had to be destroyed.

Many of the ships anchored at Gibraltar before entering the Mediterranean, but none of the men were allowed ashore. Their course now lay along the North African coast as far as Malta, where they entered the grand harbour of Valetta. Those ships which had been built for the crossing to America did not have the range needed for crossing the Mediterranean, and needed to refuel. While this was carried out, some of the soldiers were allowed ashore. For many, if not most, of them, this was their first experience of a foreign land, and they were fascinated. Even those who didn't get ashore were able to get souvenirs, for their ships were surrounded by small boats offering goods for sale. It was here that cold-weather gear was handed in to await their return from the front. On some ships everybody had to squeeze up, for there were replacements for the Royal Navy Division and the Royal Marines to be taken to Egypt.

Alexandria was even more impressive than Valetta, and had the advantage that they were there for longer and everyone got a chance to go ashore. Even better, mail was waiting for them, the first they had received since leaving Basingstoke. For most of them, it was to be their last taste of comfort for many months.

It had been decided by the British high command that simply putting extra troops ashore on Gallipoli would not help. The beach-heads were already overcrowded. Instead, they had decided that a fresh landing should take place further along the Aegean coast at Suvla Bay, where there was a series of beaches that seemed suitable. The initial landing would be by 11th Division, with 10th Division following the next day. To ensure success, the two divisions would have what had not been available for 29th Division at the original landings—the armoured landing craft known as beetles. There would also be observation balloons and seaplanes. The role of artillery was to be taken by naval guns, so the divisional artillery was to be left behind.

Most of the Irishmen were to be reunited on the island of Lemnos, at Mudros Bay. Even without the artillery, there was not enough room for the entire force, and a number had to be sent to the island of Mitylene, one hundred miles to the south-east. Here they were billeted on *Alaunia*, which was anchored off the shore. It was now that the hasty embarkation came back to haunt them. Those troops who landed off *Mauretania* discovered that they had no cookers, water carts or kettles. These had been loaded on another ship, and no-one was sure where that was. Weapons and ammunition were on yet another ship, but this was safely anchored in Mudros Harbour. There were difficulties in getting the ordnance distributed to the different units.

Most units began at once to prepare themselves for battle, under-taking night exercises and practice landings. The 5th Royal Irish Regiment, however, being the divisional pioneer unit, were given the task of building a road from the docks to divisional headquarters, no pleasant task in the blazing sun.

One of the most serious problems was that of hygiene. The local wells got polluted by seepage from the latrines. In addition, there was a plague of flies. They seemed to cover everything and some claimed that you had to be careful putting food into your mouth or you could end up chewing half a dozen of the dreadful creatures. The obvious result of this was an increase in dysentery and other gastric conditions. This exacerbated the problem, which was compounded again by the fact that the Field Ambulance Brigade's medical equipment was still some-where on the high seas. Some of the soldiers were so badly affected that they slept at night close to the latrines. Bryan Cooper said that they suffered from four plagues at Mudros: dust, flies, thirst and enteritis.

One of the few things they could look forward to each day was bathing drill, held at 6 p.m. Life for the officers was slightly better, since they had the opportunity to go for walks in the countryside, and could climb the hills for a breath of fresh air. Cooper found the experience enchanting. In the evenings they could sit in the mess-tent and drink 'Gallipoli cocktails'. These were gin, lemon, water and ice, except that they had neither gin nor ice.

At Mitylene, on *Alaunia*, they did not have these problems of hygiene, but they did suffer terribly from boredom. Men got into fights for the slightest reason, and not even regular concerts could keep their morale high. The first anniversary of the declaration of war passed and for some, the thought that they had spent a year in the army and had not yet seen active service was very depressing. They did not have long to wait.

The plan that General Stopford's staff had produced was quite straightforward. The attack on Suvla Bay would take place on 6 August, when 11th Division would land in the first wave. 10th Division would follow the next morning. As soon as they were ashore, both divisions would press inland. There was upsetting news, however. The division was to lose 29th Brigade to the Anzacs, who were fighting in the bay which now bore their name, Anzac Bay. They would be reinforcements supporting a diversionary attack from Anzac Bay that was intended to draw the Turks away from the main invasion. As part of standard operating procedure, each battalion in the brigade would leave behind three officers and 180 men, who would remain at the divisional reserve depots. These would form the first reinforcements, if that proved to be necessary.[8]

On 5 August the order came for 29th Brigade to prepare for embarkation. Each man, in addition to his weapon, had to carry: an entrenching tool; cooking utensils; extra ammunition; bombs (as grenades were then called); and basic medical supplies. In addition he had some tea and sugar, a cube of Oxo and some biscuits. Each officer carried a revolver, field glasses, a compass and a map case. He also had a mess tin to hold any food that might be offered to him. He had no way of preparing food himself. In the late afternoon they boarded their ships, the Connaughts on *Elector* and the Leinsters on *Clacton*. They had nobody from the Field Ambulance Brigade with them. It was hoped that the Australians would allow them to use their facilities. In fact, they had no detailed orders with them on what to do at Anzac and where they would fit in.

It was not long after they sailed that they began to see flashes of gunfire and could see where navy searchlights were shining on the cliffs behind Anzac Cove. The ships carrying them were ferries, rather than the large ocean-going vessels that had brought them to the Mediterranean, and there was only just enough room for each man to squat or lie on the decks. On the other hand they were able to take the men quite close to the shore, and minimise the length of time that had to be spent in the small naval pinnaces that were to take them to the beaches. Just how close they were became apparent when a Turkish sniper fired at the sound of an anchor chain rattling into the water, wounding a member of the Leinster Regiment.[9] In the absolute darkness, men began to climb down into the small boats for the transfer to shore. In the urgency, men from different companies were crushed together, and most lost touch with their NCOs. Before they were finished, the first streaks of dawn were in the sky. The sailors hurried everyone ashore, because they knew the danger of being caught in daylight in their defenceless little boats. It was also important the Turks did not find out that large numbers of reinforcements had arrived at Anzac.

As dawn broke they found themselves in a small bay. There were dugouts on the beach, with piles of rations beside each. Under cover of these they got themselves reorganised, before following a New Zealand guide. They were taken to a location ominously known as Shrapnel Gully. On the slopes on either side of these the Anzac soldiers had prepared enough dugouts to accommodate the entire brigade. As they settled into their new dwellings, it seemed as if the sound of firing was coming from every point of the compass. A set of standing orders was given to every company commander; these were examined deep in the dugouts, where no stray light could betray a position. No lights or fires were allowed after dark, and no green wood was to be used on fires at any time.

The men now began to prepare for a night attack. They had to prepare white bands, six inches wide, which they would wear on their arms, and stitch an eight-inch square of white cloth on the backs of their uniforms. They were told to rest as much as they could during the day. Resting was difficult, with the heat and the flies, so most of them passed the time reading old newspapers or watching the Australians going about their business. At about 11:30 a.m., the Turks fired some shrapnel into the gully. The men were very curious at first, especially since most of the shells were exploding high in the air. One shell took the head clean off a Connaught Ranger, and a man from the Irish Rifles was killed by shrapnel, with the result that less curiosity was shown, and the men retreated into their dugouts. Even here they weren't completely safe, and most units had several men wounded. The bombardment tailed off around noon, but started up again about 3 p.m. After an afternoon conference of commanding officers, the order was passed on that the men should be ready to move at one o'clock the following morning. Because of the continuing shelling, it was impossible for them to have a warm meal that evening, and they had to satisfy their hunger on cold bully-beef and luke-warm water.

The order to stand-to was given at 12:30 on the morning of Saturday 7 August. This was no easy task, for the men were scattered in many small dugouts, and there was no open ground on which to assemble, simply a steep slope covered in scrub. Officers had great trouble in finding their men. Eventually, when everything was in order, the men moved in single file back towards the sea. Here the column turned north along the coast and started to climb another gully. The sound of rifle fire was so great that it was impossible to talk. Just a little north, the Australians were attacking the Turkish position known as Sari Bair. The 6th Leinsters were in the lead, and an order came that they were to remain in this gully to support the Australians, while the rest of 29 Brigade was to retrace its steps. The Irish Rifles, the Connaughts and the Hampshires turned back, all the way to Shrapnel Gully, where they spent the rest of the day, wondering what was happening. At 7 p.m. the Connaught Rangers were ordered to move to the southern end of the Anzac sector, where they were to provide support for 1 (Australian) Brigade. They were in position by 8:10 p.m. One company was ordered to bury the dead that remained from recent fighting. This was an unpleasant task in itself, made worse by the fact that the position was being constantly shelled, and the burial party had a number of casualties. The following day the Connaughts were moved again, into dugouts at a place called Victoria Gully, while another company took over the burial detail. They too sustained a number of casualties. Once again the Irish units had been split up. The Hampshires were in the dugouts at Shrapnel Gully. The Connaughts were in dugouts in Victoria

Gully. The Leinsters had been detached and were now part of the reserve for 1st Australian Division in the Battle of Sari Bair, an attempt to capture the range of hills that dominated the Anzac positions.

It was not until 8 a.m. on 8 August that the Leinsters moved forward. Their orders were to go to an outcrop of the main Sari Bair ridge known as Rhododendron Spur, which was held by some New Zealand battalions. They took extra water in petrol tins and made their way up to a small knoll that gave them some shelter. Here they stopped and had a lunch of bully-beef and biscuit. Beyond this, they had to cross an open space some 400 yards across. Here they were exposed to sniper and machine-gun fire, and to the ever-present shrapnel. They crossed this section half a platoon at a time, running as fast as they could, and had only a few losses. The gully in which they found themselves was shallow, and they had to make their way bent double. It was not until 3 p.m. that they reached the foot of Rhododendron Ridge. Here they waited until dark, so that they could complete the relief of the New Zealand troops without being seen by the enemy. A and D Companies went into a line of shallow trenches, while the other companies were held in reserve. To the right of the Leinsters were 8th Royal Welsh Fusiliers and to their left 6th Loyal Lancashire Regiment.

The following morning an entire Turkish division attacked the line held by these three battalions. The Lancashire battalion was completely overrun, but the Leinsters held their ground. As the Turks came towards them the weight of Irish fire slowed and finally stopped them, and at this crucial time the remaining two companies came into the line and added their fire to the defence. After a hand-to-hand struggle, the Turks were forced back. The Leinsters settled down to bandaging their wounds and counting their dead. The ground to their left was carpeted with bodies, where the Lancashire battalion had suffered dreadfully. The Turks chose this time to attack again. Coming at the Irish, however, meant that they had to cross open ground, and every gun in the fleet started firing at them. In addition, the New Zealanders had machine-guns covering the space, and it was the turn of the Turks to die in their tens and hundreds and even thousands. They came in line after line and line after line was annihilated. Those who survived scrambled back over the ridge.

The British forces now had to modify their front line to allow for the ground they had lost. The Leinsters, after a short rest, began to dig in on their new line in the afternoon. When they saw this, the Turks began to fire shrapnel and the work had to be suspended until dark. Even then the work was interrupted regularly, as Turkish snipers crept close enough to see the digging troops. A platoon was sent out to drive the snipers away, but this platoon was shocked to discover that the Turks had sent forward so many men that the patrol was outnumbered. By the time it had extricated itself, half of its number had been left behind, killed or wounded. The enemy began attacking again, in a series of attempts to break the Irish line. There was no time for digging now; all energy was directed towards staying alive. They could not even see the enemy, and could only direct their fire towards the flash of his rifles. The exchange of fire went on through the night. Dawn brought no respite for, in the half light, the Irishmen could see the Turks massing for an attack. At 4:30 a.m. the massed ranks came forward and it became obvious that the only way to stop them was with a counter-attack. The Leinsters got up, therefore, with fixed bayonets and surged forward. The Turks hesitated as the Irishmen came on and the two forces collided. This was a chance to be positive, to pay the enemy back for all the casualties suffered from shrapnel and sniper, and the Leinsters were determined to pay back with interest. Officers pressed forward so hard that some were cut off and never seen again. The charge fulfilled its purpose, however, and the Turks' morale was temporarily broken. The day of 11 August passed quietly, and that evening the Leinsters were allowed to leave the lines and return towards the beach. They had missed two nights' sleep and had fought continuously for thirty-six hours. They deserved a rest.

The experience of the other battalions of 29 Brigade was no less exciting. When the Connaughts went to Victoria Gully, the Irish Rifles and the Hampshires—all that remained of Brigadier Cooper's command—were ordered to move to the headquarters of General Godley, commander of the New Zealand troops and the general in immediate charge of the battle. On their way they met many hundreds of wounded coming in the opposite direction. One platoon of the Rifles got caught in the open and was almost totally wiped out by Turkish fire. As it grew dark, they waited on the shoulder of the gully, getting what rest they could. It was not much and, by 9:15 p.m., they were being given orders to move forward again under the command of Brigadier Baldwin. The officers were told they had to capture Hill Q by first light. For the attack, in the small hours of 9 August, Brigadier Baldwin had the use of 6th East Lancashire and 5th Wiltshire. The New Zealand guides got lost, and Baldwin's force was late arriving.

Baldwin seems to have learned little from the lessons hard gained since the initial landings, and he decided on a daylight assault, starting from Farm B. The approach to the Turkish positions began as a gentle concave slope, covered in young wheat. For the last fifty yards or so, however, it was an almost vertical slope. Undeterred, the men went forward. The two battalions from 29 Brigade got to a position some 300 yards above the Farm, where they were held by the weight of enemy fire in the shelter of a small outcrop. Two companies of the Hampshires made their way right and linked with the New Zealanders. Two companies of the Rifles were ordered forward to attack the Turkish trenches. They were annihilated; dead and wounded lay all over the slopes.

For the rest of that day the Allied soldiers lay in what little cover from enemy fire that they could get. There was no cover from the sun and by midday the temperature was 110°F. The day passed slowly and, although nightfall brought relief from sun and machine-gun, there was no relief from thirst. Machine-gun was replaced by shrapnel, and it was under the threat of this that Baldwin's battle group tried to dig trenches as the night passed. On their right was Rhododendron Ridge, where they knew the Leinsters were in line. Ahead, a dark, shadowy bulk, was the ridge of Chunuk Bair, which they were expected to take in the morning. Before their attack could go forward, however, the Turkish attack on Chunuk Bair and Rhododendron Ridge began, as described above.

The Leinster charge threw back the Turks and the warriors on Rhododendron Ridge were given a well-earned respite. It was not to be the end of Turkish aggression, which was now focused on the men sheltering above Farm B. The destruction to their right left the men of the Hampshires dangerously exposed. One of their problems was that many officers and senior NCOs were among the casualties. Although one machine-gun was already destroyed, the almost leaderless group clung on to the hillside. On the left the Rifles were reinforced by survivors of the East Lancashires and the Ghurkhas, together with a very much reduced company of Wiltshires. Baldwin's force, even with these additions, was reduced to about a thousand men. The Turks poured their full efforts on this group, intent on driving them from the slopes. Still they hung on, though Baldwin was killed and Brigadier Hill severely wounded. Battalion cos were killed or wounded, and often their second in command survived only a little while. The Turks pressed them close, and much of the fighting was hand-to-hand. By this stage most of the junior officers were *hors de combat*. It is estimated that only eight officers and 450 men were able to fight, out of four battalions.

The senior surviving officer, Colonel Bewsher, ordered a general retirement. The retreat was orderly but, when a brigade staff captain met them and challenged them to follow him back up the hill, the survivors returned and took up their positions. Such courage in adversity should have earned a miracle, but God maintained a strict neutrality, and none occurred. The intensity of Turkish fire was no less, and they were driven back once more. The only result of their bravery was another tranche of casualties. It nearly overwhelmed the resources of the Royal Army Medical Corps.

The next morning, 11 August, the Connaught Rangers were ordered to prepare to move. The outlying companies came back, and they trudged towards the farm, passing through masses of wounded from the other 29 Brigade battalions as they went. There was an air of foreboding as they hurried on. They climbed the slopes of Chunuk and looked up at the farm they were to occupy. Before their final climb, they had something to eat and drink, and were given extra ammunition. Then they advanced. A and B Companies led the way as far as the buildings themselves. As they moved forward they were taking fire from snipers and machine-guns. There was one open sandy place about three hundred yards across. Bloated bodies of British soldiers indicated that the Turks had this area in their sights. In spite of this, the officer commanding A Company tried to sprint across, taking with him his signallers and a rifle section of about eight men. Only half made it across; the captain himself was wounded, but reached safety. Warned by this, the rest of the battalion made their painful way through the scrub. Finally they reached the farm buildings, which they attacked, only to find that the place was deserted. They dug trenches to defend the position, but received orders to retire. The area was covered with wounded, and the Turks held their fire when they saw what was happening. Right up to daligone, when the last colour had gone out of the world, the wounded were brought in. Then the Connaughts fell back.

Meanwhile, the remainder of the division had gone into action. They knew something of what was expected of them. They were to land on A Beach, near the north of Suvla Bay. Their first objective was to be a long ridge of high ground called Kiretch Tepe, which overlooked the northern flank of the bay. Here, too, orders from corps headquarters were unclear. No-one knew what the arrangements were for liaising with 11th Division. Lines of communication were going to be tenuous at best; General Stopford had indicated that he was going to remain offshore on his yacht.

Many of those going into battle were still suffering the after-effects of their gastric problems at Mudros. It is estimated that six hundred of them still had dysentery. One officer, Gordon Drage of the Munster Fusiliers, was so doped with laudanum, which he had taken to control the pain, that the whole invasion passed in a blur. The only clear memory that he was to take away from the experience was a vision of a high-explosive shell blowing many of his men to pieces. Those who were travelling to Suvla Bay were given hot tea at 3 a.m. More and more ships came closer together as they approached the bay, and they could see the flash of battle at Anzac Cove as they sailed north.

The bay into which they were sailing might have reminded some of the Irishmen of places like Killiney Bay or Cushendun, but it was not as straightforward as these. It faced west, and somewhere about its centre was a channel leading to what would have been, at most times of year, a salt lake, something more than a mile across. Although it had dried out in the summer heat, it was still not firm enough to support the weight of a man in full fighting gear. It divided the battlefield in two, so that units landing north and south of the lake would not be able to support one another. To the north of the channel was A Beach, where the two remaining brigades of 10th Division were to land. Just before the channel itself was a small hill, known as Hill 10. To the south of the channel there was a spit of land partially enclosing the salt lake. On this spit was another high point, Lala Baba. A promontory, known as Nibrunesi Point, jutted west into the sea here. To the south of this the coast curved inland again and here were to be found B and C Beaches.

Although there were still only 1,500 Turks defending the area, 11 Brigade had had great difficulty landing the previous night. It had been found impossible to land at A Beach, because the water was shallow for too great a distance from the shore, and most of 34 Brigade of 11th

Division had had to land instead on the spit to the south of the channel. B and C Beaches were under heavy artillery fire, and the entire divisional command structure was threatened. In fact, 11th Division was only able to take its first objective, Lala Baba, though they were faced only by Turkish outposts at this time.

At 5 a.m. the Irish Division received the order to land on B and C Beaches, with Brigadier Hill and his 31 Brigade landing first, together with the two battalions of Dublin Fusiliers which had been billeted in Mitylene. This meant that they were far from their primary objective, Kiretch Tepe, the long ridge which dominated the northern flank of the landing area. The landing went ahead nevertheless, until at 7 a.m. the order was changed. A new beach had been found that was suitable for landing to the west of A Beach, right at the end of Kiretch Tepe Ridge. It was also, unfortunately, right beside a Turkish outpost at Ghazi Baba. Those units of 10th Division which were still on the sea when this change of orders came were redirected to their new landing area. As a result, four battalions of Irishmen were at Ghazi Baba; another five battalions, together with the headquarters of 31 Brigade, had landed on Nibrunesi Beach, while 29 Brigade was fighting down the coast at Anzac Cove. The division, which had been designed and trained to fight as a single entity, was now scattered along eight miles of coast, under two different and independent commands. Rather than being given the chance to prove themselves, they were to be committed piecemeal to the battle.

The division of the division, as it were, almost seemed random. On the northern flank were two battalions of Munster, one of Inniskillings and the divisional pioneers of the Royal Irish Regiment. There was also Brigadier Nicol and his staff, and it was here that General Mahon would land. On Nibrunesi Beach were two battalions of Dublin Fusiliers, two of Irish Fusiliers and one Inniskilling battalion. They were not comfortable. Landmines had been laid randomly and they were under fire from Turkish snipers, who were able to get very close in the thick scrub. Around them were the bodies of Turks who had been killed when 11th Division came ashore, now in an advanced state of putrefaction. There was the smell of death, and the smell of blood as it soaked into the sand. Flies were everywhere, but silent compared to the roar of fire that was being aimed at them. Their own dead seemed like dark, motionless beetles, while the wounded crawled like ants, looking for whatever shelter they could get. To look towards the Turkish lines was to see the flash of a thousand rifles. The field ambulance men, who had to look closely at the casualties, were appalled to see what high explosives could do to the bodies of their comrades.

The 6th Royal Munsters were the first ashore on A Beach West, but 7th Munsters were close behind them. Both battalions were ordered to fight their way along the crest of the ridge, to push along it as far as possible, and to link up with 11th Manchester Regiment. This battalion had landed in the first wave and, in spite of the difficulties caused by the original A Beach, had managed to overpower the defenders at the Ghazi Baba strongpoint. They were now some two miles along the ridge.

The Turks were now firing at the transport ships lying offshore. Men of the Inniskillings, waiting to transfer to their lighters, were ordered to lie flat on the deck when their ship came under intense rifle fire. Suddenly there was a huge explosion and an empty transport, tied alongside their ship, was hit by a shell and began to settle in the water.

When 5th Inniskillings landed at A Beach West, they discovered that the Munsters had landed before them. Bodies were floating in the sea, and their boats had to bump against them as they came to the sand. There was a thunderstorm at sunset, and it was midnight before the last of them got ashore.

South of Nibrunesi Point, the landings were not without incident. The men had transferred to their lighters at 5:30 a.m. As the sun rose, Turkish artillery focused on these small targets. One lighter, carrying men of 7th Dubliners, was hit and eighteen men were killed or wounded. The first two battalions ashore were 6th Inniskillings and 5th Irish Fusiliers. Brigadier Hill was ashore by 6:30 a.m. As ordered, he placed himself under the command of General Hammersley of 11th Division and, more immediately, of Brigadier Sitwell, who commanded the men on the beach. There was a great deal of confusion as to how these unexpected reinforcements should be used. Eventually, plans were made for a joint attack on two strongpoints facing 11th Division, Chocolate Hill and, beyond it, Green Hill. The direct route lay along the south shore of the salt lake, but that side of Chocolate Hill was obviously well defended. General Hammersley ordered Hill to take his men clockwise around the lake so that the hills could be attacked from the north and east where, he hoped, the defences would be weaker. Hill was to move through the area occupied by 32 and 34 Brigades of 11th Division and to cooperate with them in the attack on the hills. Since these two brigades had already been given written orders which contradicted this, this led to further delay.[10] 10th Division was now operating under three different commands. General Mahon had the rump that had made it to A Beach West. General Hammersley effectively commanded the Irishmen on Nibrunesi Beach. Miles to the south, 29th Brigade were fighting as part of Anzac. Redmond's vision of an Irish force fighting as a unit was not going to be realised on Gallipoli.

Hill concentrated his men around Lala Baba shortly after the last of them came ashore, around noon. The troops now began their long trek around the salt lake. Their route would take them across the Cut and round past Hill 10. Although this was not as heavily fortified as the Turkish defences to the south of the lake, it had a well-built redoubt built on top of it, so the Turkish defenders had the cover of earth banks to shelter behind. It was early afternoon by this time, and the Irish were not impressed by the inertia of 11th Division troops. Eventually the Irish moved off, along the spit to the north of Nibrunesi Point. Men who strayed too close to the dried lake bed found themselves sinking up to their knees in foetid mud, able to move only in slow motion. They made easy targets for the Turks. Standing watching as they moved off was Brigadier Sitwell, who refused to take his brigade away from the beach.

Some of the Dublins had found their way to the top of Lala Baba. There were shallow trenches here, but they provided no real shelter from the Turkish artillery. They were relieved when the order came that they, too, should move to the Cut. Here they found themselves in an even worse position, for there was no cover at all, simply a stretch of open ground between salt marsh and sea. The Turks inflicted such casualties here that one Dublin wit christened it 'Dunphy's Corner' after a location in Dublin, on the road to Glasnevin Cemetery, where fast-moving hearses had been known to shed their coffins as they swung round on their journey north. The Commanding Officer of 7th Dublins, Colonel Downing, recognised the need to give a good example to his inexperienced troops in their first battle, and he stood in full view of the Turks, calmly twirling his swagger stick.[11] Thus encouraged, his men went forward.

Once across the cut, the troops reorganised for the advance on Hill 10. No reinforcements had arrived, but they did not wait, since it was already 3 p.m. As they came closer they realised that the hill was not protected solely by the redoubt on its top, but by the very terrain which surrounded it. The plain consisted of a combination of soft sand and muck; what people in the north of Ireland call glaur. At its worst, it swallowed men waist deep. At its best, its sucking texture drained the energy of men who had lost the edge of their physical fitness in the weeks since Basingstoke. Whether they were still, or moving in ghastly slow motion, they were easy targets for Turks who were now firing from the slopes of Chocolate and Green Hills.

They stacked their large-packs so they could move more freely. Now they marched in line of companies; 6th Inniskillings on the right, 7th Dublins in the centre and 5th Irish Fusiliers on the left. Behind these three battalions Hill sent 6th Irish Fusiliers in support. The broad line drove the Turks before them, although the Irish Fusiliers were now exposed to flanking fire from the high ground to the east and this tended to slow them down. For officers especially it was a worrying time, since the scrub was thick enough to hide preparations for a Turkish counter-attack or for a machine-gun that could wait to fire at their backs.[12] There was also the danger of getting too far in advance and becoming isolated. The time was now 3:30 p.m., and orders came that Hill's attack was cancelled. Another attack was planned for 5:30 p.m. At that time Hill was to attack from the north while 33rd Brigade would attack from the south-west. 11th Division's other two brigades, 32nd and 34th, would be in support. Brigadier Sitwell, who had not wanted to advance all day, was to be in overall charge.[13] While they waited on the open plain, the Irishmen dug shallow trenches to protect themselves. The casualties were so heavy now that everybody had a friend wounded or killed. The burning sun, reflecting off sand and salt, and the salty atmosphere combined to give everyone a serious thirst. There was one respite when a shower passed over, bringing for a moment the freshness of cool air and the unexpected fragrance of rosemary and thyme. Some men found a well and felt they had to fill their canteens. Stretched out and motionless, they were easy targets for the Turks, and a lesson to their comrades.[14]

At last the time came to attack. The Irishmen charged forward, supported by this time by two battalions of 11th Division. Their way was difficult, obstructed by empty water courses and ploughed fields, but they kept steady. When they reached the base of Chocolate Hill they discovered that the Turks had abandoned the trenches at the base of the hill and had retreated to the summit. Without hesitating, the Irishmen fixed bayonets, leapt over trench and communication trench and charged uphill. In spite of a stout defence in places they swept the Turks from the top. This was the first major objective captured in this sector and it had been done, in the main, by the Irishmen of 10th Division. The work was completed just in time, as the sun sank over the mountain of Samothrace to the west. Using what little light was left, outposts were set up beyond the crest of the hill and the men were reorganised into their own battalions. Work went on into the night, because food and water were needed, as well as supplies of ammunition. The dead had to be buried, and the wounded found and brought into the bivouac. This last was difficult, because there was scrub everywhere and an unconscious man might easily be overlooked.

The real problem was water. Each man had set out with one canteen of water. Few had been successful in replenishing this supply during the day. Now they were parched and might expect a Turkish counter-attack at any time. A few water lighters had evaded the shoals and managed to get to the shore, but there were no containers to take the water to those in the front line. It was not until camp kettles had been unloaded that it was possible to get adequate—barely adequate—supplies of water forward. It took all of that night, and most of the next day, before the situation was satisfactory. As the men rested and tried to recover their breath, they reflected on the cost. About one hundred of the Dublins were killed, wounded or simply missing. In terms of what they came through, and of later casualties on the peninsula, they might have considered themselves lucky. The real cost had been in senior officers.

While this was happening, those soldiers who had landed at A Beach West had begun their attack on Kiretch Tepe. They found themselves confronted by a rocky ridge, traversed in places by winding goat trails. The sides of the ridge were cut by gullies in which grew dense oak and holly scrub. Although most of the ridge was waterless, there were some springs halfway up the slope. Here, too, thirst was a major problem. The highest point on the ridge, at over 600 feet, was 'The Pimple'. The two Munster battalions led the attack, 6th Battalion in the lead. Considerable progress had been made the previous evening by 11th Manchesters, but the sooner the whole ridge was captured the better, since it overlooked the left flank of any army advancing on the plain to the south. The Munsters were ready to advance by 1:30 p.m., 6th on the left of the ridge, 7th on the right. They were supported by elements of the Royal Irish Regiment. Progress was slow, because the thickets could conceal anything from a sniper to a Turkish battalion. The Manchesters who had come that way before them had suffered terribly, and had lost almost half their numbers in casualties. By the time night fell, they had reached a position only 100 yards from the Turkish defences. The Turkish defences were on the near side of the Pimple and from here they poured heavy fire into the Irish lines. One officer and thirteen men had been killed. By 10 p.m., the Munsters had settled down for the night. All the time that the Munsters were closing with the enemy, the Pioneers of the Royal Irish Regiment were busy. Ammunition had to be unloaded and stacked on the beach. Some of them were detailed to construct a divisional headquarters for General Mahon and his staff. Another priority was to build a jetty so that supplies of fresh water could be brought in. The final job was to start building a trench system to safeguard the divisional staff.

While this was going on, soldiers from 30th Field Ambulance Brigade started setting up the tents they would need for their hospital. Stretcher-bearers were already bringing in casualties, who were left in rows along the beach. There was a unit of the Royal Engineers there as well. One party was checking the area for landmines, while another searched desperately for fresh water. This was an immediate priority, as the boat bringing in canned water from Egypt had run aground just offshore.

The Inniskillings had remained on the beach during the day, waiting as the rest of the battalion was brought ashore. Towards dark, one company was ordered to advance up the line of the ridge to a spot where some shallow trenches had been found. They were to wait here till dawn, when they were to move forward to support the Munsters. The remainder of the Inniskillings were to wait on the shore to see how things developed. The Munsters themselves had bivouacked high on the ridge, waiting for first light. Some of their walking wounded now returned to the shore and told stories of fierce fighting. On the following morning the Munsters attacked the Turkish position. A party of 6th Munsters, under Major Jephson, the battalion's second in command, finally took the knoll, which was christened Jephson's Post.

At this stage, the troops that were facing the Allied invasion were not regular troops at all, but a force that was the Turkish equivalent of the

Territorial Army, a gendarmerie whose main task was to maintain guard in less dangerous sectors. There was nothing decadent or Dad's Army about them. They were local men and they were guarding their homeland and the hill of Tekke Tepe, the Hill of the Holy Shrine, which was the first objective of ix Corps. Gradually, they were reinforced by 7th and 12th Divisions of the Turkish Regular Army, roughly seventeen thousand men, under the command of Turkey's most able general, Mustafa Kemal. These men were mostly illiterate and their rations consisted of bread, crushed wheat and olives, but they were well-armed, with Mauser rifles and 18-inch bayonets, and they, too, were defending the heartland of Turkey. As these reinforcements moved forward and got themselves organised they were vulnerable, and the only real chance of a break-out by the Allies was on Sunday 8 August. After that, the Turks would be there in sufficient strength to start dislodging the attackers. Unfortunately, General Stopford chose to do nothing.

His reasoning may have been that the main battle would take place at Anzac or at Cape Hellas. He seemed to have been impressed by the fact that the corps had actually landed and decided that his best option was to maintain a holding action. Brigadier Sitwell even ordered the Royal Irish Fusiliers to abandon Green Hill, which they had taken on Saturday, and to fall back on Chocolate Hill. General Hamilton, in overall charge at Gallipoli, was appalled at the peaceful scene he found when he visited A Beach West. Some men were actually bathing in the sea. Experienced ex-regulars in 10th Division were themselves horrified by the lack of urgency on the part of corps staff and of the men of 11th Division. The latter seemed happy to spend the day lying on the ground between the Cut and Hill 10, doing nothing.

Those Inniskillings still on the beach tried to find divisional head-quarters, looking for orders. The only orders they got were to help with the landing of rations. Some of the more alert began to get worried about the dangers of fire. Tinder-dry scrub was growing close to stacks of ammunition. Sure enough, someone dropped a cigarette and the scrub flared up. Luckily, the alert Inniskillings put it out with sandbags before it could get a proper hold. The only real sign of war was the constant stream of casualties being brought in on stretchers.

This pastoral scene was not replicated in the heights where men were in contact with the enemy. The Munsters on Kiretch Tepe ridge and the Irish Fusiliers on Chocolate Hill were under constant pressure from snipers. They too had scrub around them, and there was the danger of sparks from the shells that both sides were using to pound the hills. For some, however, the greatest danger was the madness of thirst that drove them to try to get water from the wells on Chocolate Hill or the springs on Kiretch Tepe. Once again, they offered easy targets for the Turkish snipers.

There was some relief when supplies of water reached the front line at about 3 p.m. Later, areas of scrub burned fiercely, and the Irishmen smelt the flesh of Turkish dead burning in the flames. This was unpleasant enough, but by this stage stretcher parties were finding that the wounds of men who had lain in the sun for hours had turned gangrenous. They tried to cut the infected pieces away with whatever they had to hand, but most realised that it was a hopeless task.

The Inniskillings on the beach near Kiretch Tepe spent the afternoon taking water forward to those troops who were in contact with the enemy. The Munsters on Kiretch Tepe had no shelter from the sun and the burning rocks. Once again thirst was causing problems with eating. Flies had appeared, feasting on the dead, and they were so thick that it was difficult to swallow a bite of food without swallowing flies as well. Most men simply stopped eating. It was the work done in bringing forward the water—lukewarm though it was—that allowed the front line to be held.

Some soldiers noticed how few of the top brass were to be seen, even on the beach. The generals seemed to be maintaining a silence. There was little they could do to alleviate the situation, anyway. Some equipment was so poor that soldiers threw it away to save weight. British-issue wire cutters, for example, scarcely dented Turkish barbed wire. Having to watch the mounting casualties as their comrades were hit by sniper fire was threatening to affect men's morale. Worst of all, retrieving service pay books from putrefying corpses was enough to make men vomit, a dangerous thing when the threat of dehydration hung over everybody.

On 9 August General Hamilton ordered 11th Division to launch an attack on a Turkish position known as Anafartha Heights. They were to be supported by two battalions of 10th Division, one each from 30 and 31 Brigades. These were the 6th Irish Fusiliers and 6th Dublins. They managed to take their objective and to hold on against Turkish counter-attack, but the units on either side of them withdrew and they too had to retire. The troops were so mixed together on Suvla Plain that it was impossible to sort them out. The Turks, who were growing stronger by the hour, drove back each phase of the attack. Two Territorial Divisions, 53rd (Welsh) and 54th (Eastern), were fed into the battle as they arrived, like meat being fed into a butcher's grinder, with the same result. On 12 August several hundred men from 5th Norfolks followed their co and sixteen other officers and were never seen again.

On 15 August General Mahon was ordered to take the ridge of Kiretch Tepe. The irony was that the ridge had been there for the taking on the first day that 10th Division had landed, but the kidnapping of Brigadier Hill's battalions by 11th Division had left the Irish too short-handed. Now, after mass and general absolution for the Catholics, and Holy Communion for the Protestants, they advanced once again up the steep-sided ridge, with its wooded gullies on either side. 31 Brigade moved along the ridge proper. The men of 30 Brigade had to make their way along the intricacies of its southern face. The defences they were facing were much stronger than they had been a week before, and they were manned by a much greater number of Turks. The advance was held up as they came to the first trenches and, in an effort to outflank these, Brigadier Hill ordered two companies each from 6th Munsters and 6th Dublins to move forward along the northern slops of the ridge, keeping under cover as much as possible.

This group of men actually made it to within 250 yards of the main Turkish positions at the Pimple. From here the ground was open. Undaunted, the four companies of young volunteers fixed bayonets and charged forward, under the leadership of Major Tynte of the Munsters. They went at the Turks so hard that those of the enemy who were not killed by the first bayonet thrust fled or tried to surrender. They had thought their position was impregnable. Even watchers on the ships saw this action, and cheered at its success.

The advance along the southern slopes was meeting greater difficulties. Both battalions of Inniskillings were held up by machine-gun fire, and the mountain battery that accompanied them could not pinpoint the enemy positions. They tried to assault a position called Kidney Hill, with 6th Irish Fusiliers in support. There were five Turkish battalions in the line, however, and within an hour the Irish had suffered 350 casualties. In one company, all of the officers were killed or wounded. The survivors were trapped. They could not advance, yet would not retire without orders. Officers were sent in from other battalions, but they were killed or wounded in their turn. As the day closed, no progress had been made on the southern slopes. This left the Munsters and the Dublins, on the hills above, open to flanking fire from the Turks. The casualties were as intense as any they had experienced up to this. The German General Liman von Sanders had no doubt as to the crucial nature of this fight. He saw the possibility of a victorious British attack entirely outflanking the Turkish 5th Army.

General Hamilton, on the other hand, does not seem to have been aware that the battle was going on at all. He chose this moment to change the leadership of ix Corps, sacking the corps commander, General Stopford, as well as 11th Division's GOC, General Hammersley, and Brigadier Sitwell. In Stopford's place he appointed on a temporary basis Major General de Lisle, GOC of 29th Division. This produced two complications. When the battalions attacking along the spine of Kiretch Tepe requested reinforcements, General de Lisle, unfamiliar with the local situation, delayed his decision until it was too late. As a result, only 6th Dublins and 5th Royal Irish Pioneers were able to go forward to reinforce the embattled troops as darkness fell. The other result, almost farcical in such life and death circumstances, was that General Mahon sulked. He had been passed over for command of the corps; he was a lieutenant general, a rank above de Lisle. Mahon resigned in the middle of the battle and took himself off to Imbros in a huff.

It seems as if General Hamilton had lost control of the entire campaign. Lord Granard, writing home on the day that the attack on the Pimple began, blamed Hamilton directly for the 114 officers and 3,000 men who had been killed or wounded by that time—fewer than 11th Division, which had lost 205 officers and 5,000 men.[15] By wasting troops he had ensured that any attack would be under strength. He needed to be recalled. Yet people at home knew little of what was happening. Letters and newspaper reports were censored by the army. It was not until an Australian journalist arrived, Keith Murdoch, who was supposed to report to the Australian government on the innocuous subject of postal services at Anzac, that news of the reality of Gallipoli reached London. Murdoch smuggled out a letter written by the *Daily Telegraph* correspondent and passed it on in London.

It was the beginning of the end. The British lost heart in the affair and brought it to a close in as seemly a way as possible. Troops were

removed as quickly as was decent and sent elsewhere. In a final manoeuvre that provided an inevitable contrast with the bungling invasion,
the last troops were removed in January 1916. The Irish Division had
gone long before that, gone to serve in the misery of the Balkan winter.
It was not much of a reprieve.

Chapter 4 ~

DISSENTING VOICES

Jeremiah O'Donovan Rossa was born in County Cork in 1831 into a family of tenant farmers. As a young man he became a shopkeeper in the town of Skibbereen. When he was only twenty-five he set up the Phoenix National and Literary Society which, in spite of its name, had as its main aim the liberation of Ireland by force of arms. His organisation pre-dated the Irish Republican Brotherhood, with which it later merged, by two years. It was shortly after the IRB was founded, in fact, that he was first arrested; he was held without trial for six months. When the Fenian Crisis erupted in 1865, he was arrested again. This time he was charged with high treason and was given a life sentence. He served his time in a series of jails in southern England. While he was in jail, he was nominated for the Parliamentary seat of Tipperary, and won the election by nearly nine hundred votes. Since he was an imprisoned felon, the election was declared invalid.

He was released as part of the Fenian Amnesty of 1870. It was a condition of his amnesty that he undertook never to return to Ireland. He left for New York, where he joined Clan na Gael and the Fenian Brotherhood. It was not long before he was once again involved in the Irish struggle. The most famous, or infamous, of his initiatives was the dynamite campaign which was carried on in English cities throughout the 1880s. The British government knew of his involvement and requested his extradition. The Americans refused. Yseult Dudley, an Englishwoman who hated Rossa because of his terrorist activity, took matters into her own hands in 1885 and shot him, though the wound was not life-threatening. Dudley was declared insane by a jury. Rossa's activity was not popular in Ireland where most people supported the constitutional nationalism of Parnell and the Irish Parliamentary Party.

When the last vestiges of the bombing campaign had been over for a number of years, Rossa was allowed to visit Ireland, in 1894 and again in 1904. He did not return again, possibly because of increasing illness. He died in Staten Island in the summer of 1915, at the age of eighty-three, having been confined to his bed for some time. By this time his old comrade Thomas Clarke was settled in Dublin and was the driving force behind a much more active IRB. Clarke insisted that Rossa's body be brought home, since he knew that Dublin loved such a funeral, and that it would provide the occasion for a set-piece attack on English policy in Ireland. The committee he assembled was a cross-section of anti-war nationalists, including Thomas MacDonagh, who was the Chief Marshall, James Connolly, Arthur Griffith, Constance Markievicz and Éamon de Valera.

Rossa's body arrived in Dublin a few days before the funeral, allowing time for it to lie in state. The venue was Dublin City Hall, next to Dublin Castle. In this way, the numbers attending would indicate to the Irish Administration the depth of feeling against the war and for an independent Ireland. The coffin was guarded by Irish Volunteers and many thousands came to pay their respects to the dead Fenian. As the Under-Secretary at Dublin Castle watched what was happening next door, he noted that he had an uncomfortable feeling that the con-stitutional nationalists were losing ground to the Irish Volunteers, which he called Sinn Féin, as most people did at the time.[1]

On the August day of the funeral itself there were special trains to Dublin organised from many parts of the country. The hearse was preceded by a pipe band and was followed by armed units of Irish Volunteers and the Citizen Army. The streets were lined all the way to Glasnevin, and the organisers claimed that 70,000 people were in the cemetery, close enough to hear what was going on. A requiem mass was said by Father O'Flanagan, a radical priest who had already spoken at the lying in state, and who was later to be expelled by his bishop from his parish in Cliffoney for his political involvement. When he finished, Patrick Pearse spoke, dressed in the uniform of the Irish Volunteers. He spoke well.

Firstly he explained why he was delivering the panegyric, rather than one of Rossa's old comrades. They had fought their fight, he said, and it was time for a new generation to take up their burden and to con-tinue the struggle. He praised Rossa and the other Fenians, especially those buried in Glasnevin. The seeds they had sown were now ripening in the hearts of young men of Pearse's generation, a miracle performed, he said, by God. He continued in this mystical theme, claiming that it was from the graves of patriot men and women that living nations sprang. The Defenders of the Realm thought they had pacified Ireland, that they had 'purchased half of us and intimidated the other half'. He finished with words that are still quoted almost a century later. 'The fools, the fools! They have left us our Fenian dead, and while Ireland holds these graves, Ireland unfree shall never be at peace.'

The whole affair was a triumph of advanced nationalist propaganda. Less than a year after the Irish Volunteers had appeared no more than an isolated rump of nationalism, an impediment disturbing the clear flowing stream of home rule, they had been able to take over Dublin for a period of days. They had been shown respect by thousands of Dubliners who only months before had been cheering soldiers of the British Empire on their way to battle. The reception was so enthusiastic that a decision was taken by the organisers to go ahead with launching a rising in Ireland sooner rather than later.[2] Even if it was accepted that a large number who watched along the route or who crowded into Glasnevin Cemetery were motivated by idle curiosity, the sheer numbers involved would imply that this was not the determining motive for most people. Something had changed within the Irish psyche in the previous year, and it is important to determine what brought that change about.

For much of the previous quarter of a century, Irish nationalism had been defined by the Irish Parliamentary Party and its national support organisation, the United Irish League. Its progress had not always been a smooth one; the organisation, like the country, had torn itself in two over the private affairs of Charles Parnell. The country had lacked a credible alternative, however. The National Invincibles had created a furore by murdering the two highest officials of the Dublin Castle administration in the Phoenix Park in 1882, but they stirred no nationalist uprising of sentiment. Soon the disparate factions of constitutional nationalism had gradually come together, re-merging like drops of mercury so that the fault-lines disappeared. While this was going on, a Conservative administration in London fed concessions to Irish Catholics and nationalists, as if they were trying to kill the cat of home rule by choking it with cream, a phrase allegedly coined by the Conservative Chief Secretary, Gerald Balfour. In particular the government addressed the matter of land ownership. The two Land Acts passed by Gladstone had concentrated on security of tenure. By the time these laws were enacted, however, the expectations of Irish tenant farmers had gone beyond that. Now they wanted to own their own land. When in 1898 the Local Government (Ireland) Act extended to Ireland local government reforms which already existed in England, it was a contributing factor in helping the United Irish League to win a landslide victory in the General Election of 1900. This platform in turn led to a determined attempt to solve the Land Question once and for all.

George Wyndham, Chief Secretary for Ireland, set up a Land Conference in Dublin, consisting of four representatives of the landlords and four of the tenants. Their recommendations did not include compulsory purchase, but attempted to make the arrangement attractive to both sides. The government would pay the difference between the price that tenants would pay and the market price expected by the landlord. By 1914, as many as 75 per cent of tenants had exercised their right to buy nine million acres of the land they occupied. Further legislation allowed county councils, with the help of state funding, to build cottages for agricultural labourers on the purchased land.

In a sense, the administration might have considered that the Irish problem was solved. It had seemed to be about land and franchise, and now Irishmen had both, and, it could be argued, had more government protection than their English counterparts. The only battle that the Irish Parliamentary Party had left to fight was the battle for home rule. This battle was complicated by the continued aversion to the Bishop of Rome on the part of the Protestant and unionist people of Ireland. Although the phrase 'Home Rule is Rome Rule' had been coined by Protestants worried both by their inherited picture of the Pope as a beast of the Apocalypse and the reputation of the then incumbent, Pius x, as an autocratic opponent of all things modern, it has to be said that it was a sentiment approved of by many of the Catholic clergy. Protestants did not want to become a persecuted minority in a land they had dominated for almost 300 years. The Act of Union of 1801 had, supposedly, guaranteed Protestants a perpetual majority in a United Kingdom. The unionists had seen off a challenge to this in the First and Second Home Rule Bills; the challenge in the second decade of the twentieth century was more serious. The Liberal Party, by devious means—they stood accused of not mentioning the subject during their election campaign—had agreed to support Irish home rule in return for the Irish Parliamentary Party's support in government. By that time the traditional support given to the Unionist Party by the House of Lords had been undermined by the removal of their veto on Commons legislation.

By this time many Irish nationalists were sceptical of the value of the home rulers and their party. The party had become so welded to the idea of home rule that it became a one issue party. Those Irishmen and women who sought social change saw the party as increasingly irrelevant. Its tactic of being all-inclusive meant that it had to blur the edges of its political vision. Like St Paul, it sought to be all things to all men but, lacking St Paul's missionary zeal, it became a political chameleon, a political non-entity against which no one could take exception. Its programme was aspirational rather than well-formed, and avoided controversy in the broad church that was the party's home. It was a matter of good practice to stick to vague generalities when discussing the cause, so that no one could take offence.

There was of course a value in this. It delivered votes and elected members of Parliament, and their votes in Parliament, to put it bluntly, were for sale to the party which would offer the best deal on self-government for Ireland. The amazing thing was that, in spite of all evidence to the contrary, the Irish Catholic electorate believed that the British government would pay the agreed price. Time after time the democratically expressed wishes were ignored or suppressed by the administration and time and again constitutionalists turned to the British for help. It looked as if Irish nationalists had given up physical force as a method of obtaining their political objectives. There was still much to complain of. Although, taking Ireland as a whole, almost three quarters of the population was Catholic, more than half of those who worked in insurance companies or banks, or practised as lawyers or civil engineers or auctioneers were Protestant. True, almost 80 per cent of the police force was Catholic, but 90 per cent of the RIC's County Inspectors were Protestant. Among those who wished to go beyond the limited self-government being offered by the Liberals it was frustrating and humiliating to observe John Redmond go through the hoops constructed by his supposed political allies.

When the 1911 Home Rule Bill, ungenerous and limited though it was, was placed before Parliament, it seemed as though Redmond's faith in British fair play was vindicated. Within a short time, however,

Conservatives and Unionists had mobilised to counter the threat. The Conservatives may have seen this as an opportunity to bring down a government that was all too radical, which played fast and loose with the traditional governing class of England. Irish unionists, and particularly those from Ulster, set about ensuring that the provisions of a Home Rule Act would never apply to them. The Ulster Unionist Council was confident that it could frustrate the government using four main lines of attack. To begin with, they set about inflaming British public opinion against home rule. They hoped that the resultant pressure would encourage Asquith to drop or emasculate the bill. To ensure that everybody was proclaiming the same message, they circulated briefing notes for speeches to sympathetic figures, including academics and others in the public eye, such as Rudyard Kipling, as well as to politicians. Members of the UUC were delegated to establish sympathetic links with newspaper editors. Finally, in order to reach into the homes of ordinary people, they instigated a campaign of picture postcards, leaflets, newsletters and treatises. In other words, they tried to swamp the mass media of the day with their message. They hoped that such a show of die-hard opposition would force the government to resign. But they went beyond this. The wording of the Ulster Covenant contained the implication that, in the last resort, it might be necessary to resort to arms. It was simply following the logic of the unionist position to form a paramilitary force and declare openly that they would defy the government. The Ulster Volunteer Force was top-heavy with retired army officers, many of them heroes of the Empire. Their commanding general was Sir George Richardson, who had displayed his concern for world heritage by laying waste to the Temple of Heaven in Peking in 1901. One of the chief advisors was Lord Roberts. More worryingly, the force was supported by several serving generals. Best known was Sir Henry Wilson, who was Director of Military Operations for the army.[3]

In all this the UUC was helped by a former Irish Solicitor-General, Carson, and encouraged by the leader of His Majesty's Loyal Opposition. Guns were imported from Germany and distributed throughout Ulster in an operation that involved people at the highest levels of political, business and commercial life. At this stage some officers in the General Staff claimed that the UVF was superior to the regular army in Ireland and that it could be disarmed only if reinforcements were brought from the ends of empire, disrupting troop allocations from all over the world.[4] Although there was much sabre rattling, and battleships sailed to the Clyde and patrolled Ulster's coastline, no definite action was taken against the rebels. When the possibility arose of moving reinforcements to Ulster to place a more secure guard on the arms magazines located there, senior officers contrived a crisis by implying that the troops might have to fire on the Ulster Volunteer Force. The junior officers concerned, some of whom later declared that they were unsure what was happening, said that they would resign before they would fire on their northern fellows. The matter was sorted out within a few days, but the incident gained notoriety as the 'Curragh Mutiny'. In fact, what worried the government was not the possibility of a few junior officers in a cavalry brigade choosing which orders to obey; it was the fact that general officers at the highest levels within the War Office were complicit with, or at least sympathetic to, the Ulster rebels. For the first time since the troubled days of the English Civil War a government felt that it could not trust its army.

There is also anecdotal evidence that some senior officers in the RIC were doing their best to exaggerate the strength of the Ulster Unionist Council. John McKenna was a Catholic from Monaghan who joined the RIC in the last decade of the nineteenth century. After about ten years of service in Galway, he was transferred to Ballymena, in County Antrim, which turned out to be a much busier posting. After a few years, during which he was promoted, McKenna was transferred to the small, mainly Catholic, village of Carnlough on the Antrim coast as officer in charge. There were very good relations between Catholics and Protestants in the sub-district, and a great deal of intermarriage. As the discontent resulting from the Third Home Rule Bill began to grip the north, Carnlough remained calm, and there was no sign of any paramilitary reaction among the Protestants. In early 1914 he was visited by the District Inspector, who seemed to doubt whether his reports were accurate; perhaps the Protestants were keeping their activities secret from him, a Catholic. The District Inspector ordered that the only Protestant in the station should take charge of the enquiry and report back to him. McKenna objected to passing on sealed reports, and insisted on opening them as regulations required. He found that the constable was reporting 100 Ulster Volunteers in the district.

Another order came, this time asking for the number of political clubs in the sub-district, such as Unionist Clubs, Ulster Volunteers, United Irish League and others. He took the opportunity to ask the constable for the details concerning Carnlough. The latter answered that he could not give final figures until after a meeting that was to be held that evening. McKenna already knew of this meeting, and believed that it had been organised by the Protestant constable, so he positioned himself outside the town hall, where it was to be held. He got into conversation with a couple of men, Protestants, and took note of twenty-eight individuals, men and boys, going into the meeting. One of the men with whom McKenna was talking was caretaker of the hall, and the three of them went into the storeroom to shelter from the cold. They could hear the movement of men upstairs but the three pretended that they did not know what was going on. In spite of this simulated ignorance, the three were unable to cover their surprise when the meeting began to break up after only ten minutes. The caretaker closed the storeroom door, possibly intending that McKenna would not be able to identify those leaving. The door was not soundproof, however, and McKenna was able to hear some of the men complaining that it was proving impossible to set up a UVF branch in Carnlough. A delighted McKenna went back to the station to report the truth to County Headquarters.

On reflection, McKenna decided that some senior officers were trying to inflate the level of support for the UUC and Carson in order to make the latter a greater threat to the government. This incident happened a few weeks before UVF guns were landed in Larne, and McKenna maintained that the District Inspector was at Larne Harbour that evening, calmly smoking, while the County Inspector's car was actually used to transport arms.[5]

On 10 July 1914 Carson convened a meeting of a Provisional Government in Belfast. At that meeting he expounded his theory of 'conditional loyalty'. The Protestants of Ireland owed loyalty to King and government only in so far as King and government protected their interests. If the Protestants were betrayed by those in whom they had put their trust, then they had the right to withdraw their loyalty. The precedent he took was that of the 'Glorious Revolution', when Parliament had withdrawn the crown from James II and offered it to William III. They were quite specific about what they wanted: they wanted the status quo to remain and Ireland to be governed from

Westminster. It defies logic to say that they would fight the United Kingdom in order to remain in the United Kingdom. They could not possibly win that war, since Westminster could bring the full range of artillery and cavalry against them, while they did not have even the standard machine-gun allocation of an infantry brigade. What Carson and the UUC wanted to demonstrate was that they would fight Irish nationalists rather than be absorbed into a Home Rule Parliament dominated by Catholics. When, later in 1914, the Irish Volunteers managed to smuggle a few thousand guns into Howth, the unionist editor of the *County Down Spectator* looked forward to conflict between the two forces, after which the Ulster Volunteer Force would have hegemony over the entire island of Ireland.

The sincerity of this desire of Protestant unionists to be integrated fully into the Westminster government requires examination. As it became obvious that the overwhelming majority of the Irish people would accept nothing less than home rule, unionists from Ulster began to shift their ground. First, they wanted Ulster excluded from home rule and then, when it became obvious that this would not happen, they redefined Ulster as the four counties with Protestant majorities—Antrim, Armagh, Down and Derry—and two counties with small Catholic majorities—Fermanagh and Tyrone. At this time their stance was still against home rule, but when it became obvious that the unit they had identified could be guaranteed to have a Protestant majority, they became prepared to have a home rule parliament in Belfast with the powers that would have been granted to Dublin. It begins to look as if the absolute priority for the UUC was to maintain Protestant domination of as much of Ireland as they could.

There were Irish observers who were not slow to learn the message. When the Fenians had been a threat, the government had suppressed the movement and told the Irish that all that the Fenians desired could be obtained by constitutional means. Now that it looked as if constitutionalism was going to succeed, an alliance of Orangemen and the Conservative and Unionist establishment were using the methods of Fenianism to suppress the Irish people. In defying Parliament this union was committing treason. In choosing which orders they were prepared to accept, the officers at the Curragh were allowing themselves a privilege that would get private soldiers shot in the Great War that was such a short distance away. The irony is that, by treating the parsimonious concessions of the Home Rule Bill as if they had the disruptive force of the Communist Manifesto, Conservatives and Unionists destroyed the very institutions that they wished to preserve. By denying the possibility of giving even an inch, they lost 80 per cent of Ireland for the Crown. General Maxwell, who became a bête noire of Irish nationalism after the Easter Rising, knew where the fault lay. 'The law was broken, and others broke the law with more or less success.' The success of their treason led to the destruction of constitutional nationalism. By undermining the prestige and integrity of Redmond and his party, they created an environmental niche for nationalists of a much more belligerent intent. Carson had knocked Redmond off his pedestal, leaving a free space for Clarke, or Pearse, or de Valera, or Griffith or whoever came out on top of the nationalist scrum.

The decline of the Irish Parliamentary Party was not immediately obvious, although police reports show what was happening. National and constituency structures that had kept the United Irish League in business began to fail in 1913, and membership began to fall every year from this to the election disaster of 1918. Even branches began to close, over 150 of them failing during the same period. As early as 1915 it proved impossible to hold a convention in North Tipperary to appoint a candidate as successor to the dead incumbent. Yet the deadly enemy of the United Irish League was not to be found in Ulster unionism, but in Catholics who valued what it was to be Irish. That is not to say that there was a growing militancy. Indeed, for many years those who saw themselves as the inheritors of the militant tradition, the Irish Republican Brotherhood, had been little more than a drinking club, which in 1873 had given itself a new constitution, one of the articles of which was that no military action should be taken until the majority of the Irish people had indicated that they wanted a rising.

The initial discontent came from people who thought that Irish culture was disappearing and that Ireland was becoming indistinguishable from England. These people became part of what was termed the 'Irish-Ireland' movement. Their objectives were cultural rather than political, and many of them worked through the Gaelic League and were more concerned with the cultural rather than the political domination of English. Many of the leaders of this movement were Protestant, and the Ireland that they were striving for was an inclusive one which was not split by sectarian divisions. Others saw the re-establishment of Irish as a national language as a step that would lead inevitably to a separate state in which national identity would be fostered by a sympathetic government. In the first years of the twentieth century the movement gained some success in making Irish a compulsory subject in higher education and insisting that national school teachers attended summer schools in the Gaeltacht areas. The effort of making the language relevant, even in this minor way, made the pursuit of cultural or language aims more closely identified with political, nationalist aims, and even Douglas Hyde, President of the Gaelic League and a man who prided himself on being non-political, found himself attacking the Parliamentary Party. One Redmondite MP from Kerry claimed in 1914 that nearly all Irish students were anti-party men, and complained about the 'poison' of the Gaelic League. It is interesting that Eoin MacNeill, who was to lead the Irish Volunteers, followed this progression, from non-political Irish activist and inspiration for the Gaelic League in 1893 to promoter of militancy in 1913.

Another assertion of Irish identity was to be found in the Gaelic Athletic Association. This had been established, in fact, before the Gaelic League, in 1884. Its aim was to revive Irish games, more suited than cricket or football to the soil of Ireland, according to one of the founders, the Archbishop of Cashel. The IRB were pleased to see the 'separatist' tendencies of the organisation and had soon infiltrated it at every level. Politics became more openly involved in sport when the playing of English games was banned by the GAA.

The desires of these cultural movements found expression through the efforts of some newspaper editors towards the turn of the century. Arthur Griffith had returned from South Africa at the start of the Second Boer War. A self-educated writer and a self-taught printer, he had a natural pugnacity and the ability to coin an epithet that could cut to the quick. Back in Ireland he started producing a sequence of small news-sheets supporting the Afrikaners. His views were supported by a small but vocal minority, which included Maud Gonne and her future husband, John MacBride. While unionists dismissed these activities as fringe lunacy which demonstrated that nationalists were not fit to govern themselves, the movement found enough support to be able to send two volunteer 'Irish Brigades' to fight for the Boers. Griffith went on to found Cumann na nGaedheal, the League of Gaels, which evolved two years later into Sinn Féin, a title which carried less historical baggage than the original name. Griffith argued for an independence that was economic and cultural as well as political. He felt that Irish MPs should withdraw from Westminster and form a national assembly without concerning themselves about British approval. There would then be de facto autonomy, even if it was still within the British Empire. Its method of producing these results was civil resistance, subverting and ignoring British rule. Bulmer Hobson wrote a tract called 'Defensive Warfare—a handbook for nationalists', distributed by Sinn Féin, in which he said, 'If Ireland is governed it is because the people obey. They need not obey.'

It became obvious long before 1913 that purely cultural nationalism was causing divisions within Ireland and that the combination of Irish language and games was not going to be able to deliver a satisfactory result. Many who had been activists for the language began to believe that a military struggle would become necessary. Desmond FitzGerald was born in London of Irish parents. He was a poet, like many who became part of the language and then the militant movement, and became quite well known in literary circles in London as a practitioner of the Imagist school of poetry. In 1910 he spent a period on the Blasket Islands, off the coast of Kerry, and became enthralled by the culture of the islanders and by their positive attitudes to the vicissitudes of everyday life. In 1911 he married the daughter of a Belfast whiskey merchant. Although her background was Presbyterian and unionist, she too was fascinated by the Gaelic heritage of Ireland. They spent the first couple of years of marriage in Brittany, among that area's artistic exiles, but the call of Ireland was too much for him, and he came back to Ireland in early 1913 with the specific intention of living in County Kerry and immersing himself in the Irish language. Here he met others who, like himself, were interested in the culture that they were afraid was dying out with the old people.

One in particular he became friendly with was Ernest Blythe. He was originally from near Newry. His first experience of the Irish language had been when girls from the Cooley Peninsula had come to do seasonal work on his father's farm. They had spoken Irish and he had been frustrated by the fact that he, who thought himself as good an Irishman as anyone else, had not been able to understand. When he grew up, he went to Dublin to learn the language, and had joined the Gaelic League. When the 1910 Census was published, it showed that there was a real chance that the last generation to speak Irish in Ireland was the current one. This disturbed Blythe and he saw the problem as an urgent one. He had come to Kerry and the Dingle Peninsula to absorb the lifestyle of the people. From Monday till Saturday morning he worked on a small farm in return for his food and lodgings. Only at the weekend would he speak or read English.

As the friends talked—in Irish of course—through the summer of 1913 they discussed the developing home rule crisis. It became obvious that the pressure of Ulster opposition was beginning to tell on the British government and there was likely to be some level of betrayal of what they saw as Ireland's national integrity. To them, this was the last straw; that England should be so confident of Catholic Ireland's loyalty that they could renege on promises made and have no fear of the consequences. It was as if Ireland had been absorbed into the British body politic; as if she no longer existed as a separate entity. As their friendship deepened, Blythe admitted that he was a member of the IRB, and that he had been given the authority to accept suitable candidates as recruits. FitzGerald was delighted to enrol.

The Kerry Gaeltacht was a popular destination for summer visitors from a variety of backgrounds. One whom FitzGerald already knew was Michael O'Rahilly, better known in later years as the O'Rahilly, who took a cottage near Ventry Harbour, near the house that FitzGerald rented. He was another Irish enthusiast who contributed much of his annual income of about £900 to the cause. He, too, was coming round to the idea that some sort of response had to be made to the challenge of the Ulster Volunteers.

The summer passed and the visitors went back to Dublin and their normal lives. Through his contact with the O'Rahilly and Blythe's contact with the IRB, FitzGerald was able to keep in touch with developments at the centre of things. As yet there was no openly militaristic initiative on the part of nationalists. Indeed, the most bellicose item in the nationalist armoury was the title of the Gaelic League newspaper, *An Claidheamh Soluis*, or 'The Sword of Light'. This was edited by the O'Rahilly, who had even invented a new typescript designed to allow anyone to read Irish script. Its format was to have all of its articles in the Irish language, with the exception of a leading article which was to be written in English. Eoin MacNeill, an academic and historian of mediaeval Ireland, was invited to write one of these in which he argued that the appropriate response to the UVF was to set up an Irish Volunteer organisation. Shortly afterwards, he received a message through the O'Rahilly stating that if he were to hold a meeting to establish an Irish Volunteer Force, he would be guaranteed an attendance of at least five hundred. This information, though he did not know it, came from the Irish Republican Brotherhood.

At this stage the IRB was well on the way to recovery from the low-point of its fortunes, when the government had been ruthless in dealing with the last remnants of Fenianism in Ireland. For some time in the late nineteenth century it had degenerated into little more than a drinking society. Things changed when Denis McCullough was inducted into the organisation at the side door of his father's pub. He was so disillusioned that he set himself the priority of revitalising the organisation. With Bulmer Hobson, whom he introduced into the Brotherhood in 1904, and Sean MacDermott, who was working in Belfast at the time, he founded the Dungannon Clubs, the aim of which was to promote the ideal of republicanism in opposition to the 'dual-monarchy' solution which was being supported at that time by Arthur Griffith. They also campaigned against recruitment in the British army. In spite of their early differences, the Dungannon Clubs merged with Griffith's Sinn Féin in 1907. The following year, Hobson and MacDermott, good friends, moved to Dublin. Here Hobson worked at establishing himself as a journalist. MacDermott became a full-time organiser for the new Sinn Féin, his travels throughout the country giving him an insight into the minds of the full range of nationalists. Meanwhile, McCullough stayed in Belfast, reforming the northern IRB so effectively that he was appointed Ulster representative on the Supreme Council.

In Dublin, Hobson used his organisational skills to help Countess Markievicz in setting up a youth organisation, the Fianna, to prepare boys to take part in a war of liberation—the main activities were physical fitness, scouting and even participating in military exercises. Hobson intended that suitable graduates would move on to the IRB. Within a few years there was a circle of Dublin IRB officers who had begun with the Fianna; two were executed after the Rising. Indeed, many current members of the Fianna played a crucial support role during the fighting.

What really restored a sense of purpose to the IRB was the return to Dublin of Tom Clarke. His had been a hard life, and he seemed much older than his fifty years. As a youth he had emigrated to America where he got involved with Clan na Gael. He was sent to London to blow up London Bridge. He and three others were arrested, tried and sentenced to penal servitude for life in 1883. When he was released in 1896, only four other Fenians remained in prison. His long incarceration had had a disastrous effect on his physical well-being but, according to John Redmond, who visited him in Portland Prison, 'his brave spirit was keeping him alive'. After his release he returned to New York, where he married a girl over twenty years his junior. He stayed in America, working for Clan na Gael, for nine years before coming back to Dublin in 1907. His reason for doing so was to ensure that, when next there was a war, Irishmen would neither fight in the British army nor fight for Britain's enemies in a faraway land, as they had done during the Boer War. Next time, he hoped, the fight against Britain would take place in Ireland.

He opened a tobacconist shop near Parnell Square, in what was then North Great Britain Street, and was soon in the thick of republican politics again. He was delighted at the rejuvenation brought about by the northerners, Denis McCullough and Bulmer Hobson. With a great deal of political cunning, he used a resolution deploring an intended visit to Dublin by Edward VII to mount a coup against Fred Allen, and succeeded in having the latter toppled from the leadership of the Supreme Council. Later, Clarke took Hobson under his wing, together with Sean MacDermott. With the latter he established a friendship which, in many ways, was the key friendship of the revolutionary years. The older man's frailty became matched in MacDermott's case by the after-effects of an attack of polio which he suffered in the first year of their friendship. After that, MacDermott always need a cane when he walked anywhere.

The little shop was soon a humming centre of revolutionary talk. It was so small that no more than six men could stand at the counter, while there was room at the side for two more. The lighting was very bright, and the place was kept extremely clean. Most of the men who met there had very happy memories of the place; some even thought of it as a shrine. The man behind the counter was the centre of attention. Although the years of imprisonment gave him the appearance of a man ten years older than he actually was, the general impression given was of keenness, of an internal fire. He was particularly interested in the steps being taken by Carson and the unionists, and always rubbed his hands with glee when he spoke of the UVF.

Since McCullough continued to live in Belfast, where he would eventually become a medical doctor, he found himself slightly out of the loop. It was inevitable that a man of Clarke's spirit and reputation should be co-opted onto the Supreme Council. It was also inevitable that the inert old guard should be displaced from the council, some for alleged financial misconduct and others for attempting to block a more active programme for promoting republicanism.

The organisation was not a rich one, and depended very much on £300 sent each year from Clan na Gael, which supplemented the subscriptions of members, of which there were roughly two thousand. The IRB did have its own newspaper, *Irish Freedom*, until it was suppressed in 1914. It would not have been effective, however, for the IRB to be too forward in promoting a paramilitary counterpart to the Ulster Volunteers. It was Bulmer Hobson who came up with the idea of getting Eoin MacNeill to write his article for *An Claidheamh Soluis*. Although MacNeill was so respectable that he was almost staid, it was a brilliant choice. He argued that the arming of Ulster Protestants was an opportunity rather than a threat; that a government that did nothing to disarm unionists could not then disarm nationalists; that unionists were effectively taking responsibility for their own territory, and so should nationalists. England would see the way the wind was blowing and leave Ireland to her own devices. MacNeill was sure that England would react in the same way as she had about the Ulster Volunteers, and that the threat of force would be enough.[6] Respectable citizens listened.

Patrick Pearse had different ideas. He was coming to the view that 'bloodshed is a cleansing and a sanctifying thing'. It is important to remember that, when he first spoke these words, it was not his own or his colleagues' blood that he was referring to. He was actually talking about the number of people that his forces might kill, and making an excuse for the possibility that they might kill too many, or the wrong people. He was not offering himself up as a sacrificial lamb, nor was he saying anything messianic, at least not as the word is used by most Christians.[7] Observers noticed at the time a sort of desperation entering his speeches. They claimed that his imagery was showing an almost pathological lust for violence. Others saw it as exultation. One of his pupils, Desmond Ryan, remembered his burning and intense speech, and his claim that he was the most dangerous revolutionary in Ireland.

It was decided that 'a selected few' would be invited to Wynn's Hotel on 11 November. This elite formed itself into a provisional committee. Of the ten members, four were also members of the IRB. When, at further meetings, the committee expanded to thirty members, twelve were in the IRB. When, hardly three weeks after the publication of MacNeill's article, a public meeting was held at the Rotunda, thousands attended and within a very short time 4,000 recruits had attested for the Irish Volunteers. By May 1914 the numbers had risen to 75,000. The trouble was that they were an army in name only, almost totally lacking in funds and in arms. To make matters worse, the government, alarmed by the spread of militarism to the south, prohibited the import of arms to Ireland. Buying arms was the initial problem, however, because the Irish Volunteers, unlike their Ulster counterparts, did not have access to the privy purses of rich industrialists. In April 1914 the UVF demonstrated the sophistication of their finances and organisation by smuggling a cargo of guns and ammunition into ports along the east coast of Ulster and distributing them to holding depots around the province. This brought a reaction in the south, and recruiting for the Irish Volunteers soared; but unless the Volunteers became an armed force, they would be dismissed as paper tigers.

The problem was solved by a group of people whose origins were in what was to become a despised and mocked stratum of Irish society, the Anglo-Irish. Alice Stopford Green, a London socialite who was the daughter of a Church of Ireland Archdeacon, and Roger Casement, a Protestant ex-diplomat who had been knighted for his services in the Congo and Peru, formed a 'London Committee' to raise funds. In a short time, £1,500 was available. Darrell Figgis, an Anglo-Irish journalist, and Erskine Childers, a member of the Royal Navy Reserve, went to Germany to buy the guns. They obtained 1,500 Mauser rifles and 45,000 rounds of ammunition. Childers organised the transport of the guns in two yachts, *Asgard* and *Kelpie*, crewed by a mixture of Anglo-Irish, English gentry and women. Other than Childers himself, few had a long-term commitment to an armed struggle. It seems that their liberal or vaguely home rule sentiments, together with a sense of adventure, led them to try to provide a counterbalance to the arming of Protestant Ulster. On most of their parts, it is debatable whether they considered the possibility that the guns might be used in anger.

While the operation to bring guns to the Volunteers was in progress, MacNeill had to face opposition from an unexpected quarter. Under pressure from his senior colleagues, John Dillon and Joe Devlin, John Redmond moved to bring the Volunteers under his control. He told MacNeill that he would establish his own volunteer organisation if the constitution was not changed to give his nominees numerical control of the Provisional Committee. His argument was that home rule was soon to be granted and that it was reasonable that any armed forces in Ireland should be under the control of those who would have responsibility for controlling Ireland. After some delay, and a great deal of pressure, MacNeill submitted. One who urged him to do so was Bulmer Hobson, who maintained that to do otherwise would be to cause a disastrous split in the nationalist ranks that might even prove fatal. In doing this, Hobson burned his boats with his old colleagues in the IRB. Tom Clarke never forgave him. He asked Hobson, 'How much did the Castle pay you?' and never spoke to him again, always referring to him as the devil incarnate. Hobson felt that his only option was to resign from the IRB's Supreme Council. He still kept a great deal of influence within the IRB, but he came to realise that he had been the victim of a coup. By forcing him to resign, Clarke and MacDermott had effectively hijacked the Supreme Council. By accusing him of being in the pay of Dublin Castle, Clarke knew that enough dirt would stick to Hobson to ensure that he had less influence within the IRB than his record would have entitled him to.[8]

Since the operation at Howth was to provide counter-propaganda to the Larne gun-running, it was important that it should gain as much publicity as possible. This would also draw attention away from the disproportion between the shipload that arrived in Ulster and the two tiny yacht-loads that were to arrive in the south. Bulmer Hobson was in charge of the practicalities, and he arranged that *Asgard* should arrive in Howth Harbour on the morning of Sunday 26 July. Waiting for the boat would be the Volunteers, together with the Fianna. Everything went as planned, and the Volunteers started to march back into Dublin. They found their way blocked by police and a detachment from the King's Own Scottish Borderers. This check turned into farce. As the Volunteer leaders argued with the police, the rank and file simply left the road, walked through the fields and rejoined the road when they had bypassed the soldiers, so that very few rifles were actually confiscated. A secondary objective of Hobson's was that the operation, as a gesture of defiance towards the authorities, would encourage recruiting for the Volunteers. This indeed became a more likely outcome when, that evening, through malice or mal-management, members of the King's Own Scottish Borderers shot dead three people and wounded many others on Bachelor's Walk in Dublin. One man died of bayonet wounds some days later. Hobson may have felt vindicated by the fact that, by the end of August, the Irish Volunteers numbered almost two hundred thousand. By that time, however, the Great War had started, and it was an entirely different game.

While mobilisation was taking place and the preliminary battles of what was to become the Western Front were beginning to destroy the youth of Europe, John Redmond held to a position that could be accepted by almost all nationalists. He saw these new Volunteers as carrying out the same duties as the original Irish Volunteers in the eighteenth century: guarding the shores of Ireland in order to release the regular army for overseas duty. There would be no need for them to take the oath of allegiance, even. Then, without warning, he changed his mind. He was on his way home from London immediately after the Home Rule Act had passed—and been suspended. It may have been a sense of euphoria resulting from seeing his long-awaited ambition fulfilled. It may have been that he felt that he had to match Carson, who had already encouraged the uvf to enlist for overseas service. It may simply have been that he spoke off the cuff, without thinking through the implications. Whatever the reason, at Woodenbridge in Wicklow he called on the Volunteers to fight, 'wherever the firing line extends'.

Carson was more open in his use of the uvf as a bargaining counter. He refused to support recruiting until he had obtained assurances that home rule would be suspended. When he was sure that the Union was safe for the time being, he negotiated a deal whereby the uvf would be absorbed into the army as the 36th (Ulster) Division, under its own officers and with its own structure. It is interesting to contrast this with the army's welcome of Volunteers of a Catholic and nationalist background. The National Volunteers were not incorporated as a unit and Redmond had no control of the 16th Division. The division's officers were chosen with no regard for Catholic sensibilities. Its commanding general rejected most applicants for a temporary commission as being socially unsuitable and most of the rest because they had not attended Officers' Training Corps. Even John Redmond's son was rejected. Although almost every member of the rank and file of the 16th Division was Catholic and nationalist, only 20 per cent of the officers were Catholic.[9]

The Woodenbridge speech, unsurprisingly, produced a crisis in the Provisional Committee. The Redmondite representatives were expelled and the resulting split in the Volunteers left only 11,000 members loyal to Eoin MacNeill. Those who followed Redmond soon reorganised themselves and took the title of National Volunteers, trying to minimise any sense of sectionalism within their ranks. Undaunted, the rump retained their original title of Irish Volunteers and now set about reorganising themselves. As well as a General Council which would draw its members from every county in Ireland, there would be a smaller Central Executive consisting of the President and eight other members, who would be elected at the annual convention. Crucially, these members had to live within ten miles of Dublin. This Dublin-centric arrangement matched the distribution of the majority of Volunteers. Outside the capital the only two areas with substantial organisations were the south and west. This skewed distribution became even more pronounced as 1916 approached.[10] The lack of national distribution did not matter, however, since Dublin was becoming the cockpit of nationalist politics. What was more worrying was that the National Volunteers had control of most of the guns that had been brought in at Howth. Fewer than five hundred were in the hands of the Irish Volunteers, and most of these were single-shot Mausers. Even the ammunition for these was unsuitable, as the bullets were explosive.[11]

The Central Executive appointed a headquarters staff whose task would be to make a military force out of citizen Volunteers. MacNeill, as befitted his dignity, would be Chief of Staff. Hobson had demonstrated that he would make an excellent Quartermaster General, while the O'Rahilly was given the post of Director of Arms. What turned out to be the three key positions, however, were given to a trio of poets and Gaelic enthusiasts: Patrick Pearse, Thomas MacDonagh and Joseph Plunkett. These three were, or shortly became, members of the IRB, so already that secret organisation had gained control of the day-to-day running of the Volunteers. Yet the three were an unlikely set of warriors.

Pearse was born near Trinity College, in the street that was then Great Brunswick Street, one of two sons and two daughters of his English father's second marriage. He was obviously a bright lad and he worked his way through the Christian Brothers School and Royal University, taking a degree in law. Under the influence of the Brothers, the shock-troops of the Irish language as Joyce's Jesuits were the shock-troops of the Counter Reformation, Pearse developed a love for Irish. He regarded education through the English language as a form of colonialism, and an examination-centred education as a murder-machine, so his response was to set up a school in which Irish held equal sway with English and the curriculum focused on education rather than schooling. Not unexpectedly, this was a difficult ambition to finance, and he had to rely on his family and friends for help in financing and staffing the school. The words of Cú Chulainn emblazoned on a fresco in the school seem to sum up his own attitude to life: 'I care not though I were to live but one day and one night, if only my fame and my deeds live after.' In a way it is as if Pearse was the narrator and hero of his own epic, prophet and prophecy in one. One observer, who was not an admirer, spoke of the contrast between the Pearse of the family and St Enda's, quiet and full of school business; while as a public man he took great trouble with how he looked, his uniform always perfectly tailored, his hair sleeked to his skull. One biographer feels that this was the result of the inevitable tension between Pearse the reflective educationalist and the Pearse that he hoped to be, with his obvious abilities in literature and oratory being matched by achievement as a man of action.[12]

Pearse became a member of the physical force camp because that was where the logic of his narrative drove. Like MacDermott, he was moved by the plight of Dublin workers during the lockout, but this did not shake his core doctrine. He called himself Catholic and nationalist, and did not see the problem in terms of a starving workforce being brought to its knees by the employers, who were also Catholic and nationalist. The desperate poverty of Dublin, he believed, was the result of the foreign domination of Ireland. A free Ireland would not have such conditions. It was a condition of manhood to fight for one's rights. Perhaps he even believed that rights granted were of an inferior nature to rights obtained by struggle. He was one of the first Irish Volunteers, and was a founder-member of the Provisional Committee. Tom Clarke was wary about him, because of his record of political moderation. He was converted by listening to Pearse give the oration at a republican commemoration. By the end of 1913 he was a member of the IRB, sworn in by Bulmer Hobson.

Pearse had only lately become convinced of the necessity for physical force. His main contribution to the Volunteers, other than his oratory, was a booklet called 'Defensive Warfare', which was largely copied from ideas of Bulmer Hobson's, in which he laid out a sequence of events leading towards guerrilla activity. On the strength of this he was given the position of Director of Military Organisation. This not only allowed him to develop a blueprint for the Volunteer army, but to allocate IRB members to key positions within it.[13] In the event, the structure was taken straight from the British army, with one minor exception. Pearse seems not to have liked the title 'colonel', and substituted for it the crisper-sounding 'commandant'. A structure based on battalions and brigades may not have seemed appropriate over the country as a whole, but in Dublin and in some areas of the south-west there were enough Volunteers to give the organisation a semblance of reality. There were four Dublin City battalions, with another in the countryside of north County Dublin. Of the five battalion commanders only one, Éamon de Valera of the city's 3rd Battalion, was not already a member of the IRB. This exception was only made after Pearse interviewed de Valera and reassured himself that he could be trusted to obey orders without question.[14] Thomas MacDonagh was placed in overall command of the Dublin Brigade. With these commanders in place, Pearse was confident that the new Volunteers would follow him into insurrection. It is likely, however, that the majority on the Executive of the Volunteers was opposed to armed action except in self-defence.

Joseph Plunkett came, as they say in Ireland, from a good family. His father was a Papal Count, given the title for building work he had done near Rome, and Director of the National Museum in Dublin. The family had a tradition of active Catholicism, and the martyred Oliver Plunkett had an honoured branch on the family tree. Joseph had not had a healthy childhood, and had spent much of his time in the Mediterranean. He decided that he wanted to learn Irish and he met MacDonagh in 1910, when he was looking for someone to act as a tutor. MacDonagh's origins were less exalted. Originally from County Tipperary, he had qualified as a teacher. His interest in Irish came from his days as a student and he became deeply committed to the language. He cooperated with Patrick Pearse when Pearse set up St Enda's as a bilingual school before going on to take a degree at University College Dublin. He did so well in this that he was taken on as an assistant lecturer by UCD and might have looked forward to a comfortable life, combining academe and the theatre; even before taking his degree he had had a play produced by the Abbey Theatre. What jolted him out of this easy prospect were the bloody events that took place on the streets of Dublin during the lock-out of 1913, when the treatment of strikers by the police was simply brutal. He was one of the first to join the Irish Volunteers. Here he demonstrated his organisational abilities when he helped Bulmer Hobson to organise the Howth gunrunning. This work impressed Tom Clarke so much that MacDonagh was given full control of the funeral of O'Donovan Rossa, as we saw above.

It was the trio of Pearse, Plunkett and MacDonagh which began to formulate the plan which saw its fulfilment in April 1916. They were well known in nationalist circles and beyond, but the nature of what they were doing was not. Indeed, they were like a centrepiece to a set of Russian dolls, hidden from the world by the IRB, the Volunteers, the Gaelic League, Sinn Féin, Irish nationalism and Irish Catholicism.

The first concrete steps towards an armed rising were taken even before Redmond made his crucial speech at Woodenbridge. A committee of Clan na Gael met with the German ambassador to America in August 1914. They told him that there would be a rising in Ireland during the course of the war and asked for military aid. The Supreme Council of the IRB also decided that there should be a rebellion. In early September, before the Home Rule Act had passed the House of Lords, a group of advanced nationalists, which included James Connolly and Arthur Griffith, met in Dublin to discuss the possibility of a rising. Sir Roger Casement appointed himself Irish ambassador to Germany, got funding from America, and proceeded on an adventure that might have been scripted by John Buchan. The sum total of his achievement was obtaining permission to recruit an Irish Brigade from among captured soldiers. There were few volunteers. He spent much of his time in Germany suffering from depression and vulnerable to a series of illnesses.

About eleven thousand Volunteers chose to stay loyal to the principles of MacNeill. Although this was still a substantial number, it was a pitifully small percentage of the body as a whole. For the first months of the war the organisation, which continued to use the title Irish Volunteers, actually increased in numbers and by the time of Rossa's funeral was very close to the peak it reached in early 1916 of about sixteen thousand. It was MacNeill's intention to keep this as a force in being, highly organised and well-disciplined, ready to act as a pressure group after the war, when he thought they would be joined by thousands of disillusioned ex-soldiers. There were only two factors which would justify open revolt. One was the possibility that the authorities might try to disarm the Volunteers. The other was if conscription was extended to include Ireland. The provisional plans devised by MacNeill, with the help of the O'Rahilly and Bulmer Hobson, did not include pitched battles on Dublin streets. They looked towards an extended period of guerrilla warfare across the entire country. In the meantime, the Volunteers should continue to arm and train.

This was not what Joseph Plunkett had in mind. It is difficult to establish Plunkett's credentials as Director of Military Operations. As an individual he had been less in the public eye than most of the other players. His poetry was highly spiritual, and he was engrossed in the ideas of St John of the Cross and St Catherine of Sienna. Before the war he also edited a weekly journal called the *Irish Review*, with contributors ranging from W. B. Yeats to Arthur Griffith, as well as Plunkett himself. In politics he had been a supporter of home rule, an ally of Tom Kettle, but this changed by the end of 1913. From the establishment of the Volunteers he changed the content of the *Review* so that it became an unofficial organ for the Volunteers, said to be much more readable than the *Irish Volunteer* itself. Friends noted a change in his personality after he made this commitment to the Volunteers; once considered taciturn and reserved, he was now described as outgoing and happy.[15] One area of Irish history that he studied closely was the abortive rising of Robert Emmet in 1803. His conclusion from this was that Dublin had to be seized if an insurrection was to have any chance of success. As the Volunteer movement had grown in mid-1914, this had begun to seem possible; but the likelihood of success shrank rapidly after the split. Plunkett had also studied Clausewitz, seen by many to be the prophet of modern military thought. Clausewitz believed that the defender always carried the advantage, and this had proved even more to be true with the development of accurate modern rifles. In addition, keeping the inexperienced Volunteers in defensive positions would make it easier to control their fire. A final point was that Clausewitz believed, like Napoleon, that a campaign could hinge on a single battle, leading Plunkett to believe that a successful Battle of Dublin might be enough to drive the English from Ireland. It is a pity that he had not studied the more recent American Civil War, where battle after battle— some estimate ten thousand in all—failed to deal a fatal blow to the enemy, and it was only after Sherman's burnt earth march through Georgia and the Carolinas that the South's will to fight was extinguished. Some others on the headquarters staff of the Volunteers may have tried to learn the lessons of the Civil War and of the Franco-Prussian War, in that they advocated the use of guerrilla tactics. In America, guerrilla forces, many of them unofficial, had proved a constant strain for both sides, while in France a continuing guerrilla war had denied the Germans a clear-cut victory.

Redmond and the Irish Parliamentary Party found themselves becoming much more closely aligned with the administration at Dublin Castle. The very fact that this administration had not followed the evolution of Whitehall in the nineteenth century tended to under-line Ireland's status as a colony within the United Kingdom, different not only from England, but from Wales and Scotland. The Irish Secretary, Augustine Birrell, became Redmond's closest ally in the government. Part of the reason for this was that Birrell saw his as a caretaker administration, keeping things ticking over until the time that Redmond took up the post of Prime Minister of Ireland. Certainly he listened carefully to advice from Redmond, while his deputy, Sir Matthew Nathan, cultivated John Dillon in Dublin. Nathan, nominally Undersecretary, was the man who ran Ireland on a day-to-day basis. It was on the advice of Redmond and Dillon that Birrell played down the importance of the MacNeill Volunteers.[16] It was the increasing identification of the Irish Parliamentary Party with the government, combined with the fact that Carson, but not Redmond, had become a member of the Cabinet, which allowed Redmond's opponents to portray him as a mere recruiting sergeant for the British army. Yet this close identification brought some benefits to Ireland. Birrell negotiated some exemptions from wartime regulations for the Irish Liquor Trade, as well as some amelioration of the provisions of the Defence of the Realm Act (DORA). When increasing militancy on the part of advanced nationalists goaded the authorities into action, Birrell kept repressive measures to a minimum, and was careful not to make martyrs of the activists. For a time this seemed to be working and there was no great build-up of militant nationalism till after Easter 1916.[17]

But this was in the future, and in 1915 MacNeill had a problem that he didn't know existed. Within the Volunteers, most of the key positions were held by members of the IRB. The triumvirate of Pearse, Plunkett and MacDermott on the headquarters staff was joined by another IRB member when Eamonn Ceannt became Director of Communications shortly after the O'Donovan Rossa funeral. Ceannt was a clerk in the Dublin City Treasury Department. Educated by the Christian Brothers, he had grown into a dour and distant individual who had little time for debate. He had been brought into the IRB by MacDermott, to whom he had a fierce loyalty.[18] The IRB were now well-placed to keep a tight grip on any developments. They ensured that it was one of their members, Plunkett, who went to Germany to organise a shipment of arms. They squashed loose talk of a premature rising. They even set up their own Military Council, initially comprising Pearse, Plunkett and Ceannt and later joined by Clarke and MacDermott. Later, James Connolly and Thomas MacDonagh were co-opted onto it. These were the seven men who, in April 1916, would sign the Proclamation of Independence. When this group eventually decided on a date for the rising, the timing was hidden not only from Eoin MacNeill, but from Denis McCullough, President of the IRB's Supreme Council. All these levels of concealment may have been necessary to save the operation from informers, but such lack of communication weakened the chain of command within the IRB itself and led to confusion throughout Ireland when the time of action eventually arrived.

There was a great deal of confusion when the Dublin Brigade had a field day at Stepaside, then open country south of Dublin, at Easter 1915. Pearse had prepared detailed orders running to four closely typed pages, which prescribed in detail the conduct of the attack. The exercise was a shambles. Not a single objective was reached. Ginger O'Connell, who was Director of Inspection on the Volunteers Staff, having been replaced by MacDonagh as Director of Training, saw the problem as resulting from the doctrinaire way in which people like Pearse viewed the insurrection, so that they put the Volunteers in a strait-jacket which would not allow the men to adapt plans to the local situation. He also thought that a great deal of effort was being wasted in trying to organise places considered to be of strategic importance, like Kildare. The effort should be concentrated on areas where men were easily organised, he said. Once large groups of men were armed and trained, that area would become of strategic importance, able to operate in areas where the authorities had difficulty in exerting their strength.[19] It is probably true to say that O'Connell, who had served with the US army, thought Pearse and Plunkett were playing at soldiers.

Yet when Thomas Clarke in May 1915 established a Military Council, the very existence of which was a closely guarded secret, its members were Pearse, Plunkett and Ceannt. MacDermott was in prison at this stage but he joined the others in September when he completed his sentence. These individuals had formed a sort of advisory committee for the IRB Supreme Council even before this. The council kept no minutes of its meetings, and, although it produced the plan for the Rising, no copies of the final plan survive; indeed, it is thought that there were only three copies ever made. The plan, which Plunkett seems to have formulated, was based on the idea of seizing a defensive perimeter within Dublin and fighting a purely defensive battle. He thought, presumably, that this sort of battle would neutralise the numerical advantage of the British army. When Desmond Fitzgerald raised the possibility that the British would simply stand back and shell the defensive positions, he was assured by MacDonagh that the British would never use artillery in the city, since they would be 'injuring their own supporters'.[20]

There was a growing tension within the organisation between those who advocated this city warfare, with the seizure of iconic buildings, and others who believed in fighting in the countryside. Hobson was one of the most prominent of the latter group, and he and Pearse had heated arguments on the matter. O'Connell, as Director of Inspections, set up training camps which focused on the skills of guerrilla warfare, but these were 'tolerated' by Pearse and Plunkett only on the grounds that they did no harm, even if they would serve no useful purpose. It is also possible that Pearse thought that these activities would encourage the authorities to expect trouble in the provinces and to lower their guard in Dublin. For a time it looked as if O'Connell and Hobson were winning the argument, since the umpire's report on a field day at

Coolock, held in November 1915, emphasised the need for special training to prevent units being broken up in close country. This encouraged O'Connell to publish a series of articles on 'hedge-fighting' for small units in the *Irish Volunteer*, but these were totally ignored by Plunkett and the others.

By this time the Military Council's thinking was going in the opposite direction. Without minutes, and with no official report to anybody, it is difficult to establish what exactly their thinking was. Geraldine Plunkett, sister of Joseph, claimed to have heard some of the discussions of the Military Council.[21] She said that Plunkett and the council wanted to see success in Dublin before the Rising was extended to the country as a whole. In addition, rural rebellion was the norm in Ireland. Some senior officers in the Volunteers did want to fight their campaign in the hills. She dismissed these people as being afraid of getting caught like rats in a trap among the streets. They had, she said, a fantastic idea of the accuracy of big guns and of machine-guns; they thought such weapons mowed you down. Perhaps, if the military authorities had not been so reluctant to release details of fighting in Gallipoli and the Western Front, the conspirators might have had a more realistic appreciation of modern weapons.

It is important to remember the odds that were stacked against the success of any insurrection. In spite of the claim that England's difficulty would be Ireland's opportunity, the build-up of army numbers in Ireland meant that there was probably less chance of success than there would have been before the war. Almost the entire Catholic population of Ireland supported the war effort, so much so that Desmond FitzGerald felt that Ireland had been 'absorbed into Britain', leaving a true Ireland only in the west where, incidentally, most of the anti-Redmond Volunteers lived. Worst, from the advanced nationalist point of view, was the fact that the Irish were prospering as a result of the war. Farmers had greatly increased profits and the level of unemployment among the working classes was falling. For allies, the Volunteers had only the Citizen Army, which had suffered from low morale from the days of the Dublin lock-out.

It is unquestionably the fault of the British government that this level of goodwill was squandered. Almost no information came from the battlefields, other than the horror stories brought home by wounded soldiers. A certain amount of military censorship was probably necessary for national security, but the practice went far beyond what was reasonable. Kitchener banned photography at the front and suppressed reports of the gallant fighting of Irish troops in the Gallipoli Peninsula. As a result, those negative reports that did reach Ireland, and the growing evidence of casualty lists, could not be countered by tales of Irish heroism. It seemed as if Irish lives were being squandered in a pointless demonstration of incompetence, while there was no official recognition of Irish achievements. It is not surprising that recruitment fell as 1915 progressed, and by the autumn was far below the numbers needed to maintain the reserves of the Irish battalions. Kitchener put pressure on the authorities in Dublin Castle to estimate the number of single men of military age who had not yet joined the forces. Dublin Castle came up with a figure of 100,000 men 'readily available'.[22] A series of recruiting drives brought poor results, and by February 1916 the number enlisting fell to just over 300 per week.

Long before this, the threat of conscription became a common topic in the Irish countryside, and led to a heightened, almost neurotic atmosphere. This contributed to a debate within the Catholic Church concerning their support for the Allied cause. Although the bishops had been almost unanimous in their support for Catholic Belgium, they were less enamoured of the anti-clericalism of the French army. A story circulated throughout Ireland of a wounded Irishman in a French hospital who had to make a written declaration that he was a Catholic and wanted to receive the sacraments before he could be visited by a priest.[23] Cardinal Logue entered the fray in July 1915 when he claimed that Britain had deliberately destroyed Irish industry, forcing young men and women to emigrate. Now the government was looking for men, but they weren't there to be had. At the end of July Pope Benedict xv denounced the war as futile and called on all Christians to make peace. One the first anniversary of Britain's declaration of war, Bishop O'Dwyer of Limerick wrote to Redmond stating that the prolongation of the war beyond what was necessary was a crime against God and humanity, and calling on him to follow the Pope's advice. Redmond deflected the bishop's call by blaming the Germans for continuing the war.

In November there was an incident which took place in Liverpool which brought the conscription issue once more to the fore. A group of about seven hundred young Irishmen, most of them from the west, tried to emigrate to America. Because of restrictions on shipping routes after the sinking of *Lusitania*, they had to join their ship in Liverpool. Both Cunard and White Star Lines refused to embark them, since they felt that they should be going to the Western Front instead. Nationalist Ireland was outraged. Redmond attempted to defuse the situation, claiming that the emigrants' fears of conscription were groundless. He then went on to score an own-goal, saying that it was cowardly of them to try to emigrate. It was, once again, Bishop O'Dwyer who challenged him. These were peasants, the bishop said, who only wanted to grow their crop of potatoes. They knew nothing of the causes of the war; their only crime was that they did not want to die for England. Redmond, he went on, had betrayed the trust given to him as a national leader by refusing to stand up for his own countrymen. His final shot was probably the most deadly. Redmond claimed to have delivered home rule, whereas anyone with intelligence could see that what was on offer was only a pretence at home rule, and even that would never come into operation. This was a challenge to the very raison d'être of the Irish Parliamentary Party, and it was seized on by Redmond's opponents. The bishop had evaded strict Dublin censorship by having his letter published in provincial papers. Now it was re-published as a handbill, and proved so popular and widespread that there was no point in prosecuting people who had it in their possession. Although even at this stage anti-British clergy were in a small minority, it was a sign of things to come.

While this exchange was going on, the fortunes of the Volunteers were undergoing a change. Terence MacSwiney was second-in-command of the Cork Brigade. For much of the year he had despaired of increasing numbers in the brigade. He felt, however, that men from Cork and Kerry would be against conscription and this proved to be the case. When, at the end of November, a parade of Volunteers was held in Cork City, 1,500 turned out. Even the police began to notice the change in atmosphere and confidence. For the time being there were several counties where the Volunteers still had not established units— Carlow, Leitrim, Longford, Sligo and, for all practical purposes, Roscommon—but units in the west and south were gaining in strength. Some units of National Volunteers were transferring their allegiance to the Irish Volunteers. An interesting point is raised in a report from east Galway; here the police considered that most of the population disapproved of the Volunteers, but were afraid to oppose them because they had no confidence in the government's power to protect them. In this way, the Volunteers began to have an importance out of proportion to their numbers.[24]

Clarke decided that something needed to be done to persuade the Germans that Irish nationalists were serious about staging a rising. The first initiative in the great Hiberno-German Alliance, that undertaken by the ex-British diplomat, Sir Roger Casement, had ended in humiliation. The grand total of volunteers for Casement's Irish Brigade was fifty-four. Most of the prisoners of war were home rulers and would not countenance fighting on the side of a Protestant country which had attacked Catholic Belgium. Those few who had heard of Casement considered him to be a traitor.

Plunkett, the one who would cause least unease to the British if he visited the continent, was chosen to undertake another John Buchan adventure, leaving Ireland in April 1915 and not returning till July. He entered Germany by train from Switzerland and arrived in Berlin, where the German authorities put him in touch with Casement. This was fortunate since he could speak almost no German and he might well have been arrested as a spy. Together, the two men tried to compose a document that would persuade the Germans to cooperate. This memorandum analysed the present condition of Ireland, the mistakes made by the French during the invasion of Mayo, so that they would not be repeated, and the glittering prizes that awaited the country daring enough to invade England by the back door. All this could be obtained by giving 40,000 rifles to the Volunteers and landing a German infantry division of 12,000 men on the shores of the Shannon estuary. Thousands of Irishmen would bear arms for their German allies, they claimed. British forces in Ireland were not as strong as their numbers would indicate, since they were in scattered garrisons and training camps. It is doubtful whether the Germans would consider moving so many men on a long voyage from Kiel to Shannon through seas controlled by their British enemy, to land on an island so easily reinforced from the huge numbers of Kitchener's armies now at an advanced stage of training in England, whereas the invading Germans would be almost impossible to resupply. There were aspects of the plan which were frankly disingenuous; Plunkett claimed that the countryside was suitable for guerrilla warfare—not something the Germans would have wanted to hear, with their experience of *francs-tireurs* in the Franco-Prussian War—and that the Volunteers were training for this sort of action. He also claimed that the Military Council had plans for the destruction of British railway bridges, canals and viaducts.[25]

It is doubtful whether Plunkett was really upset when he realised there would be no German troops on offer. It was probably of more importance to Casement's ambitions than his own. Plunkett and his co-conspirators, after all, were focusing all their attention on Dublin, far away from the Shannon. Pearse, however, nursed a hope all through Easter Week that the Germans would arrive. His last letter to his mother confirms this. Sean MacDermott also claimed that the leaders 'had been sure [the Germans] would be there'. Another clue is in the wording of the actual Proclamation, where Pearse spoke of 'our gallant allies in Europe'. This phrase made enemies of the Republic all those who were currently fighting against the Germans; it seems hardly worthwhile to alienate a large proportion of the adult male population of Ireland in return for a shipload of obsolescent guns which was already at the bottom of Cork Harbour. What led Pearse and MacDermott to believe in German reinforcement? Did Plunkett return to Ireland with an over-optimistic estimate of what the Germans were offering, or did he deliberately mislead his co-conspirators, confident in the ultimate success of his plan?

Perhaps Plunkett and the Military Council believed that the landing of arms was the key to success. If that were so, then there should be signs of detailed preparations, the mobilisation of Volunteers in the south-west to ensure that the guns were brought ashore and sent where they were needed. Plunkett himself said, after he was captured, that nothing was forgotten.[26] What traces of plans that can be found in the evidence are fragmentary and contradictory. First to be assigned the task of moving the guns was the Limerick battalion, under the command of Sean Fitzgibbon, who had been sent down from Dublin for this purpose. Fitzgibbon was considered a 'talker' by MacDonagh, however, and secret orders had been sent to IRB men in the Limerick battalion to let Fitzgibbon think he was in charge until the moment for action came, when they were to take matters into their own hands.

It can be no surprise that there was so much talk that Eoin MacNeill actually overheard a conversation in Limerick in September 1915, where some of the Limerick battalion were discussing instructions issued by

Pearse 'in the event of war in Ireland'.[27] He was concerned, but not concerned enough to make any serious effort to establish what was going on. Pearse, perhaps, learned of this breach of security, for he sent Diarmuid Lynch soon afterwards to look into the possibility of changing the landing site to Kerry. It was he who, in consultation with Austin Stack, the Kerry commander, decided on the deep-water pier at Fenit, near Tralee. This may have rung some alarm bells with the Military Council, as the local Volunteer commander had already been removed from office twice for laziness, but there was nothing better on offer.[28]

Diarmuid Lynch was obviously a very trusted colleague of Pearse's. As mentioned before, an absolute minimum of the Military Council's deliberations were committed to paper. In January 1916, it became important for the commanding officers of Volunteer units around the country, at least those who were also members of the IRB, to know what they would be expected to do when the rising occurred. Rather than sending written orders, Pearse briefed Lynch in fairly general terms of the dispositions for each county force, so that these could be passed on to the officers concerned. In the circumstances, Lynch was unable to pass on this information since he was confined to Dublin under Defence Regulations.

Another complication was caused by the stance of James Connolly. He wanted to make war immediately, and there was a real danger that the rising would go off at half-cock, with only the Citizen Army taking to the streets. In January 1916, Pearse invited Connolly to a meeting— there was talk of kidnapping, but none of the major players ever used the word. By the end of the meeting, Connolly had been persuaded to coordinate his plans with those of the IRB and to join the Military Council in its planning activities. He accepted, and a union between the political left and the religious right was established.

Eoin MacNeill's interference was more difficult to deal with. In view of his indecisive behaviour in Holy Week 1916, and of his less than celebrated performance in the Boundary Commission, MacNeill is sometimes dismissed as a puppet concerned about his dignity. In fact he was a very intelligent man who had set as his target the maintenance of a military body to oppose the UVF at the war's conclusion. He didn't want the Volunteers frittered away in a pointless rising that would leave the field open to the cold calculations of Carson and Craig when the soldiers returned from the battlefields of Europe. There were regular appeals in the north for Protestants to keep up the strength of the UVF, so that they would be ready to take up the final great task of keeping Ulster British.

Pearse had managed to keep his secret so far, and he may have thought that MacNeill would be dealt with easily. MacNeill had written a letter, asking for clarification of the apparent orders that he had overhead in Limerick. Pearse tried to deal with the matter by reading the letter to the Volunteers Headquarters Staff while the Chief of Staff, MacNeill, was absent and would not be able to press the matter. Not to be denied, MacNeill called a special meeting and prepared a memorandum to go with it. This was a closely argued document, still in existence. In it he accused insurrectionists of being people who sought to repeat the ready-made arguments that had led previous generations to their deaths—that Ireland had to strike during the present war; that Ireland always struck too late; that the initiative went to the side that struck first—because they could not think of anything better. The first, he said, could not be proved. The second was completely untrue; most Irish risings failed because there had been inadequate preparation; the third was a nonsense, because the initiative ultimately lay with those who could bring the greatest forces to bear: the British. Clinging to these ideas relieved Pearse and his friends of the responsibility of thinking for themselves. If the Volunteers of 1798 had concentrated on remaining a force in being, who knows what they might have secured? Anyway, the world had changed in a hundred years, and the momentum was with nationalism. They must stick with the real world and reject fantasy; they must reject the vanity that they were right and the Irish people knew no better.

They might have sat like rebellious schoolboys, being lectured by their dogmatic history master. But they didn't; they didn't even hear it. Before MacNeill could say anything, Pearse denied that any preparations were being made for war and reproached those on the HQ Staff who thought otherwise for their suspicious nature. Not prepared to force the issue—and probably another split within the Volunteers—MacNeill said nothing more about his memorandum.

Chapter 5 ∿

| TO THE WESTERN FRONT

When it was established, the 36th (Ulster) Division was desperately short of NCO instructors. The army had been, traditionally, a career for Irish Catholics, so most old soldiers had enlisted in the 10th or 16th Divisions. Before the war, the UVF had paid ex-NCOs to act as drill sergeants, but these were mostly reservists and had been recalled to the colours. Others had enlisted in the 10th Division, impatient with the political manoeuvring of Carson and Craig. For the time being, volunteer NCOs kept control, but Major Crozier was sent to Horse Guards Parade in London to try to persuade better-qualified NCOs to opt for the 36th Division. Most of those he did persuade were relatively old men and, although keen enough, were out of date. This unpromising condition, however, was more than offset by the enthusiasm of the soldiers and by the fact that most were serving with neighbours and friends. Whole platoons might come from the same Belfast street; a valuable arrangement in this early stage of the division's history, but one which concentrated tragedy in the dreadful days of July 1916.[1]

It did not take the division long to begin looking like soldiers. Craig had ordered the thousand uniforms directly from a military outfitter. This gesture, paid for by friends of Ulster in England, meant that 36th Division did not have to go through the indignity of doing their drills while still wearing civilian clothing. Most of them had already learned the basics of drill, anyway, either in the UVF, or in the Scouts or Boys' Brigade. The real advantage that they had over other recruits to Kitchener's armies was that many of them had had practice in using rifles. Indeed, while other units were still using wooden drill rifles, men of 36th Division were firing live rounds, using Mausers belonging to the UVF, at targets on ranges which were also owned by the UVF. Although this was strictly against regulations, as long as the men were in Ireland, inspecting generals tended to ignore this as an administrative inconvenience. At this stage, very little was done to prepare the men for the realities of modern war. Their lesson on digging trenches could be summed up as: eighteen inches wide and straight down.

Right from the start, it looked as if Redmond's hopes of a shared war bringing Protestant and Catholic together were in vain. When the division was formed, there was a shortage of army accommodation in Ulster. Craig went directly to Kitchener, and was persistent enough for Kitchener to order that all the division's requirements should be met. This led to a most distasteful result. The staff officer assigned to the division to liaise about the construction of hutted camps was a Dublin Catholic. This was discovered through the Ulster Club. Major Crozier, in his memoirs, simply says that a letter was quickly sent to a 'friendly general in England' and the offending blot was removed from the landscape. The result was that the camps built for the Ulster Division at Ballykinler, Clandeboye, Newtownards and Finner only had tents for accommodation. It may have been an avenging deity who subsequently sent an Atlantic gale to Finner Camp that autumn of 1914 and levelled the tents, soaking the inhabitants. The winter that followed was particularly wet and cold and the ground was turned to the consistency of porridge. In spite of their youth, many of the men succumbed to illness. There were more deaths in the 36th Division during this period than there were in the other two Irish divisions.[2] It became so bad that something had to be done, and as many of the units as possible were moved to available barrack accommodation, though this meant breaking up brigades. The 10th Inniskillings, the Derry battalion, remained in Finner during the wildest of the weather, only leaving at the beginning of May 1915.[3]

When the Derrys did eventually leave Finner, it was to take a long march across the Ulster countryside, from the Atlantic Ocean to Belfast Lough. The unit weaved its way through as many towns as it could on this trek, including Derry itself, because its task was to encourage recruits to come forward. On 8 May, the entire 36th (Ulster) Division was inspected at Malone, south of Belfast, before parading through the city. It was a day of festival, and many unionist luminaries, including Carson, had come from London to witness the event. People had come from all over the province by special train. It was like an early Twelfth of July, with streamers and bunting in the streets and cheering crowds everywhere. There must have a sense of anti-climax after this, as they were ordered back to quarters, where they had to remain another two months before being transferred to Seaford, on the Sussex coast. Even then there was disappointment for some; 9th Inniskillings, from Tyrone, were sent to Ballycastle to get over an outbreak of measles.[4]

The 16th Division also had its difficulties. It had been formed as part of Kitchener's Second Army, but had not originally been intended as an Irish division. Under pressure from Redmond and others, Kitchener was finally persuaded that such an organisation would encourage recruiting from the Irish National Volunteers, and he first cleared a brigade for Irish recruits, before clearing the entire division. Its commanding officer was Lieutenant General Sir Lawrence Parsons, born in what was then King's County, now Offaly, in the Irish midlands. He had had a long and distinguished career in Africa and India, and had served under Kitchener during the re-conquest of Sudan. Now fifty-four, he had retired in 1909. He set up his headquarters in Dublin, but was sent south to Munster because 10th (Irish) Division had first claim on accommodation and facilities. His new headquarters was set up in Mallow by early October.[5]

47 Brigade headquarters, under Brigadier General P. J. Miles, was established in Fermoy. Its first battalion, 6th Royal Irish Regiment, was raised around Fermoy that October. Their accommodation was shared by 6th Connaught Rangers. This was the battalion to which most Belfast nationalist recruits were assigned, and it had a northern commanding officer, Lieutenant Colonel J. S. M. Lenox-Conyngham, from Springhill House near Moneymore, in County Derry. He had spent thirty years with the Rangers.

Both battalions recruited well, and by spring of 1915 each numbered about sixteen hundred men. One surprising group of recruits for 6th Royal Irish Regiment came from Guernsey, who had been impressed by the regiment's 2nd Battalion when it had been stationed on the island before the war. There were enough to found a Guernsey company, D Company. The fact that half of them could only speak French was made up for by their enthusiasm, and they turned out to be of immense value when the battalion was in France. A less-travelled company was B Company, which was comprised of nationalists from County Derry.

In spite of being overwhelmingly nationalist in the ranks, 6th Royal Irish Regiment had only two officers who were nationalist in politics.

One of these was John Redmond's brother, William, who was a captain. This was also the rank of Stephen Gwynn, another nationalist politician. Although he was the son of the Church of Ireland rector in Rathmullan in County Donegal, Gwynn was IPP MP for Galway City. In spite of their politics, these two MPs proved extremely popular in the officers' mess.

7th Leinster Regiment, also based in Fermoy, was built around a nucleus left behind by 6th Leinsters. Recruiting was slow, with most recruits coming directly from Belfast or from the regimental depot in Birr. Its commanding officer, Lieutenant Colonel Wood, set up an officers' cadet company, which allowed him to train junior officers. This was the route that Stephen Gwynn chose to become an officer. The winter of 1914/15 was a bad one, as we have already seen. Yet, in the middle of this, 7th Leinsters were forced to leave the overcrowded barracks at Fermoy and march to Kilworth. Although the total journey was only seven miles, it was undertaken in near-blizzard conditions, with full packs, and the last four miles was a steep climb. They arrived to discover that almost nothing had been done to prepare for their arrival. It is possibly lucky that 7th Leinsters got a new commanding officer soon afterwards. This was Lieutenant Colonel G. A. McLean, a New Zealander by birth, who had explored Patagonia and had taken part in Shackleton's 1908 expedition to the Antarctic.[6]

The final battalion in 47 Brigade was 7th Royal Irish Rifles. This battalion had been established in Belfast, but had been moved to Ballyvonare Camp in County Cork soon afterwards. This area, and the Ballyhoura Mountains nearby, gave them excellent terrain for training. This battalion also had an unusual group assigned to it. In March 1915 six officers and 225 men from the Jersey Militia arrived. This brought the battalion up to its wartime complement.

48 Brigade headquarters was set up in Fermoy, while its four infantry battalions were all stationed at Buttevant. This made the accommodation at Buttevant very crowded. The overcrowding was only relieved when three extra training camps were built, at Ballyvonare, Fermoy and Mitchelstown. Luckily, these had hutted accommodation, so 48 Brigade did not have to endure the wet canvas of their comrades in 36th Division that winter. Even before this concession to personal space had come on-stream, the brigade trained for eight hours every day whatever the weather threw at them. Battalions within the brigade

were: 8th and 9th Royal Munster Fusiliers; and 8th and 9th Royal
Dublin Fusiliers.

9th Munsters had as its second-in-command Major Sir Francis
Vane. He got into a dispute with his brigade commander, Brigadier
General K. J. Buchanan, and his divisional commander, Lieutenant
General Parsons, and was relieved of his duties. He became a recruiting
officer, and was to make a controversial contribution to the story of the
Easter Rising. This unit had another interesting officer in its number.
This was Tom Kettle, who had been MP for East Tyrone, and had been
in Belgium during the German invasion. He witnessed the atrocities
committed around Louvain, which had been closely associated with
Ireland in the sixteenth century, and this convinced him of the
necessity for the Irish to fight on the side of civilisation. He saw Irish
participation in the war as a crusade.

49 Brigade, the third in the division, had its headquarters in
Tipperary Barracks. All four of its battalions originated in the north,
and the move to Tipperary took them far from their traditional recruiting areas. The country was now divided militarily into two districts,
North and South, which impeded recruiting for these battalions even
more. On 2 October, 7th Inniskillings had only six officers and eighteen
other ranks. By March 1915 there were still only 400, and a party was
sent to Fermanagh to drum up recruits, with little success. Many
northern nationalists were hesitant about joining regiments which
were closely associated with 36th (Ulster) Division.[7] It looked for a
while as though the battalion would be amalgamated with another or
even disbanded, but the CO of 7th Inniskillings was made of stern stuff.
At his own expense he spent the month of June collecting men in
Ireland and in his estates in the north-east of England. A total of 670
recruits were obtained in this way, but the battalion did not reach full
strength until January 1916, when it got reinforcements from English
and Scottish regiments.

The Royal Irish Fusiliers did rather better in the matter of recruiting,
but even so had difficulty reaching full strength. As the ranks of its four
battalions—7th and 8th Royal Inniskilling Fusiliers and 7th and 8th
Royal Irish Fusiliers—gradually filled up, some men were moved into
the local workhouse for want of accommodation.[8] Tipperary Barracks
itself had been designed for the use of one battalion and was hopelessly
overcrowded. A new hutted camp was built west of the town, and

officers were allowed to use empty married quarters, and this relieved some of the pressure.

Pressure on housing was relieved in a most unwelcome way in June 1915 when 49 Brigade lost 1,200 men to 10th (Irish) Division, which was due to go overseas to Gallipoli. It was as if the brigade was going to have to start over again. Redmond got involved in the controversy, arguing that all Irish Catholic recruits should be sent to the 16th Division; the War Office would hear none of it. There was a double problem caused by the fact that many northern nationalists were unwilling to sign on for 16th Division. They opted for the reserve battalions of Irish regiments, as this seemed a quicker way to see some fighting. It seemed as if 16th Division might never leave Ireland. Some members of the Parliamentary Party feared the same thing; that their 'Irish Brigade' might be kept in Ireland permanently, as some sort of holding formation.[9] There was even talk of 49 Brigade being disbanded and replaced by a brigade of South Africans.

Lacking generous well-wishers in England, 16th Division had to wait before getting its allocation of equipment, and its early drills were performed in a motley of clothing. One sergeant in 7th Inniskillings paraded in a bowler hat, a civilian jacket and khaki trousers. To complete the ensemble he wore boots and puttees. Any resemblance to a music hall act was belied by the work required in an average day. The day began with a run shortly after reveille, at 6 a.m. Two periods of drill took place each day: three and a half hours in the morning and another two and a half in the afternoon. About three times a week there would be a route march of up to five miles. There were usually three lectures a week, held at 4 p.m. There were also night exercises. There was a limit to what could be done until proper equipment arrived, and the concentration was on military discipline and fitness.

Drill purpose rifles arrived at the end of November. These were obsolete weapons which could no longer be fired safely. When bayonets also arrived there were a few more drill exercises that could be taught. In the New Year leather equipment arrived. Although this American-made equipment differed from the army's standard webbing, it meant that the division could now carry full kit into the field for extended marches and exercises. As spring approached, the pace of training increased. Route marches were no longer a few miles and were undertaken with the full discipline of field service marching order. Proper rifles arrived and companies in turn were marched to the rifle ranges to learn that mastery of fire power that was the pride of the army. To give a bit of edge to this, shooting competitions were organised and a healthy rivalry developed among the different units. The downside of this was service in the butts, below the targets, reporting back on a soldier's accuracy and repairing targets. It was a long, noisy, boring business, often in cold and wet conditions, but it could be enlivened by occasional exercises in wit: 'Tell the man on number one target that the only way he'll hit anything is to fix bayonets and charge.'

Also in the spring, officers and NCOs were chosen for specialist training. They were sent to England on courses and, when they returned, took responsibility for preparing their special elements for war, whether they be transport, machine-guns or signals. Proper equipment for most of these had not yet arrived, so most of the training was on improvised equipment. There was a great shortage of junior officers throughout the army, intensified by the losses on the Western Front. The War Office sought to relieve this shortage by commissioning experienced NCOs and warrant officers (sergeant majors). In the main, these were made very welcome in the officers' messes of 16th Division, and recognised as men who knew the business of war.

In the early summer of 1915, the War Office made the sort of thoughtless decision that did so much to negate the efforts of John Redmond and others in encouraging nationalists to join the army. 16th Division, having already lost 1,200 infantrymen, now lost all three Artillery Brigades, two Engineer Field Companies and the Divisional Signal Company. All were transferred to the Guards Division. The other Engineer Field Company was sent to 7th Division, which had suffered badly in the spring battles of that year. The division's three Field Ambulances had already been sent to France.

Even before this blow, as we have seen, recruitment to 16th Division was disappointing. Redmond and his close ally, Joe Devlin, wanted to recruit Irishmen living in English cities. General Parsons disagreed, referring to such émigrés as slum-birds and corner boys. Tyneside was one area that had large numbers of Irishmen. By the time Parsons allowed recruiting there it was too late; they had already formed a Tyneside Irish Brigade, uselessly destroyed like so many others on the first day on the Somme.[10] Strenuous efforts by different battalions within Ireland produced few new recruits. In the context of these shortages, with 10th (Irish) Division and 16th Division both desperate for men, an entire battalion, 10th Dublin Fusiliers, was sent to fight as part of 63rd Royal Navy Division. Once again, the War Office showed little concern for Irish sensibilities.

The lack of central information, together with the fact that its commander seemed more concerned with matters of dress and regimental procedure than preparation for war, meant that training tended to be outdated, more suited to the days of Empire than the cruel realities of the Western Front. At divisional level the training was patchy at best. Although the divisional area was eminently suitable for divisional exercises, the division itself was not concentrated for collective training until November 1915, and then only at the insistence of Aldershot Command. Parsons did not even visit some of his infantry battalions until September 1915, almost a year after they were established.

Even at brigade level there were deficiencies. 49 Brigade, still struggling for recruits, received no training in trench warfare. The lack of equipment could not be used as an excuse, since all the equipment required was a spade. Although the officers of the brigade had had lectures on static warfare in France, the lessons were put to no practical use. The basic tactics of trench warfare were not taught, nor even mentioned to regimental officers, most of whom were inexperienced. The Germans had already used gas as a weapon of war, yet there was no introduction to gas warfare, nor was there any anti-gas training. When, in September, the soldiers had the opportunity to shoot on the Aldershot ranges, much time was wasted, and hundreds of soldiers not actually on the ranges stood around with nothing to do. The best of the training was at battalion level, where a sense of unit pride, of traditional regimental spirit, spun a net which would hold its men together in the tribulations that were to come.

One way in which General Parsons offended Irish sensibilities was in the matter of granting temporary commissions. His common sense told him that his junior officers had to be good, which meant that those who did get a commission in the division had a solid grounding in military matters. Unfortunately, his snobbery and complete lack of tact made it impossible for him to explain his thinking in a sympathetic way. Only gentlemen, he said, could be officers.[11] To the Irish public, it looked as if he was only granting commissions to those who had passed through an OTC course at university or public school; in effect,

Protestants. His snobbery was seen as sectarian prejudice. He did not make enough of the fact that he had set up a Cadet Company in 7th Leinsters, which turned out to be a great success. From November 1914 until December 1915, 161 cadets from this company, most of them nationalist and Catholic, had gone on to gain commissions in 16th Division. Parsons preferred them to temporary second lieutenants sent by the War Office.[12]

One of those who came through the cadet company was John Hamilton Maxwell Staniforth, who had come down from Oxford in 1914. Although an ancestor had been a junior member of Wellington's staff at Waterloo, Staniforth enlisted in the ranks of 6th Connaught Rangers, arriving in Galway in mid-October 1914. It did not take long for him to become disabused of the idea of starting at the bottom. Within two weeks he went to his brigade commander and applied for a commission. When the brigadier general had satisfied himself that Staniforth was of the right stuff—he had been to a good school (Charterhouse) and was a keen sportsman—he recommended strongly that the young man be given a commission. On 12 November he joined C (Officer Cadet) Company of 7th Leinsters. In this company he was responsible for twenty men. Young though he was, he was soon lecturing these men on soldierly spirit, esprit de corps, discipline and smartness. Every evening, cadets were required to attend the officers' mess, and the whole ritual of this affected him deeply. By mid-December he could see progress in the men he was instructing. They had begun route marches of up to eight miles and, unlike some of the other battalions, had begun trench construction. He was amazed to find the amount of science backing up what he did: 'two feet wide, ten feet deep, with all sorts of traverses, revetments, recessing, drainage and other delights'.[13] Even in such a well-run battalion, however, signs of impatience began to show.

By June, Staniforth was impatient for the move to England. When the orders finally came, in September, there were aspects of the journey which were almost farcical. When his company arrived in Kingstown, two of his squad of fifty simply disappeared. They were both Dubliners, and perhaps wanted a last home leave. When the remainder arrived in London, however, the scene took on the atmosphere of a nightmare. They had to cross the city by underground railway. This was entirely a new experience for his men, who wanted to miss nothing. It was difficult enough to persuade them that they had to catch the train to a particular destination, but getting to board the actual train seemed almost impossible. Used to the leisurely ways of Irish branch lines, they would stroll up and down the platform looking for a good seat, and the train would leave without them. Staniforth had a sharp word with them, speaking so emphatically that they stampeded aboard the next train, making themselves extremely unpopular with commuters who suddenly found their carriage swamped by fifty men in full kit, carrying rifles.[14]

When the 16th Division was concentrated in mid-November in order to prepare for a ceremonial inspection by Queen Mary, the army commander, General Hunter, was horrified to discover that the division had not received any training in ceremonial drill. Worse, many of the senior officers were more familiar with the traditions of their regiments than of the modern drill book. Two weeks of precious training had to be postponed in order that the soldiers could receive rudimentary ceremonial drill.[15] In spite of everything, the parade itself went off reasonably well, and all battalions were congratulated. However, it was shortly after this fiasco that Parsons was relieved of command. It is tempting to think that this was a result of his training shortcomings, but General Richardson of 36th (Ulster) Division was also relieved of command. A more likely explanation is that experience in the Dardanelles had shown the folly of sending soldiers into battle under superannuated generals who had had no experience of modern warfare. In future, commanders would have to have proved themselves in the cauldron of France. The man replacing Parsons, Major General William Hickie, from County Tipperary, was fifty and had already served in the Western Front as a brigade commander. This was not enough to prevent great dissatisfaction among the troops. It is, perhaps, worthy of a footnote that Kitchener inspected 10th (Irish) Division once and 36th (Ulster) Division no less than three times. He did not inspect 16th Division at all. On the other hand, Cardinal Bourne, Primate of England and Wales, spoke to the Catholics of the division before they left for France.[16]

The orders for the move had come just before the Queen's Parade. General Parsons was not the only one who would have to remain behind. It was decided that 49 Brigade needed to remain behind in Aldershot Command to receive some intensive training and some extra numbers to bring it up to strength. It was also to get a new commander. As well as that, some of the officers and men throughout the division had proved unfit for active service and were redeployed. The rest of the division was to be in France within a fortnight and 49 Brigade joined them in mid-February.

The 16th Division left Aldershot by train on 17 December. General Parsons watched them off and noted drily, 'One man left behind drunk.' They boarded ship in Southampton that evening and, by early the following morning, were disembarking at Le Havre, and they had arrived south of Béthune by 22 December. This was the last division of Haig's 'Second New Army' to arrive in France and this was lucky. To begin with, these new divisions had been flung into battle as soon as they arrived, with the intention of blooding them. Hickie now wanted his men to be blooded gradually, and not before they had got used to the new conditions and to Boche habits.[17]

This was not the only change General Hickie had in mind. As the year turned into 1916 he weeded out every senior officer whom he considered to be too old or too weak to fight a modern war. He sent home all brigade commanders and many battalion cos. Although Parsons complained that he was too ruthless, the commander of IV Corps, Sir Henry Wilson, accepted that the changes were justified.

The shrunken 16th Division was posted to the Loos Sector as part of the First Army. To begin with, each brigade was attached to an experienced division as an introduction to the front line. Each battalion was then allocated to a brigade. The weather was dreadful, with snow and ice, and on this first tour of the trenches 16th Division lost one officer and five men killed, seventeen wounded and two missing. They were already becoming aware of the dreadful attrition of life in the trenches, even when there was no battle taking place. Between tours of duty at the front there were lots of other jobs to do, such as improving trenches and burying communications cable. During this period they were inspected by General Joffre, who appreciated the fact that, for the first time in over a century, there was an Irish brigade fighting for France.[18] Another interesting inspection was by General Wilson, who visited 47 Brigade. He was intimately involved in the unionist cause, but seems to have found nothing that he could criticise; in fact, his diaries make no mention of his inspection. He was under a cloud of his own at the time. Now commander of IV Corps, he had upset his divisional commanders by telling them that the French were better fighters than the British, and the Germans better leaders. After this, even General Haig became concerned about the morale of IV Corps.[19]

British trenches at this stage of the war were normally three lines, known as front, support and rear lines. These lines were linked by an intricate network of communications trenches. The line of the main trenches were never straight for more than a few feet before zigging or zagging, in order to make it impossible for an enemy machine-gun to fire along its length; it also limited the distance that shrapnel would fly if a shell fell in the trench. The front trenches were narrowest, only wide enough to allow two men to pass. There were usually duckboards on the floor of the trench, but in wet weather these could be covered with water. Dugouts and latrines were usually scraped out of the side of the trench. At intervals along the trench there were short passages called saps. These led out to listening posts, where a soldier would listen for unusual noises from the enemy lines. Finally there was a ledge, known as the fire step, which allowed soldiers to see over the parapet and to fire at the approaching enemy. Trenches were easily damaged by enemy fire, or by particularly bad weather, and much of the daily grind was in keeping them in good repair. The trenches which 16th Division inherited on the front line were particularly bad, and the subject of many complaints.

Being in the front line trenches enforced a routine of its own. Each battalion was responsible for a length of front from 800 to 1,000 yards long. One hour before daylight every available man was required to man the trenches, standing on the fire step. This was known as standing to, and it was necessary because the half-light of dawn was the most likely time for a German attack. When full daylight came, most of the men were able to stand down, leaving only a few sentries to keep an eye on no-man's-land, which could be anything from a few yards wide to nearly half a mile. Since most activity took place at night, those who were not on sentry duty would spend the day looking after their equipment, cooking, brewing tea, but mainly resting. At the coming of night, things got busy again. Firstly there were working parties. Trench parapets were repaired, barbed wire in front of the trenches was repaired or improved, and food and water were fetched from the nearest transport dump.

Two of the most frightening duties were working at the barbed wire, well away from the shelter of the trenches, and going on patrol. Those working on the wire were conscious of every clink made by their tools and were aware that at any moment the enemy could send up a flare that lit the area as bright as daylight. When that happened the only protection the men had was to lie absolutely still; to move risked catching the attention of a German sniper. Most patrols consisted of an officer and half a dozen men. They would make their way to a spot near the enemy lines and listen for enemy activity, staying for a few hours before returning. Larger, fighting patrols were sometimes organised, to obtain some German prisoners or to bomb the Germans out of one of their forward positions.

For Tom Kettle, the horror came from the very routine of things, changing every few days, but with casualties at every change, and disease, and the losses coming like the teeth of a saw, so that a strong unit could become a weak one before you knew it. The physical and mental toll was enormous. Each time they marched to the front, they knew that three or four, or more, would not return. Death was a random visitor, not meeting you head on, but coming out of blindness. In the trench there was waiting; in no-man's-land there were shell holes and enemies and unburied men. Patrols came and went. On the wire were blood-stained strips of uniform. The near daylight of flares was replaced by utter darkness, and eyes of sentries ached as they tried desperately to adjust, for strange things came from no-man's-land, and they had to be seen.[20]

Front line training began in earnest at the end of January 1916, before 49 Brigade had rejoined. The Loos Sector was a salient pointing into German lines and was continually under shell-fire. At that time, it was second only to the Ypres Sector in terms of German activity. There were continual attacks. In early February, the Royal Irish had their first experience of mines, when huge explosions opened two craters in front of their lines. Shortly afterwards 49 Brigade arrived and 16 Division was up to strength. On 16 March, the division became fully operational and took over its own section of front on the Hulluch and Puits sectors of the Loos salient. The trenches were in poor condition; they were flooded and stank. The general air of filth was not helped by the sight of swarms of rats. The Irish worked constantly at improving the defences, but bright moonlight and the domination of the front by German heavy artillery meant that it was an unremitting and dangerous task. There were daily casualties. In their spell in the front line from 9 to 16 April, Royal Irish lost one officer and eight men killed; one officer and nineteen men wounded.[21] This was in spite of the fact that the troops opposite were Bavarians and, as the Leinsters decided, easy-going and non-belligerent. This was to change later.

The standard deployment of a division in the line, at that stage of the war, was to have two brigades in the front line and one in reserve. Each brigade had two battalions at the front and one in reserve. A battalion on the line had two companies in the main trenches, another company in a support trench about two hundred yards behind that, with a fourth about a quarter of a mile further back still. Each brigade was at the front for eight days before being relieved to spend four days in reserve behind the line. This was not a rest period. During the days in reserve the troops went on work parties required by division or brigade, or worked on the repair of roads, trenches and lines of communication. When they weren't doing this they were training in grenade throwing, sniping, wiring and general trench routine. Then, when the short respite was over, it was back to the front line, first along slippery pavements, then through the tedious zig-zags of the communications trenches, sometimes taking twelve hours to complete the journey.[22]

At Easter a German deserter brought information that the Germans were planning a massive gas attack. The easy-going Bavarians had been replaced by Prussians, who had already tried to dominate no-man's-land with rifle grenades and offensive patrols. At night there were vicious exchanges of fire at short range between neighbouring shell craters. The men had to camouflage themselves in white because of the chalk exposed by shellfire. News of the coming attack was confirmed by intelligence reports, and by rats which were also deserting the German lines, trying to escape from leaking gas cylinders. General Hickie ordered all necessary preparations to be made. Blankets were soaked in an anti-gas agent known as Volmerol and used to cover the entrances to dugouts. Personal protection was pretty basic. Gas helmets at this stage of the war were made of sacking and did not protect the individual completely; they merely slowed down the rate of asphyxiation. The men did not realise this, and probably were more confident than they should have been. On 26 April heavy shells began to fall on their lines. The barrage moved backwards and forwards, in a pattern that indicated that the Germans were trying to obliterate the British forward observation posts and lines of communication, trying to blind and paralyse the British defenders before the attack went in.

On the right of the Irish line was 48 Brigade, with 9th Munsters and 8th Dublins in the forward trenches. To their left was 49 Brigade with 7th Inniskilling Fusiliers and 8th Irish Fusiliers in the forward trenches. Each brigade had two further battalions in immediate reserve, while 47 Brigade acted as divisional reserve. To the left of the Irish forces was 9th Black Watch. Divisional artillery waited to be given a target. Engineers struggled to improve defences. Deep in dugouts, signallers crouched over their equipment. Back in their different headquarters, General Hickie and his brigade commanders waited. All along the line, men waited.

The long night passed, and streaks of light were beginning to light the eastern sky. A slight breeze blew in the faces of Irish sentries. At 4 a.m., most of the Irish in the forward trenches withdrew, leaving a small screen of sentries. At 4:35 the Germans opened fire with machine-guns, expecting the defenders to mass in the trenches, ready to repel an attack. At 4:45, when they judged the trenches would be fully manned, a new barrage of shell-fire began. At the same time gas was released from saps which the Germans had dug forwards from their own lines. A cloud of mixed gas and smoke drifted across no-man's-land. When it passed over the front lines, visibility was reduced to no more than three yards. At 5:15 the bombardment lifted from the front lines and began to fall near the artillery positions. At the same time, shells filled with tear gas were lobbed into the reserve lines and into the communication trenches. This was the time for the Germans to attack, and the Irish opened fire. They were firing blind, however, and the Germans were using the cover of the smoke to get as near as possible to the Irish lines before charging. In places the smoke lifted a little from the ground and the defenders fired at approaching legs.[23]

When the Germans did launch their assault, many of them penetrated the front line and desperate close-quarter fighting began. At one stage the attackers managed to get between the Inniskillings and the Dublins, and it took fifteen minutes for contact between the battalions to be re-established. In the meantime, the Germans took many prisoners, shooting anyone who resisted or tried to escape. When the trenches were secured once more, it was found that, although there were some gas casualties, most of the damage had been inflicted by artillery shells. These explosions had also cut telephone communications, and runners had to be used to ask for reinforcements. Handicapped by their gas helmets, the runners found it difficult to make their way about. Many officers in the support trenches used their own initiative to send reinforcements forward. Eventually the enemy withdrew, under cover of a small mine that they exploded in no-man's-land. Four hundred and fifty German dead were counted in front of the Irish lines.

There was a repeat of the gas/high explosive bombardment about two hours later, but this was beaten back before it could reach the Irish lines. Then the gods intervened. The wind turned completely round and started blowing the gas back towards the German lines. The Germans were unprepared for this, and terrified. They found that they could not turn off the gas cylinders in time. Many began jumping out of their trenches and running to their rear. The British corps commander ordered all the artillery that he had under his control to fire on the Germans opposite the Irish sector. Further mayhem was committed by battalion machine-guns. By 11 a.m. the battle was over.

When the men had a chance to look around them, the sight was devastating. The front line trenches were completely smashed. Parapets had been levelled and trenches filled in. Pieces of personal equipment lay all over the battlefield. Everywhere there was the stench of chlorine. Every rifle, machine-gun, cartridge, and every metal of whatever sort was covered in a green arsenic film, which was corrosive and had to be cleaned off at once.[24] Worst of all, fire-bays and dugouts were full of dead and seriously wounded. Those who could, tried to help. There were lines of walking wounded, many of them gas cases with blind streaming eyes, who vomited green bile, making their way back to the Casualty Clearing Stations. One of the worst jobs was disposing of the dead. The weather was hot and the corpses had begun to stink. Lieutenant Lyon of 7th Leinsters had the job of collecting the dead in his battalion. He was struck by the way that many of them were holding hands, like children. Their faces had turned purple and some who were not quite dead were gasping out a green foam. Those he could find, some sixty or so, he arranged to be buried in a large shell hole. Where wisps of gas still hung in the air, it killed all the vegetation.[25]

The Dublins were due to be relieved by the Connaughts on the night of 28/29 April. At 5 a.m. the Germans released gas, catching many of 8th Dublins and 8th Irish Fusiliers. The machine-gun section of the Connaughts was caught; an officer and three men died, while five others were seriously gassed. Private D. Lynch was also gassed, but continued firing on the Germans even when companies on either side had been reduced to a few men. His shooting stopped a German attack and knocked a gas cylinder back into a German trench. Once again the gods favoured the Irish and the wind changed, blowing the gas back towards the Germans, who were once again forced out of their trenches. The Irish expected another attack the next day, or the day after that, but the Germans seemed to have had enough of their own gas for a while.

16th Division had survived its first test, but at a cost. In the three days of battle they had lost 570 killed and over 1,400 wounded. Most of the damage had been inflicted by gas, yet all the gas-dead were found to be wearing their gas helmets properly. It was obvious that there was something wrong with the design.

In spite of their success in holding off the German attacks, the soldiers of 16th Division came in for a great deal of criticism at senior levels. The general officer commanding 12th Division claimed that he had been unimpressed by their gas drill, and that their general level of efficiency left a lot to be desired. This idea of bad gas discipline was mentioned by others. There were reports of soldiers losing their heads and refusing to wear gas helmets. There were even the beginnings of Irish jokes about men cutting a hole in their masks so that they could enjoy a smoke. Much of this was put down to Irish temperament, which found any restraint irksome. The official historian of the war on the Western Front repudiated these allegations, pointing out that not one of 16th Division's dead had been found without a gas mask on. At the same time he reported that the sacks which were glorified by the name of gas mask at the start of 1916 had little use against concentrations of gas; they were only serviceable when the gas had thinned out. They also lost what little effectiveness they had when they were subjected to gas for long periods. When the British Commander-in-Chief, Douglas Haig, visited the 16th Division in May he said that the gas attacks were the most severe that the army had so far suffered, and that 'the Irishmen did very well'.

Why then, was there the verbal sniping? Just a few days before the German attacks, the Easter Rising had broken out in Dublin. Officers such as General Gough, the 16th Division's corps commander, had never really trusted home rulers, and questioned their loyalty. Other officers took their tone from this eminent Irish unionist and regarded Irish troops with the gravest suspicion.

Chapter 6 ∾

DUBLIN SUNDERED

By mid-January of 1916 the Supreme Council of the IRB had met and decided that the insurrection would take place on Easter Sunday of that year. A courier was sent to America to pass the message on to Devoy. The choice of day was not meant to be symbolic. The Volunteers had had a field day, albeit a disappointing one, on Easter Sunday of the previous year, and it was considered that the authorities would be expecting another one in 1916. As a result, they would not be alarmed at the sight of Volunteers on the streets. The choice of date also seemed to give plenty of time for preparations, since Easter was late that year, and there was the added bonus of the St Patrick's Day holiday, when there could be a trial mobilisation. It was not long before the rank and file in Dublin knew that something was up, as preparations intensified. In workshops around the country munitions were being prepared.

The St Patrick's Day mobilisation went extremely well. In Dublin there was a turn-out of 1,400 Volunteers, armed and in uniform. They took control of Dame Street from City Hall, just outside Dublin Castle, to the Bank of Ireland, where Ireland's Parliament had met before the Act of Union. They stayed there for an hour, allowing no traffic through. Even greater numbers, 4,500, mobilised in the provinces. At subsequent meetings of the Volunteers, some of the commanders warned their men that there was a time coming when they might have to shoot to kill. The administration was beginning to feel the tension. Lord Wimborne, the Lord Lieutenant, was one of these. When he raised the matter of the sheer scale of the Volunteer mobilisation, he was told not to worry; only half of those who turned out in the provinces had weapons, and only a quarter had rifles. In addition, onlookers had lacked enthusiasm, probably frustrated at being delayed for an hour. The policy of the administration seemed to be that they should avoid causing alarm.

Almost two weeks after St Patrick's Day, on 30 March, the small steamer SMS *Libau* sailed from Hamburg, under the command of Lieutenant Karl Spindler; she was carrying arms and ammunition for the Irish Volunteers. There was no radio on board, so that all the time she was at sea she would be out of touch with Germany—and with Ireland. She made her way through the Kiel Canal and entered the Baltic Sea at Lübeck. She had been disguised as a Norwegian ship, *Aud*, in the hope that this would help her to slip through the naval blockade that the British maintained in the North Sea. Lieutenant Spindler brought her through the Skagerrak on 10 April and then tried to lose himself and his ship in the vastness of the sea to the north of the British Isles. Two days later, Roger Casement boarded the U20 in Wilhelmshaven. With him was an ex-army captain and supposed military expert called Monteith, who had been supposed to help in the organisation of Casement's Irish Brigade. At first it looked as if Casement was going to have as little luck with his submarine as he had had with the Irish prisoners of war; two days out the U20 developed mechanical problems and had to turn back for repairs. The Irishmen were transferred to the U19 and were at sea again by 15 April.

Meanwhile, back in Ireland, preparations for Easter went on. As early as 10 April, Austin Stack, commander of the Kerry Volunteers, warned his men that a rising would take place in Dublin at Easter. Since it would be his responsibility to organise the collection and distribution of the German guns it may have been necessary for him to give his men this advance warning, but it seems a very serious breach of security. Even Pearse did not seem able to contain his excitement. On 15 April he warned a meeting of the Dublin Brigade that no one who was afraid of losing his job should come out on Easter Sunday. There were route marches on Palm Sunday and in Holy Week Volunteer meetings were held every night. On Spy Wednesday MacDonagh told his men that they should bring three days' rations with them on Sunday as they were going out and not all of them would be coming back. The following night he told them that they would have to obey every order given to them on Sunday.

There was another cause for excitement that week. At a meeting of Dublin Corporation, Alderman Tom Kelly read from what came to be known as the Castle Document. This seemed to authorise the arrest of a wide range of nationalists and the imposition of a severe curfew in

Dublin. Liberty Hall and the headquarters of Sinn Féin, the Volunteers, the Gaelic League and the Irish National Foresters were all to be occupied. In addition, Mansion House, the Archbishop's Palace, St Enda's School and the homes of O'Rahilly, MacNeill and Plunkett were to be isolated. Kelly said that the item had come, in code, from a sympathiser within Dublin Castle. At first the document was accepted as genuine, although some of the targets seemed so arbitrary that, on reflection, many people started to doubt its authenticity. MacNeill considered that it was a threat to the very existence of the Volunteers and issued an order that any attempt to disarm them should be resisted by force. This order was distributed on 20 April. Desmond Ryan, a pupil from St Enda's who was very close to Pearse, said afterwards that the document, in the form that it appeared, was a forgery. Eugene Smith, however, who later admitted that it was he who had smuggled the document out of Dublin Castle, claimed that what Kelly had read out was practically identical to the original, although Plunkett had pretended that it had been authorised by the Chief Secretary. Grace Gifford remembered writing it down as Joseph Plunkett, her fiancé, decoded it. Sean MacDermott swore to a priest, a few hours before he was shot, that the document was genuine. The nature of the plan is open to question, nevertheless. It seems likely that it was a draft of a provisional plan, produced by the army, one that might be put in place if certain conditions arose, such as an actual rising. The trouble was that the army had cast its net so wide that MacNeill finally came to the conclusion that the Castle Document had been forged by Joseph Plunkett to trick the Volunteers into premature action.

MacNeill had been certain for some time that he was out of the loop as far as planning was concerned. At the start of the month he had received a letter from America warning that there was a plot afoot that would deluge Ireland in blood. MacNeill decided he would wait and see. Now it became obvious that the time for waiting was running out. Ginger O'Connell and Eoin O'Duffy met with Hobson on the evening of Holy Thursday. They told him that orders being given out to the Dublin companies could only mean that the rising would take place on the coming Sunday. Although it was late, after ten, they decided to go to MacNeill's house at Dundrum and pass on their suspicions. When MacNeill heard what they had to say he decided, for once, on immediate action, and all four drove to St Enda's where they met with Pearse. It was not an easy meeting. Pearse admitted straight away that there was to be a rising and that MacNeill had been deceived but said that it was necessary. MacNeill said that he would do everything in his power to stop the insurrection, short of telling the authorities. Pearse replied that MacNeill had no power; that the Volunteers were under the control of the IRB. Desmond Ryan says that Pearse had very different feeling for each of the people facing him. For MacNeill he had some contempt, believing as he did that the older man could have found out at any time that an insurrection was being planned, but he had decided to see no evil and hear no evil. He felt that MacNeill was striking a pose even then, at this midnight meeting in Pearse's study. Ryan felt that Pearse underestimated O'Connell's abilities and was too confident in the book-learned military science of MacDonagh. He had genuine respect for Hobson, but their different views of politics had driven them apart. Pearse said to Hobson that night that reason and logic might decide it was the wrong time for a rising, but he knew he was right. After his visitors had left, he told his mother that he had had a little trouble with MacNeill, but that it would be all right in the morning.[1]

It was obvious that they were at an impasse, so the four returned to MacNeill's house, where they drafted three orders. The first recalled and cancelled all orders given by Pearse. The second stated that the only orders to be obeyed in future would come from MacNeill alone. Finally, O'Connell was given command of all Volunteers in Munster. Hobson was to command the rest.

The following morning, Good Friday, Pearse, together with MacDonagh and MacDermott, went out to Dundrum to meet with MacNeill, who told them of the orders he had drafted. The others said that, if the orders for the rising were to be cancelled now there would be a disaster, since there was a ship bringing arms from Germany. MacNeill's reading of the situation was that, when the British discovered the shipment, the administration would move against the Volunteers, so he agreed to do nothing for the time being, though, after meeting with the O'Rahilly that afternoon, he felt unsettled once more.

The Military Council had decided that Bulmer Hobson, with his sharp intellect and great organisational skills, was their most serious threat within the Volunteer movement. On the afternoon of Good Friday, Hobson was called to a meeting in Dublin's Dawson Street, where he was arrested by order of MacDermott. Although he was treated well, he was not released until Monday evening. When O'Rahilly heard of the arrest, he went straight to Pearse's study at St Enda's and drew his pistol. 'Whoever comes to kidnap me', he said, 'will have to be a quicker shot.' Pearse persuaded him to put away his gun, and they spoke for some time.[2]

Meanwhile, *Libau/Aud* was still at sea. With British auxiliary cruisers patrolling the waters he was navigating, Spindler took a course that brought him close to the Arctic Circle, where the ship managed to survive hurricane-force winds. He arrived at his rendezvous in Tralee Bay on the afternoon of Holy Thursday, expecting to meet up with the U20. She was not there, nor was there any sign of a reception committee on land. The lack of radio had prevented her from receiving a message from the military committee, through John Devoy, that it was vital that the arms should not be landed before midnight on 23 April, Easter Sunday. Devoy had passed this message on, but does not seem to have known that there was no way of contacting Spindler. That could explain the lack of reception committee, but it does not explain the fact that the U19, which arrived just after midnight, was unable to find *Aud*. After searching for two hours, the submarine withdrew to wait for the next day.

That Good Friday in Kerry was a beautiful spring day, with perfect visibility, yet neither boat could see the other. There is some evidence that Spindler was not a good navigator, and may have been as much as seven miles away from the rendezvous, but that is not a great distance, given the quality of German binoculars. *Aud* cruised round the bay, at one time coming within 600 yards of the long finger of Fenit Pier, showing the green light that was the pre-arranged signal. The local pilot, who had been warned that he was to bring *Aud* into harbour, later reported seeing a ship on Thursday night and again on Friday morning, but since she made no signal that he could see, he did nothing about it. Since he had been told to look out for a ship of about one hundred and fifty tons, while *Aud* weighed over a thousand tons, he thought the boat had nothing to do with him.

Some preparations had been made on shore. Austin Stack had had his usual meeting with the Tralee battalion council on the night of Monday 17 April. Their discussions must have been very secret, as no minutes were kept. The previous week his deputy, Paddy Cahill, had gone to Dublin for discussions with Pearse, and before that again had gone to Dublin to collect two signal lamps. For some reason, these never reached Tralee. Stack had a plan for unloading the arms at Fenit Pier and organising their distribution around the country, but he told no one about it and no copy survives. Although he took the trouble of going to Cahirciveen to brief a radio operator on how to alert America when the rising took place, he does not seem to have thought it necessary to put a watch on the coast at the original time arranged for the landing, just in case the delaying message had not got through.

On Good Friday morning, Stack was having breakfast with Con Collins, a wireless expert sent down from Dublin. Before they were finished a message came that two strangers were at his father's shop and were anxious to talk to him. They finished their breakfast at a leisurely pace, and it was an hour before they reached the shop. Here Stack recognised one of the men as Monteith; the other's name was Bailey. They told him that Casement had landed with them north of Tralee, at Banna Strand, although Monteith had not known the name of the beach. Their boat had capsized in the surf and Casement had collapsed, probably through a mixture of stress and cold. The others left him there and walked into Tralee.

Stack took Collins and they set off by car. They drove as far as Ballyheigue, at the north end of Banna Strand, before being alerted by the sight of an RIC search party checking the dunes behind the beach. A passing walker had seen the upturned boat and the lines of footprints heading towards the dunes and had told the police. By this time Casement had already been arrested, although the police had no idea who he was. The two Volunteers started driving back towards Tralee, but they had not gone far before they were stopped by an RIC patrol and Collins was arrested. Stack followed him into the police station and, at gunpoint, rescued him. At a meeting that afternoon he heard that Casement was being held at the police station in Ardfert, although he was to be transferred to Tralee that evening. Stack vetoed a motion that there should be an attempt at rescuing Casement. Later in the evening he heard that Collins had been rearrested and went to the police station to see him. This time his luck had run out and he too was arrested; so he and Collins spent the night in the same police barracks as did Casement, before the ex-diplomat was transferred to Dublin on Saturday morning.

The tragic farce was not yet over. Sean MacDermott had planned an operation to seize the radio equipment from the station at Cahirciveen and to set up a rebel station in Tralee in order to keep in contact with the German ship bringing arms. Con Keating was a wireless specialist who came with four others to Killarney to carry out the operation. Two cars were waiting and they divided themselves between these before heading off on the road through Killorglin to Cahirciveen. In Killorglin the driver of the second car took a wrong turning and drove off Ballykissane Pier straight into the sea. The driver survived, but his three passengers, including Keating, were drowned. The driver of the first car noticed after a while that the following lights had disappeared. He waited a few miles west of Killorglin, but when it became obvious that the second car was not coming, they abandoned the operation and returned to Dublin.

Even Spindler's operation ended in total failure. Two armed trawlers had appeared, and he decided to make a break for the open ocean, where he could operate as a commerce raider. He was too slow in putting this plan into operation, however, and two naval sloops appeared, faster and better armed than he was, so he was compelled to follow them to Queenstown, now called Cobh, in Cork harbour. The following morning, at 9:28, he scuttled his ship, apparently in an effort to block the channel. Even in this he failed. The naval part of the Irish insurrection was over, thirty-eight hours before the Military Council had thought it was due to begin.

In Dublin, late on Friday night, Pearse must have felt that it had been a long day. It was not yet over. A car arrived at the school, very late, to take Pearse to an emergency conference at Liberty Hall. It was here that he learned that Casement had been arrested and that the arms ship had sunk without unloading its cargo. He was also told of the arrest of Stack and Collins. After a short sleep, Pearse and MacDermott went to see MacNeill the following morning, Saturday, and told him of these developments. Although he upbraided them once more for keeping him in the dark, they left MacNeill's house thinking that they had persuaded him not to interfere, since they had to preserve unity in the face of a British clamp-down. In fact he had not yet decided what his next step should be. He read in the newspapers of Casement's arrest, but claimed to think that the emergency was receding. Although he saw little chance for its success, he was prepared to take part in the insurrection. That afternoon, however, he had yet more visitors. This time it was the O'Rahilly, together with Sean Fitzgibbon and Colm

O'Lochlainn. He now learned that the arms shipment was lost, that the Castle Document was a forgery and that Hobson had been kidnapped. For what was to be the last time, the group went to St Enda's. They found Pearse in an excited and aggressive mood. For the first time he was openly rude to MacNeill. 'We have used your name and influence,' he said, 'for what it was worth, but we have done with you now. It is no use trying to stop us.' When MacNeill said that he would forbid the Sunday mobilisation, Pearse retorted that the men would not obey.[3]

Even yet MacNeill, whose motto seems to have been, like Asquith's, 'Wait and see', had not made up his mind. Although he drafted an order saying that the Volunteers had been deceived and Sunday's mobilisation was to be cancelled, before he sent it out he called a meeting at the house of a friend in Rathgar Road. Arthur Griffith, Sean Fitzgibbon, Joseph Plunkett, Thomas MacDonagh and some members of the Volunteer Executive attended. One of those present, Liam O'Briain, wrote later that it was a very informal meeting, but that MacNeill was very agitated. When he told the meeting that he intended to stop the mobilisation, both Plunkett and MacDonagh warned him that that would not stop the rising without disaster to the whole movement; they were going ahead anyway. They now said they were going, but would return later with a message. When they left they got in touch with MacDermott and Pearse and arranged to have a meeting of the Military Council on Easter Sunday morning.

Those who remained must have been puzzled and somewhat alarmed at these exchanges. MacNeill now told them what he had learned of the plans for insurrection, emphasising that he had only learned of them three days earlier. He also told them of the sinking of the arms ship and said that it was his duty to try to save the Volunteers from useless slaughter. Leaving the meeting, he sent off copies of his orders by messenger to all parts of the country. Typically, the O'Rahilly took a taxi to west Munster. Even then, some of his friends urged MacNeill to put an advertisement in the *Sunday Independent*, to make assurance doubly sure.[4]

Perhaps the IRB had become too complacent about MacNeill's reluctance to act, because the rescinding order came as a dreadful shock to many of them. Eamonn Ceannt had told his wife at six o'clock that Saturday evening that there would be an insurrection the next day. His place would be in the South Dublin Union. He gave as the reason that the British Parliament was meeting in secret session to impose conscription on Ireland; the Volunteers could not let that move go unchallenged. He was back at three in the morning complaining that MacNeill's order had 'ruined us'. While he had been away he had heard of the meeting with MacNeill from Cathal Brugha. He had gone straight to Liberty Hall, but Connolly's loyal Citizen Army refused to waken their leader. From there Ceannt went to the Metropole Hotel where Plunkett was staying, but Plunkett had given orders that he wasn't to be wakened before nine. There was nothing to do but return home and try to get some sleep himself. As he lay in bed he told his wife, 'If I sleep now I could sleep on dynamite.'[5]

When the *Sunday Independent* was being delivered and read over Sunday breakfasts, the Military Council was already in session in Liberty Hall. They had their Proclamation of the Republic, signed by seven of them, with Clarke's name at the top, and printed on the presses of the *Worker's Republic*. While Constance Markievicz brandished her pistol and told Connolly that she would shoot MacNeill, the rest of them reacted more thoughtfully. Clarke wanted to go ahead that evening, because most of the men would have dispersed and the British would be off their guard. The rest, even Pearse, voted against that. Even Connolly, who could in theory have gone ahead, accepted the need for delay. This probably turned out to be a mistake; there was a much larger turnout that Sunday than there would be on Easter Monday. Without the benefit of hindsight, however, the Military Council issued two orders. The first confirmed the cancellation of that day's mobilisation. The second said that there would be a new mobilisation at noon on Easter Monday. It may have been that the combination of orders produced a confusion that ensured that fewer men would attend the Monday mobilisation.[6]

Clarke was right in one thing; the British authorities were beginning to react at last. On Easter Saturday the Under-Secretary, Nathan, wrote to Birrell in London telling him of the *Aud* incident; that the man captured on Good Friday was thought to be Roger Casement; and that Stack and Collins had also been arrested. He also mentioned Sunday's mobilisation but felt that there were no signs of a rising. When Nathan met Wimborne later in the day, he found the Lord Lieutenant convinced that the capture of arms meant that any danger of insurrection was postponed, since he thought that the guns were a necessary part of any rebel plan. He thought Casement was the key to the business and that his removal would bring the whole thing down. The danger, for now, was over. The question now was what to do with the Volunteers, now that it had been proved that they were in direct collusion with the enemy. Nathan was reluctant to do anything that Saturday night, other than to arrange for some special constables, known from their age and their GR armbands as the 'Gorgeous Wrecks', to support the police in some public buildings, including the GPO.

The following morning Nathan got a message that another man who had landed at Banna Strand had been captured and had made a complete statement. This was Bailey, who had served in the Royal Irish Rifles; he named Monteith as a third man, but he was missing. The statement included details of the arms mission, gave Sunday as the day of the rising, and implicated Stack and Collins in the arrangements. To set against this statement was the advertisement in the *Irish Independent* calling off the mobilisation. Nathan went to his office in Dublin Castle, where he felt nearer the centre of things. Here he had news that Volunteers had stolen 250 pounds of gelignite from a quarry in Tallaght and had taken it to Liberty Hall. The police who had followed them were keeping the premises under close observation. He phoned Wimborne to tell him of this and to tell him that he would arrange for the police to raid Liberty Hall, together with two other arsenals of which they were aware, that night. The Lord Lieutenant did not think this went far enough. He wanted the ringleaders arrested and the Castle guard to be strengthened. Nathan declined to do this and they went on to discuss whether there was likely to be any action that day. It was now eleven in the morning and both men felt that it was too late for any insurrection that day, as if fighting could only begin immediately after breakfast. In the end, Nathan sent a telegram to his chief, Birrell, asking if it would be legal to arrest the Volunteer leaders and intern them in Europe.

Wimborne wrote to Birrell at the same time, complaining that the Volunteers were being treated too gently. It now looked as if they had stirred a hornets' nest yet weren't prepared to do anything about the hornets. He asked Birrell to 'ginger Nathan', because the chance to arrest them that was now offered might not recur.[7]

If Nathan and Wimborne were confused, so were the Volunteers. In Dublin and countrywide, Volunteers went to their meeting points, unaware of any orders from MacNeill or Pearse. Two hundred men from 5th (Fingal) Battalion of the Dublin Brigade met at Saucerstown, near Swords. There was also a good turnout of 2nd Battalion at Father Mathew Park in Fairview, where the park's pavilion was being used as an arsenal. They were told to stand down when a message came from Miss Ryan, MacNeill's secretary, and that only the Citizen Army was going ahead with manoeuvres. This left the problem of what to do with the arsenal, which also held equipment for 1st Battalion and GHQ. In the end it was left to 2nd Battalion to guard it. There were police spies everywhere, so the battalion officers got little sleep that Sunday night. Liam Tannam was OC of E Company in the 3rd Battalion, and he assembled all but two of them in Oakley Road in the south of the city at three that afternoon. This was de Valera's battalion, and Tannam refused to accept an order to stand down that came from MacNeill. Tannam was about to march his men off when an officer from 4th Battalion, which was commanded by Eamonn Ceannt, came by on his bicycle, wearing full Volunteer uniform. The cyclist told Tannam that he had received the stand down order directly from Ceannt, so that they could take it as official. Stubbornly, Tannam still refused to dismiss his men, but his brother arrived at about 3:45 with an order from MacDonagh countersigned by de Valera. Soon after that MacDonagh himself arrived with both Pearse brothers, who were on their way home.[8]

Nathan was still busy. At around six that evening he contacted two officers of the GOC's staff, since General Friend himself was in England. He explained about the stolen gelignite and the need to raid Liberty Hall. It was likely that there would be a great deal of fighting, since there were still many Volunteers about, and the fighting could spread to their parts of Dublin. Their first reaction was that they would need a field gun to get into Liberty Hall. One could be sent from Athlone, but Colonel Cowan, the senior officer, said he would like to consult the police, the rest of the staff and Major Price, the Military Intelligence Officer. They agreed to meet again at ten that night. In the meantime, Wimborne cancelled a trip to Belfast that was scheduled for Easter Monday.

When the group met again at ten, Wimborne said that he saw no point in raiding Liberty Hall unless there was a round-up of the leaders; he wanted sixty to one hundred of them in jail that night. Anything less was simply stirring the hornets' nest. Nathan refused, saying that he would do nothing until he had checked that it was legal and that a charge could be sustained. The agreement of the Home Secretary was needed before a charge of hostile association with the enemy could be brought. Wimborne countered that there needed to be a significant number of the Volunteers disarmed, probably six or seven hundred. He conceded that this could not be done that night, but he felt that it was possible to arrest 100 particularly prominent members. It was eventually agreed that nothing would be done until Nathan got his reply from the Chief Secretary and a list of those to be arrested could be drawn up. The meeting broke up at 11:30 p.m.

Easter Monday proved to be another beautiful day. Men and women were on the streets in holiday mood, some of them looking forward to a day at the races because this was the day of the Irish Grand National. Eoin MacNeill rode on his bike through Rathfarnham to visit his friend, Dr O'Kelly, expecting a quiet day after the excitement of the weekend. He met the local Volunteers assembling, and stopped to have a word with their officers before going on. Further on he met with Sean Fitzgibbon, who was on the Volunteer Executive, and Liam O'Briain, who had wanted to buy a bayonet in anticipation of action, but had made do with a Spanish knife that was now lying beside his rifle and knapsack. When MacNeill mentioned the fact that he had seen the Rathfarnham Volunteers assembled, Fitzgibbon volunteered to go on a bike to see what was happening, while MacNeill and O'Briain went into the doctor's house. Here MacNeill brought the others up to date with what had happened in the last few days, and told them that he thought there was now no danger of a rising. It was his belief that the reason the Volunteers were out that morning was to assure Dublin Castle that things were going on as normal. There was a distinct shock when Fitzgibbon returned to say that the fight was on. MacNeill was so shocked that he refused to believe it, so O'Briain went to get definite news.

Sir Matthew Nathan had looked a little troubled when he left home that morning, but he had a short meeting with Wimborne before going into his office at Dublin Castle, reaching there about ten o'clock. The chief of Military Intelligence in Dublin, Major Price, also made his way to the Castle, enjoying the air of a spring day and the sense of Dublin being on holiday. Although the shops were shuttered for Easter Monday, and the quays were still, not everyone had gone to the races at Fairyhouse, and the streets were lively with people. Many of them were soldiers, on leave or waiting to be posted. It was eleven o'clock before he turned through the Castle gate. He settled down with Nathan to begin the list of those to be arrested.

After a little while Nathan phoned the GPO and asked for Arthur Hamilton Norway, the Secretary of the Post Office in Ireland. He had a number of things of a technical nature to discuss. Norway expected nothing unusual to come of this. He already knew of the 'prisoner of consequence' who had been arrested in Kerry the previous Friday, and he learned, as soon as he entered the room, that this was Sir Roger Casement, who had already been taken to London under guard. Nathan wanted to be able to limit the use of the telephone and telegram in the south and west of the country to the military and the navy. Norway saw no difficulty in this, but needed a written instruction. Norway was writing this out for Nathan's signature when shots crashed outside the window. The rising had begun.

It was not only holiday crowds that were moving round Dublin that morning. From 10 o'clock Volunteers began to muster at different locations around the city. This was not a smooth operation, because the confusion of the day before had proved the truth of the old saying, order plus counter order equals disorder. Fairview was supposed to be the muster point of 2nd Battalion. This was now changed to Stephen's Green. Those who had stayed there overnight were only told at 10:25 that they should have been on the other side of the river half an hour earlier. Other officers overslept and only discovered when they had been awakened by impatient couriers that mobilisation was on again. Sometimes units met and moved off, to be joined by stragglers later.

Ned Daly commanded the 1st Battalion, most of whose men came from the north-west of the city. Daly was a brother-in-law of Tom Clarke, and his own family had impeccable republican credentials. Most of the men, about two hundred and fifty, gathered in Blackhall Street, but D Company, under Captain Sean Heuston, formed at Mountjoy Square. These men were to work directly under James Connolly. The rest of the battalion was to occupy and defend an area based around the Four Courts and stretching north as far as Phibsboro. They were to expect attacks by the British from the west, where both the Marlborough and Royal Barracks were located.

MacDonagh himself commanded the city's 2nd Battalion, and this was the area where the greatest confusion occurred. About two hundred men obeyed the order to go to St Stephen's Green. From here they were to go on to Jacob's Biscuit Factory, on Bishop Street. About half of those who mustered remained behind to guard the large quantities of stores that were kept at Fairview Park. These were joined by some latecomers as the day progressed, before all of them were told to report to the General Post Office in Sackville Street, which even then was becoming known as O'Connell Street, because of the bridge at one end.

In the south-east of Dublin, Éamon de Valera, an American-born schoolteacher, commanded 3rd Battalion. Unusually, he had been given command of the battalion even before he joined the IRB, but only after a personal interview with Pearse. He was now having difficulty getting his men together; only 130 turned up to begin with. This was a pitiful number when compared to the task the battalion was set. The men had to neutralise the threat of British soldiers in Beggars Bush Barracks and to prevent any army reinforcements that might be landed at Kingstown from getting access to the city.

Arguably, 4th Battalion had the most difficult task. They had the largest battalion area, covering the city south from Kilmainham and centred on the South Dublin Union, the largest workhouse in Ireland. Any reinforcements for the army would most likely come from the Curragh, and would detrain at Kingsbridge Station, just to their west. Only 100 men mustered at Dolphin's Barn before their commanding officer, Eamonn Ceannt, marched them to their posts.

One irregular group was that known as the Kimmage Garrison. This was made up of Irishmen who had returned from England. They had bivouacked in the grounds of Count Plunkett's family estate and had received basic training. They were commanded by Captain George Plunkett. It was they who made the most stylish entrance to the Rising. Plunkett used his gun to persuade a tram driver to stop, then asked the conductor for 'Fifty-two two-penny tickets to the City Centre, please.' One of the young men who boarded the tram was Michael Collins.

Most of the Citizen Army, in their dark green uniforms, had spent the night at Liberty Hall, but some had been given leave to spend a last night at home, and these now hurried back to the building on the quays. Scouts had been sent out by Connolly to watch the army barracks for any unusual movements. Here too came Tom Clarke, after a breakfast at home, walking through the streets with two armed bodyguards. Out and in came Volunteer couriers, distinguishable in their grey-green uniforms. Sean MacDermott arrived, like Clarke, on foot. The Pearse brothers arrived on bicycles. Joseph Plunkett, whose health was really poor, arrived by car from the Metropole Hotel, only a few hundred yards away. Another who arrived by car was the O'Rahilly, who had discovered that the Rising was going ahead and was determined not to miss the 'glorious madness'. On a practical level, he had brought several rifles with him in the car. The Supreme Council met, although MacDonagh had already left, and the members reconstituted themselves as the Provisional Government of the Republic of Ireland. At 11 o'clock Connolly bade farewell to his daughter.

Sometime before 11:45, a bugler sounded the stand-to and the men hurriedly formed up outside. There were two groups who had particular missions. Patrick Daly had already left with his team, cycling in ones and twos along Bachelors Walk. Their task was to blow up the Magazine Fort in Phoenix Park. When they arrived at the gate of the park, they started a kick-about game of football with a ball they had picked up on the way.

Another group was led by Sean Connolly of the Citizen Army. His task was to occupy City Hall, which stands in front of Dublin Castle and could limit access to Ship Street Barracks. As well as City Hall, the original plan envisaged occupying the Corporation rates building, the Evening Mail offices and a pub that was opposite the lower gate of the Castle. Since Sean Connolly was employed in the motor tax office in City Hall, he knew his way about it.[9] Constable O'Brien of the Dublin Metropolitan Police was on duty at the near or lower gate of the Castle. Seeing a group of armed men coming towards him, he tried to slam the gate shut, but Sean Connolly shot him dead; the first fatality in the rising was an unarmed Irishman. This was the shot heard by Nathan and the others. It was exactly noon, and the Angelus bells sounded around Dublin. A group from the Citizen Army now forced the gate. A sentry looked as if he was going to fire, but thought better of it and retreated into the guardhouse. The Irishmen followed him so closely that the rest of the guard, only ten in total, surrendered. They were disarmed and tied up with their own puttees.

The team working in Nathan's office were shocked, but both Nathan and Price recovered quickly. Price started firing at the rebels with his service revolver, while Nathan alerted the soldiers at nearby Ship Street

Barracks. They then closed both castle gates and released the sentries. For Price, it was a matter of great relief that the Citizen Army had not realised how poorly garrisoned Dublin Castle was. It would have been a tremendous coup for them if they had captured the seat of government in Ireland, as well as the second most important political figure in the country. Sean Connolly withdrew his men from the guardroom and entered City Hall. Although this building seemed solid and safe, it was a poor choice. The roof in particular had no protection and Sean Connolly himself was shot dead here by a sniper a few hours after the action began. The garrison had to be removed the following day to the Daily News offices across the street because of the sustained fire they came under.

In the Phoenix Park, at about 12:15 Daly picked up the football and walked over to the sentry and asked if there was a football pitch nearby. While he engaged the soldier in conversation, another Volunteer jumped on the unsuspecting man from behind and disarmed him. Daly and two others rushed the guardroom, where the astonished men raised their hands in surrender. One soldier who tried to fight back was shot in the leg. There was an unpleasant surprise in the guardroom. As well as the soldiers, the Volunteers found themselves guarding the wife of the British commandant and her two sons. Daly took the fort's keys from a cabinet. While he opened the ammunition, paraffin, oil and tools stores, he sent another man to open the guncotton store. There were tin-can bombs which he distributed to his men before he saturated the premises with paraffin. But none of the keys fitted the guncotton store. He had to be content with the damage the paraffin could do. He released the commandant's family, telling them the fort was about to blow up. He also released the guard, warning them that they would be shot if they tried to reach Islandbridge Barracks, just across the Liffey. The Volunteers then left, planning to make their separate ways back. One of them saw one of the commandant's boys running towards a house, presumably to raise the alarm, and shot him dead. The rising's second fatality was an unarmed boy. His name was Playfair.

Shortly after Sean Connolly and his men had left, James Connolly turned to his Chief of Staff, Michael Mallin. Mallin had been a trade union organiser and before that a soldier in South Africa. Connolly ordered him to take about one hundred men and to occupy St Stephen's Green and the College of Surgeons. When Mallin marched off, he had only about thirty-six men and some women for support.[10] Not all of them had uniforms and some had only got shotguns. One girl, Margaret Skinnider, who was actually Scottish, cycled ahead to check for British troops, but found none. One policeman thought about intervening as the column marched past singing nationalist songs, but was put off by the determined look on the marchers' faces. When the men reached the top of Grafton Street and crossed to the Green, Mallin ordered that the gates be closed and the area cleared of civilians. This was easier said than done, as the Green was full of mothers taking advantage of the good weather to let their children play on the grass. Some of the women even threatened to call the police; how much good that would have done was demonstrated when a constable refused to leave his post and was shot dead. At around this time Countess Markievicz appeared on the scene. She was supposed to act as liaison between St Stephen's Green and the GPO, but Mallin invited her to act as his second in command and she was nothing loath.

Douglas Hyde, the founder of the Gaelic League, had been buying cigarettes and had thought the sound of gunfire was merely the sound of cars backfiring. He realised that it was something more serious as he cycled past the Green. He watched what was happening for a minute, but he was threatened by a young fellow with a rifle and, wisely, cycled home.

Back at Liberty Hall, only about one hundred and fifty of the battalion that was to guard the GPO had turned up.[11] About one third of these were from the Citizen Army and others were drawn from the four city battalions. The biggest element, however, were the seventy-five men of the Kimmage garrison. All of them formed up, this time with Connolly at the head of the column, as befitted the Commandant General of the Dublin Division. Close behind him was Patrick Pearse. Even the terminally ill Joseph Plunkett joined the column, unsheathing his sword-stick as he did so. As a concession to age on the one hand and infirmity on the other, Clarke and MacDermott had gone ahead by car, and were waiting at the corner of the GPO. Attracted by all the activity, quite a crowd of onlookers had gathered and, when at 11:50 the order 'By the left, quick march' was given, a cheer went up. The column turned left into Abbey Street, followed by a single cab carrying supplies and ammunition. Sackville Street was the first main thoroughfare that they came to and here they wheeled right towards the GPO. As they drew level with this, another order was called out and they charged the building.

Anyone found in the building was hustled out, but a number of British soldiers, some of whom were guards, others who had called in on business, were taken prisoner. A group of Volunteers had been designated to go to the roof to act as snipers, while the others set about fortifying the building.

Only about a third of Ned Daly's 1st Battalion turned up at the muster point in Blackhall Place. All of them were surprised when Daly told them that they were going into action that day for the Irish Republic. He suggested that they might want to leave the muster, but only two did. Because of the size and importance of the area, key buildings had been identified as outposts, and groups of men left to take control of these. The main column marched towards the symbol of British justice in Ireland, the complex known as the Four Courts. They found a single policeman in occupation; the courts had been suspended for the holiday. The unfortunate constable was made to open the gate and hand over the keys before being taken prisoner. A caretaker was located in the basement, and he was sent home, before the Volunteers began to consolidate their positions. Daly established his headquarters in the entrance hall of St Joseph's Convent, nearby. The 1st Battalion was the first unit to fight a proper action that day. A convoy of five lorry-loads of ammunition was being brought from Marlborough Barracks along Ormond Quay to be deposited in the Magazine Fort. It was escorted by fifty lancers. The British had been allowed to pass Liberty Hall, the end of Sackville Street and City Hall, because the men at the Four Courts would be in the most favourable position to deal with them. When the soldiers came under fire it was as if they were dazed.[12] Desperately trying to get their horses under control, they turned into Charles Street without firing a shot. The lancers had only been issued with five rounds of ammunition each, so had to be careful not to waste shots. They cut their horses loose, turned over the lorries to form barricades and settled down for a siege. It was to be three and a half days before they were relieved.

This action had happened so soon after the excitement of beginning that the Volunteers realised the seriousness of what they had undertaken and worked feverishly to complete their preparations. They blocked the bridge at Church Street, placed units on the North Circular

Road and on Cabra Road, and built barricades at North King Street and North Brunswick Street. These barricades were made of whatever could be gathered from local builders' yards and other premises, and were fairly insubstantial. The sheer number of them rendered them effective, however, in this area 'which resembled a rabbit warren than a battlefield'.[13]

The most important of 1st Battalion's outposts was just across the river on Ussher's Island. This was the Mendicity Institute, once an elegant building which now displayed signs of a steady decline, and was now the daily haunt of 'the poorest of the poor'. The garrison here was commanded by Sean Heuston. He entered the premises at one o'clock and cleared out the occupants. Other outposts were located in 'Reilly's Fort', a public house at the corner of Church Street and North King Street; Moore's coach works; Monks's bakery; and Clarke's dairy. In taking over these posts there were more disagreements and, inevitably, more casualties, and a seventy-year-old man was shot through the eye. The combination of outposts gave a clear view north towards Broadstone Station. This had been one of the battalion's objectives, because it was here that troops from Athlone and Galway would detrain, but the poor turnout made this impossible, and it was soon in the hands of the military.

Those of Thomas MacDonagh's 2nd Battalion who had received the up-to-date orders had gathered at St Stephen's Green, only moving on when Mallin's force arrived. MacDonagh's second-in-command was Major John MacBride, whose fame as a fighter in South Africa and the man who married Maud Gonne had slowly washed away as rumours of his drinking and his marital problems had become known. He had sunk to unemployment and alcoholism before getting a job as a water bailiff for Dublin Corporation. Once a member of the Supreme Council of the IRB, he had been squeezed out to allow a place for Sean MacDermott. He had not been part of the original planning for the Rising, but MacDonagh wanted to take advantage of his military experience. The two met fortuitously in the city centre and MacDonagh offered him the post. It was perhaps the fact that he was over fifty and that this might be his last chance to redeem his reputation that made MacBride accept.

Most of the battalion marched to Jacob's Biscuit Factory, a huge building which dominated the area between Dublin Castle, a quarter of a mile north, and two military barracks, Wellington and Portobello, three quarters of a mile to the south. The height of the building would allow snipers to command Portobello Bridge, across the Grand Canal, Portobello Barracks itself, the roof of Ship Street Barracks, Dublin Castle and a good portion of St Stephen's Green. The main body of Volunteers got into the factory by the simple expedient of taking a sledgehammer to the front gates. About forty men, however, were sent to occupy three outposts on Malpas Street and one opposite the police station in Kevin Street. The people in Malpas Street, near the Coombe, were among the poorest in Dublin, and children still got a daily handout of a cup of cocoa and a bun.[14] The Volunteers who went here had to endure a great deal of hostility from a crowd which sang pro-British songs and threw stones. One local died after being shot and bayoneted when he tried to grab a Volunteer's rifle. Many of the crowd were women whose husbands were in the army, the only job available to most of them. Known as Separation Women, these women had a reputation for drinking the weekly allowance they received from the army. The hostility was so persistent that the Malpas Street outposts were abandoned that evening.

In the 3rd Battalion area, the men concentrated around Earlsfort Terrace, south of St Stephen's Green. By 11:30 a.m. less than one hundred and fifty had turned up—and seven of these deserted that day, taking a large quantity of supplies with them. Those men present moved off at 11:50, the majority of them to occupy Boland's Bakery in Grand Canal Street. Fourteen of C Company, under Lieutenant Michael Malone, turned off along the canal bank to Mount Street, a middle-class area where they had been told to establish outposts. The main part of the battalion went on to the bakery, though parties were detached to take control of Westland Row Station and Boland's Mills, a stone building which covered the narrow bridge between Great Brunswick Street, now known as Pearse Street, and Ringsend Road. The workers were ordered out of the bakery, though a small group volunteered to stay until the current batch of bread was baked. There was some slight difficulty getting rid of the company doctor and his wife, who lived above the dispensary, but they too finally left.

The party sent to Westland Row Station was commanded by Capt. McMahon of B Company. He cleared and locked the station before ripping up a portion of the line. He then had his men dig in about three

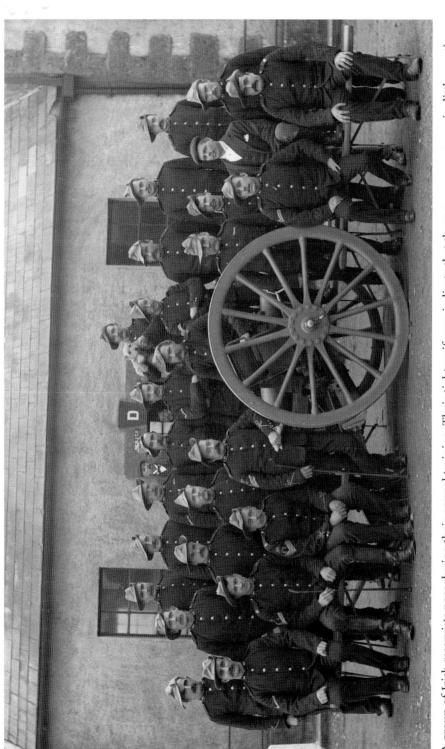

A group of Irish reservists pose during their annual training. Their tight uniforms indicate that these manoeuvres require little exertion. (*National Library of Ireland*)

John Redmond at a Home Rule meeting. It was his success in getting the government to agree to Home Rule that brought relations with the unionists to a head. (*National Library of Ireland*)

Arthur Griffith began by seeking a joint monarchy between Ireland and Great Britain, on the model of Austro-Hungary. It is ironic that the name of the pacifist movement which he initiated, Sinn Féin, should be applied to an armed uprising. (*National Library of Ireland*)

Edward Carson, seen here in 1915, used his skills as a barrister to redefine treason in such a way that Irish unionists could see their actions as defending the British constitution. (*Popperfoto/Getty Images*)

An early example of an armed, if not an armoured, car. The UVF demonstrates its fire power. (*Sean Sexton Collection/Corbis*)

The nationalist response. Members of the Irish Citizen Army receive sniper training on a Dublin rooftop. (*Hulton-Deutsch Collection/Corbis*)

Although these nurses come from Ulster, there were volunteers from all over Ireland, including the woman that went on to establish the Medical Missionaries of Mary, Mother Mary Martin. (*Getty Images*)

The Irish became used to the sight of wounded soldiers from early in the war. These soldiers seem relieved to be spared the fighting at Gallipoli, if only for a few weeks. (*Stapleton Historical Collection/Hip/TopFoto*)

The funeral of Jeremiah O'Donovan Rossa gave the first hint of the strength of advanced nationalist support. Patrick Pearse, beside the altar boy, is putting his notes into his pocket. (*National Library of Ireland*)

Founded to protect workers from violence by the Dublin Metropolitan Police, the Irish Citizen Army soon found common cause with the Irish Volunteers. (*TopFoto*)

Patrick Pearse surrenders to the British forces. (*National Museum of Ireland*)

Relatives were allowed to visit prisoners in Richmond Barracks three times a week, bringing food, letters and fruit like apples as a treat. (*TopFoto*)

Finding a silver lining: children drag home wood from ruined buildings to use as fuel. (*Press Association Images*)

This iconic shot of the Royal Irish Rifles waiting to go forward at the Somme shows the squalor in which the soldiers lived, and the stoicism with which they endured it. (*TopFoto*)

The change from fighter to politician: Éamon de Valera campaigns in Ennis, County Clare. (*Hulton Archive/Getty Images*)

The British response, one: the recruiting of Auxiliaries, seen here being inspected at their depot in Phoenix Park. (*National Library of Ireland*)

A soldier's eye view of the Battle of Cambrai. Soldiers of the 16th Division are escorting German prisoners back to British lines. (*Popperfoto/Getty Images*)

The British response, two: troops try to impose their presence on the Irish country. (*National Library of Ireland*)

The urban Irish saw few benefits from the war. Some, however, found employment in the National Shell Factory at Parkgate Street, in Dublin. (*Imperial War Museum*)

The War among Brothers: Éamon de Valera inspects a large contingent of IRA fighters. (*TopFoto*)

Although it appeared to be a spectacular success, the attack on the Custom House cost the IRA dearly in terms of personnel. A cool head might have described it as an own goal. (*Bettmann/Corbis*)

The Civil War gave many veterans of the British army an opportunity to legitimise their experience by joining the ranks of the Free State Army. Commandant Ned Daly here inspects recruits in a variety of headgear. (*National Library of Ireland*)

Even before he lost his life, Michael Collins had paid a high personal price. Here he inspects the ruins of his family home in Clonakilty, County Cork. (*National Library of Ireland*)

Sir James Craig (*front row, centre*), first Prime Minister of Northern Ireland, relaxes among his Cabinet colleagues. (*TopFoto*)

It took longer for Éamon de Valera to prevail, and he looks much less relaxed as he sits among his colleagues (*front row, centre*) on the day that he announces the freeing of Irish political prisoners. (*TopFoto*) hundred yards from the station. A Company, under the command of Captain Joseph O'Connor, had already stopped and emptied a train, and had taken prisoner a very surprised British army officer.

Eamonn Ceannt's 4th Battalion was to cover the south-western approaches to the city. Among its number were some of the most interesting of the Volunteers. His second in command was Vice-Commandant Cathal Brugha. He was already getting the name of being a hawk whose main argument was resource to his gun, which he claimed uttered the only effective sound in Irish politics.[15] Another firebrand was Con Colbert, whose Puritan attitude to smoking and drinking he had derived from Irish history. He had a simple explanation for the failure of every Irish rebellion: drink and want of discipline and loose talk.[16] At 11:30, the battalion made its way to its main base, the South Dublin Union, where St James's Hospital now stands, while detachments went to the three main outposts: Watkins's Brewery in Ardee Street; Jameson's Distillery in Marrowbone Lane; and Roe's Distillery in Mount Brown. Ceannt and Brugha took the main group and travelled along the canal bank to the Rialto Bridge, and entered the Union complex from the rear. They took the keys from the porter and then cut telephone wires. Ceannt remained here with ten Volunteers while the rest went round to the front entrance, where they were reinforced by some stragglers. There was an amusing incident at Watkins's Brewery. Tom Young had been sent out with half a dozen men to make sure there were no soldiers in the vicinity. When he came back he discovered a police inspector and some constables waiting for the Volunteers to come out so they could be arrested for breaking and entering. The policemen were taken aback to find themselves arrested at gunpoint.

Nathan had reacted quickly to the first shots in Dublin Castle. He and a storekeeper opened the armoury, intending to distribute arms among the few members of the Metropolitan Police who were on duty as Castle guard. They found revolvers, but no cartridges, so the police remained unarmed. The Chief Superintendent of the DMP had an office in the Castle, however, and he sent out an order that all men should assemble, together with cars and ammunition. Few did so, and a later order that police should stay off the streets was superfluous, since most individuals had already done so.[17] Nathan sent a telegraph to Birrell in London, describing all that he was aware of. Birrell already knew most of it, because he had been at the Home Office when Lord French had come with the news that rebels had seized the GPO. For the time being, Birrell seemed more concerned about being questioned in Parliament than the situation in Dublin, which he does not seem to have considered serious.

The senior British army officer in Dublin was Colonel Kennard, but he was out of contact when the first shots were fired and the explosion occurred at the Magazine Fort, at which point the authorities became aware that something was happening. His adjutant, Colonel Cowan, telephoned the Portobello, Richmond and Royal Barracks at 12:10 to let their commanders know that something was afoot. He also told each to send their stand-by units, each of about a hundred men, to Dublin Castle in order to defend it till the full city garrison was mobilised. He then telephoned Colonel Hammond at Marlborough Barracks to investigate the situation at Sackville Street, from where he was getting confused reports. The next person to be alerted was Brigadier General Lowe, commander of 3rd Reserve Cavalry Brigade at Curragh Camp, who immediately ordered the three regiments under his direct command to entrain for Dublin immediately. Further reinforcements were requested from Belfast, Athlone and Templemore. Finally, a plain-clothes officer went to Kingstown so that a message could be sent by radio to the War Office in London. This was the message that had brought Lord French to the Home Office.

At the GPO a Tricolour was now flying at the Henry Street Corner, while a green flag with a harp and the words IRISH REPUBLIC was at the Prince's Street end. Inside, a screen had been used to set up a hospital, and a store area was stocked with arms, while another had boots, trousers, shirts and overcoats. The tables in the sorting room were used for beds, and an area was set aside for Fr Flanagan from the Pro-Cathedral to hear confessions. Upstairs, the captured British soldiers worked preparing food. Other buildings in Sackville Street had been occupied. There were Volunteers in Clery's Store, the Imperial Hotel and the shops on the corners facing O'Connell Bridge. The GPO was to be a magnet for Volunteers who had lost contact with their own units, and the original garrison of 150 men rose to slightly over 400.

At 12:45 Patrick Pearse went outside, with an armed guard. One disadvantage of the GPO is that it has no steps leading up to it, so Pearse was forced to speak on the same level as his listeners. He read out the Proclamation of the Republic to an audience which, while not openly hostile, was not friendly. His sense of drama seems to have left him and what he read out, one of the finest evocations of the spirit of the national struggle,[18] seems to have fallen on unappreciative ears. When he had finished, there was a muted response, though a few cheers rose from the crowd. As he returned to the GPO, hundreds of copies of the Proclamation were posted around the city centre or taken to the other garrisons. In spite of the lack of enthusiasm in the crowd, the wording of the Proclamation is extremely important, since for the first time it gave an indication of the Ireland to which Pearse and his co-signatories aspired.

Pragmatically, only the title was in Irish. The main purpose of the Proclamation was to communicate with the people, and what was now the Provisional Government of Ireland realised that there were few Dubliners fluent in Irish. The tone is elevated, like a poem or an invocation to prayer, or like a hymn that can be moving even to unbelievers. It proclaims the continuity of the Irish nation, through 'the dead generations', as a separate entity, and calls on her sons to rally round her at this time of ordeal. The personification of Ireland as a woman also claimed a continuity through Irish culture, where Ireland could be Róisín Dubh or Cathleen Ní Houlihan or even the Old Woman of Bearra. With this justification, the Provisional Government now proclaimed that the Republic of Ireland was a sovereign inde-pendent state, guaranteeing civil and religious liberty and with equal rights and opportunities for all its citizens. It would cherish all children of the nation equally and be oblivious to the differences 'carefully fostered by an alien government'. It struck only one sour note. In its reference to 'our gallant allies in Europe', it declared as an enemy of Ireland every Irishman serving in the British army. While proclaiming unity, it was already establishing differences.

The seven signatories of the Proclamation, while most of them had military rank, do not seem to have divided the powers of government among themselves. Tom Clarke's widow maintained that Clarke was the President of the Provisional Government, since his name came first on the Proclamation. Most others thought that Pearse was the President and a newsletter published on the Tuesday, 'Irish War News', gave him that title. The other signatories seem to have considered their role as being purely military. The mixture of men who had turned out that Monday was referred to by their leaders as the Army of the Irish Republic. It was not long before Irish usage had changed this to Irish Republican Army, a name which was to remain significant for many decades.

Colonel Hammond in Marlborough Barracks had sent a detachment of cavalry to find out what was happening in Sackville Street in response to Colonel Cowan's request. They arrived at the Parnell Square end of the street about half an hour after Pearse had read the Proclamation and started to ride towards the crowds around the GPO. When the first horses had drawn level with Nelson's Pillar, the rebel garrison opened fire, killing three soldiers and fatally wounding another. The rest of the troopers withdrew at speed and in some disorder. One horse was also killed and its gradually putrefying body contributed an unpleasant ambience to the scene for the rest of the week.

The elation felt by the Volunteers because of their success in this first action was turned to hilarity when someone discovered the RIC pigeon holes in the sorting office and discovered the latest police reports on the Volunteers, none of which gave any hint that a rising was imminent. Even after the shooting, there was still a group of soldiers' wives outside, trying to force their way in. Gradually they left, as friends and family dragged them away. More stores were transferred from Liberty Hall in a convoy of fifteen lorries and cars. Liberty Hall itself was locked and deserted, but the flag of the Irish Citizen Army, the Starry Plough, was still flying above it. All through the afternoon reinforcements kept trickling in, including a group calling itself the Hibernian Rifles, consisting of Irish-Americans, and two sailors, one Finn and the other Swedish, who explained that they hated the English. Some women also arrived, and they were allocated to nursing or kitchen duties by Connolly.

O'Connell Street was situated very close to some of the poorest parts of Dublin. One thing that the Volunteers had not considered was the possibility of people from these areas seeing the Rising as an opportunity to help themselves to some of the good things of life. There seemed no way of stopping them short of shooting some as an example, because they ignored shots fired over their heads. Things ranging from sweets to motor bikes were taken. In the end, the Volunteers entered into an uneasy truce with the looters, although their presence made it difficult to get on with the business of preparing a defence. Much of the afternoon was spent establishing outposts in houses in Henry Street and in the block opposite the GPO. On the streets, barricades were being built of whatever materials came to hand. One was made of rolls of linoleum and carpets, designed to collapse if anyone tried to climb over it. Another was made of thousands of bicycles, jammed into one another and almost eight feet high. A third was made of piles of marble clocks, of the sort so common in business and commercial premises.

That evening, Hobson was eventually released. He had been held at gunpoint to the very last.

In the South Dublin Union, Ceannt and one party took over the night nurses' home, while another went to the boardroom. The Union authorities, confronted with such a drastic disruption to their routine, decided that it was impractical to evacuate the inmates. Instead, they were moved into a number of buildings which were draped with Red Cross flags. Some of the inhabitants could not comprehend what was happening; one old nun opened a door to a Volunteer and asked if he had come to read the gas meter.[19] Although both sides tried to minimise the danger to civilians in the Union during the fighting, it was almost inevitable that some would be killed.

Ceannt had no more than sixty-five men, but he had an instinct for warfare and he chose defensive positions that would ensure the army would have to fight hard to take the Union. As they were taking up position and improving their defences, they could hear a military band playing in Richmond Barracks. 'They don't know yet,' said Ceannt in an amused tone. Suddenly the music stopped, and the Volunteers realised that news had reached the barracks. Ceannt knew that the British had to attack the Union in order to clear the way for the reinforcements that would soon be arriving at Kingsbridge Station. Close to the Union stood the Royal Hospital, Kilmainham, official residence of the British Commander-in-Chief. Anyone looking out of the general's window could now see a large Tricolour flying like a challenge at the nearest corner of the Union buildings. For most of the day, a machine-gun on the roof of the Royal Hospital kept this west wing of the Union under fire.

The Volunteers in the Union had as their first target a column of about thirty soldiers moving along James's Street towards the city, presumably on their way to defend Dublin Castle. Their officer was wounded and the remainder took cover. Shortly afterwards they scattered a party of the 3rd Royal Irish Rifles, when they fired at point-blank range.[20] Fighting was almost continuous after that. After being reinforced, the Rifles overwhelmed the small outpost, manned by fourteen Volunteers whom Ceannt had established in sheds and other buildings in the grounds, although the fighting lasted for two hours. These men had to retreat to one of the hospitals, but a quick-thinking soldier smashed the door with a lawn-mower and they were captured. Ceannt then concentrated his men at the James's Street end of the main building. Inmates were paid to move all the ammunition here, and the job was completed in ten minutes. Already there were casualties among the non-combatants. A nurse was shot by soldiers while she was checking patients on the ground floor. An inmate was shot dead in the kitchen. Soldiers threw a hand-grenade through a window which fell among eight inmates who were gathered around a fireplace. One was killed and the rest were wounded.

One handicap that Ceannt's men laboured under was that there were not enough of them to maintain communications between Ceannt's headquarters at the James's Street end of the buildings and his remaining outposts. The British too were having difficulties. Major Sir Francis Vane, who we met before, was ordered to take charge of Portobello Barracks. Here he found the Ulstermen of the Royal Irish Rifles, as well as small parties of soldiers from different regiments and young officers who had not yet experienced war, giving him a total of about six hundred men.[21] His first concern was for the security of the barracks itself. He established pickets in the direction of the insurgents, making sure that they had clear lines of retreat if they came under attack by superior forces. He also established an observation post in the top-heavy clock tower of Rathmines Town Hall. He did not take personal charge of the attack on the Union till the next day, Tuesday.

At Jameson's Distillery in Marrowbone Lane, the Volunteers had filled a large vat with fresh water in preparation for a siege. There seemed to be rather a lot of women there, from a nearby branch of the Gaelic League. One man, Holland, who was well acquainted with rifles, was sent to the top of one of the grain storehouses with a Lee-Enfield and a Mauser, and with Josie McGowan as a loader, prepared to cover the ground to the west of the distillery. He had views of both sides of the canal banks as far as Dolphin's Barn.

At Roe's Distillery, to the north of the Union buildings, C Company of 4th Battalion occupied a much less useful building. It was overlooked by the buildings of the Royal Hospital. When the building came under fire from the British, the Volunteers discovered that the ground floor windows were too high to shoot out of, while windows on the upper floors were so low that a rifleman had no protection.[22] Things became really bad when grain in a side building threatened to catch fire. Although the Volunteers managed to move the smouldering sacks, British fire was so heavy that they could not move about in the open. The same British fire, coming straight along Mount Brown, cut them off from the Union buildings as effectively as if they were in another country. The bodies of three dead Volunteers lay on the road. A fourth was still alive. From time to time he tried to drink from his water bottle, but he was too weak.[23]

MacDonagh's 2nd Battalion were in action within an hour of taking over Jacob's Factory. A group of about thirty soldiers were seen coming along Camden Street and the Volunteers had time to set up an ambush for them at the junction of Redmond's Hill and Bishop Street. They managed to wound the officer and six men, and then braced themselves for a major assault that they thought must come soon. They were wrong, however. The British saw no great military value in Jacob's and had made the decision that it would take too great an effort to assault. Instead, they would use psychological warfare on the defenders, with sniper fire being used steadily and armoured cars racing round the streets in low gear, making it difficult for anyone to sleep. It looked as if the last minute change of plan for the Fairview men had been a mistake.

Éamon de Valera was frustrated because the small turnout in his sector meant that he had to abandon many of his objectives. He was a gentleman who had difficulties in dealing with women, and refused to allow women to get involved in the action. A section of Cumann na mBan had assembled in Merrion Square, but de Valera neglected to send the promised courier. As a result Volunteers had to take turns in the kitchen, and the doctor had to work without any nursing help. (One man was even assigned to look after the bakery's thirty horses.) His armament was even worse; he had fifty rifles of different makes and calibre and a mixture of ammunition. In fire fights, time was wasted while men sorted out the proper bullets for their rifles. There were some shotguns, but these were so corroded as to be useless. Someone had provided home-made hand-grenades, but these were so heavy that the thrower was in as much danger as the target, since he might be the one nearer the explosion.[24]

One of his outposts was at Mount Street Bridge, covering the approaches from Kingstown. This was under the command of Lieutenant Malone. These men were to take part in one of the saddest actions of the day. There existed in Dublin a unit of the Irish Association of Volunteer Training Corps, known to Dubliners, as noted above, as the Gorgeous Wrecks. Its members were respectable pillars of the community, many of them doctors or lawyers, and many of them above military age. They had spent a glorious day on manoeuvres in the Wicklow hills until they had met a cyclist who told them of the exciting events in Dublin. It would have been perfectly understandable if they, like the DMP, had made their way home discreetly, but they wished to do what they could to help and started back towards their depot in Beggar's Bush Barracks. Although some had rifles with them, none had ammunition. Some little time before four o'clock they were told that St Stephen's Green was in rebel hands, but that their barracks had not been taken. Their commander, Major Harris, split his men into two columns. The smaller of these came under fire from Volunteer outposts in Northumberland Road. Four were killed and several wounded before the survivors managed to scramble into neighbouring houses, where they were looked after until they could get away. The larger column, under Major Harris, managed to get into the barracks, although one corporal was killed. Here they found only members of the Catering Corps, with a total of twenty-seven rifles among them. The Wrecks took over defence of the barracks and, when they had sorted out arms and ammunition, they started firing at the rebel positions.

Since de Valera could not carry out his original plan of occupying Kingstown Station and harbour, at midnight he ordered one of his officers to set up a blocking position on the road that came from Blackrock and Ballsbridge to the capital. Just before they set off he changed his mind and called them back. Perhaps he remembered that he already had a post in Mount Street.

In St Stephen's Green the insurgents were having difficulty taking control of the situation. Crowds of onlookers kept getting in the way and ignoring orders to keep moving. While trenches were being dug, some of the rebel women set up a kitchen in the summer house. As well as blocking the gates, men started building barricades in streets round about. Vehicles, from wheelbarrows to lorries, were used for this. Some men went round with a handcart, distributing shotguns and ammunition. Some extra reinforcements drifted in as the afternoon passed, and Mallin set about setting up outposts. The most important of these was the Royal College of Surgeons, where Mallin was particularly interested in getting the rifles which belonged to the OTC. Unfortunately, a thorough search revealed none, but Mallin ordered a party under Frank Robbins to occupy the building, and soon the Tricolour was flying from its roof. For some reason, Mallin chose not to occupy the Shelbourne Hotel, which dominated the Green, although Connolly had identified it as a suitable place to establish a garrison, with its ready-made accommodation and supplies. Although the hotel was booked out, it was almost empty that afternoon, since most of the guests had gone to the races.

Volunteers were stopping cars and using them to solidify barricades. No one who lived in this part of Dublin seemed to support the insurrection, and many were reluctant to part with their property. A group of women had gathered who were encouraging drivers to ignore these rebels and to drive on. Even municipal tram drivers did not co-operate, one throwing away his control handle and another performing the difficult task of changing direction under fire. As the Volunteers became more frustrated, the mood became more dangerous. Michael Cavanagh had a vehicle carrying theatrical effects which was taken. He asked permission to recover some of his property but, when he was pulling at the shafts of the lorry, some gunmen told him to stop. Three shots were fired over his head before he dropped the shafts and walked towards the gunmen, waggling an admonitory finger. A voice said, 'Put that cart back or you're a dead man. Go before I count to four. One, two, three, four', and then he fired. Cavanagh was killed with a shot to the forehead. The crowd surged forward and some men lifted the unfortunate old man. Women began to keen and to kneel on the road and pray. 'We'll be back for you, damn you,' shouted one of the men carrying the body.[25]

With all the shooting, unintended targets began to be hit. A Shelbourne guest was shot as he went through the hotel's revolving door. Another was shot in the leg as he took his lunch. After that, the front of the hotel was locked and guests moved to the rear of the premises. The Green and the square around it began to look like a battlefield, although most of the casualties so far were non-combatants. There were prisoners taken, and these were kept in the bandstand at first, but then moved to a greenhouse beside the College of Surgeons. After a while, most of them were released, but one man was held all week because he had been seen going into an army barracks and might have been an informer. Another, a police sergeant, was told he could go but was then shot. He lay on the pavement for five hours before being taken to hospital by some students.

During the afternoon twenty-five members of the Irish Citizen Army under the command of Captain Richard McCormick arrived at the Green. They had had an exciting day so far. They had been sent in the morning to establish outposts south of the Green. One of these was Harcourt Street Station. Here they had ordered the members of the public to gather on the platform, but women and children had panicked and some men had locked themselves in the ticket office. A British staff officer had been captured and a recalcitrant old man had had his top hat shot off his head. An attempt to block the track was frustrated by a quick-thinking signalman. The party had gone on then to block Portobello Bridge. They took up position on two railway bridges and in Davy's Public House. From here they could even cover the entrance to Portobello Barracks. When British forces brought a machine-gun into the equation, however, the ICA men retreated to St Stephen's Green.

To provide extra security, a squad was stationed in some houses in Leeson Street. Snipers were placed on the roofs to cover Portobello Bridge. Soon after midnight a force of twenty men arrived from Jacob's Factory as reinforcements. After the beautiful day it had begun to rain. Most of the women took shelter in the summer house, but Constance Markievicz sought privacy in the car of Dr Lynn, the ICA's medical director. The men bedded down in what shelter they could find, confident that the Rising was going well.

Actually, the military was doing well, after a poor start. On Monday morning, as was normal practice, there was an 'inlying picquet' of one hundred men at each of the four major barracks in Dublin: Richmond; Marlborough; Royal; and Portobello. All, except the cavalry at Marlborough Barracks, were from Irish regiments. The 3rd (Special Reserve) Battalion Royal Irish Regiment was stationed in Richmond; the 10th Royal Dublin Fusiliers were in Royal; and 3rd Royal Irish Rifles were in Portobello. These were the men who would be expected to deal with any outbreak of trouble. Although there had been a widespread expectation of manoeuvres the previous day, no specific orders had been given to these men; such orders would have been useful as a basis on which to react to the sequence of events starting midday on Monday. Although many policemen witnessed the mobilisation of the Volunteers from Monday morning, not one seems to have reported anything unusual.[26] The army tried to cover its embarrassment by claiming that the 'Sinn Féiners had collected quietly in Dublin' possibly disguised as Bank Holiday trippers.

Once the alarm had been raised the first priority was to safeguard Dublin Castle. The Royal Irish Regiment, eventually totalling 300, spent most of the day fighting Ceannt at the South Dublin Union, though after dark Colonel Kennard, Dublin garrison commander, took over eighty of them and reached the Castle through Ship Street Barracks. The picquet from the Dublin Fusiliers had also come under fire, from Sean Heuston's men in the Mendicity Institute, but, under covering machine-gun fire, had crossed Queen's Street Bridge and from there had been able to move unimpeded to the Castle, reaching there about two o'clock. About the same time, fifty of the Rifles arrived, having driven the ICA group out of Davy's pub at Portobello Bridge. They had also taken fire from MacDonagh's men around Jacob's Factory.[27]

Having secured the Castle, the army set about establishing some more defensive positions. At Trinity College, the gates had been closed and a rifle with fifty rounds of ammunition had been distributed to the members of the OTC who were in the grounds. There were too few of these to defend the entire perimeter, but they prepared a fall-back position in the pavilion. The sports grounds were overlooked by the railway viaduct, manned by rebels, and there were rebel forces just over the road in Westland Row Station. A few more members of the OTC, together with officers who were home on leave, made their way to Trinity during the afternoon. It never came under serious rebel attack, however, and it remained as a serious obstruction to movement between different insurgent outposts for the rest of the week.

On Monday night, the first 150 reinforcements from Belfast were arriving at Amiens Street Station. Men were also expected from the Curragh and artillery was requested from Athlone. Brigadier General

Lowe, commander of the 3rd Reserve Cavalry Brigade, arrived from the Curragh, about an hour after the first of his troops detrained at Kingsbridge Station. He took over command of the troops in Dublin and immediately set about crushing the insurrection. He saw that he would be able to establish a line of communication which would run from Kingsbridge Station to the North Wall and Trinity College. His next step would be to isolate the rebel positions, so that no strongpoint could support another and the leaders of each battalion would be starved for information of the general picture. Although General Friend arrived later on Tuesday morning, he did nothing to interfere with Lowe's operations.

The civil administration was in disarray. The Chief Secretary was in London, the Under-Secretary penned in Dublin Castle and the third of the triumvirate, Lord Wimborne, was on the periphery in the Phoenix Park. Being on the periphery was no barrier to Wimborne. Having been proved right in his concerns, he was glad of the opportunity to do the right thing now. Firstly he wrote a letter to the War Office, giving his view of the situation. This letter was sent by hand and arrived in London early on Tuesday morning.[28] Since the DMP were inoperative, he felt justified in declaring martial law in Dublin and now did so. This took the crisis to a plane that had not been seen for a century in Ireland; the last time martial law had been declared in Ireland was around the time of the Act of Union. Wimborne risked alienating moderate nationalist opinion by this step, when he already had the powers he needed under the Defence of the Realm Act (DORA). At another time, a Liberal government might have looked unfavourably on such a step. In the middle of the Great War, crushing the rebellion was paramount.

Monday night was not without incident on St Stephen's Green. The sentries were alerted about two in the morning, when a line of figures was seen approaching from the south along Leeson Street. Unsure of who they were, the sentries held their fire, which was just as well. It was a party from 4th Battalion making their way to reinforce the GPO. The reinforcements passed on and shortly afterwards a machine-gun which British soldiers had quietly positioned on the roof of the Shelbourne Hotel opened fire on the Green. While the Volunteers had been looking south, soldiers had come up Kildare Street from the north and crept into the hotel from the rear. They also occupied the nearby Hibernian United Services Club. Barely thirty yards from the Green, there were snipers stationed at every window. These opened fire at the same time on the shocked Volunteers below, who had expected an attack from the south, from the direction of the army barracks. Trenches were facing in the wrong direction and were no protection from fire from above and behind. Men abandoned their trenches and sprinted to the shrubberies, where they could not be seen but had no more protection from bullets. Most of the Green's garrison had been positioned at the Shelbourne end, and it was here that the mayhem was greatest. The women were slightly luckier, in that there was an embankment near the summer house that gave them some measure of protection.

Surprisingly few rebels were killed, given the fire power of the British. The officer in charge claimed that eleven had been killed, but James Stephens, the Irish poet, who worked in the National Museum, saw four bodies, and a wounded man who lay in the rain, his arm raised feebly to call for help. Whatever the number of casualties was, it was enough to persuade Mallin that the park was untenable and he ordered a transfer to the College of Surgeons. Not everyone was able to escape; some remained in the trenches, and it was some time before the Green was under full military control. The British too had received fire, as Mallin's snipers shot at the Shelbourne windows. The residents of the hotel settled down for a siege in the back rooms; some of them even covered for staff who were unable to reach the hotel. The Ascendency was showing a stiff upper lip.[29]

The transfer to the College of Surgeons was not only handicapped by British fire. One rebel was attacked by a crowd armed with crowbars and at least one hatchet. Others merely suffered verbal abuse, while Miss Skinnider claimed that people helped her to safety. There were now about one hundred and twenty-five people in the solid but cold buildings, the rooms of which were draughty, and decorated by jars of human organs collected as specimens by the students; there was a stench of formaldehyde. The men went about converting it into a usable building. The windows were barricaded using desks, benches and even books. A large lecture hall on the ground floor was converted to a living area, where people could eat, relax and sleep. Rugs and carpets brought from the other rooms had to do for bedding. There was a small kitchen in the care-taker's quarters to cook what food was available. A sick-bay was set up in one of the laboratories. Finally, a mortuary chapel was improvised where the dead could be laid out on slabs and there were seats for any mourners that could be spared from other duties. Mallin stationed his best marksmen on the roof and with them he assigned spotters with field glasses.

At the South Dublin Union the fighting had gone on through the night. The battleground was a maze of dark corridors along which attackers and defenders moved as quietly as possible. There were innumerable hiding places, and no one knew if he was about to be shot from point-blank range. Cannier ones removed their boots and listened at doors and partitions for noises on the other side. For one British soldier it was too much. He was hiding in a carpenter's shop when he saw the body of a comrade being put in a hearse by Union officials. He slid into an empty coffin and waited to be transported to safety.[30] As Tuesday dawned the knowledge that you could see danger was cancelled by the sense that others could see you. Both sides fought grimly all day. The Volunteers were heartened to get small packages of cooked food thrown over the wall to them. They prepared themselves to receive a full-scale assault on the main buildings but, for some reason that has never been properly explained, the soldiers were pulled back to reassemble in Kingsbridge Station.[31] The only reasonable ex-planation is that they were moved to help protect Army Headquarters, which had now moved to Kilmainham.

MacDonagh, in Jacob's Factory, had sent out two groups at two o'clock on Tuesday morning, with instructions to set up outposts. He hoped to get into the fight by ambushing British troops. These came under attack later in the day when fourteen soldiers surrounded the outpost in Byrne's stores and started firing into the building. At the same time the outpost in Delahunt's just across the way came under attack and soldiers forced an entry. All they found were weapons abandoned by the defenders. In Jacob's itself, effective authority devolved on the larger than life figure of Major MacBride. Although MacDonagh dressed the part of a commander impeccably, he was at heart a poet and academic and lacked the ruthless streak and singleness of vision required by men who lead others to war.[32]

In de Valera's sector there were a few interesting developments. Malone, in command of the post at Mount Street, decided to cut the tram wires leading into town, producing a fireworks display as the live wires bounced along the ground. A fishery protection vessel, *Helga*, which had been converted to an anti-submarine role by having a three-inch gun fitted, began to shell the forces around Boland's—'Hurrah, rotten shot,' exulted de Valera—but did not continue firing for long. During the day a few more Volunteers arrived in the sector, a few of them bakers who wanted to make bread for the neighbourhood. Increased sniping by the British made it impossible to carry out this plan. At any time the Volunteers expected an attack from the direction of Lansdowne Road, but the only incident was when a group of Irish Rifles took up a position on the railway line. The weight of rebel fire drove them back. In the afternoon, de Valera selected a detachment which he intended to send to Mallin at St Stephen's Green, but the order was cancelled when it was learned that the Green had been abandoned. Although the morale of 3rd Battalion was high, one man at least was concerned when he heard that the *Daily Mail* was on sale in the city. If the ports were open and British newspapers could get through, there was nothing to stop British reinforcements following.

At the Four Courts, the snipers on the roof were nervous. In the darkness of early Tuesday morning they saw a party of soldiers making their way along Usher's Quay and opened fire. The soldiers fled, leaving behind them some weapons which the Volunteers collected. For the rest of the night it seemed 'as if every chimney pot was a soldier'.[33] From first light Daly's outposts, especially those on the Cabra and North Circular Roads, came under serious attack. They were impeding Lowe's plan to establish a link between Kingsbridge and the North Wall, and had to be cleared away. The British attack intensified on Tuesday afternoon when soldiers from Marlborough Barracks attacked with the support of artillery and machine-guns, driving the Volunteers out of their positions. This left a military cordon round the north side of the city. Daly tried to counter this by sending to see if it would be possible to seize Broadstone Station. A priest blessed them before they left, but the British were already firmly established at the station and the Volunteers were forced to retreat and had to be satisfied with sniping at the station from positions in North Brunswick Street.

Across the river, the Mendicity Institute came under gradually increasing pressure, especially from sniper fire. This tailed off each evening, but, through the night, at least half of the garrison remained on duty in the hall, on the stairs and on the first floor.

One of Daly's problems was the number of prisoners he was taking. One of these was Lord Dunsany, the peer-poet-soldier who had been reprimanded for being too friendly with the men he commanded. This was a pleasant situation to begin with but, while other sectors were already beginning to contract, Daly's men continued on the offensive for most of the week, continuing to take prisoners as they went.

At the GPO, Dick Humphries noted the time of sunrise on Easter Tuesday: four o'clock. There was a slight breeze coming from the building's open windows. He had spent the night in shelter, and it seemed a beautiful morning. The street outside was empty of people, but littered with the detritus of looting. In a sign that not everyone had grasped yet the seriousness of what was happening, a group of postmen formed outside, obviously debating whether to enter the building. They left when one of their number approached the door and was threatened by a man with a bayonet. Connolly ordered that barbed wire be placed across O'Connell Street in order to discourage civilians from wandering about. Overhead tram wires were blown down and used to reinforce the barricades. Breakfast was served in the restaurant, guards were set and Jim Ryan, a medical student at UCD, checked that the hospital was operational. During the morning some Volunteers took a car for the short drive to Parnell Square, where the National Volunteers had their headquarters, and helped themselves to the rifles they found there. Other rifles were brought in during the day from dumps around the city. Because army activity was concentrated in the south and west of Dublin, there was almost complete freedom of movement.

Within the GPO stocks of bombs were being built up and Volunteers instructed in their use. Men filled sandbags in the courtyard. Fire extinguishers were placed at key points and an internal telephone system was set up, which had a line to the roof so that Connolly could keep in contact with his snipers. Large rolls of newsprint were man-handled from the Irish Times offices to reinforce the defences. At this stage, women couriers were still able to maintain contact with the other garrisons, so that the leaders had some sense of what was happening in the city.

Although the defenders of the GPO were relaxed—some of the younger ones were performing tricks on the bicycles left behind by telegraph boys—discipline was strict, and there was an almost puritanical attitude to alcohol. Round the corner in Henry Street, looters were making their way through the stock of a public house. An old woman staggered across to the Volunteers and offered them a few bottles of stout. An officer appeared and warned he would shoot anyone he saw drinking.

At 9:30 a.m., Pearse had released a statement claiming that the British were suffering the heavier losses in the fighting and—his tongue must have been buried in his cheek—the people of Dublin were overwhelming in their support of the insurrection. This message was repeated in the four-page 'War News', which cost one penny. In the afternoon, Pearse climbed a table on Sackville Street and read a statement saying that the insurgents were holding the line everywhere, and outlining the ways in which civilians could help the Volunteers.

As MacBride had taken effective command at Jacob's, Connolly dealt with military matters in the GPO and the Sackville Street area. A mixed group of Citizen Army and Volunteers occupied Clery's department store and the Imperial Hotel. The hotel was the property of W. M. Murphy, who had been the arch-villain in the Dublin lock-out of 1913. Other buildings were occupied, including the Metropole Hotel beside the GPO, and men were positioned so that they covered three approaches to the GPO itself: Middle Abbey Street; Lower Abbey Street; and Sackville Place. Finally, he ordered the small detachment that was still at Fairview to come to the GPO. For most of Tuesday the garrison was left in peace to complete its defences, which included breaking holes in intervening walls so that defenders could move between positions without going into the open street.

The British, too, were completing their preparations. On Tuesday evening troops of the Leinster Regiment took over the defence of Trinity. At the same time four 18-pounder guns arrived from Athlone. The young men of the OTC were reluctant to leave and six of them went outside in civilian clothes to dig gun pits in Tara Street. Curious bystanders were told that they were repairing drains, information that was received with some scepticism. The job proved too much for the students anyway; the cobblestones were too densely packed to be removed by amateurs.

A much more worrying incident occurred on Tuesday evening. When the rebels had abandoned Davy's pub, the British had occupied it. Their orders were to defend the position, but to avoid conflict if possible. Towards dark, the junior officer who was in charge saw a small crowd approaching. They were led by a man no Dubliner would have had any difficulty recognising: Francis Sheehy Skeffington. A pacifist and a feminist, he was now trying to establish an organisation that would prevent people from looting. Because Skeffington was obviously the reason the crowd had gathered, and because he thought that martial law required him to do so, the young officer arrested the pacifist and had him sent to Portobello Barracks. Here there was little organisation; 3rd Royal Irish Rifles was under the temporary command of Major Rosborough, the second in command, and most of the officers who had joined him he did not know. A subsequent board of enquiry was unable to establish which officer was in charge of the guardroom when Skeffington was brought in.[34]

Certainly there was a heightened atmosphere in the barracks. The troops, certainly, were not under control; they were firing without orders, accepting as true every rumour that was going around. Some of the officers were little better. Captain J. C. Bowen-Colthurst, an experienced officer, decided on his own initiative that he was going to lead a raiding party on the premises of Alderman James Kelly. Bowen-Colthurst probably mistook this man, who was a Unionist, for Alderman Tom Kelly, who had produced the 'Castle Document' at Dublin City Council. He collected forty men and a subaltern and, as he was passing the guardhouse, decided he would take Skeffington as a hostage. When Skeffington refused to pray, Bowen-Colthurst ordered his men to remove their hats and prayed, 'O Lord God, if it shall please thee to take away the life of this man forgive him for Christ's sake.' If his men were surprised at this, they must have been shocked at what happened next. Just outside the barracks, Bowen-Colthurst stopped a passing youth, told him that martial law was in force and shot him dead, without waiting for a reply. At Portobello Bridge he left twenty men and Skeffington with his lieutenant, while he took the rest to Kelly's tobacconist shop in Harcourt Street. They threw a grenade in the door and arrested the two shocked men they found there, Thomas Dickson and Patrick McIntyre. They returned to the barracks with all three prisoners.

During the night Bowen-Colthurst read some documents that he had confiscated in the shop and was persuaded that he had caught three very dangerous men. At nine o'clock on Wednesday morning he went to the guardroom and removed the prisoners. He ordered seven soldiers with loaded rifles to follow the prisoners into the yard. Once there, he ordered the soldiers to shoot Sheehy Skeffington and the others. They did so. They were only obeying orders, as members of a different army would claim, a few decades later. 'They might have escaped,' was Bowen-Colthurst's explanation.[35]

The inhabitants of Dublin would have been forgiven for thinking that Bedlam had come to their city that Wednesday morning. *Helga*, which had been ineffective against the Boland's garrison the day before, was now anchored off Sir John Rogerson's Quay; it opened fire on the empty Liberty Hall. Its gun did little damage to the building, but it was soon joined by the 18-pounders, which had been moved to Tara Street. The blast of the guns shattered every piece of glass in the street and shook buildings to their foundations. Liberty Hall was quickly reduced to a ruin, but it was a symbolic bombardment, designed to show that rebellion was going to be extirpated from Dublin.

In Kingstown, reinforcements had landed in darkness during the night. In the rush, they had left their hand-grenades in barracks at Watford. At 10:35 they started their advance towards Dublin. In total there were four battalions of Sherwood Foresters, most of whom were young recruits, only eight weeks in uniform. They had only just been issued with rifles, and two of their Lewis guns were now sent to Arklow, together with a company of soldiers, in order to protect an arms factory. The remainder marched through cheering crowds to the edge of town. They had been split into two columns, following the two roads closest to the sea. After the rain of Monday night the weather was continuing fair, and they marched through a fine spring morning towards Dublin. The 5th and 6th Battalions, following the inland route, reached Kilmainham and Kingsbridge without incident. For the other two battalions, following the coastal route, things weren't quite so simple.

Although there was only a small number of Volunteers at Mount Street Bridge, they had taken up excellent firing positions. Five men went into Clanwilliam House, which overlooked the bridge from the city side. Another three went into a parochial hall just over the bridge. Four, including the group's commander, Michael Malone, went into the corner house, 25 Northumberland Road. Three went into the schools. By Wednesday morning, Malone had improved the disposition of his men. The men in the schools had been sent back to the bakery. There were now two men in number 25, Malone and James Grace; four men held the parochial hall; while seven Volunteers defended Clanwilliam House.[36]

The Sherwood Foresters, meanwhile, had halted at Ballsbridge. The majority of the force remained there. Another group was left behind at the junction of Lansdowne Road and Pembroke Road. This group was soon relaxing, but some Volunteers fired a volley of revolver shots in its direction and the soldiers soon withdrew into cover. The advance guard came along Northumberland Road, a line of skirmishers on each pavement moving ahead of the main body, which was marking four abreast.

Malone and Grace opened fire from the basement of number 25 as soon as the advance guard came level. The crash of the shots scattered the troops for a minute but they soon reformed and tried to take the house at bayonet point. In the confusion they did not realise at first that they were also receiving fire from Clanwilliam House. Some soldiers went to the rear of the building, while others climbed the tower of Haddington Road Church, which overlooked the rebel positions. Even when they realised that Clanwilliam House was also an objective, they concentrated on taking number 25. Sniper bullets came through every window in the house, and hand-grenades were thrown through the empty frames. Eventually, the two Volunteers were driven from the basement. For a while they remained in the hallway, shooting through the locked doors, front and rear. There was a loud explosion in one of the back rooms when a grenade set off a box of 500 cartridges.

The fact that Malone and Grace had had to abandon the basement meant that the main body of soldiers could now pass and attack Clanwilliam House. The two in number 25 must have heard the heavy sound of machine-gun fire, but there was nothing they could do to intervene. They mounted their bayonets and decided they would meet their end at the stair head. Just then soldiers burst in, on the middle floor, and the two were separated. Malone was on the stairs above the soldiers, while Grace had barricaded himself in the kitchen. Malone started to descend but was shot dead. Grace could not believe his luck when the soldiers seemed to check every room in the house except the one he was in. After dark, he slid into the garden, where he hid in a tool shed. Although he tried to get away a few times, every attempt was frustrated by patrols of soldiers and he was forced to remain in the area. He was eventually caught in a roundup later in the week.

The others had taken up the struggle. The main British effort was to capture Clanwilliam House. They seem to have been unaware at first of the firing that was coming from the parochial hall, which was set back from the footpath in a deep recess. As the young soldiers crept forward to Mount Street Bridge, showing a determination that belied their lack of training, they were hit time and again on the exposed flank. The few who managed to escape the four men in the hall were hit on the bridge itself by point-blank fire from Clanwilliam House. The defenders, even, became sickened by that continuous movement towards death or disablement. There was even supporting fire from Volunteer snipers on the railway line and from the water tanks at the locomotive yard near Boland's Mills. Eventually the garrison in the parochial hall were forced to give up their position and retreat to Percy Place. Here they found their way blocked by soldiers trying to reach Clanwilliam House from the flank, and they were captured.

Fate was now closing in on Clanwilliam House. One man had his rifle shot from his hand. Another was shot dead while firing from the window. Some of the machine-gun bullets were tracers, and these started small fires. Yet another man was shot at a window. Then the roof caught fire. Then, inevitably, ammunition ran short. With an encouraging word, George Reynolds, who had commanded the post, distributed the last ten rounds per man. He was shot dead soon afterwards. The roof was now fully ablaze and soldiers were close enough to throw grenades through the windows, driving the four survivors to the basement. They were nearly trapped here, because it was securely barricaded; Reynolds had intended escaping through the roof. They eventually escaped into the back garden and climbed wall after wall until they reached safety. They had given such a good account of themselves that the soldiers did not advance until the next morning.

There was one other post where the military had exerted overwhelming pressure that day. The Mendicity Institute was the closest post to Kingsbridge Station, where the first reinforcements had arrived. It had already given a good account of itself, from a Volunteer point of view, and had inflicted serious casualties on the soldiers. Although it is probably true to say that there was no overwhelming need for the British to capture the Institute, since they could easily have by-passed it, the Volunteer commander, Heuston, believed that up to four hundred soldiers were engaged against him. The defenders, although they had been reinforced by twelve men from the GPO on Tuesday, were completely outgunned. On Wednesday, Heuston discovered that he was out of contact with the other posts. His men were weary, without food and short of ammunition. He decided to surrender.[37]

Across the river, Daly at the Four Courts was having more success. Until now, most of his fighting consisted in exchanges of sniper fire. That Wednesday, Daly looked for ways to strengthen his position. An attempt to take Broadstone Station was beaten back, but Linenhall Barracks, occupied by forty unarmed members of the Pay Corps, was captured, as was the nearby police station. In Daly's judgement, trying to hold these positions would have stretched his garrison too thinly, but he did not want the British to be able to reoccupy them. The solution seemed to be to set them alight. This was not the good idea it seemed at first. The fire was spectacular. During Wednesday night the flames spread, including a building where large drums of oil were stored and these in turn caught fire, and a dirty smoke filled the neighbourhood. The fire burned all day Thursday and into Thursday night.

The build-up of troops in Trinity College was complete by midday on Wednesday. Machine-guns mounted on the college roof fired directly down Sackville Street; the rebels could only move about through holes they had dug in walls connecting building to building. At two in the afternoon troops moved out from Trinity against outposts in Westmoreland Street and D'Olier Street, moving inexorably towards O'Connell Bridge. They reached the bridge within fifteen minutes and were now in a position to engage rebel positions in Sackville Street. What was worse, from the insurgent point of view, was that the British troops were supported by artillery. Some of Connolly's outposts had to be abandoned, as they were too exposed. The Metropole Hotel was hit, and its chimney stack crashed to the ground. The Imperial Hotel was also attacked by machine-gun fire. The firing quietened slightly at about six o'clock but the defenders found it difficult to relax. Towards dusk an armoured car tried to move up Sackville Street, but it was immobilised and was eventually towed away by another armoured car.

Once more, the night brought limited respite. The two battalions of Sherwood Foresters which had taken the inland route and reached Kilmainham unscathed moved to Dublin Castle at four in the morning on Thursday and went on from there to reinforce the attack on Daly's positions at the Four Courts. The first twenty or so British soldiers who tried to advance along Usher's Quay were turned back, but the assault gradually intensified and the Four Courts garrison became more vulnerable to sniper fire. Daly now expected an imminent attack and strengthened his defences. Volunteers reinforced windows with corrugated iron and bags of meal. They scrutinised every move of the British that they could see and tried to analyse its implications.

Since they were strangers to the city, the Sherwood Foresters took the trouble to obtain a map of Dublin from a newspaper office and used that to shape their tactics. They occupied Capel Street and Parnell Street, thus separating the GPO from the Four Courts. At each junction on Capel Street they built barricades on both sides, so that they could repel an attack from either direction. Around midnight on Thursday, Daly was so worried about his isolation that he held an officers' conference, to decide whether to try to break through to the GPO. The trouble was that, under the thick smoke of the burning oil, the flames were so bright that any movement in that direction would provide easy targets for British snipers.

From first light on Thursday, the British had begun to move troops around the city in the protection of improvised armoured cars—flatbed lorries which had boilers from the Guinness brewery fitted. This allowed them to strengthen the east to west cordon in the north of the city. By nine o'clock, elements of the Foresters were making sure that no outlying rebel posts remained north of this cordon. The British artillery was used once again against Sackville Street. A number of 18-pounder shells hit the Irish Times paper store, setting fire to a number of rolls of paper. These burnt with a thick smoke and British soldiers took advantage to move onto Sackville Street until fire from Middle Abbey Street halted their progress. Connolly was proving a very energetic commander, issuing orders and responding to reports from his outposts. He was wounded twice. The first was a clean shot, and a captured British captain who was helping the medical staff dressed it for him. Connolly was not so lucky with his second wound. A round ricocheted off the ground and smashed into his ankle. There was no hope of hiding this wound, and he was propped up on a mattress in the public hall.

At noon, two battalions of the South Staffordshire Regiment left Trinity and began to work their way along Lower Mount Street; as they moved along, sniper positions were chosen from where marksmen could fire directly into de Valera's positions at the Boland's Bakery and Mills positions. This had the effect of fixing the defenders in place until enough troops could go together for an assault. It is probably true to say that with a determined push the British could have overwhelmed de Valera and his men, but the fate of the Sherwood Foresters on

Wednesday weighed heavily on their officers, who knew that their men had received no training in street fighting and did not realise just how small a force de Valera had under his command.

While the South Staffordshires were engaging de Valera, those Sherwood Foresters who had survived the Mount Street Bridge fighting were ordered to Kilmainham via the southern suburbs. The march passed peacefully enough, but as the leading troops crossed the Rialto Bridge towards the South Dublin Union, they came under fire from Ceannt's outposts. They took what cover they could; this was beginning to have uncomfortable echoes of the previous day's fighting. The British troops were less constricted than they had been in Northumberland Road, however, and the open ground meant that they were able to keep moving forward. A captain of the Foresters took a fighting patrol forward to engage the Volunteers and keep them busy while the remainder of the troops went on to Kilmainham. He wrote later that it was worse than being in no-man's-land on the Western Front. At least there, he said, you knew where the enemy was. In Dublin you could be shot at from any direction. Once the Foresters were in the building, they tunnelled their way from room to room, using any tools they could find. Once they had got into the nurses' home itself, a small party went ahead with grenades.

Ceannt's men were not finding things easy. He had lost a dozen as prisoners and a further twenty as casualties, including Cathal Brugha. Firing now was at close hand, with Ceannt trying to turn the cramped conditions in the rooms and corridors to his advantage. The badly wounded Brugha lifted the Volunteers' spirits by singing republican songs at the top of his voice. The two forces were separated only by a doorway when, as darkness fell, the British were ordered to withdraw. Another Volunteer battalion had been saved at the last minute.

As darkness fell, the flames of the Irish Times building and those of the Linenhall Barracks competed for attention. At about ten o'clock, both fires were eclipsed when Hoyte's Druggist and Oil Works, on the opposite side of Sackville Street, exploded in a column of flame. There were fires, too, in the GPO, and hoses were being directed on any surface that might catch fire. Although wounded, Connolly still gave orders, and was still in command of the forces in the building.

The nemesis of republican Ireland arrived in Dublin at two on Friday morning, one of a small group of officers landed by a British warship on the North Wall. The officers climbed into three waiting cars and General Sir John Maxwell KCB KCMG, the new commander of the British army in Ireland, was driven to his headquarters at Kilmainham. When he got there, he confirmed the orders and tactics used by Brigadier General Lowe, while also ordering moves against the besieged garrisons at Boland's and the Four Courts. The drama of Dublin was now moving into its final act.

It was as actors that Pearse and Connolly spoke to the GPO garrison at nine on Friday morning. They told of success on all fronts and of a popular rising throughout the country. Soon afterwards, an 18-pounder was brought up to Great Britain Street, now known as Parnell Street, where it started to shell Arnott's Department Store, which backed on to the GPO. A noose was tightening around the Provisional Government and its headquarters, as it was around each of the surviving garrisons. Connolly's belief that the British would not shell property was proving as much a fantasy as talk of a country-wide rising. There was not going to be an assault of infantry on the GPO or any other building occupied by the Volunteers. It was much easier to shell them. As the truth of this dawned, it was decided to evacuate all the women in the GPO under the protection of a Red Cross flag. In spite of this, many of the women refused to leave.

As Friday passed, the fires in the upper storeys of the GPO burned out of control. It became obvious that the building would have to be abandoned. At seven, all prisoners were told to make a run for safety. At 8 o'clock that evening, the wounded were moved through a tunnel to the Coliseum Theatre. The O'Rahilly had volunteered to take a party of men along Moore Street to occupy a factory in Great Britain Street which could be used as a new headquarters. In Moore Street, however, his group came under fire from soldiers behind a barricade. The small force was scattered, and O'Rahilly himself was killed. He was the only senior member of the Volunteer movement to be killed in action. By nine most of the survivors were crowded into a greengrocer's shop in Moore Lane. Their only hope of getting to the factory was by tunnelling from house to house, but it was desperately slow work. By early morning they had reached number 10 Moore Street, and here the Provisional Government decided to establish its last headquarters.

Not far away the 6th Battalion of the South Staffordshire Regiment reached King Street, where they completed the cordon around the

Volunteers at the Four Courts. An armoured car had screeched down Bolton Street and stopped outside the technical school. The soldiers stormed this and it was used as battalion headquarters. The soldiers also captured corner houses at the junction of Bolton Street and North King Street. The objective now was to advance along North King Street towards Church Street. Their commanding officer was Lieutenant Colonel Henry Taylor, and he took some time to confer with officers of the Sherwood Foresters, who had been operating in adjoining streets. Like most officers in Dublin, he wanted to keep his casualties low, so he used the Volunteer tactic of tunnelling from house to house, while at the same time troops exchanged fire with insurgents behind barricades. They seem to have had little more success than their enemies in Moore Street and, by midnight, were starting to get frustrated. There were casualties caused simply by confusion, and there was a constant danger of troops firing on one another by mistake.

The constant pressure began to tell, however, and the Volunteers were forced to abandon their barricades. It was now possible for the British to make their way along North King Street towards Capel Street, moving all the time from house to house by the connecting tunnels they had dug. Since the Volunteers still occupied the houses on the other side of North King Street, the opponents were now firing at each other at almost point blank range. Taking the first barricade had cost the soldiers fifteen casualties. Casualties were still being suffered as they kept up the pressure. There were many deaths among civilians; Volunteers claim that they were killed deliberately; they were particularly incensed by an incident in number 175 North King Street. Here George Ennis had been dragged away from his wife, stabbed with a bayonet and left to bleed to death.[38] Daly moved his headquarters, taking arms, ammunition and stores to the Four Courts. The army prisoners were taken to the Bridewell station and the police who had been captured there were released. More and more men arrived in the Four Courts as outlying strong points were overrun. As Saturday progressed, the firing gradually died down. The operation had cost the South Staffordshires sixteen dead and over thirty wounded.

In Moore Street, the members of the Provisional Government were divided on what to do next. As some of his colleagues wavered, Clarke remained determined to fight on. It was Pearse who made the final decision, when he saw a family trying to escape from a burning house, waving a white flag, only to be cut down by machine-gun fire. He sent word to as many of the insurgent forces as he could reach that there would be a ceasefire of one hour while he tried to contact the British authorities. At 12:45 p.m., Nurse Elizabeth O'Farrell went to talk to Brigadier General Lowe. It was over.

Chapter 7

THE BIG PUSH

The officers and men of 36th (Ulster) Division had little time to worry about the events in Dublin. They had been in France for about six months and had, by this time, developed into an efficient fighting machine, used to the ways of the trenches and disciplined enough to be trusted with a major task. The task that faced them was to be part of a major offensive in the area of the Western Front known as Picardy. The Germans had started a major attack against the fortifications of Verdun, further south, with the intention of bleeding the defenders to death through attrition; the French suffered 90,000 casualties in the first six weeks. The French asked the British to join with them in an attack in Picardy which would force the Germans to ease the pressure on Verdun. Later, the British were asked to take full responsibility for the attack.

The section of line allocated to the Ulster Division was intimidating, to say the least. It sat astride the River Ancre, in a low valley with a swampy floor. As the river passed through the forward trenches, flowing east to west, it was more or less in the centre of the sector, dividing the line equally. Towards the German positions, however, it swung to the north, so that soldiers attacking north of the river would be cramped by the marshes, while those on the south of the river would find the front opening out in front of them. Behind the front, on the south of the river, was Thiepval Wood, a favourite target for German guns when they were not required elsewhere. On the Ulster left was the 29th Division, which, as we have seen, had proved its fighting efficiency in Gallipoli. On the Ulster right was the 32nd Division. The most important position facing the 36th was the Schwaben Redoubt, named for the Germans who manned it, to the south of the river. This was a German strongpoint, consisting of trenches, dugouts and machine-gun posts, situated on the highest ground overlooking the river. It was protected by four lines of trenches and numerous rows of barbed wire; there were sixteen in places on the German front line and five on the second line. German dugouts in the chalky soil were up to thirty feet deep, so the German defenders were well protected from shellfire. The ground towards the redoubt had a gradient of slightly over 8 per cent: 250 feet in 1,000 yards. Having taken the redoubt, the attackers were expected to go another 1,500 yards to capture the German fourth and fifth lines.

To the north of the river, the Ulstermen were to cross a ravine, take three lines of German trenches and capture Beaucourt railway station. They were also to capture a mill on the riverbank near the station, and to detach a platoon to patrol the marshy ground to the north of the river. This task was entrusted to the Armagh Volunteers, 9th Royal Irish Fusiliers, and the Mid-Antrim Volunteers, 12th Battalion, Royal Irish Rifles.

The much more difficult task to the south of the river had more men allocated to it. The Down Volunteers, 13th Royal Irish Rifles, and the South Antrim Volunteers, 11th Royal Irish Rifles, were to attack the northern slopes of the redoubt, with the North Belfast Volunteers, 15th Royal Irish Rifles, in support. Special detachments with mortars and machine-guns would clear captured trenches north towards the river and the road between St Pierre Divion and Grandcourt. The southern flank was the task of four battalions from 109 Brigade, attacking in several waves. First to go over would be the Derry and Tyrone Volunteers, 10th and 9th Battalions, Royal Inniskilling Fusiliers, whose job it was to advance as far as the German fourth line, which they would hold. The Belfast Young Citizens, 14th Royal Irish Rifles, and the Donegal & Fermanagh Volunteers, 11th Royal Inniskillings, would follow. They had to consolidate the trenches captured by the first wave, but also to capture a strategic trench junction known as The Crucifix. When this was achieved, a third wave, consisting of the other three Belfast battalions, 8th, 9th and 10th Royal Irish Rifles, would advance through these positions and take the German fifth line, with East Belfast on the north, West Belfast in the centre and South Belfast on the right.

To help the attackers, there was to be a bombardment of the German positions that would last five days. This was aimed at cutting the wire and at the same time trapping as many of the defenders underground as possible. The rate of fire would be doubled an hour before the British attacked. Even then the firing would not stop. As the British advanced, a line of artillery fire would move before them, forcing the Germans to keep their heads down. The men of Kitchener's new armies would advance at a good pace, but not a run. At the head of the Ulstermen would be their officers, carrying a blackthorn stick and, if they wished, a revolver. Commanding officers were ordered not to take part in the attack. It would be a fine, if noisy, morning stroll.

That was the theory.

For a sensitive soul, and there were many in the 36th Division, the preparations for dealing with the wounded must have been disconcerting. There were only thirty-two stretcher-bearers to each battalion; on rough ground; that meant that only eight casualties could be moved at a time. For casualties north of the Ancre, a special trench was created from Hamel Village along which stretcher cases and walking wounded could be taken to the road, where they would be sent on to dressing stations. 110th Field Ambulance manned Clairfaye Farm and would deal with walking wounded. 108th Field Ambulance was at Forceville, and would deal with more serious cases. South of the Ancre, walking wounded would assemble and be taken by horse-drawn wagon to Clairfaye. Stretcher cases would receive initial attention at an advanced dressing station at Aveluy Wood. They would then be taken by motor lorry to Forceville.

The valley was beautiful that June, with the yellow of mustard flowers predominating. Through this yellow, which one soldier described as looking like cloth of gold, clumps of red clover were uncomfortably like patches of blood. The hedges were white with elderflower and heavy with its scent. The good weather was good for morale, and the troops participated in the final training with enthusiasm and efficiency. On 1 June, two brigades were taken to the rear area for special training, while the third, 107 Brigade, held the line. A dummy trench system had been built near Clairfaye Farm and here the troops practised until the layout of the German trenches was familiar to them.

On 5 June, the Mid-Antrims went forward to conduct a large-scale raid on the German lines. The intention was to attack a German trench in order to get a feeling of the general layout and standards of fortification. The trench chosen was one to the north of the river, running parallel to the railway. This was shelled heavily before the Antrim men advanced and, when they broke through, it seemed as if the artillery had done a good job and a sustained bombardment would be able to destroy German defences. The problem about this interpretation was that the trench that had been raided was not a typical German trench. It lacked machine-gun nests and deep bunkers. It was a bad example from which to generalise.[1] In revenge for this attack, the Germans, five days later, launched a raid against the section of line held by the North Belfasts, but they were easily repelled.

By the middle of June the level of planning had got to the stage of individuals being chosen for special duties during the battle. Anyone chosen as a runner, whose job it would be to take information of the battle back to headquarters, had a red stripe sewn on either sleeve, to distinguish him from anyone simply fleeing from the battle. The Young Citizens battalion was set to work with the Pioneers, carrying ammunition to gun positions. Other battalions were involved in digging gun emplacements for a French regiment of field artillery. The French were unable to contribute any infantry, but at least they could help with the bombardment.

While this heavy labour was going on, the weather changed for the worse. In spite of this, ammunition had to be brought forward. It was an unpleasant task, because a stray German shell could blow a party of men and their load to indistinguishable fragments. They tried to work in silence. Mules that were used for part of the journey wore special boots and were muzzled, while the carts they pulled had their wheels covered in anything from old rubber tyres to old coats and blankets to keep noise to a minimum.[2] In the short nights men struggled to bring two loads forward and get back under cover before dawn.

One of the pleasures available to the men in their short rest periods was a swim in the river, downstream from the front line. Even here it was not always safe, as random shells could land nearby. Nevertheless, they enjoyed the chance to forget war for a time, to rid themselves of vermin-infested uniforms and splash or race in the relatively clean waters. At other times they simply sat on the riverbank in the shade of the trees and enjoyed talking. These intervals were few enough. Working parties were digging assembly trenches in Thiepval Wood, which was a frequent target for German guns. Many of the Ulstermen were wounded by shrapnel. Even for those bivouacked at night, the German nuisance firing went on, with machine-gun fire stripping the trees and shrapnel shells exploding overhead.

Preliminary orders came through on 19 June, and were passed on to
each battalion's officers by their CO. The weather had turned warm
again, and many officers and men chose to sleep in the open. To protect
themselves from machine-guns, some of the men dug slit trenches. One
officer did so as well, and made it big enough to contain his camp bed,
but was chilled by the resemblance to a grave. The weather turned wet
again towards the end of the week and, by the evening of Friday 23 June,
the Tyrones and the South Antrims had taken position in Thiepval
Wood, while the Armaghs were in the Hamel trenches. As the German
artillery opposite realised that the Big Push was coming, they concentrated their fire on these sectors and the Ulstermen suffered
grievously.

The following morning, the British bombardment began. It was
probably the loudest man-made noise yet heard on earth and could be
heard in the relative quiet of a London night as distant thunder.
Soldiers' ears became sore, and even began to bleed. They watched the
field gunners behind them. It had continued raining—it would rain for
five days—and the recoil of the guns splattered the gunners with mud.
All the soldiers were wet, with cold and swollen feet and with chilled
hands.

It was still raining on Sunday. Some COs gave their final operational
orders to their officers, although they still did not know when zero
hour would be. The great weight each man would be expected to carry
caused concern. In order to minimise this, packs and greatcoats would
be left behind. Haversacks were to be worn containing shaving and
washing kit, one pair of socks, iron rations and full rations for 'Z' Day.
A waterproof sheet and a cardigan were to be carried in a roll at the
back of the belt. There would be two grenades for each man, carried in
side pockets, two sandbags tucked into the belt and 170 rounds of
ammunition. There were also wire cutters, barbed wire, iron screw
stakes to fix this, picks, shovels and even signal flags to be brought
forward. Orders were given as to who would carry these. In this matter
the runners were lucky; their burden was to be kept as light as possible,
and they were even issued with scouts' shorts.

Another raid was planned for 26 June, this time to be undertaken by
the Down Volunteers. There were casualties when German shells fell on
Thiepval Wood just as the Down men were working with gas. The raid
went ahead anyway and thirteen prisoners were taken, including an

officer. There were more casualties on the way back, when a machine-gun caught them in the open. They took shelter in a stretch they called the Sunken Road, but it gave them little cover. Six Ulstermen were killed and another nine wounded.

On Wednesday, after two days of rain, it was decided to postpone the assault for at least two days in the hope that the weather would improve. This meant that there had to be enough extra shells to be brought up to the guns to extend the bombardment for another two days. It also meant that the battalions holding the front line had to be relieved. This needed men to be out in the open while the German counter-bombardment was taking place. A single shell caught both No 11 Platoon of the Down Volunteers and the battalion headquarters staff as they marched out of Martinsart. Fourteen were killed on the spot and almost all of the remainder were wounded, including the battalion's second in command. A group of South Antrim Volunteers took charge of clearing the devastation. As they worked into the dawn, they could see the huge crater in the road, bloodstains everywhere and pieces of bodies dangling from statues on the wall of the chapel.

The men who had returned from Thiepval Wood were particularly relieved. They were cold, wet and dirty; they had had little or no hot food for days. Worst of all, the best shelters in the wood had been full of supplies for the coming battle, so they had had to make do with slit trenches. Thursday had been the day planned for the attack. Now, the weather improved and there was a beautiful sunset. Many of the men took advantage to write to family or friends. The night stayed fine, and early Friday brought hopes of another fine day. General Haig decided that the attack would take place the next day. Zero hour would be 7:30 on the morning of Saturday 1 July.

As Friday warmed, steam rose from the damp earth. During this lovely morning, each battalion received its final briefing for the morrow. The divisional headquarters staff moved to their report centre and here the senior officers of each battalion came to be given their orders. They in turned briefed their junior officers, who briefed the NCOs. The one imponderable was the bombardment. Although it had deafened the Ulstermen for a week, there was no way of knowing if it had been successful in its tasks of clearing a way through the German wire, destroying the German defences and keeping the German soldiers deep in their dugouts.

By the afternoon, final preparations were made. Drinking water was brought up to the lines. Letters for home were collected. The Medical Corps checked and re-checked the medicines and equipment. In trench mortar batteries, bombs were fused and food and water were issued. Some officers distributed cigarettes and other cigarettes were passed on by neighbouring English soldiers, who had had a special issue.[3] There were religious services held in various locations and, although attendance was not compulsory, most men made an effort. Even the few Catholics attached to the division were given the opportunity to attend a service. They were taken by ambulance to 29th Division, where a priest from the west of Ireland said mass.

In the early evening the men were given a hot meal and were encouraged by the NCOs to eat as much as possible. Afterwards men got their battle packs ready; some of them took a few moments to write what might be a final letter home. Just before dark some of the machine-gunners fired off a few rounds. In one case, the gun kept jamming no matter what the team did to try to cure it. In the end, that team went into battle carrying rifles.

It was dark enough to see the first stars when the men were moved up to their assembly trenches. Their paths through the countryside were marked by small green and red lanterns. Near the front there was a halt, while officers dismounted and had their horses sent back. The Germans were still firing random shells and some of the men thought the wood looked like a mass of flames. It was difficult to rest for the night; it was difficult to get comfortable, difficult to talk to a neighbour, painful to think of home. One soldier compared the experience to waiting for a death; wishing it was over.[4]

At about one in the morning, adjutants reported to their brigade headquarters and were told the time of zero hour. Watches were synchronised before the adjutants returned to inform the battalion officers. By 3 a.m. battalions had reached their forward positions. There was enough of a lull for men to hear noises of the natural world—moorhens splashing and, maybe, a nightingale singing. The CO of the West Belfast Volunteers drank tea and ate sandwiches with the CO of the South Belfast battalion. Both men were concerned about the possibility of Thiepval Village, on their left flank, remaining in German hands. They decided that, in such a case, they would have to lead their men personally into no-man's-land.

Dawn broke at about 4 a.m. It was still early enough in the year for
there to be a dawn chorus. There were the dim sounds of the company
cooks preparing breakfast; in the case of the West Belfast battalion, this
was sweet tea, rashers, fried bread and jam. Men came along with a
hand cart, doling out fresh water. It brought to some minds the image
of a milkman doing his daily rounds. Not everyone had as pleasant a
start to the day. Hugh Stewart, a South Antrim Volunteer, had shared a
breakfast of bully beef, biscuits and cold water. Some of them had little
appetite as they looked at the gradually lightening ground in front of
the trenches. They knew it reasonably well, and were confident that
they could find their way in the half-light. Why was zero hour so late,
they wondered, when the sun would be high in the sky and they would
make easier targets for the Germans.

The German bombardment of the front lines increased in intensity
at about 6 a.m. Hugh Stewart belonged to a Lewis gun team which was
hit by a German shell. The gun was beyond repair, but Stewart wondered why the ground felt spongy underfoot; it took a moment to
realise that he was standing on the body of his mate, with whom he'd
been drinking tea a few minutes before. He was given a rifle and told to
join the rest of the battalion for the assault.[5] At 6:25 the hurricane
bombardment by the British began, bringing a renewed sense of awe to
those waiting in the front line. On a normal morning this went on till
7:45, but this morning it would stop at 7:30 in the hope that the
Germans would be caught by surprise.

Among the Young Citizens, Billy McFadzean from Lurgan was one
of a group of bombardiers sharing out grenades. A box he was working
with fell to the floor and two grenades rolled out, losing their pins as
they did so. McFadzean threw himself on top of these and was killed
instantly in the explosion. His action saved the rest of the men in his
team and he was awarded the Victoria Cross, the first to be awarded in
the Battle of the Somme.[6]

There was a bonus for some of the soldiers when the rum ration was
distributed; many of the men in the Ulster Division were teetotal and
passed their rations on to friends. Some men from rural backgrounds
had even managed to smuggle poteen in their gear, and this was also
passed around. Though the men were far from gay, many looked to
celebrate the anniversary of the Battle of the Boyne, which had taken
place on 1 July in the old Julian calendar. Some even managed to find

orange lilies to wear, but most made do with any flowers they could find by the wayside. The truly faithful had brought their orange sashes.

Special groups now crept forward from the trenches to cut lanes through the British wire. At 7:10, the first of the Ulstermen climbed out of their trenches. General Nugent, the divisional commander, believed that this would save them precious minutes when the order to advance came. Each wave went at five-minute intervals, so the fourth wave was in position by 7:30. Troops from the support battalions now moved forward to man the empty trenches. In the sudden silence when the bombardment stopped, there was a dramatic pause before the first officers blew their whistles. The men rose to their feet, formed up as if they were on parade, and advanced towards the German lines.

South of the river, the walk forward became a charge as the first wave approached the first line of trenches. There were cries of 'No surrender' as they reached the trenches; at that moment machine-guns opened fire from Thiepval Village and from the Schwaben Redoubt, and even from the high ground on either side of the river. The later waves suffered most, because they had more guns ranged against them. Officers were shot, breaking the chain of command. Men took shelter in the Sunken Road, watching men in front dropping like marionettes with cut strings. Now the German artillery shortened its range and began firing into no-man's-land. Although many took shelter in craters, others were determined to press on.

The Down Volunteers were taking heavy fire from north of the river and had lost most of their officers even before they reached German territory. As one veteran said, the bodies were lying like sheaves of corn. Men caught on barbed wire were doomed, shot before they could tear themselves free. Once in the German trenches it was a matter of hand-to-hand combat with any Germans they met, and of using grenades to clear any dugouts or bunkers they came across. It was not until they reached the third line that the real fighting started. The first two lines had been held by skeleton forces. Here it could take fifteen minutes to clear 100 yards of trench. They discovered too that the grenades they dropped were falling into spiral stairs, so that the full force of the bomb was not reaching the main dugout. The strict timetable to which the Ulstermen were operating meant that they did not have the time to check dugouts and bunkers. There were many German survivors, and it was to cause great difficulty later.

The second wave was already on its way, starting ten minutes after the first attack. The machine-guns from Thiepval to the south and Beaumont-Hamel to the north caught them in a crossfire. Jim Maultsaid, of the Young Citizens, staggered under the shock and gasped for air. He was aware of the hissing of metal in the air, of the screams of casualties. Two good friends were killed near him. The disadvantage of Pals' Battalions, that it was neighbours and friends dying around you, was becoming very apparent. Some of those carrying heavy loads simply abandoned them and went forward with their rifles. All seemed confusion, and survival became an individual struggle. At best it was a matter of small groups. Messengers had a particularly hard task, crossing the open killing field of no-man's-land not once but several times.

The Donegal and Fermanagh battalion was tackling the Crucifix strongpoint. It had taken them some time to get to the German positions because heavy shell fire had meant they had to crawl from crater to crater as they went forward. One boy remembered an officer shouting, 'What the Hell kept you?' The laconic reply was, 'Sorry, Sir. We were delayed coming through Hell.'[7] It was in this hell that the stretcher-bearers operated. There was plenty of work for them just in front of their own parapets, where men got shot as they rose out of the trenches. Later arrivals lessened the target they presented by rolling out of the trench, then getting their bearings before they moved off. Stretcher-bearers took longer getting to casualties nearer the German lines. Some of the men noticed that casualties would huddle together, as if it comforted them to have others dying around them.

For many units, command had devolved to NCOs. One sergeant took over his platoon, gave them a talk about what trench fighting would be like and then arranged them in pairs, each pair following twenty seconds behind the other. Because of the closeness of the fighting, some soldiers took their bayonets in their hands and slung their rifles, not wanting to be handicapped by the rifle's length in the confined space of a dugout. Few prisoners were taken; there was the problem of what to do with them. The heat of battle, the emotion of seeing friends killed, had removed all sense of human sympathy.

The Ulstermen pressed on, and the German fourth line was reached by 9 o'clock, and the strongpoints of the Crucifix and the Schwaben Redoubt had been captured. The Belfast Brigade was coming now, and was due to attack the fifth line at ten. The problem was that neither of the flanking divisions had made any progress at all. The further forward the 36th Division went, the bigger target they were offering to Germans north and south. One request was made by the divisional commander at 8:35 to cancel the attack on the fifth line but a message came from corps headquarters that the neighbouring divisions would soon be advancing and the attack should go forward as planned. At about 9:20 another order arrived, stating that the Belfast Brigade should postpone their attack until the situation on the flanks had improved. Unfortunately, it proved impossible to pass on this order to the Belfast men, and the attack went ahead anyway.

Crozier, the CO of the West Belfast battalion, had seen the ranks of the 32nd Division break on the defences of Thiepval Village, and was aware of the implications for his men. The South Belfast battalion was taking casualties because of the inadequate cover in Thiepval Wood; the trees had been stripped and they were in plain view of the Germans. At about 8:30 there was a slight easing of the shelling and both battalion COs ordered their men forward by squads to the Sunken Road and, after a rest, forward towards the fighting. The men from East Belfast, many of whom were shipyard workers, were the last to go forward. Some of the men were shot as soon as they left the trench. Those who left the trench safely made their way quickly forward. Some felt the red hot kiss of shrapnel without being seriously wounded. Others were shot without realising it, only becoming aware of their condition when they tried to walk.

It was very frustrating to hang back, knowing the battle that was going on for the fourth line, yet not being allowed to get involved. One Lewis gunner from West Belfast got so impatient that he started firing on German prisoners being escorted back to the British lines. 'They're only Germans,' was his comment when rebuked.[8] The Belfast men were determined to get as close to the German fifth line as possible before the barrage lifted. Some of them pushed forward, ignoring the bullets that raked around them. Some of the British fire was falling short, and many were killed by what nowadays is called friendly fire. And they did take the fifth line, making the 36th the only division on the Somme to reach so deeply into the German defences. They held it for a while too, although only the most aggressive and the fittest survived the hand-to-hand struggle. This was not the place for conventional weapons. One man fought with a pick-handle onto one end of which he had attached a lump of cast iron.[9]

There were too few to hold the line for any length of time. The Germans had got themselves organised and were beginning to counter-attack. The men at the fifth line had to fall back on the fourth shortly after noon. Surrounded now by enemy fire, the 36th Division found itself besieged in the four German lines they had taken. Beyond the trenches, men who had been wounded by bullet or shrapnel lay in the heat of midday with nothing to ease their final hours. A runner reported three to four hundred wounded in no-man's-land. Medical orderlies, helped by some walking wounded, set up a forward aid station in Thiepval Wood, while a call went out to the nearest medical depot for more morphine. One of the greatest trials of the wounded was thirst, and orderlies went around with clean water and, sometimes, hot sweet tea.

As each casualty was brought in, he was examined by a doctor. Those already dead were put to one side. Those who were obviously going to die were placed in a tent, given an injection of morphine and some cigarettes. Nothing more could be done for them. It was very affecting for an orderly to light a cigarette for a soldier and watch the man die before he had finished it. Minor wounds and amputations were carried out at the advance aid post. Anything more serious was sent to the main dressing station.

There was a desperate feeling of being out of contact in the various command posts behind the line. The second in command of the Fermanagh Volunteers, a Major Peacocke, was sent across no-man's-land to try to gain control of both the Derrys and the Fermanagh men. Together with Major Gaffikin, he tried to consolidate the hold on the German third line, but Germans were filtering into their old front line and attacking the Ulstermen from the rear. To try to find a safe way to bring reinforcements forward, Pioneers began to dig a shallow trench across no-man's-land. The Germans simply concentrated their fire on this work for a while and the Pioneers had to give up. The decision was now for people at the highest level. The only significant gains on the entire Somme battlefront were in the sector assigned to the 36th Division. The division was now surrounded, but seemed to be holding their positions securely. It seemed unthinkable to give up what had been won at such cost.

But the men at the sharp end, those in the Schwaben Redoubt, were reaching the ends of their tethers. Exhausted and numb, their faces were yellow as jaundice from the explosives; they could hardly even recognise one another. Hugh Stewart tried to speak, but found that his tongue was swollen and his throat dry and parched. Incongruously, a man near him took out a flute and began to play, in defiance of the devil.[10]

Things were no easier in the action to the north of the river. As the frontline troops went forward through no-man's-land, they had to cross a ravine that was seventy yards wide and up to twenty feet deep, with steep sides. When they had crossed this they decided that walking gave the Germans too much time to recover, so they charged towards the German wire, which was fairly well cut. In this first line of trenches there were few defenders, and they were soon in Ulster hands. One group of men simply kept going until they reached Beaucourt Station and the German third line. The Germans were ready for the second wave, and these later troops were strafed by machine-gun fire, in particular from Beaumont-Hamel, on their left flank. Each subsequent wave found it harder, with many getting no further than the lip of the ravine.

Where the Mid-Antrim Volunteers reached the German line there were huge rolls of barbed wire, still largely intact. German machine-guns were trained on the few gaps that did exist. Fewer than ten reached the trenches; scores became casualties. The only cover available was in the ravine, and here the men hurried. Those men from Armagh who, with the help of some Antrim men, had reached Beaucourt station found themselves surrounded as Germans worked their way behind them. The report to the divisional commander said that those who were not already casualties were trapped, pinned down by enemy fire, and the Germans were once more in control of their front line. There was such a severe bombardment of the Ulstermen's own front lines that no reinforcements could come through. The position was made worse by the failure of many of the Lewis guns. Without orders, survivors made their way back in ones and twos from the German trenches. To do this they had to jettison heavy equipment. Those who stayed were killed or captured in German counter-attacks. Surrendering was not an option for the men whose battle cry was 'No surrender!' The wounded were faced with a terrible prospect. Lying in the sun, they were glad when their retreating comrades tried to get them back to the lines. They were carried on men's backs or dragged along on capes or blankets. The jolting and the sudden drops as men had to take cover must have been agonising, but it was better than being left to die in the open.

The battle to the north of the Ancre gained nothing, won nothing; the flanking fire from the Germans made it impossible to hold any objectives. In one short morning, the Armagh Volunteers were decimated. About six hundred had gone over the parapet, led by fifteen officers. By the end of the day they had lost fourteen officers and five hundred and eighteen men killed, wounded or missing.[11] Only eighty-three returned to the lines unscathed. A resource that had been built up over more than two years was simply squandered.

To the south of the river, the glory that was gained in the early fighting also turned out to be a waste. From 1 p.m. it became apparent that the Germans were building up their forces for a counter-attack. German reinforcement could be seen arriving by train at Grandcourt, fresh men more than ready to face the exhausted Ulstermen. By 2:45 p.m., they could be heard making their way along the communication trenches towards their third line, still held by Belfast men. The fourth line had been captured. Some of the men were tempted to run, but were dissuaded by officers' revolvers. Most of them simply waited, ready to fight on. At 3:45, the Germans concentrated their attack on a trench in the southern side of the redoubt; it took them an hour to force it. William Montgomery, an officer in the West Belfast battalion, thought that all was lost, but he received word that reinforcements would arrive at 6 p.m. This information was only partly correct. The Belfast Brigade was expected to be reinforced by 146th Brigade. But two battalions of this Yorkshire brigade were already being used to attack Thiepval and by the time enough Yorkshiremen had been collected to make a difference, eight companies of them, they were an hour late, not arriving at the redoubt till 7 p.m.

The German counter-attack was gaining momentum. Some of their attacks came to nothing, and entire groups were wiped out, but still they came. The Ulstermen were forced back to the German first and second lines. Although some men settled here for a last stand, more and more of them had had enough. Montgomery thought that the crisis came shortly after 9:30 p.m.; large numbers of men simply turned their backs on the enemy and headed for their own lines. Although he and Major Peacocke did try to rally some of them, it was only a temporary remission, and they left again about twenty minutes later.

Even as night fell, some of the Ulstermen remained in the German trenches. They collected what ammunition they could from the dead around them. In the British lines too, men were working with dead bodies. Tommy Russell was gathering identity discs from corpses when he realised that one of the corpses was still alive. He managed to get the still alive soldier from the dreadful pile and sent for stretcher-bearers. While they were putting the man carefully on his stretcher, another soldier came over, his face very pale. He was the wounded man's brother.[12] Unfortunately, the Germans were still shelling Thiepval Wood and the little party never made it to the dressing station. Doctors were being worked off their feet. The wounds made by machine-gun fire were horrendous, 'so big you could put your fist into them'.[13] All night and into the next day the medical staff worked, taking only short breaks for a drink of water and a bite to eat. Many of the casualties needed limbs amputated, and the smell of blood was all-pervasive.

The officers in the command posts were despondent as the full extent of the disaster became apparent, but, as the sun warmed the Sunday morning, they were surprised to see that a group of Ulstermen was still holding out in the German lines. General Nugent decided that they had to be supported. Fresh ammunition and water, and more machine-guns, were sent forward. Pioneers worked at gathering this material and getting it as near the front line as possible. When they had done that, they were sent into the fighting line. About four hundred men altogether were assembled, together with two machine-guns. They were a mixed bag, collected from where they could be found, and they were sent forward under the command of Major Woods from the West Belfast battalion. Some of those who had been in action the previous day were terrified that they would have to face the inferno again, but the survivors of the Young Citizens were sent back along the causeway to Martinsart Wood, only 120 men and two officers.

For Major Wood's party, the journey forward was no easier than it had been the previous day. They were carrying supplies not only for themselves but for the men trapped in the German trenches, and they were greatly overloaded. As a man fell, his nearest comrade took as many of his supplies as he could manage. It was well that some of the fitter soldiers could carry twice the weight of supplies they started off with, because over a third of those who set out did not arrive. The defensive position in the German trenches was much improved, and was improved again when Pioneers brought bombs from Thiepval Wood. It now seemed possible to hold out against the counter-attacks. It was just a question of holding out, however, and at nightfall the order came for them to withdraw that night. In the dark hours of Sunday night and Monday morning, 49th Division took over 36th Division's responsibility for this stretch of front line.

The various battalions tried to reform and then started back to the rest areas around Martinsart, where they tried to sleep through the noise of the continuing battle. When Monday's daylight came, it was time to start counting the cost. In the West Belfast battalion, only seventy remained. A Young Citizen thought that his company was only a shadow. In the Down Battalion, it seemed as if only one man in ten answered his name. Field postcards were distributed and men wrote home, if only to let their families know they were still alive. General Nugent sent orders of the day to each battalion, saying he was 'proud beyond description' of their 'sublime courage and discipline'.[14] He visited each of the brigades in turn to reinforce this message. Late on Tuesday the rain had returned and small parties of men were sent to Thiepval Wood to see if they could find any more living casualties. A group of Young Citizens who went to the Sunken Road at 9 p.m. were amazed to find twelve men still alive.

It was a week later, on Tuesday 11 July, that 36th Division left Picardy, and left 5,000 casualties behind them.

Before this, news had begun to filter home. On Monday 3 July the Belfast *News Letter* reported that the long awaited offensive had begun. On Thursday, the same paper published the Order of the Day that General Nugent had issued before the battle. On Friday, it reported that the Ulster Volunteers had played a central role in the offensive and that they had 'won a name that equals any in history'.[15] A report by a correspondent hinted at great loss of life. The most concrete inform-ation of all was a list of the dead and wounded from the battle. Individual information began to arrive as well; small buff-coloured envelopes addressed to the next of kin were delivered in the normal post. One postman, seeing two of these envelopes addressed to the same woman, held one back till the next day, in case finding the full extent of her loss at the one time should be more than she could bear. The writer's father-in-law told him of witnessing the Presbyterian minister arriving in a hayfield to take the bad news to a farming family.

It was not the first time in the war that Belfast and the north had suffered losses; professional soldiers had fought in the first year of the war and men who had gone to the 10th (Irish) Division had fought and died in Gallipoli. This time, however, the deaths were more concentrated in specific areas, even specific streets. It was a horror that pulled people towards the windows of newsagents, who would paste each day's casualty list to the glass. Occasionally, people would find a loved one's name on the list before the official notification reached home.

On Monday 10 July, the *Belfast Evening Telegraph* began to publish letters from wounded men who were in hospital in England. These were often stilted, anxious not to cause too much worry at home; they glossed over the horrors and emphasised the high morale that still existed in the division. This effort was cancelled out by the obituaries that were now beginning to fill the papers, simple expressions of grief and loss. Small advertisements also began to appear, where families sought details of loved ones who were missing. Very occasionally, there would be good news and someone supposed to be dead would be discovered in hospital.

Whereas these insertions expressed a natural and genuine emotion, some of the tributes made by political figures were high in praise but low in empathy. They stressed the nobility and loyalty of those who had fought and died 'in defence of those liberties and rights which have been the heritage of all British citizens'. Another wrote, 'Ulster Protestants took their stand where their fathers stood (in) costly self sacrifice to the Empire.'[16] It may have been a genuine attempt at finding consolation for the widespread bereavement by placing it in context, but it smacked of trying to make political capital out of what was in reality a military cock-up. Colonel Blacker of the Armagh Volunteers was annoyed. 'The Division behaved magnificently and the point does not want labouring,' he said.[17]

The Orange Order, which had lost so many members in the battle, cancelled the 12 July parades. Instead, there was a five-minute silence all over Ulster, starting at noon. Blinds in buildings were shut in mourning, people stood bare-headed in the streets among the stopped traffic. Even nature seemed to mourn, and the flags which hung at half mast dripped in the pouring rain.

The Ulster Volunteer Force still existed as an organisation and its commander, General George Richardson, issued an order of the day expressing sympathy to the relatives of those who had died. Carson sent a message to 'the Ulster people' expressing sorrow for the loss of so many friends and comrades. More personal was the sympathy expressed across the religious divide; many Catholics prayed at mass for the sons of neighbours and friends.

Chapter 8 ～

॥PUNISHMENT

There is a famous photograph of the discussions between Patrick Pearse and General Lowe which led to the surrender of the insurgent forces. It is 2:30 in the afternoon of the Saturday after Easter, the sixth day of the Rising. Pearse stands, uncomfortably, in the 'at ease' position, feet slightly apart, hands held behind back. He wears a slouch hat, the chin-strap of which is tightly in place. It seems small for his large head. His coat is a long greatcoat, reaching well below his knees. The cut is not flattering and it gives the impression of a man who is beginning to succumb to middle-age spread. Beneath it, incongruously, are four legs and four feet. The effect, for someone who has watched television in the late twentieth century, is of an illustration from *Monty Python's Flying Circus*. The explanation is much more prosaic. Pearse is accompanied by Nurse Elizabeth O'Farrell, who is to play a crucial role in the entire surrender process. It is her legs that hang so strangely from Pearse's greatcoat. Whether she is so tiny that she is hidden completely by Pearse, or some picture editor has tried, carelessly, to airbrush her out of history is impossible to say.

Facing the couple are General Lowe, who has fought the Rising almost to a standstill, and the general's son, John Muir Lowe. The two are 'standing easy', each with one knee cocked in a relaxed pose. The general holds Pearse's sword stick and pistol, which he has just accepted from the rebel commander as a token of surrender. He has a pleasant, open face, and it is recorded that he was very polite in his dealings with Pearse, and he seems to be speaking politely now. The son, John, seems much more informal as, perhaps, befits a cavalry officer who has served at Gallipoli. He is reading Pearse's typewritten letter of surrender, while a cigarette dangles from his mouth. There is a sense, in the out-of-focus shadows in the background, that Dublin, and Ireland, is being filled with soldiers.

General Lowe, after the Rising, seems to have disappeared into the War Office.

His son went back to fight in France, was captured and spent the rest of the war in Germany. After the armistice he stayed on, changing his name to John Loder. He loved acting and appeared in several films made by Max Korda in the 1920s. Up to the beginning of the Second World War he had minor parts in many films, first in Hollywood, then in Britain. In 1939 he returned to Hollywood, where he had some more important roles in films. He even married the beautiful Hedy Lemarr, which lasted for three years. Finally he married a rich Argentinian and retired to her ranch, where he died in 1988.

Nurse O'Farrell was less lucky. She was one of very few women imprisoned by the British, even though General Lowe wrote a note emphasising the help she had given in organising the surrender. She was a republican activist for most of her life and died in Bray, when only in her sixties.

Patrick Pearse had only four days to live.

The man chosen to take charge of the much increased Irish garrison was Sir John Grenfell Maxwell. He got the job almost by accident. He had recently returned from the Middle East where he had commanded the defending forces along the Suez Canal. In fact, he had spent most of his service in the Middle East. As a young officer he had gone to Khartoum with Lord Wolseley's relief column and had stayed on with the army of occupation in Egypt. He stayed with the Egyptian army until they finally retook the Sudan at the Battle of Omdurman, where Kitchener commanded the joint British and Egyptian armies and the young Winston Churchill had a minor role as a young cavalry officer. Maxwell remained in Egypt till 1899, when he went to South Africa and commanded a brigade during the Boer War. He became military governor of Pretoria and the Western Transvaal. He must have done his work to a satisfactory degree, because he was appointed to the staff of the Duke of Connaught, third son and seventh child of Queen Victoria. The Royal Duke at that time was General Officer Commanding (GOC) Ireland, so Maxwell was based in Dublin. He served the Duke until 1907, when, after a short period as Major General in the General Staff at Whitehall, he was appointed GOC Egypt. He remained in Egypt till 1912, when he returned to the General Staff in Whitehall. When the Great War started, he was posted to the Suez Canal, as noted above. His part in the Dardanelles adventure was, as is noted in a previous chapter, largely a matter of trying to prevent British troops being transferred from his command to reinforce Gallipoli.

His regiment was the Black Watch; indeed, he was appointed Colonel-in-Chief of the Black Watch in 1914. This is a regiment with a long history. It was formed soon after the 1715 rising in Scotland. Its members came from the loyal clans on the highland fringe. The Campbells and the Munros were prominent among them. Its task was to keep an eye on the hills, to watch against disaffection and breaking of the penal laws. The soldiers gained a reputation for trapping Catholic priests. The reputation for religious partiality stayed with them when they were incorporated into the Royal Highland Regiment late in the nineteenth century.

In 1916, having finished his tour of duty, Maxwell returned to England. He took advantage of this to have a medical examination for suspected gallstones. It so happened that his letter to Kitchener, reporting that he had been passed fit and requesting a posting, arrived on the great man's desk more or less at the same time as the decision was taken to replace General Friend. The fact that Kitchener's old regiment was also the Black Watch may have been irrelevant, but Maxwell was chosen as the new GOC for Ireland. Kitchener, apparently, thought highly of his 'racial understanding'. His experience of fighting minor wars in obscure corners of the empire persuaded him that firmness was the most important quality in dealing with insurrection and his first proclamations when he arrived in Dublin set the tone for what was to come. Soldiers on the street soon fell into his way of thinking, a fact not always appreciated even by those loyal to the Crown. One loyal citizen who had been ordered away from his own window by a soldier 'brandishing a heavy revolver' thought that this was how German soldiers would behave.

Maxwell took his authority from the declaration of martial law, which had been extended to the entire country by the Cabinet. He was in effect military governor. Lloyd George was worried that an unconsidered action taken by a junior officer under the new powers might set the whole country ablaze, and so Maxwell was told in writing that the ordinary processes of the law were to be followed except where he personally felt that the powers available under martial law were required.

Maxwell, meanwhile, ordered that nothing but unconditional sur-render was to be accepted from any rebel unit. When he heard that the officer commanding the Queenstown garrison was prepared to allow the Tralee Volunteers to surrender their arms to a responsible third party and go home, he telegraphed at once that no terms or guarantees were to be offered to anyone found in arms. He met with Birrell and Wimborne and told them that he did not like to interfere more than was necessary but that they were under his orders and he hoped they would do what he wished of them. A joint appeal to Asquith availed the pair nothing, and the Cabinet confirmed the extension of martial law to the entire island of Ireland. So far Maxwell fits the picture, subsequently painted of him, of a right-wing martinet sent to Ireland to put Catholic nationalists in their place. This, however, is an over-simplification; Maxwell was a much more complex man than this.

It was his opinion that the trouble in Dublin and elsewhere had been the direct result of the feeble way in which the government had dealt with the Ulster crisis right from the beginning. If the Ulster Volunteers had been stood up to, the Irish Volunteers would never have come into existence. A government should never allow itself to be coerced by physical force. It should never even negotiate with those who support physical force. The different ways in which unionists and nationalists were treated allowed the Irish Volunteers to claim that only force or the threat of force would achieve anything with the British government. Maxwell asserted that it was becoming more difficult to separate Sinn Féin supporter from constitutional nationalist and the younger generation was likely to be more extreme than the one that had undertaken the Rising.

As soon as the official surrender had been made, Maxwell tightened security in Dublin. The city was divided into two area commands, one north and one south of the river. Each had a brigade of infantry, two field guns, and two armoured cars. They were to snuff out any resistance and to identify rebel strongholds and arms dumps. Since there continued to be sporadic firing in the city, particularly around Ringsend, for a few days, this was probably a wise tactic. The troops carried out house-to-house searches for arms. It was his intention to use these captured weapons to arm the DMP. He reasoned that if they had been armed they would have been able to resist the insurrection at its very beginning. The politicians frustrated him. The Treasury argued that to arm the DMP, which was a force paid for by the rates of Dublin, would mean that they would have to be taken under the control of—and paid for by—the government. That would be an expense too far.

'To understand all is to excuse all' is not a phrase that finds a welcoming shelter in the military mind. Duty is all. Maxwell might understand what had led to the Rising, but he was not going to take that into consideration when dealing with the results of it. At the heart of Maxwell's problem was the world view of two peoples. The British, at least the British establishment, saw Ireland as an integral part of the United Kingdom. If, then, the Irish were to take arms against the government, they would be rebels, fighting against their lawful rulers. For Irish nationalists the picture was completely different. They saw Ireland as a separate nation, voluntarily sharing the struggle of the Great War with Britain. If Irishmen or women were to take arms against the British government, it was as one nation fighting another, and any prisoners should be treated as prisoners of war. For Maxwell, Pearse and his fellows were traitors and murderers. They had shot down soldiers in the streets of Dublin. It was his duty to see that they were tried and the guilty punished. Constitutional nationalists saw them as patriots, even if they were misguided. They should be kept in prison to reflect upon the errors of their ways; no more than that.

A reluctant Cabinet allowed him to proceed. They did not want the matter drawn out, however, and insisted that any death sentences should be carried out as quickly as possible. They then pushed the door ajar again by telling him that he should do, of course, what he thought necessary.

Far more people were arrested than had taken part in the Rising: 3,500 men and seventy-nine women. A good many were released after preliminary inquiries had been made, but 2,000 men and six women remained in custody. Maxwell was relieved when he was told that most of the women who had been arrested seemed to lack any ideology. It allowed him to be shot of those 'silly little girls' whose courts martial might have inspired sympathy in the English press. Eventually only one woman, Countess Markievicz, was selected for court martial, together with 186 men. Well over one thousand of those men who were sent to be interned in Wales were quickly released. The reason given was that they were 'low level dupes' who had been tools of Sinn Féin. Most of the rest were released by Christmas 1916, while the rest had their freedom in July 1917. Ironically, to justify their detention at all they had to be classified as 'enemy aliens', implying an acceptance of the view that Ireland was a separate nation.

That was in the future. The courts martial began almost immediately. Each case was judged by a panel of three officers; no officer was required to have legal training. The prosecutor in most cases was William Wylie, a son of the manse, who, though he had been born in Dublin, was educated in Coleraine. The appointment of a Northern Unionist may seem to have been yet another example of crass thoughtlessness on the part of the authorities, but in fact Wylie was scrupulous in his efforts to ensure that the accused had a fair trial. He wanted the trials to be public and wanted the accused to have access to a defence attorney. The Solicitor-General vetoed these suggestions, but did, eventually, allow defendants to call witnesses.

Almost all of the proceedings took place in Richmond Barracks, close to the Kilmainham Hospital Headquarters of General Maxwell. Thomas Kent, who had been arrested at his home in County Cork, was tried in the Cork Detention Barracks, while James Connolly was tried in the Red Cross Hospital in Dublin Castle. The first trials began on Tuesday 2 May. As it turned out, almost everyone was faced with variations of the same charge: that they had taken part in armed rebellion and that they had waged war against the King with the intention of assisting the enemy. All of those charged, with the exception of Willie Pearse, pleaded not guilty. It was not considered acceptable to plead guilty to part of the charge. Again, this was a political judgement. It was important for the authorities to be able to claim that the rebels were betraying their compatriots at the front.

Most of the witnesses for the prosecution were officers who had been captured by the insurgents and were, therefore, in a position to identify those in command, or at least those who gave orders. Others testified concerning the rank that an individual had given at the time of his surrender. Policemen gave evidence of past involvement in 'extreme nationalism'. In the case of Patrick Pearse, a letter which he wrote to his mother on 1 May, after the surrender, was said to prove that he had been in contact with the Germans as well as being a leader of the insurgents.

Pearse was the first to be tried. He was brought under escort from Arbour Hill that morning. His tribunal was headed by Brigadier Blackader, who later told the Countess of Fingall that he found Pearse one of the finest characters he had ever come across. 'There must be something very wrong', he said, 'in the state of things that makes a man like that a rebel.' Blackader found it hard to condemn Pearse to death but, as a soldier, he knew where his duty lay. Pearse was sentenced to death by being shot, as were Clarke and MacDonagh. They were then taken to Kilmainham Gaol to await Maxwell's decision as to whether the sentence should be confirmed or commuted. The old gaol was a disgrace, disused for years until the army had taken it over as a detention centre. The cells lacked furniture; there was only a groundsheet on the floor for sleeping and a bucket for sanitation. The only light was provided by candles or bare gas mantles. The most important space in the gaol was the old stonebreakers' yard, where those who had been sentenced to hard labour had stretched out their days. Now it was to be a place of execution.

Pearse had not long to wait. He was informed by an officer that his sentence had been confirmed and that he would be shot at dawn the following morning. The officer told him that he could write last letters to friends and family and that he could have a priest to stay with him. Cars would be provided, if he wanted, to bring relatives and friends for a last visit. As it turned out, the military vehicle sent to collect his mother was unable to get through because of continuing unrest in the city. He had a priest, however, and received Holy Communion for the last time. Standing orders issued later were that the priest should be allowed to remain with the condemned men but, on this first morning, they were made to leave before 3 a.m.

At about 3:30 on the morning of 3 May the executions began. Each man was taken from his cell. As he reached a long corridor which led down to the execution yard he was blindfolded and had his hands tied behind his back. A piece of white cloth was pinned over his heart. He was then led out into the yard. Some of the condemned were asked to sit on a soap box. Twelve soldiers faced him at a distance of ten paces. The rifle of one of them was loaded with a blank; the other eleven had live ammunition. None knew who had the blank, so each soldier could believe that he had not fired the fatal shot. The front rank knelt, the rear rank stood and, at a visual signal from the officer in charge, they fired. Each body was certified dead by a medical officer, had a name label attached and was then taken to a waiting ambulance. When that day's quota had been shot, the bodies were taken to Arbour Hill Barracks where they were buried in quicklime, without coffins. Maxwell, mindful of Pearse's words at the funeral of O'Donovan Rossa, was determined that there should be no martyrs' graves to be visited by future patriots. An officer took note of where each body was placed, and a priest was allowed to conduct a funeral service.

Already, nationalist politicians saw the danger and began to protest. Redmond, during the day, protested to Asquith that continuing executions would make things impossible for any constitutional party in Ireland. Yet that day no fewer than fifteen rebels were sentenced to death, although only four had their sentences confirmed. One of the unfortunate four was Willie Pearse, whose only sin had been to idolise his brother. The others were Ned Daly, Michael O'Hanrahan and Joseph Plunkett, who was allowed to marry his fiancée, Grace Gifford, before the sentence was carried out in the early hours of 4 May. He had pleaded guilty to the charge laid against him but, as he said himself at his trial, he was no more than an aide-de-camp. Major MacBride followed the next day, disappointed that they insisted on blindfolding him, when he wanted to look death in the eye. By this time even the *Daily Chronicle* carried a leader saying that the executions should be stopped.

Perhaps the unluckiest were those who were sentenced to death on Friday 5 May, since they were forced to remain in Kilmainham over the weekend, while death was taking a holiday. Sean Heuston, Michael Mallin, Con Colbert and Eamonn Ceannt were allowed to take Holy Communion together on Sunday, before being told that sentence of death had been confirmed and taken to adjoining cells on the ground floor. Capuchin priests from Church Street tried to give them religious comfort, and they had final visits from their families. This was particularly hard in the case of Mallin, whose wife was pregnant. The poignancy of the situation was enough to cause a young soldier who was holding a candle to weep, according to Mallin's son. The atmosphere of death was beginning to permeate everything. The four were shot at dawn on Monday morning.

On Tuesday, in Cork, Thomas Kent was shot. MacDermott and Connolly were tried and sentenced to death.

On the next day, Wednesday the 10th, MacDermott and Connolly were told that their death sentences had been confirmed. At this stage Asquith intervened. He was travelling to Dublin on Thursday night and wanted the executions delayed for a day. On the morning of the 11th, Kitchener contacted Maxwell and told him that he should go ahead with the executions on Friday the 12th, unless he heard further from Asquith. No further stay of execution was received and the final firing squads were assembled on the Friday morning. Connolly, last of the leaders to be shot, was taken to his place of execution on a stretcher, in the back of a van, and propped on a chair in front of the firing squad. The executions were over in two working weeks. It was not the end of the courts martial. They went on till the end of May. Even MacNeill was sentenced to penal servitude for life, though it could be argued that he had done more to frustrate the Rising than any British officer.

Maxwell decided that it was best to assure Asquith that all those executed had taken a significant role in the Rising and that the evidence against them had been overwhelming. He prepared a memorandum to that effect. It was certain that, given the scale of the disruption to life and property, those who signed the Proclamation would be executed. Possibly, too, those who commanded battalions could expect little mercy. There were others executed, however, who had nothing like the same level of authority. It was claimed that Willie Pearse was a commandant in the Volunteers, which was untrue. All that could truthfully be said of him was that he was in the GPO with the others and had surrendered with them. O'Hanrahan had served at Jacob's Factory, where little fighting had taken place. MacBride had bumped into the rebellion at St Stephen's Green, but had fought against the British in the Boer War. Kent had shot a policeman after the surrender. There was a message in his execution: anyone who tried to continue the armed struggle would be shown no mercy.

There was one court martial which caused difficulty, that of Eoin MacNeill. MacNeill had presented himself at military headquarters to secure an interview with Maxwell when Major Price, the ex-RIC man who was the head of military intelligence in Ireland, had grabbed his arm and arrested him as a rebel. During his interrogation, MacNeill was struck by how little Price knew about the Volunteers, especially since the Volunteers themselves had been a very open organisation— with the exception of the IRB core. Maxwell was advised by his law officers that it would not be a good idea to allow a public trial of MacNeill. This was probably true, because the public would then have grasped the disparity between the trivial charges—attempting to spread disaffection and interfering with recruiting—and the magnitude of the sentence: penal servitude for life.

For all that he had tried to bring the matter of the Rising to a quick close, for all that he had overturned the majority of death sentences handed down by the courts, Maxwell was rapidly becoming a butcher in the eyes of the Catholic and nationalist majority in Ireland. His good intentions had created the worst of many worlds and had made him a bogeyman. His haste in holding the courts martial, their secrecy and the fact that none of the defendants had anyone to act in his defence smelt of a cover-up. The apparently arbitrary nature of the decision to confirm the death sentence on some of the prisoners, in particular Willie Pearse, spoke of vindictiveness. Finally, the way the executions were drawn out over two weeks, with no end announced, was seen as the extension of a policy of deliberate killing that had begun with Francis Sheehy Skeffington. In truth, however, sympathy among the general population had started shifting towards the rebels when Dubliners saw them being herded into confinement at the Rotunda. Upon this resentment was added the trauma of the executions. John Dillon spoke vehemently in Parliament, implying that the Prime Minister had lost control of Maxwell, and stating openly that prisoners were being threatened with death if they did not testify against their colleagues.

To ensure control of the rest of the country, on 3 May it had been divided into three. The northern area consisted of the nine Ulster counties plus County Louth. The central area stretched from there south to a line 'five miles north of the railway running from Ennis to Limerick to Clonmel and by a straight line from there to Arklow'. The rest of Ireland was the southern area. The southern area was under the control of the commanding officer at Queenstown, who was to send small columns of infantry and mounted troops to various centres and, gradually, to sweep the entire area. The central area had more substantial forces and there were mobile columns set up in four centres. Each column consisted of two companies of infantry, a squadron of cavalry, an 18-pounder gun and an armoured car. A 'disloyal' area was to be surrounded by cavalry and then searched by the infantry. They were to collect all arms. They were also to gather as much information as possible on anyone who might have taken part in the Rising. Ominously, anyone who resisted arrest might be tried by court martial 'on the spot'.

The columns were not very effective at finding guns, since they were forbidden to do house-to-house searches other than in Dublin. They were rather better at arresting people. Their officers had been instructed to differentiate between nationalist and Sinn Féin, and to give the benefit of the doubt on the side of the nationalists. Almost immediately Maxwell had to make another order saying that only Sinn Féin leaders and those who had been known to bear arms should be arrested. By 14 May he complained that in some districts Sinn Féin followers were being arrested who could not be described as 'leaders exercising dangerous influence'. Only those who had actually taken part in the Rising or those who were inciting others to retain arms or resist authority should be taken into custody. In spite of these orders, Maxwell was inclined to believe reports that were coming from MI5 which suggested that it was impossible to differentiate between Sinn Féin and Redmondites, and it is possible that he was simply covering himself. Certainly some of his subordinates didn't worry themselves about such niceties. In Omagh, County Tyrone, a raid on houses in a nationalist area which was undertaken without consulting the police resulted in turning many people who had been against Sinn Féin into opponents of the government.

Dillon wrote to Maxwell on 8 May condemning the policy of large-scale searches in areas where there had been no trouble. In Parliament on 11 May he said that Maxwell had enough to do in Dublin without making work in the rest of the country. The searches in Limerick, Clare and Mayo were 'maddening the Irish people'. 'If Ireland were governed by men out of Bedlam you could not pursue a more insane policy.' The life work of the Irish Parliamentary Party was being washed away in a sea of blood. The secrecy of the trials was poisoning the air in Dublin and turning thousands of people against the government. His attack was taken up by the nationalist press. Even the *Freeman's Journal* had to be threatened with prosecution under the Defence of the Realm Act. Maxwell blamed Dillon, saying that his speech had inflamed racial feelings.

Since the resignation of Birrell, the task of setting up a new civil administration in Dublin was in a sort of limbo. Not able to find a suitable candidate as Chief Secretary, Asquith decided to take on the duties himself for the time being. In this capacity he came to Dublin in mid-May. One of the first places he visited was Richmond Barracks, where he spent some time with the prisoners. He saw that most of them were countrymen who had taken no part in the Rising and who should not have been brought to Dublin. Presumably as a public relations exercise, he ordered that the prisoners be provided with the best of food, no matter what the expense to the public purse. This did not raise his popularity with the Sherwood Foresters, who provided the guard for the prison. According to some of the captives, this produced a situation where hungry soldiers were begging for food outside the prisoners' cookhouse.

Asquith also ordered that a process of weeding out should begin immediately. Serious political damage had already been done, most seriously in the claim made that he had not known of the shooting of Sheehy Skeffington till the end of the first week in May, while, as was pointed out by Dillon, it had been witnessed by up to four hundred soldiers and was being spoken of around Dublin within a day of the killing.

The killing raised two main issues. Firstly, it showed how a junior officer could abuse martial law powers. It is interesting to note that Maxwell excused Bowen-Colthurst, who had ordered the shooting, by saying that he was a 'hot-headed Irishman'; no racial stereotyping there! The other issue was the slowness with which the military authorities reacted, although all accepted that what Bowen-Colthurst had done was illegal. There was advice from the Judge Advocate General's Office that, since the offence had been committed within the United Kingdom, the matter could not be settled in a court martial, but would require a civil trial. Things were looking bad, but the Irish Attorney-General simply reversed the original judgement and said the army could go ahead with the court martial. Asquith insisted that proceedings should be open to the public and press. The legal team representing Hanna Sheehy Skeffington protested that this was not enough since, although they could attend the proceedings, they could not intervene. Sure enough, Bowen-Colthurst was found guilty but insane. The Sheehy Skeffington solicitor, Henry Lemass, complained vehemently to Asquith that the evidence had not been properly presented. Asquith simply kicked the ball into touch. He set up a Royal Commission under Sir John Simon, which reported that the entire fiasco had resulted from an honest misunderstanding of martial law on the part of a number of junior officers.

There were other accusations of unlawful killing to be dealt with. Thirteen civilians had been shot in the fighting in North King Street. Maxwell claimed that it was done in the heat of battle. Subject to constant sniping, the soldiers had killed any males they came across as they moved from house to house. Anyway, if the men had been innocent, he wrote, why did they not leave their homes? In this, he was being somewhat disingenuous, since it is hard to imagine that the streets were any safer than the houses. This matter was dealt with by a military court of inquiry and the president, Brigadier Maconchy, found the battalion concerned, 2/6th South Staffordshires, 'a quiet and very respectable set of men'. He decided that it was impossible to apportion blame to any individual soldier. Maxwell was more forthright. He said that the deaths were the fault of those who resisted the troops who were simply trying to carry out their duty. A senior Home Office official, Sir Edward Troup, thought differently. In one case at least, he thought there was evidence that a sergeant should be tried for murder. In the other cases, the problem was that the soldiers had been told to take no prisoners. This order was illegal, since to shoot an unarmed rebel who had been taken prisoner was murder. Neither could a person be shot simply on suspicion. He concluded, however, that it was best not to publish the evidence, since there were those who would make mischief with it.

It was also decided not to publish the proceedings of the courts martial. Ostensibly, this was to protect the lives of witnesses who testified at them. Equally likely, however, is the possibility that the War Office was concerned that some of the evidence used was 'extremely thin'. There were aspects of procedure that would not look too well on the front page of a newspaper. Ceannt, for example, had wanted to call MacDonagh as a defence witness, only to be told that he would not be available since he had been shot that morning. The feeling among senior officers was that publication would not do, and a galaxy of reasons was found to justify continued secrecy.

As far as weeding out internees was concerned, it was unfortunate that proper records had not been kept in most cases, and even in the cases of men who had been caught red-handed, it was going to prove difficult, if not impossible, to ascertain who the arresting officer was. This caused particular difficulties with those prisoners that Maxwell had sent to Britain. It was pointless to take them to court martial, yet the 'worst' of them were too dangerous to be allowed their freedom in Ireland. It would be much too expensive to gather evidence to try them in Britain yet, if they were given the civil trial they were entitled to in Ireland, it was certain that no jury would convict them. At the time of Asquith's visit to Dublin, there were already 1,600 Irish prisoners in Britain. The only quasi-legal way in which they could be kept there, as we have seen, was by classifying them as enemy aliens under the Defence of the Realm Act.

By early June an intelligence report prepared by Colonel Brade declared that many people who had originally condemned the Rising believed that those involved had been punished too severely. The reason he gave was the silence which the army maintained on the facts, coupled with the publication of the unsatisfactory court martial proceedings concerning Sheehy Skeffington's killing. The language of official dispatches gave the impression that the army was glossing over 'a bad record'.

Even Maxwell began to realise that the extreme nationalists were by no means cowed, and that the public was beginning to say that those imprisoned should be released and to see those who had been executed as martyrs. As is the way of things, he blamed everyone else, the cranks and faddists and in particular the Catholic clergy. Some of the last, he claimed, were extremely disloyal, and he wondered whether the Pope might be approached with a request to silence them. He was particularly concerned about the changing self-image of the prisoners, as shown in their letters to family and friends. At first their tone had been almost apologetic, but by mid-June they had become defiant and totally unrepentant. Maxwell had foreseen his growing unpopularity. He claimed that his skin was too thick for the insults to penetrate, but the fact that he mentioned them at all shows that he was upset. 'I am dead sick of this job,' he wrote. His writ ran in Ireland for about three months altogether, before Asquith appointed the Unionist Henry Duke as Chief Secretary. Wimborne was reappointed soon afterwards. Maxwell's career was not blighted, exactly, but he never afterwards achieved a battlefield command, although he was promoted to full general after the war. He never understood the Irish reaction to the way he dealt with the Rising.

The last of the executions was beyond Maxwell's bailiwick, though not beyond his influence. It was decided that Casement should have a civil trial, in London. Here, on 29 June, he was found guilty of High

Treason and sentenced to death. There was evidence that his mind was 'abnormal', though not certifiably insane. The Home Secretary brought the possibility of leniency to the Cabinet for discussion. Asquith would have liked to grant a reprieve based on the medical evidence, but was concerned that he would look weak if he dealt more mercifully with Casement than Maxwell had dealt with the other leaders in Ireland. Casement was hanged in Pentonville Prison on 3 August. The Cabinet decided that there would be no more discussion of the Irish Question till the war was won.

It was doubtful whether it could be put to one side like that. Pearse had written to his mother on 1 May:

> You must not grieve for all this. We have pursued Ireland's honour and our own. Our deeds last week were the most splendid in Irish history. People will say hard things of me now but we shall be remembered by posterity and blessed by unborn generations.

The change came more quickly than Pearse might have hoped. By June of 1916 Sinn Féin badges were being worn openly. When released prisoners were returned to their native towns, there were demonstrations in support of the rebels. The congregations of several churches in Dublin united to march past Trinity College and Dublin Castle, waving small flags of the Irish Republic and booing the soldiers. Some of this derived, not from admiration of the martyred dead, but from the way martial law was applied. The inhabitants of Ireland were divided crudely into loyal and 'disaffected', without anybody in authority realising that most people in Ireland simply wanted to get on with their lives. They did not need to be encouraged or cowed by martial law; they simply found it irritating and offensive. As far as nationalist politicians were concerned, its existence benefited only Sinn Féiners.

To begin with, most priests were cautious in their comments about the Rising. Two priests from the Limerick Diocese were more outspoken, however, and Maxwell wrote to their bishop, Edward O'Dwyer, saying that they were a threat to the peace and safety of the country and inviting him to remove them from their parishes. He chose the wrong bishop. Bishop O'Dwyer said that his priests had broken no laws, even though they held strong nationalist views. Maxwell, on the other hand, was a cruel and oppressive military dictator. He contrasted the way in which the British government had sought mercy on behalf of the Jameson Raiders, but would entertain no plea for mercy on behalf of those who had surrendered in Dublin. Maxwell's abuse of power was 'as fatuous as it was arbitrary'. The letter was published as a pamphlet.

For many historians this confrontation between general and bishop marks the moment when the rebels achieved the status of martyrs. There has been a widely accepted idea that the people of Dublin were initially hostile to the Rising, but changed to support them and even romanticise them. It was never as clear-cut as this. In the better-off parts of the city, sympathy was undoubtedly with the troops. In the poorer parts of the city people were more ambiguous. There were those, such as the much-maligned wives of soldiers serving in the army, who saw the Rising as a stab in the back. For most of the community, however, there was a great deal of sympathy for the rebels. This was particularly true after the surrender, and the sight of the defeated and dispirited young men herded like cattle into the cages at the Rotunda stirred pity in many hearts. These boys were, after all, their own people.

For people in the rest of the country the main reaction was puzzlement. All during Easter Week the authorities had been minimising the scale of the problem in their briefing of the press. This made the shock caused by the scale of the punishment incomprehensible. If it was such a pitiable affair, why were so many being executed so quickly? It might have been possible to reassure the public by releasing more details of what happened and, in particular, the nature of the evidence against those condemned. As we have seen, however, the authorities chose not to do this. More and more unionists, including George Russell (AE), asked the Prime Minister to consider the effect on a population which saw young men of most respectable families being sentenced to long periods of imprisonment without having any real idea of what they were supposed to have done. It is possible that in many cases what had been a latent anti-English prejudice was becoming more definite but certainly the public was becoming alienated from the authorities. In Mullingar, a film of the Rising was shown in the local cinema. This was in July, at the height of the Battle of the Somme, when hundreds of Irishmen were dying daily on the Western Front. In spite of that, the audience cheered the rebels and jeered at the soldiers on screen. The manager of the cinema, mindful of the strictures of the Defence of the Realm Act, did not show the film again.

For priests all around the country, the stand that Bishop O'Dwyer took against General Maxwell acted like a rallying call. By August there were police reports of priests giving sermons which sympathised with the rebels. Some of the sermons were openly seditious. The situation was not helped, as far as Maxwell was concerned, by the number of articles appearing in local papers, many of them copied from the American press, which showed the Rising in a sympathetic light. Photographs of the executed leaders were on sale, as were copies of letters written on the eve of execution. Young people in particular had taken to wearing Sinn Féin badges. Even establishment figures such as James Stephens and W. B. Yeats commented on the calibre of the dead leaders, those whom the authorities were calling 'irresponsible hare-brained adventurers, rainbow-chasers and hooligans'. Lily Yeats condemned 'this shooting of foolish idealists'. Ireland and England, she said, 'can never understand each other'. Yeats himself, in a poem that he wrote that summer but did not publish till the following summer, made the point that the leaders, as a result of their act, were 'all changed, changed utterly'.

There was one bright side. There were no disciplinary problems amongst the Irish regiments serving in active theatres. Southern union-ists saw the Rising, predictably enough, as a stab in the back. One unit which might have been particularly outraged was the 16th Division, which was in the front line near the village of Hulluch. On the night of 27 April, the Germans launched a gas attack against a battalion of the Royal Inniskilling Fusiliers. They disguised their attack by sending over smoke to begin with. Since visibility in gas masks is poor enough at the best of times, and many of the Irishmen presumed that the Germans were going to sneak forward under cover of the smoke, many soldiers removed their masks. The Germans released chlorine gas ninety minutes into the battle and the Inniskillings suffered horrendous casualties. Other battalions, including the Royal Irish Rifles, the Royal Munster Fusiliers and the Royal Dublin Fusiliers, moved forward and stemmed the attack. The Germans launched another attack two days later, but on that occasion the wind changed and blew the gas back in their faces. After the three days, 16th Division had lost over five hundred dead and nearly sixteen hundred wounded. The Germans in the line opposite the Munsters stuck up a placard about the Rising claiming that the English were shelling Irish wives and families, and inviting the Irish to give themselves up and escape the war. The Munsters shot up the sign, and a raiding party stole the remains from the German trenches during the night.

When news of Sheehy Skeffington's murder and the execution of the Rising's leaders reached the troops, it brought a change of mind to many individuals. Nationalists who had enlisted began to reconsider the part they were playing. They wondered whether they could trust Britain to the extent that John Redmond had told them. Equally, they wondered how they would be viewed—whether they would even be trusted—by their own people. Lieutenant O'Connor Douglas of the Army Service Corps had taken part in the gun-running at Howth. He had enlisted because he believed Redmond's assurances. Now he wondered whether he had taken a wise step. Francis Ledwidge was recuperating in Manchester from a back condition that he had developed during a long winter campaigning in Salonika. He was distraught to think that men whom he had counted as among his best friends, men who were practitioners of his own craft of poetry, could now be dead. When he returned on sick leave to his home in Slane his mood was very low. He told his brother that he didn't feel like fighting Germans even if they were climbing the wall into his back yard. His sense of depression was reinforced by the fact that he was posted to Richmond Barracks, where his friends MacDonagh and Pearse had been sentenced to death. From there he was transferred to Ebrington Barracks in Derry. He was able to express the anguish that he felt in some of the loveliest poetry that he ever wrote.

A more positive reaction was felt by Tom Barry. He was campaigning in the Middle East when he heard that guns had been firing 'at the people of my own race by soldiers of the same army with which I was serving'. His indignation burned through the rest of his time in the war, and he joined the IRA when he was demobilised.

Anthony Brennan was with the Royal Irish Regiment, based in a quiet part of France, when news of the Rising came. The men discussed what had happened, but nobody saw it as anything serious. When they remained in the area a few weeks more than had been intended originally, the men came to the conclusion that they were distrusted, and that the army was concerned about any sympathetic reaction in support of the rebels. This seemed to be confirmed after the Kaiser's Offensive of 1918, when 16th Division ceased to exist. At a local level it led to Irish battalions being labelled 'Sinn Féiners'. The situation was worse for Irish soldiers serving in non-Irish battalions, as they were open to more direct hostility. When Monk Gibbon, in a supposedly informal discussion with his commanding officer in the mess, tried to defend a speech that John Redmond had made after the Rising, his senior officer's reaction was to declare that Gibbon should be 'drummed out of the British army'.

For most Irish soldiers in Irish units, their concentration was on their own situation, with the prospect of the 'Big Push' in the summer. They were too concerned about their own survival to worry about the lives of the men in Dublin. Even some individuals who later took part in the War of Independence felt that the Rising was a mistake. For the time being, those who were lucky enough to get leave in Ireland found that they were being treated with the animosity that had been reserved for the Irish Volunteers in 1914 and 1915. In the Ireland that arose from the War of Independence and the subsequent Civil War, only those who had purged themselves by swapping the army for the IRA could be accepted into the New Jerusalem.

Chapter 9

NATIONALIST IRELAND ON THE WESTERN FRONT

The 16th Division had been blooded at Hulluch, in the major gas attacks that the Germans launched in April 1916, and it was in this sector that they remained for the early part of the summer. It was not a pleasant posting, because the trenches were notoriously bad. It was hardly the fault of those who dug them, or who tried to maintain them. The area was flat, low-lying and waterlogged. Even in June the trenches were wet, with water ankle-deep in the bottom.[1] The land had been fought over a number of times, and it was not unusual to find a sandbag being filled with parts of a badly decayed corpse. Although the muddiness of the terrain made sure that there was little mobile warfare, German sniping was intense, and it was hard to feel protected in trenches that were shallower than the norm. In June General Hickie was reprimanded on the state of his defences. He replied that the trenches had started off bad and were constantly being damaged by German shellfire. The excuse was not accepted and Hickie was made to give regular updates on improvements that had been made.

High command decided that there should be no more 'live and let live' sectors during the Battle of the Somme, in order to prevent the Germans moving troops away from quiet areas to reinforce the main point of attack. This meant a series of large-scale raids. The Commander of the First Army, to which 16th Division belonged, was Sir Charles Munro, and he was a great believer in aggressive raids. 16th launched several of these each week from the end of June. The first of these was mounted by 7th Leinsters on the night of 26/27 June. They surrounded several German posts, undertook a great deal of hand-to-hand fighting and remained in the German trenches for up to two hours. They took heavy casualties in this piece of bravado, including a young officer killed. There soon built up among the junior officers in the division a detestation of these raids, which were undertaken, as they saw it, so that a senior officer could have a feather in his cap or a ribbon on his breast. Lieutenant Lyon of 7th Leinsters was ordered to take a patrol into enemy lines. He told his company commander that there were no gaps in the German wire, but that was not considered an acceptable excuse. Lyon took out twenty men and, at the cost of losing half of these as casualties, eventually returned with one prisoner.[2]

Few of the raids achieved much success; possibly the most successful was the one undertaken by 1st Munsters on 5 July. The raiders were split into specialist groups and carefully briefed. They moved carefully to a position 100 yards in front of the British lines. A ten-minute bombardment by British artillery was the prelude and halfway through this, a smoke barrage was begun to protect the torpedo party as it went forward, with soldiers to give them covering fire if they needed it. The torpedo was a long explosive designed to cut a way through barbed wire. The assault party followed close behind, went through the gaps in the enemy wire and bombed the German dugouts. On the other hand, 6th Connaught Rangers, on 28 July, on what they thought was a weak spot in the German lines, advanced without a bombardment in order to achieve surprise. One party of eleven men, led by a second-lieutenant, cut their way in undiscovered. A second group was spotted by the Germans and came under heavy fire. They extricated themselves, but found that they had left behind a badly wounded NCO. A sergeant and two junior officers went out to retrieve him, but he died of his wounds. Another six men were wounded in the raid. In a raid on 31 July, 7th Royal Irish Rifles lost four killed and six wounded.

One of the reasons that 16th Division was so enthusiastic about this phase of raiding is that, in the minds of the officers, it fitted the stereotype of the Irish fighting man, and the divisional staff believed that their men could dominate and torment the enemy. Whether the stereotype was true or not, the opposing Germans did become very quiet. The most aggressive raids came from 47 Brigade, commanded by Brigadier General Pereira, who combined a fire-eating personality with a great concern for his men.[3] He reviewed every raid, particularly those where something had gone wrong. On the night of 29/30 July, 8th Munsters conducted their fourth raid in ten days, attacking German saps and a machine-gun emplacement. The raid failed because the torpedo group could not cut the German wire. One success occurred when the blocking group got through older gaps in the wire and reached the German front line. They drove the German defenders before them into an ambush by bombers. The four raids cost the Munsters ten killed and thirty-five wounded, but Pereira was satisfied that they had done much to lower enemy morale.

For all Pereira's fire-eating demands that his battalions should dominate no-man's-land, it is unlikely that the raids had much effect on the enemy. In fact, given the serious losses in junior officers and in NCOs, it is arguable that all this activity blunted 16th Division's effectiveness as a fighting force, rather than sharpening it. Even before the policy of raiding, the division had lost almost 3,500 casualties that year, including 740 of them killed. From then till the end of August, 6th Connaught Rangers needed more than three hundred men to bring it up to strength. From January to August, 6th Royal Irish had lost more than half its established strength, including nineteen officers. There was a problem in finding Irish recruits to replace these losses. The 9th Munsters had already been disbanded in May and its place taken by 1st Munsters, a regular battalion.

During most of this activity, the major focus of attention in the Western Front was the Battle of the Somme. What had started as a plan which would lead to a breakthrough into open country had developed into a stalemate where one division after another was fed into the mincing machine. Other Irishmen than those of the Ulster Division had taken heavy losses; the Tyneside Irish Brigade suffered 3,000 casualties and didn't get across the start line. It was only a matter of time before the 16th Division became involved. 47 Brigade was attached to the 20th (Light) Division as reserve. Guillemont was the divisional objective. Guillemont had been on the right flank of the British line since the middle of July, and had been attacked without success during August. Progress on this eastern flank of the British line was essential if the French and British were to cooperate properly north of the Somme. By the start of September the capture of Guillemont was becoming more urgent, as the plans for a major attack north toward Flers and Courcelette began to take shape.

The successful attack on Guillemont was made by XIV Corps, and was led by the 20th Division, with the 5th Division to their right. Their target was Leuze Wood, nearly a mile beyond the village, on a ridge overlooking the village of Combles. The southern part of the attack on

3 September suffered the most heavily. There the 13 Brigade had been relying on the French for a final bombardment of their objective, Falfemont Farm, but the French became stuck in Combles Ravine, and were unable to make any progress. The leading waves of the first battalion to attack were wiped out by German fire. To their left the 95 Brigade (5th Division) captured its first three objectives, and reached a line east of Guillemont.

One of the 20th Division's brigades had attacked the village from the north and had suffered such heavy casualties that it had to be withdrawn to be replaced by 47 Brigade. By the time the Irishmen arrived, the village had disappeared, to be replaced by a network of craters. Shell holes only went so deep, however, and below this the German dugouts survived. In addition, there was a complex of underground galleries connecting the different wells, so the enemy had freedom of movement out of view of the British army.

The surface was strewn with dead bodies and wrecked equipment. On 3 September the Irishmen approached their start line over the detritus of previous fighting. The ground was like sludge, and you did not know when you might step on human remains. The artillery bombardment began at 8:15 a.m. and the Germans replied immediately. Many of the British shells were falling short, so it felt as if the troops were being bombarded from both sides. 6th Connaughts lost 200 before they even left the start line and their co, Lenox-Conyngham, was forced to supplement his attacking companies with his reserve companies. A shell hit the door of his dugout during his briefing and killed one of his officers. The medical officer had a break-down when a shell hit a man he was treating, tearing off the casualty's face and spreading it like a mask on the trench wall.[4] In spite of all the chaos around him, Lenox-Conyngham walked calmly among the men, reminding them that they had trained for this.

Zero hour was at noon, when the bombardment was reinforced by attack from the air. The Connaughts, possibly having learned by the example of the Ulster Division, started off just before zero hour and caught the Germans by surprise. Onlookers described their attack as a wild rush, but those taking part maintained their parade ground ranks until they had to split up to avoid shell holes. By that stage, said one officer, it looked like a post-match mob invading a football pitch.[5] There were very few Germans still alive to surrender. On the left, the 7th

Leinsters were attacking south from the remains of the railway station. They had been crouching in shallow, improvised trenches since 3 o'clock that morning. Glad to stretch their legs, they dressed their line and went forward at walking pace. They took the German forward trench easily, and were able to continue forward to take all their objectives. They took position in a sunken road to the east of the village and waited for the expected counter-attack. The two follow-up battalions came forward at 12:50. 8th Munsters passed through the Connaughts and captured a good section of the village, establishing their headquarters among the ruins. During the night, three German counter-attacks were beaten back. At 2:45 on the morning of 4 September, the advance began towards the next target, Ginchy.

The 16th Division had won its first battle honours, and its first vcs. Lieutenant John Holland of 7th Leinsters, an ex-officer of the Volunteers, led his bombing party to capture several German dugouts. Private Thomas Hughes of 6th Connaught Rangers had captured a machine-gun post and several Germans, although he had been wounded himself. Over three hundred German prisoners had been captured, together with six machine-guns and a trench mortar. But it had been done at a cost. The Connaughts had lost their co, Colonel Lenox-Conyngham and were reduced to 400 officers and men. 47 Brigade as a whole had suffered over a thousand casualties out of 2,400 who attacked that day. The Army Commander and the Divisional Commander both noted their thanks in special orders of the day.

The fighting was not over yet. Haig was insistent that high ground to the north of Ginchy and around Leuze Wood were of vital importance. The 16th Division was expected to play its part, but, like the 10th (Irish) Division at Gallipoli, it was not going to be allowed to fight as a single entity. 47 Brigade was returned, with thanks, from 20th Division, but 7th and 8th Royal Irish Fusiliers, of 49 Brigade, were placed under the command of the 5th Division, while the entire 48 Brigade was put under the command of 20th Division. 16th Division was being fed piecemeal into the mincing machine.

The 1st Munsters, the regular battalion which had been assigned to 48 Brigade, was the first in action. Asked to defend a location known as Bernafey Wood on 4 September, they found that there was no shelter except what they could scrape out of the sodden ground. They were under continuous bombardment, with a large proportion of gas shells being used. One gas shell hit battalion headquarters, and seven officers, including the CO, were affected. The CO insisted on staying at his post, but the twenty-four hours they spent in the woods cost the battalion twelve officer casualties and 200 from the other ranks.

7th Royal Irish Fusiliers, who were attached to 5th Division, were ordered to attack the German trench at Combles at 4 p.m. on the same day. The battalion was required to advance through waist-high cereal which had been sown with belts of wire. Stuck in the open, they were standing targets for German machine-gun fire. In spite of this, they tried another attack that evening. This had no more success. The two attempts had cost the battalion eleven officers and 240 men killed or wounded.

That night 8th Royal Irish Fusiliers were brought forward to attack along the Combles to Ginchy road the following morning. Their battalion chaplain, Fr William Doyle, went with them. 'The first part of the journey lay through a narrow trench, the floor of which consisted of deep, thick mud, and the bodies of dead men trampled underfoot.' When they emerged, they found themselves surrounded by British and German corpses locked together in a fighting embrace. The smell was of a charnel house.[6] Fr Doyle based himself in a dressing station in a dugout. When the battalion attacked, some of the troops got further than others, penetrating Leuze Wood, a major objective. Unfortunately for them they were isolated when Germans were able to work their way round them. These forward troops were stuck without food or water, unable to get the wounded back to their dressing stations. To add insult to injury, the British artillery started shelling Leuze Wood, unaware that there were Irishmen in it. Some of the British guns had been used the entire length of the Somme Battle and their mechanisms were worn; as a result, many of the shells fell short and onto the main body of fusiliers.

The Germans counter-attacked at about 7 p.m. Although the battalion on the fusiliers' flank broke and ran, 8th Battalion held, although they were forced to give some ground. By this stage they had lost eleven officers and about one hundred and fifty men.[7] Fr Doyle tried to make his way around as many of the casualties as possible, giving absolution to the wounded and dying. He believed that it was a priest's duty to save souls, so he insisted on being in the action. In order that he could be recognised easily, he refused to wear a steel helmet unless he was specifically ordered. It is true that the men in the 16th Division were very careful in their observation of religion. Willie Redmond noted that they would often line up for a religious service even though they might have come off a long and exhausting duty on the front line. Before any attack, priests would be busy for hours hearing confession. They had a dispensation to receive the Eucharist without having to fast, though many refused to do so, considering that it would be a sin.[8]

The war was not all gallantry and prayer. Between 4 and 8 September, the 8th Royal Irish Fusiliers lost four officers killed and five wounded; thirty-six men killed and ninety-five wounded; and forty men missing. In the fighting in Leuze Wood noted above, they had three company commanders killed and the fourth wounded. Altogether they had suffered 180 casualties. They suffered another on 15 September. A fusilier was shot for leaving his post twice during the battle. There was little sympathy for human frailty among the higher echelons of command.

The casualties continued. On 5 September the 7th Inniskillings took positions between Guillemont and Leuze Wood. They were shelled heavily as they tried to improve their defences. By the morning of 7 September only two officers remained in battalion HQ and one of them had trench fever.

One encouraging aspect was that the British had by now built up sufficient quantities of guns and shells to give the Germans as good as they got in terms of artillery fire. One officer whose position allowed him to look round the battlefield was Lieutenant Colonel Rennie, a staff officer with 16th Division. He found it difficult to get through the lines of guns, which were almost wheel to wheel and which gave off terrible concussions when they were fired.

On 9 September, for the first time, the 16th was given the opportunity to undertake a divisional attack. The village of Ginchy was still in German hands, although it had been subject to constant attacks. The Irishmen were now given the chance. The bombardment started at 5:50 a.m., though zero hour was not until 4:45 p.m.

It was a sadly depleted force that went forward in the evening of 7 September to the start positions. The new CO of the Connaught Rangers, Colonel Fielding, could only muster 250 men. They received general absolution before moving out of their positions in Carnoy. A guide was needed to take them through the devastated landscape: 'Not a brick or stone to be seen, except it has been churned up by a bursting shell. Not a tree stands. Not a square foot of surface has escaped mutilation.'[9] When they eventually got to their position they discovered that they had lost the rear company but, to everyone's relief, the missing men turned up just before daybreak. They spent that night and the next day preparing for the attack.

The British bombardment began on schedule, but Fielding was not impressed. Many of the shells failed to explode in the sodden ground. Many others fell short of the German positions. The Irish trenches were too short and too shallow, and it was difficult for men to move without exposing themselves to machine-gun fire or to the attention of snipers. In addition, there was the usual last-minute change to the orders, which would produce disaster. 47 Brigade were ordered to delay their attack for two minutes, until 4:47 p.m., so that there could be an extra few minutes of bombardment on the German lines. Unfortunately, the order did not reach 48 Brigade, which went over the top on schedule. When the Germans saw this movement, they started a counter-barrage, which caught 47 Brigade just as they were coming out of their trenches. As the leading battalions of 47 Brigade, 8th Munsters and 6th Royal Irish Regiment rose out of the ground they were cut to pieces by close range machine-gun and rifle fire. The German front trench, which everyone had thought to be empty, and therefore had not troubled to shell, was in fact heavily manned and had been completely unscathed.

Ginchy was part of the line held by the 19th Bavarian infantry. The attack of 48 Brigade rolled up one company in the middle of the Bavarian line, and allowed the brigade to occupy Ginchy within an hour of zero-hour. On either side of the village the German lines held, and the British salient in Ginchy was subjected to an unsuccessful counter-attack by another battalion of 19th Bavarians. 48 Brigade captured 200 prisoners during the advance into Ginchy, but suffered heavily casualties during the fight, amongst them two of the six battalion commanders: Lieutenant Colonel H. P. Dalzell-Walton of 8th Royal Inniskilling Fusiliers and Captain W. J. Murphy of 9th Royal Dublin Fusiliers. A series of further battles would soon push the front line away from the village. Despite the popular image of the Battle of the Somme as a total failure, the battle of Flers-Courcelette was actually a minor success, although an expensive one.

Both brigades were shelled heavily during the night, with countless rockets and star-shells from the enemy, wild machine-gun fire and rifle fire.[10] The different battalions improvised trenches by linking shell holes one to another. They were cold and thirsty and had nothing to eat but what they took from German haversacks: black bread and sausage, cigarettes and cold coffee. The 16th Division was relieved by the 3 Guards Brigade early the next morning. The 7th Leinsters were so depleted in numbers that they had to ask the Grenadier Guards to collect the Irish dead. Even the handover was no simple task, as there were still pockets of Germans in the area who had to be dealt with.

In spite of this, most of the infantry were carrying some trophy they had captured; even men on stretchers clung grimly to German helmets or bits of equipment. When the two brigades reached their bases, hundreds from all over the camp who had missed the fight ran out to meet them, standing in silent lines as the exhausted men passed. This time even the generals noticed what had been achieved, and the 16th Division left the Somme with their reputation and honour enhanced. They left behind over one thousand soldiers killed and over three thousand five hundred wounded. Whether it was worth it was an imponderable as far as the soldiers were concerned. The German General Ludendorff said that the later fighting on the Somme was some of the most fiercely contested of the war. When the Battle of the Somme was officially ended on 18 November, the British army as a whole had suffered 420,000 casualties.

The division was now seriously under strength and recruitment in Ireland was poor, for a number of reasons. There was a real danger that its numbers would have to be made up using English troops. In October, 7th and 8th Royal Irish Fusiliers were amalgamated and in November, 8th Munsters were disbanded altogether. Their place in the division was taken by another regular battalion, 2nd Royal Dublin Fusiliers. This pattern continued within the division until March 1918, by which time only two of its original battalions remained. It could be said that Guillemont saw the end of Redmond's Irish Brigade. Its soil provided the graves of many of Redmond's most idealistic supporters. Those who fell might have provided a counterweight to Sinn Féin's advanced nationalism, but it was probably too late. Tom Kettle, who died leading his company into battle on 9 September, had felt so. Kettle was a journalist, a barrister, writer, poet, politician and a man with a drink problem, who had campaigned for Irish support for Belgium. He was not really fit for active service, but felt that he had to match the dangers of those he had encouraged to enlist and had turned down at least two opportunities to leave the front. He knew that, after Easter 1916 and the subsequent executions, 16th Division would be an irrelevance to most people in Ireland. In a letter to his close friend Joseph Devlin he wrote, 'I hope to come. If not, I believe that to sleep here in the France that I have loved is no harsh fate, and that so passing out into silence, I shall help towards an Irish settlement. Give my love to my colleagues—the Irish people have no need of it.'[11]

The 16th Division had earned a rest, and they were allowed a week to rest and refit. After that, they were transferred to IX Corps, part of the Second Army. On 19 September the men mounted trains and were taken to a sector south of Ypres. Before the series of Somme battles, Ypres, with its finger of British-held land sticking into the German lines, had been accepted as the hell-hole of the British front. The Germans held the high ground on three sides of the city, and the ruins of the cathedral, which could be seen from the Irish lines, were a reminder that the enemy could hit any point he wanted within the salient. Divisional HQ was set up at Locre, about a mile behind the front line. The staff officers stayed and were fed in the local convent, looked after by two nuns who had become experts on the British army. A few miles behind Locre was Bailleul, where there were restaurants, a few hotels and bars, shops, a club for the officers and the inevitable ordnance store. It became known as Ballyhooly by the troops.

After the terrors of September, they had a quiet introduction to their new home. Although it seems to go against common sense, the fact that the opposing trenches were so close in this sector was a blessing; neither side could shell the other without grave risk to their own troops. It was not all play, however, because the trenches themselves were in a dreadful state, and it was a full-time job simply maintaining them. The extremely hard winter also discouraged a war-like attitude; staying warm and dry seemed a much greater priority than killing, or even provoking, the enemy. This state of affairs persisted well into 1917. This was lucky, because it gave time for the induction of a great number of junior officers who arrived in the division. Senior officers of each battalion strove to get their units up to strength and to peak efficiency.

The 7th Leinsters did extremely well, with a trench strength of thirty officers and 1,000 men. On parade, other officers commented on their physique, smartness and general appearance. The 2nd Dublins were a regular battalion which had joined the division in November 1916; in May 1917 their trench strength was nearly a thousand men. These were the strongest battalions, however, and many were much worse off.

18 December was the first anniversary of the division's arrival in the trenches, and General Hickie told his men how pleased he had been with their performance that year. In honour of the original Irish Brigade that had fought for France for over a hundred years, 16th Division now adopted their motto: 'Everywhere and always faithful'. Christmas cards printed in green and with the new motto inscribed with a shamrock badge were distributed to the troops.

With Christmas over, activity on 16th Division's front began to escalate. There were daily exchanges of fire, known as 'hates'. In the improved conditions of early spring, training, particularly of young officers, took on a new priority. By April the trench mortaring was getting hotter and hotter every time troops returned to the line. The Germans were using artillery more freely and in one tour of duty in the trenches the Dublins lost half their number as casualties.[12] There was also increased pressure from divisional HQ to mount raids against the German lines. These were warmly detested by junior officers because any risk incurred seemed to fall heaviest on them. It was not simply the risk of physical danger; any raid could turn into a fiasco, and an officer's reputation could suffer. One such raid was launched by the 6th Connaughts on 19 February. They had set off cheerfully enough, under cover of a dense fog, and with miniature Irish flags tucked into their caps or buttonholes. The Germans put up such a stiff resistance that the Irishmen were unable to make any progress, yet lost one officer and eight men killed, two officers and seventeen men wounded, and one officer and six men missing. In a spirit of chivalry that was not always apparent on the Western Front, the Germans allowed a local armistice, and German soldiers helped the Rangers to recover their wounded. General Hickie considered this fraternisation with the enemy and was enraged, but this just emphasised the psychological distance between divisional staff and the soldier in the front line.

The Germans launched their own raid on 8/9 March. There was a fierce bombardment, and the raiders penetrated the division's lines at several points. The 7th Royal Irish Rifles, who had a strength of only two officers and 300 men, were particularly hard hit and lost a further seventy casualties. The Germans made off with twenty-five prisoners and two Lewis guns. The corps commander demanded to know what had gone wrong, but the subsequent report exonerated the 16th Division, saying that the German fire had been particularly accurate and had put several Lewis guns out of action straight away. Brigadier Pereira thought that this had been the worst bombardment his men had undergone since the Somme. He also thought that it had inspired his officers and NCOs with a keen desire to get their own back.

Ironically, it was at this time, when John Redmond's political influence was in terminal decline, that one of his dearest ambitions was fulfilled: that of Irishmen from north and south fighting side by side. The 36th (Ulster) Division was also part of IX Corps and, when 16th Division had a grand dinner on 4 June, there were officers from the Ulster Division present. There were some speeches, and Willie Redmond prayed for 'the consummation of peace between the North and the South'.[13]

By this time preparations were under way for an attack on the ridge south of Ypres, named after the town of Messines. This was to be a limited operation, undertaken to straighten the southern portion of the Ypres front before a major campaign could be launched that would advance as far as the Flanders coast. The ridge itself was of no great height, nowhere higher than 200 feet, but in such low-lying country it gave a tremendous advantage to the Germans, who could see everything that was happening on the plain below. A German order, dated 1 June 1917, stated that the villages on the ridge, Messines itself and Wytschaete to the north, were so important that they must not fall, even temporarily, into British hands.[14]

Preparations for the assault were meticulous. As early as April, 49 Brigade was taking part in full-scale rehearsals on trenches that were replicas of the ones they would face. There was even a line of flag-waving soldiers to represent a creeping barrage. The pressure was heaviest on officers from the rank of company commander down, since they not only had to have an accurate grasp of orders for themselves, but had to be sure that the orders were passed on to subalterns, NCOs and men and that they were understood at each level. On top of that there was the seemingly endless demand for raids to obtain information on the condition of the Germans. In one raid by the 2nd

Dublins, which involved almost half the battalion strength, thirty Germans were captured and another fifty reported killed at the cost of fifty-two casualties. The 6th Connaughts made another large raid on Wytschaete Wood; their seven prisoners and sixty Germans killed cost them three officers—two dead and one blinded for life—and forty casualties among the men.

Plumer, the popular commander of Second Army, had managed to assemble 800 heavy guns and 1,500 field guns, and these opened fire on 21 May. At the end of May, the rate of fire was increased. The attack was to take place on a fairly narrow front, and it was intended to penetrate only a mile or so into enemy territory. Three intermediate objectives were identified where attacking troops could reform while waves of fresh troops leapfrogged their positions and continued the advance. Tanks would be used in conjunction with the infantry. The 16th Division had on its right the 36th (Ulster) Division, and on its left the 19th Division. It was to assault with two brigades forward, 47 Brigade and 49 Brigade. Each brigade would have two of its battalions in front, with the other two in support. As well as its own 48 Brigade, 16th Division could call on a brigade from 11th Division as extra reserve.

One piece of planning for the attack went all the way back to 1916. Mines had been used before, but the scale of the operation surpassed everything previously used. For eighteen months miners attached to the Royal Engineers had been tunnelling under the heights, constructing a system of passages leading to underground chambers. These chambers were each filled with about thirty tons of explosive, a total of 600 tons approximately. These were set off at 3:10 on the morning of 7 June. The Irishmen were shocked by the power of the explosions; the ground rocked back and forwards, water surged up and down trenches. The contrast with the few minutes before was almost literally incomprehensible. The men had been issued with bombs and specialist equipment the previous evening, and had moved forward to their jump-off positions at 10 p.m. British gunfire had died off about 2 a.m. and by 2:45 it seemed as if the whole world was asleep. Now, although the sound of the explosions was muffled by the depths at which they were buried, the men looked aghast as 'trees, mud earth and all manner of articles' went sky-high.[15] One mine went off twelve seconds late, and this caused casualties among 49 Brigade, who had already set off. The air was so thick with dust the Irishmen could scarcely see; some even put on respirators.

The mines had broken the German defences; their wire was smashed to pieces. The few Germans still alive were dazed and in no position to defend themselves. In some of the less damaged dugouts, they found breakfast served but uneaten. In 49 Brigade the 7th Inniskillings had taken their final objectives by 4:45. They had attacked with nearly six hundred men and had suffered twenty-two killed and 150 wounded or missing. The combined battalion of 7th/8th Royal Irish Fusiliers found it no harder. When, at about 8:30, they tried to push forward with B Company to reconnoitre the junction with 36th Division, to their right, they were held up by a German machine-gun post. The Fusiliers eventually captured the post, together with its garrison officer and thirty men. The morning had cost them twenty-seven killed and over one hundred and fifty wounded and missing. At 6:50 the 2nd Royal Irish passed through the lines to take up the attack, aiming for the northern outskirts of Wytschaete. They captured 300 Germans for the loss of eighteen killed.

In 47 Brigade, the 7th Leinsters suffered the shock of losing their co just before zero hour; their battalion HQ was hit by a shell and most of the senior officers were casualties. A captain took command for the attack. As they moved forward they took casualties from machine-guns in Wytschaete village, but they reached their objective at a cost of fifteen killed. The survivors were amazed at how well they could see every detail of the British trenches below them. The 6th Royal Irish Regiment had as its objective Wytschaete village itself, and to go on from this to clear Wytschaete Wood. Two companies were assigned to each task. The village had been converted into a fortress, with an outer and an inner line of trenches. On 3 June, however, the village had been bombarded with a mixture of high explosive and gas shells, and the Irishmen had no trouble taking it. The wood was another matter. Although it too had been saturated by high explosive, enough posts survived for the Germans to be able to make a fight of it. One German position in a ruined hostel to the north of the wood held out till 6:48. The Royal Irish simply bypassed it. The battalion had lost thirty killed and seventy wounded, a light casualty rate considering their task. The 1st Munsters— they had been supposed to have tanks with them, but they all broke down—passed through and reached their objective according to timetable. The 6th Connaught Rangers lost only four killed, but one of those was a grave loss to Ireland as well as to the Rangers.

Willie Redmond was a popular figure in the 16th Division, and was well known throughout Ireland. He was fifty-six years old, possibly the oldest man of his rank serving in the front line. Against his wishes, he had been made a member of the divisional staff—rations officer was how he described himself—but had been granted permission to go forward with the 6th Connaughts that morning on condition he returned when the first objective was reached. He did in fact return, but the call of action was too much for him and he started back towards his old company. A shell splinter hit him in the back just after he left the trench. By a poignant coincidence, it was a stretcher party from 36th (Ulster) Division who brought him back, though he died shortly after reaching the dressing station. He was so well thought of that there was a collection taken by the 36th Division to raise a memorial for him, and chaplains from both divisions officiated at his funeral, while troops from both divisions fired a salute over his grave. He was buried in the garden of the convent at Locre.[16]

Perhaps the 16th Division had performed too well at Messines, because they were now chosen to receive special training as storm-troopers. The GOC of Fifth Army, Gough, specially requested that they be transferred to his army. Gough was of a completely different character from Plumer; in particular, he was not so careful of his men's lives. This was the man who had been given charge of the great attack that had so long been awaited in the Ypres sector. The division spent the month of July receiving their special training. As in the case of Messines, they practised the attack 'forward, backwards and upside down till we could do it in our sleep', according to Fr Doyle.[17]

The Third Battle of Ypres began with a bombardment on 31 July. To an infantryman waiting to attack, the sound of his own guns, no matter how loud, is a friendly one, 'fierce and beautiful beyond imagination'. Unfortunately, the rain began at the same time. It started with the gentleness of a summer shower, but it lasted for most of August. The ground soaked up the rain, and the constant to-ing and fro-ing of guns, troops, wagons and all the impedimenta of war reduced the country-side to a glutinous porridge underneath which there was a sticky glue-like clay that hung on to anything that entered it. One man with the 2nd Dublins wrote, 'Mud awful, no trenches, no shelter, no landmarks, all movement by night.' The horses and mules that were attached to the artillery suffered worst; horses sank up to their breasts in mud. Nothing could move except on properly metalled roads. In the neighbouring 177 Brigade, two men were drowned in shell-holes.[18]

Theoretically, 16th Division was in reserve, not supposed to take part in the battle till 14 August, but long before that the Irishmen were used in forward areas for reinforcements or as carrying parties or carrying out fatigue duties. All this was done in deep mud under the direct gaze of German artillery. By the time the division was scheduled to attack, it had lost one third of its strength through sickness and casualties. The 6th Connaughts lost another CO when Colonel Fielding was hurt in a riding accident and had to be invalided home. The Connaughts had been involved right from the start; on 1 August they were ordered forward at an hour's notice to support 55th Division in an attack on Pilckem Ridge. When the first company went through the German bombardment in single file, following their company commander, and lost only one man wounded, the other companies copied his example. The Irishmen helped to bring in wounded, a task that was appreciated by 55th Division's GOC. Later, they supported 15th (Scottish) Division, when the mud in the trenches was so bad that both rifles and machine-guns jammed again and again. For the days they were asked to hang on they were under constant gas and shell attack. Although it missed the 16th Division's own attack on Langemarck, simply holding the line cost the battalion 250 casualties.

The 7th Leinsters were required to send twenty officers and 500 men forward on 31 July. Their unenviable job was to dig trenches and bury communications cables. They took fifty casualties while doing this. That evening they were sent further forward to support the attack on Pilckem Ridge. Under their oilskins they carried packs, rifles, bombs and spades through the heavy rain. To minimise the danger from shells, each platoon advanced fifty yards behind the one in front. To their side were dead mules and horses, wrecked transport and artillery; most poignant were two mounds of clothes with a stretcher and a third mound in between.[19] They took over the trenches of the Gordon Highlanders, who were down to one officer and sixty-six men. The support trench that they took over was crowded with men: sappers; stretcher-bearers; burial parties; fatigue details. It took five minutes to move fifty yards through the clinging mud. There was a German dugout fifty feet deep, shored up with old timbers. On

3 August they were moved to the front line. Here they were manning the remains of the Frezenberg Redoubt. It was scattered with German maps and bottles of cold coffee, but the rain had flooded the lower layers, so it did not provide shelter against shellfire. The Germans knew the positions of their old lines to the inch, and it was a foolish man who moved about in the open. Tin cans did duty as latrines. They had only the water and iron rations they had brought forward with them. Most who were there thought it was worse than the Somme. By the time they were relieved on 5 August, most of the men were suffering from trench foot. They lost so many men that they were forced to accept a transfer of 100 lads from the Shropshire Light Infantry, nineteen-year-olds who had been conscripted the previous year. In the battle to come, they proved themselves worthy of the regiment.

It took eight days for Fr Doyle and 8th Dublins to reach the front line. They took up their positions around a German blockhouse which, of course, the Germans were able to shell with pin-point accuracy. Fr Doyle spent the next few days wandering around the district with a spade, burying what dead he found. One corpse horrified him particularly: an Irish soldier who had been burned by mustard gas. The priest later wrote, 'His hands and face a mass of blue phosphorescence flame, smoking horribly in the darkness.'[20] Although they were lucky enough to be well supplied with tinned food and with a spirit lamp to make tea, their feet were always in the water, which was a foot deep in the battalion aid post.

The 7th Inniskillings were in line by 6 August, based at Square Farm, about five hundred yards from the Leinsters. This too had been a German command post so, although it was reinforced with concrete, and had a fine view of the surrounding countryside, its position was so well known to the Germans that they used it to calibrate their guns.[21] Snipers and machine-guns covered the ground so effectively that the Skins could not move about till it was completely dark. Platoons could not communicate with companies and these could not communicate with battalion HQ.

After all this, the 16th Division was required to attack Langemarck on 16 August. The attack had been postponed to allow the attacking troops a little rest before their next Calvary. It was to be an attack that should not have taken place. To begin with, the British guns, in spite of firing millions of shells, were not able to silence the German batteries.

At this stage in the war, German airplanes had mastery of the skies and could pass information about troop or transport movements directly to their own gunners. The roads along which British supplies and reinforcements had to be brought were shelled to obliteration. The ground over which the attack was to be made was already soaked. Gough, however, was no Plumer. As a man with a mission who had glory in his grasp, he insisted that the attack went forward exactly as planned. The attack was to go in at daybreak on 16 August.

One comfort was that on their left was a division they could trust, 36th (Ulster) Division, their comrades in arms if not in politics. They were in little better shape than the Irish Division. Both divisions had objectives on the Zonnebeke Spur. To reach this, they had to cross a mile of open country, where the Germans were experimenting with a new type of defensive line. Instead of lines of trenches, roughly in parallel, they were now using a system of strongpoints and pill-boxes, made of iron-reinforced concrete that was impervious to most British shellfire. Even quite large shells seemed to bounce off them, according to the war diary of 8th Dublins.[22] Each concrete position contained thirty to forty men. Each was accessible only through a small entrance at the rear and they were positioned so that each fort was covered by several others. The skill to deal with this new obstacle was beyond most NCOs and junior officers, yet these were the very people who were the key to unlocking such a defence.

49 Brigade had the 7th and 8th Inniskillings in front, with the amalgamated 7th/8th Royal Irish Fusiliers following behind. Not a single battalion was up to strength; the 7th Inniskillings had only nineteen officers and 470 men. There were few senior NCOs or warrant officers, who usually provide the backbone of an infantry battalion. Some of the men had only been told of the attack at 11 p.m. the night before. To add to their difficulties, the brigade HQ had been shelled in the night and most of the senior officers had been gassed.

Nevertheless, the two battalions launched their attack at 4:45 a.m. They captured the main German strongpoint in the area, Beck House, in five minutes and had taken another two strongpoints, Iberian Farm and Delva Farm, before the heavy German machine-gun fire blunted the momentum of the attack. Another fortified position, Borry Farm, defied them. This was held by a full company of Germans reinforced with three machine-guns. It was at this stage the small numbers of attackers began to tell. In the surge forward, they had not been able to mop up the German positions that they had passed. Now they found themselves being sniped at from the rear. The Germans launched a major counter-attack at 8:30 and both battalions were forced back because they were in danger of being outflanked. At 1:30 p.m., an order came from 49 Brigade ordering 7th Inniskillings to take Borry Farm. This was an impossible task, but they tried anyway. The Irish Fusiliers were sent in to support them, but that too was pointless. Unwilling to learn the lesson, the acting brigadier sent in a company of the 2nd Royal Irish Regiment, but they too failed. The 7th Inniskillings had casualties of sixteen officers and 370 men. It was effectively wiped out, because at the end of the day it had one officer and 'no formed body of men'. The Irish Fusiliers took 200 casualties. All there was to show at the end of the day was a vc won by a corporal in the 2nd Royal Irish.

48 Brigade, fighting with 36th Division on their left, had no more luck and, once again, it was largely because of the small number of men they were able to muster. The 2nd and 8th Dublins were amalgamated, yet still numbered only 400 men. The 1st Munsters had to be transferred from 47 Brigade to make up the numbers. As soon as they left their trenches they came under attack from three separate strong-points. Although some isolated parties made progress to within 300 yards of their objectives, a totally unexpected counter-attack launched by the Germans at 9 a.m. drove at them. The forward battalions—7th Royal Irish Rifles; 9th Dublins; 8th Royal Inniskillings—fought on till they were killed or overrun. The few who remained withdrew to the start line.

The corps commander asked for another attack, but the commanders of both 16th and 36th Divisions told him that it was impossible. Not only were the men of both divisions simply exhausted, but the largest brigade had fewer than five hundred men. In the first twenty days of August the 16th Division had lost 220 officers and 4,000 men, almost half of them in the three days 16–18 August. In the quagmire, it took eight men to a stretcher when bringing in the wounded. There were over seven hundred missing, many of whose bodies would never be found. Among the dead was Fr Doyle, who had ignored an order to stay at battalion headquarters in order to be with his men in their agony. Some in the battalion believed that he had been recommended for a vc, but being Irish, Catholic and Jesuit, he was carrying too many disqualifications.[23]

Gough, seeing glory somewhat further off than he had hoped, blamed the 16th Division for the failure of the attack, but Haig believed that the men were exhausted from the way they had been used. The corps commander was full of praise, saying that they had fought well, but the hardships they had been put through before their attack had not been helpful. Gough was to maintain his position, complaining that he knew the 16th Division was not of the highest standard, but giving no reason for his judgement. Since 36th Division had done no better, but were politically secure, they seem to have been safe from criticism.

The division needed the opportunity to recover. They were taken away from the front for some days of rest. After that they were moved to another sector, where they became part of vi Corps of Third Army, under General Byng. Here they had a fairly quiet time for most of September, though it was disturbing to notice the line of tin discs along the trenches, showing where soldiers had been buried in the parapet. The trenches, not surprisingly, were crawling with rats. It was not until October that the division began to build up. In that month there were drafts of Irish NCOs and men from other units. To build up their aggression, they took part in a series of raids. One of these was carried out by 7th Leinsters on a section of the Hindenburg Line known as the Tunnel Trench. This was wide and deep and, every twenty-five yards, a staircase led down into a tunnel some thirty feet below ground. This ran for almost a mile under the trench. At the bottom of each stairway were explosives, primed to be set off if the tunnel was captured. An engineer officer was able to gather valuable information, valuable because it was this trench that the division was to attack during the Battle of Cambrai on 20 November.

The attack of the 16th Division was a diversion, aimed to take attention away from the main attack which involved a concentration of 400 British tanks and six infantry divisions. The corps commander, General Haldane, was known for his meticulous preparation, and his two attacking divisions, the 16th and the 3rd, were well prepared. They had days of rehearsal over replica trenches. This time there was to be no last-minute slog to the front line. The attacking troops began to assemble on 18 November; by 2 a.m. on 20 November they were at their jump-off positions; and at 6:20 a.m. they left their trenches and started following the creeping barrage towards the enemy lines. All three brigades were attacking at once, each of them with two battalions in front and one in support.

47 Brigade was on the right. It had the 6th Connaughts and 1st Munsters in front, with 7th Leinsters behind them. Some of the shells fired had released smoke to make the Germans think it was a gas attack. Sure enough, when the Connaughts reached the German line they found many of the defenders wearing gas masks. The Irishmen soon captured the two forts that were their immediate objectives. When they reached the Tunnel Trench, they found a muddy ditch with curtains covering the entrances to the stairways. It was only when they got into the trench that they realised how well it was constructed. Once the electric wires to the explosives had been located and cut, the Connaughts set about clearing the tunnel itself of Germans. They captured 120 within an hour but, shortly after 7 a.m., they came under attack from Germans on their right flank. The tunnel was supposed to be closed here by a party of Royal Engineers, but their officer had been killed and the job was not done. These Germans were stormtroopers; they had not defended the trench and were well rested and ready to fight. They used copious hand-grenades. An officer and twenty-six men of the Connaughts' right hand platoon were captured. The Connaughts fought hand-to-hand for several hours, but all the time they were being pressed back.

This scare on the right was the only untoward episode in the fighting. The other brigades reached their objectives and large numbers of German prisoners were taken. Later, the land on the flank lost to the Germans was retaken. Most of the 700 Germans captured that day had been taken by 16th Division. Some 500 Germans had been killed, many still wearing their gas masks. Nearly three thousand yards of the Tunnel Trench had been captured. The corps had lost 700 casualties, most of them from 16th Division. It rankled then, that 16th Division was not given a battle honour for Cambrai.

It was time to work out a trial balance for their time in the Western Front. Since they had arrived in December 1915, they had suffered 20,000 casualties. Among their characters, Tom Kettle, Willie Redmond and Fr Doyle were dead, and so were 3,000 other soldiers. It was bad enough that they had got little credit for their achievements from the army hierarchy. Worse, they were becoming an irrelevance, even an embarrassment, to the people at home.

Chapter 10 〜

BACK HOME

For most Irish people, war became a reality when they saw injured soldiers home on leave. Frederick MacNeice was Rector of Carrickfergus on the north shores of Belfast Lough. Here William of Orange had landed in Ireland, and in this part of east Antrim political opinions were strongly held. The Rector had ideas of his own; he had refused to sign the Ulster Covenant and later, when he was Bishop in Belfast, he refused to allow the Union Flag to be draped over the grave of Sir Edward Carson in St Anne's Cathedral. At this early stage he already saw that the cost of war was not something which could be paid in a few years. 'For a generation or more there will be living memorials who have suffered loss in their bodies,' he wrote. 'An eye, a hand or a leg; men who will suffer all their days on earth . . .'[1]

For others, there were social deprivations. Olive Armstrong had been in Ballycastle for her holidays in the summer of 1915. She found the place quiet, but discovered that girls of her age had enjoyed the attentions of young officers of the 9th Inniskillings, who had been in the town in July, with whom they had had a 'gay time'. The absence of men was a serious handicap at social events. Even the number of marriages declined.[2] This was in spite of the almost complete halting of emigration to America, although it could probably be said that the young men who normally emigrated to America would hardly be seen as fit companions of ladies who socialised with the King's officers. In the more industrialised east and north of Ireland most of these frustrated emigrants found employment. In the rural south and west, however, there were fewer jobs and more frustrated emigrants. It is no accident that these were the areas which acted as reservoirs of support for Sinn Féin and the Volunteers in the years after 1916.

To begin with, there was great concern about the economic consequences of the war. The disruption of inessential industries, however, was more than compensated for by the demand for munitions and goods essential for the war effort. Belfast's linen industry was an obvious example, since linen was used to cover the frames of aircraft. Even building construction increased and it was obvious that there was plenty of employment in Ireland for those who were prepared to be adaptable. Industrial relations remained good for most of the war, because many of the more militant trade unionists had been forced to join the army by what Connolly called economic conscription.

The war was to bring one particular advantage to Ireland. The German U-boat campaign cut off Britain from many of its traditional suppliers of agricultural produce; Ireland was well placed to make up some of the deficit. Even before the submarine blockade had time to take effect, the 1914 harvest achieved the highest prices since the 1880s.[3] The wealth of the rural economy gave Ireland a stake in the war; it also gave a good reason for not allowing sons to enlist. Even that most neglected class, the farm labourer, benefited, since there was great demand for farm workers. For the urban worker this produced a problem, since food prices doubled in the years of the war. While wages rose, they could not keep pace with that level of inflation.

The beginnings of a welfare state were starting to take form in the early part of the century and became extended in Ireland, as in Britain, largely because more people qualified for insurance through their jobs. There was statutory protection for those who worked in the munitions industries, although these workers had to accept restrictions on their freedom to change jobs and were not allowed to belong to a trade union. At a domestic level there were advances in mother and child welfare. There was free milk for schoolchildren. There were clinics established for mothers and babies, and breast-feeding was encouraged. A negative aspect to this government involvement in everyday life was the introduction of rationing. Beer and bread became scarce and more expensive. By 1918, there was only one shop in Belfast selling butter over the counter.[4]

Although liquor became more expensive and pubs had restricted opening hours, the influence of the liquor lobby ensured that it was easier to get drunk in Ireland than in Britain. Lloyd George was concerned that excessive alcohol consumption by civilians diminished the quality and quantity of their work. He intended to place supertaxes on spirits, beer and wine. This would have had a disastrous result in

Ireland. Outside the six counties of the north-east, brewing was the largest contributor to the Gross Domestic Product, and distilling was also a significant contributor. In Dublin, Guinness alone had a work-force of 3,500. The supertaxes were dropped in favour of bonding of spirits less than three years old. It was made illegal to buy a round of drinks. Opening hours for pubs were restricted. Even the output of beer was restricted, and pot distilleries like Powers were closed completely in 1917. The amount of beer produced in Ireland halved between 1916 and 1918. The result, as was probably intended, was that there were massive redundancies, with men and families facing destitution or the front.[5] The Director of National Recruiting made this clear when he told men who were losing their jobs that 'he was anxious to find employment for them'.[6] The opposition of the nationalist trades unions did not avail; by 1915 half the membership of the Irish Transport and General Workers' Union (ITGWU) had enlisted.

The Irish Trades Unions Congress (ITUC) was an all-Ireland body, and efforts were made to avoid splits between nationalists and union-ists at all costs. For this reason the executive of the ITUC were less outspoken in their opposition to the war than they might have been. Employers' organisations were mostly in favour of enlistment, and many employers offered to keep workers' jobs till the end of the war, while some even paid allowances to the families of men who had enlisted. At the same time they warned those who did not enlist that they could not be sure of a job even if they stayed, since no one could predict the effects of the war on the economy. Some were reported as dismissing workers so they would have to enlist.[7]

Having lost the battle to persuade their members not to enlist, the trades unions took as their next priority the battle to maintain the welfare of workers; specifically, how to safeguard wages against the demands of higher food prices and of inflation generally. It proved impossible to fight inflation, but the fight for better wages was more successful. This was partly due to the way industrial relations operated during the war. Where in the past employers could use the lock-out to pre-empt any demands for higher wages, they now had to meet the workers' representatives around the negotiating table. If the sides could not come to an agreement, the case was referred to compulsory arbi-tration. Although membership of trade unions in some cases doubled during the war, employers resented what they saw as bureaucratic interference in their affairs. The power of the unions was also increased by the shortage of manpower, particularly after the introduction of conscription in 1916. With that power there was an increased militancy in the membership, who resented the harsh levels of inflation. The *Irish Times* reported the threat of a strike from bakers, actual strikes by gas-workers, grave-diggers and coal-porters, and a strike of railwaymen resolved; all this in one day. After the Easter Rising, this militancy seemed to increase.

Labour organisation reached into areas never before covered by regulation; the world of the landless labourer was one of these. The Corn Production Act became law in August 1917. It set up an Agricultural Wages Board which was designed to ensure that agricultural labourers were paid a minimum wage; it also capped the hours that a man could be asked to work and the rent he could be asked to pay for his cottage. This opened the way for the ITGWU to get involved, and by 1920 some 60,000 agricultural workers had become members.

In some places workers dealt with profiteering shopkeepers by setting up co-operatives. This was just one sign of increasing local cohesion and an increasing solidarity within the labour movement.

A really negative aspect of wartime restrictions was the restriction on building work. For many urban and rural dwellers, their dwellings, bad at the start of the war, were in a horrendous state by war's end. Together with the rise in fuel prices, this negated much of the effort to improve child welfare. It also became harder to get around the country; a shortage of trains made it difficult to organise GAA matches, mostly rural, or monster meetings. This was a source of grievance to much of the nationalist population, even before the vicissitudes of Easter Week 1916.

For many Protestants, the sense of shared hardship, combined with the elevated emotions produced by shared prayer, produced a sense of splendour in the gloom of war. Olive Armstrong, back from her holiday in Ballycastle, had forgotten about holiday romance. She was moved by the singing of the Russian National Anthem at Sunday Service and found the way that people—she meant women—were participating in war work 'perfectly splendid'.[8] Women were drawn more and more into economic life as the war persisted. Irish girls served in Irish as well as British munitions factories, to the benefit of their purses but at the cost of their complexions. In Ireland, as in England, women served as bus conductors or ambulance drivers. From 1917, women undertook heavy farm work. Even before that they worked as clerks or even as department store supervisors. Hundreds served as nurses, many of them, including Maud Gonne, working in hospitals just behind the front line. In 1917 the Dominican convent school in Blackrock had a hockey match against volunteer nurses from the convalescent home at Linden Hospital. Many of the nurses were old girls, and the satisfying result was a draw.

There was one group of women held in unfair contempt for much of the war. Women whose husbands were in the army received regular maintenance payments from the government. By February 1915 the separation allowance was 12s6d for a wife, plus 5s for a first child, 3s6d for a second, and a flat 2s per child for the rest. The fact that their husbands had been forced to join the army from economic necessity was not given consideration. These women were in the very unusual position of having control over their own money. They became a target of nationalist condemnation, as drunk and unnatural mothers, and many became quite literally the target of Volunteer rifle fire during the Easter Rising. Whether this antipathy rose from political concerns, or whether it was that era's reaction to women who took command of their destiny, might be debated. Countess Markievicz, with her revolver and her faintly masculine uniform, was not popular outside the Citizen Army, whereas the passive Grace Gifford, who became a bride to Joseph Plunkett but could never be a wife, was almost sanctified.

Women who donated their time and work to charities received much more general approval. Donations were so generous that by early 1915, at least one charity stopped collecting warm clothes for those at the front.[9] One woman wrote how disappointed she was, because in knitting she felt that she had been 'doing her bit'. At the same time, many educated women felt slighted at being asked only to fulfil women's traditional roles. Yet an examination of what women did in their nursing roles showed that they had plenty of scope for initiative and authority. Women in Ireland had been nursing since before the turn of the century, so the presence of professional nurses was nothing new. What was new was the new class of temporary volunteer nurses, known as Voluntary Aid Detachment (VAD) nurses. These had three months' training in first aid, taught by the Red Cross or St John's Ambulance. In the first month of the war, a ship-load of nurses had left

Dublin and, by 1915, nurses who had been trained in Dublin's Mater Hospital were working in France, Britain, Salonika and Palestine. There was even a slight shortage of trained nurses in Ireland as a result of the rush to volunteer. It has been estimated that 4,500 served in one capacity or another.

Catherine Black from Ramelton in County Donegal had been living in the East End of London when she volunteered for the Queen Alexandra Nursing Service in 1916, aged thirty-four. Marie Martin, of Monkstown, Dublin, oldest daughter of a wealthy family, was accepted as a VAD in 1915, aged twenty-three. She was sent to Malta. Here she found the work anything but glamorous. Mosquitoes and sand-flies played havoc with her face, while she had to stand so much that she suffered from fallen arches. There was the daily grind of having to maintain a sterile environment when so many people were suffering from dysentery, or simply diarrhoea, and sheets had to be scrubbed daily. Most upsetting of all was to see the young men torn and dying. Catherine Black spent most of her war in dressing stations, often just behind the front and in range of enemy artillery. She wrote of the ageing effect of dealing with so much suffering.[10]

Marie Martin was in Dublin on leave at Easter 1916. Her mother sent out tea and rhubarb to the soldiers barricading the end of their street. After that intermission she went to northern France, where she served for a year. Even after that, she volunteered to serve in a hospital for war injured in Leeds.[11]

There was plenty of nursing to be done in Ireland. Soldiers needing long-term care were sent home from France, and new hospitals were established in Britain and Ireland to look after their convalescence. It was fairly common for wealthy people along the east coast of Ireland to donate their grand houses as hospitals. In places like these, both trained nurses and VADS were needed. VADS from Trinity College helped to run a hostel for Belgian refugees in Belvedere Place, as well as doing stretches of six months in the temporary hospital at Mountjoy.

It is likely that most of these nurses and VADS came from the middle and upper-middle classes. But for women of the lower-middle class and of the working class, getting work was not so straightforward. There were traditional patterns of female employment, and these were not affected. Since male unemployment was high at the start of the war, jobs made vacant by those joining the army were normally taken by other men. There was never the chronic shortage of labour in Ireland that occurred in England, because conscription was not extended to Ireland. In Ulster's textile and shirt factories, the female workforce rose by 20 per cent by 1916. Together with the growth in ship-building and other heavy industry, this meant that the north-east's economy boomed, although this involved working longer hours in many cases.

The increase in war-related work in the north-east was offset by a fall in luxury trades, such as the production of lace or ladies' gloves, over the country as a whole. Committees under the patronage of Lady Aberdeen and Lady Dufferin and Ava set up a few enterprises which catered for women who became unemployed as a result of these changes. For all the good intentions of the titled ladies, some of these schemes seem to have been little more than exploitation. In the Donegal relief workshops of 1915, women earned a ten-penny voucher for producing a piece of work that would have earned 15 shillings in Dublin before the war. To be fair, they got their dinner—bread and tea—but they had to redeem their vouchers in the company shop. The Congested Districts Board wanted the people of the west to continue their practice of migrating to Britain for seasonal work, but they were not prepared to do anything about wages or working conditions. Those who did go slept in barns, women and men together, where, packed as close as the farmer could get away with, they ate, slept and sat around when it was too wet to work.

The Ministry of Munitions was set up in 1915 with the purpose of establishing national ordnance factories all over the country. There was little attempt to situate new factories for war work in Ireland. There was little practical reason to place munitions factories in Ireland, and there were good logistical—and security—reasons for not doing so. Many Home Rule MPs tried to put pressure on the government to give Ireland its share, but by the winter of 1917 there were still only five national factories in Ireland, employing a total of over two thousand people. A factory producing 18-pounder shells was set up in Galway in 1917. Here about forty girls were divided into three 8-hour shifts. In a munitions factory which was established in Parkgate Street in Dublin, judiciously surrounded by army barracks, there was a nurse on duty at all times, and a canteen stocked around the clock by lady volunteers. The government was very concerned that the prospect of employment should not tempt men away from enlisting, so there were strict ratios concerning the number of men or boys employed; it could be as low as 5 per cent.

Interestingly, there was no great transfer of women from domestic service to other industries; there was no great rise in advertisements for servants during the war. On the other hand, demand for women in agricultural service was so great that by 1915 young women were earning between one shilling and sixpence and three shillings for a day's work. Although they might not be employed for more than thirty days in a year, the money involved was an important contribution to a family's income. An advantage that rural women had over their urban sisters is that there was less need for them to budget for increased food prices. In 1916, eggs cost 2s per dozen, and a city woman on a separation allowance might not have been able to afford enough eggs to make a difference to her children. Although neither hens nor cows were as productive as they are in the twenty-first century, most countrywomen would have kept poultry and would have had access to local milk at local prices. In towns, milk was so expensive that some tradesmen succumbed to the temptation of watering it.[12]

Although Dublin had the highest death-rate in Ireland, in Ireland as a whole the infant mortality rate was lower than in England and Wales for the duration of the war. In Ireland the rate fluctuated between 8.7 and 8.8 per cent, although there was a peak of 9.2 per cent in 1915. Maternal mortality rose from 0.3 per cent in 1914 to 0.5 per cent in 1916, falling back to 0.4 per cent in 1918.[13] Poor nutrition during the war years, high blood pressure and low iron levels made women more susceptible to puerperal fever, toxaemia and haemorrhage. Women in the higher levels of society had expended much energy in improving the condition of working-class mothers since 1890, but now had other priorities. In Omagh, the Women's National Health Association was more interested in gathering sphagnum moss for making field dressings for soldiers.

One unusual task that was taken on by a number of Dublin's philanthropic women was to patrol the streets of Dublin to protect the morality of the city by discouraging young women and young men— mostly soldiers—from making too free with one another. One woman was absolutely horrified at the boldness of the men and girls. She did not even try to describe what she saw when she shone her electric torch into dark doorways, which makes one wonder what she expected to see. Mothers were not abandoning their babies; there was no increase in infanticide or female drunkenness or even illegitimacy in the war years that have sparked fears of a society breaking down. Perhaps it was prurience, or perhaps it was simply too good an opportunity to see how the other half lived.[14]

The fashions that exemplified the new, liberated woman were more common in the moneyed than in the working classes. Women's silhouettes narrowed and skirts shortened. The new woman did not want to be handicapped by her clothing; she wanted to be able to walk, cycle, get off and on buses and to walk in a busy street without blocking half the pavement. Although they still wore their hair long, women now had swept-back, simple hairstyles. In keeping with this, hats were much smaller. A jacket and skirt combination became almost a uniform for young women.

Many of the women who had tasted freedom during the war never returned home. Nurse Black found that she had accumulated quite a sum of money, since there had been no way of spending her salary in France. She worked on, however and, Ulster Protestant that she was, she was probably delighted when she got a position with the British royal household. Marie Martin's experiences had increased her sense of spirituality, and she worked for a while as a missionary in Nigeria. In the 1930s she founded the Medical Missionaries of Mary, who still bring nursing skills to the needy throughout the world. These two were perhaps unusual, in that their lives out of the home became well known. Millions of men had died in the Great War, producing an imbalance of the sexes which meant that very many more women would have to adjust to life without the prospect of marriage. At the end of the war women over thirty who had a certain amount of property were given the vote. In Ireland north and south there was an increase in certain types of work for women: white collar, retail, industrial and professional. There was great male resentment at this, because this was a time of high male unemployment. More women acted independently of the family home and self-confident young women became a feature of every town and city.

Artists, writers and musicians also wanted to do their bit, as entertainers or as propagandists. Even Yeats, who wanted to be neither, was drawn into writing poems in memory of his friend, Major Robert Gregory.

At this distance, it is difficult to disentangle the thread of Irish politics that wound through all of this. At the war's beginning there were hopes that the shared enterprise would bring together Irish people north and south. This was in spite of the disappointment of having home rule deferred for an indefinite period. As the war progressed and it seemed as if Irish units and Irish efforts were being belittled by the War Office, these hopes diminished and began to be replaced by a certain cynicism. The restrictions, which amounted to group penalties, that followed the 1916 Easter Rising—mass internment, suspension of common-law rights, banning of fairs and markets—reinforced this cynicism and coloured every future initiative by the government in the eyes of nationalists.

There were other developments that happened in the aftermath of the Easter Rising. The Russian Revolution in 1917 encouraged a growing interest in socialist politics in some areas, and a Socialist Party of Ireland, originally formed before the war by Connolly, was reformed in 1918. About ten thousand people attended a meeting at the Mansion House to celebrate Russia's November Revolution. For all the rhetoric engendered at such an event, it was not the revolution itself that made a difference to Irishmen, but the fact that Russia pulled out of the war shortly afterwards. The British and French were now faced with the transfer to the Western Front of all the German armies that had been fighting the Russians. There was a cry for more soldiers, and the only source of these, now that conscription had bled Great Britain dry, was in Ireland. Conscription in Ireland once more became the order of the day, and this was reinforced when the great German offensive in the spring of 1918 seemed set to wipe out the British army before the Americans came into the war. Conscription in Ireland became law in April 1918.

If there was one issue guaranteed to unite the different threads of nationalist Ireland it was this. It was made worse by the fact that conscription was introduced without any formal link to immediate home rule. Ordinary people were angry. The full range of nationalist opinion was represented at an anti-conscription conference at the Mansion House, held with the blessing of the Catholic hierarchy. In a direct copy of the Ulster Covenant, the conference produced its own pledge, to oppose conscription 'by the most effective means at our disposal'.[15] The ITUC tried to get the help of the British labour movement to oppose Irish conscription, but this came to nothing, even though a few Labour MPs opposed the measure.

At a special Labour convention held on 20 April, it was decided to call a general strike for three days later. The strike was a success, with only banks, law courts and government offices operating that day. Many employers even backed their workers, though others threatened to sack them. There were hundreds of meetings across the country, though Dublin citizens were reticent about gathering in large numbers given what had happened in 1916. In the north-east, the strike call was ignored. Even with this, the weight of opposition meant that there was no chance that conscription would be enforced in Ireland. Lloyd George had managed to bring about the worst possible result for his government; he earned the contempt of Irish nationalists by trying to introduce a highly unpopular measure; and he had not got a single Irish soldier conscripted into the army. The trade union movement earned great credit for its organisation, and entered a brief summer basking in the approval of the people, before things moved on and anti-socialist undercurrents of Irish society once more asserted themselves.

In spite of these excitements, the war left little legacy on the nature of the Irish economy. Unequal wealth at the end of the war encouraged the Irish worker to get organised. It was a long way from the Dublin lock-out of 1913. Yet Ireland had not seen the levelling of the classes that had occurred in Britain.

Soldiers coming home brought the same physical and mental scars whether they lived in Britain or Ireland, whether they lived in Belfast or Dublin. What they found when they got there, however, displayed significant differences between the two islands. In Britain there were many social problems to face and overcome, but in Ireland the soldiers were returning to a country where a very different sort of war was in preparation. Demands were made on these veterans that put them in invidious positions. It is not surprising that individuals reacted in different ways.

As noted above, veterans had been seen around Ireland for some time. Fewer than five thousand Irishmen had been discharged as disabled before the Great War's end, but many thousands more had come to Ireland to convalesce or to die. Over twelve thousand were transported by hospital train from Dublin's docks to different hospitals around the country. Convalescents wore a distinctive blue uniform and became a common sight in the streets of Ireland. Those whose convalescence took place after the Rising of 1916 experienced a degree of animosity, especially in the streets of Dublin.

One of the more troubling conditions suffered by soldiers on the Western Front was shell-shock, or neurasthenia. The first Irish hospital designed to deal with this condition was opened in Lucan in 1917. In the belief that a healthy body would induce a healthy mind, they slept in the open air, were taught crafts such as basket-making, looked after pigs and rabbits, and were encouraged to use the golf course. Two more hospitals for shell-shock were opened, one for the UVF in Belfast and another in Leopardstown. People had an almost guilty curiosity about these and other damaged soldiers. In 1919 two different models of artificial hands and arms were compared at a summer fete, where amputees demonstrated activities from chopping wood to cutting up food properly.

Some veterans seemed to be able to ignore their disabilities. In spite of having been blinded, Captain Gerald Lowry retrained as a masseur and osteopath and took up boxing as a hobby. He lived a full and very active professional and social life, and there was even a film made of his exploits. Not all veterans were capable of displaying such determined self-improvement. One ex-rugby player, who had served in Gallipoli and Salonika, placed himself in front of a train at Dalkey and was killed, only a month after being invalided out of the army; he had been suffering from severe depression. Others survived longer. A Lurgan weaver killed himself two weeks after his mother's death in 1921. The inquest heard that he had problems sleeping and had resorted to alcohol. Grief at the loss of his mother was the final straw. Even when veterans did not resort to self-harm, many of them took a long time adjusting to home. One of the saddest cases was of a UVF veteran who lived in East Belfast. During the Belfast Blitz of 1941 the strain was too much for him. When the bombing started he disappeared, and the neighbours found him next day in his allotment, where he had excavated a slit trench in which to spend the night.[16]

Many Irish veterans found that the unofficial distrust of them that had been apparent from the War Office during the war had now become official policy. In an effort to ensure that ex-army weaponry did not reach the Volunteers, Irish servicemen were discharged from the army in Britain. Here they were given their discharge papers, one month's pay and civilian clothes. They were allowed to keep their army greatcoats, but had the option of turning it in for £1 at a railway station. In unionist communities they were welcomed home for having done a dangerous job well. Matters were more ambiguous in nationalist areas. In Belfast, the veteran nationalist Joe Devlin hosted a reception in Celtic Park, but nationalist troops boycotted the Peace Day parades on the grounds that the promises of 1914 had not been fulfilled. In Derry, they went a step further and marched in a joint Hibernians/Sinn Féin parade held on 15 August.

For most men, family relationships were more important than political gestures. Most of the men had lived in an all-male society for years, working within a set of mores very different from those within a household. Most wives, especially, had been their own bosses, making their own decisions. Mothers and fathers had said goodbye to young lads and now were greeting grown men with minds of their own. Given the violence of their lives over the past years, it is, sadly, understandable that domestic violence often marred the attempt to re-establish married life.

There was also the necessity of finding employment, especially for those who were disabled. Even by 1920 there was no government agency which could give reliable figures for the number of disabled in Ireland. A civil servant from London who visited Cork in that year was horrified to find that nothing had been done to process thousands of applications for financial assistance that had been made in Munster alone.[17] Although Irish veterans were entitled to the same benefits as their equivalents in Britain, the political climate in Ireland after the war made it a matter of luck as to whether they received them or not. In local authority areas controlled by Sinn Féin, ex-soldiers were refused admission to technical colleges, hospitals and asylums. The premises of the War Pensions Committees came under attack and so did the premises of the two main veterans' associations, Comrades of the Great War and the Federation of Discharged and Demobilised Soldiers and Sailors. Where the government initiatives were allowed to operate, veterans were able to undertake courses at university as well as technical colleges, and could seek placement on farms or in factories.

Unemployment among ex-servicemen was higher in Ireland than in Britain, where only 10 per cent were out of work by the autumn of 1919. In Ireland 46 per cent of veterans were living on twenty-nine shillings a week, the out of work donation.[18] A year later, the figure had risen to 50 per cent. The donation period was due to expire in 1920, and many Irishmen took advantage of subsidised resettlement in the British colonies.

Although the situation in the north-eastern counties was not quite as severe, veterans of the UVF had a much better chance of finding employment than others. As the Irish Revolution developed, Catholics in particular were vulnerable in the heavy engineering industries in Belfast. Among the many Catholics expelled from the shipyards were men who had served in the 10th and 16th Irish Divisions. Loyalists even threatened Catholic patients who were being treated for shell-shock in the UVF clinic. Twenty had to be moved for their own safety.

In Great Britain there was a scheme whereby employers undertook to hire disabled veterans. This scheme was never extended to Ireland, on the grounds that Sinn Féin would make it unworkable. Even in Northern Ireland, where it was introduced after 1922, there was a very poor take-up by employers; only in the Northern Ireland Civil Service did disabled veterans find preferential treatment. Many were reduced to becoming organ-grinders, or door-to-door salesmen. An ex-soldier wanting to become a jarvey or porter could get a small grant towards buying a pony and trap. A parish priest in County Galway managed to extract loans for ex-navy personnel to buy fishing boats. When the British Legion came to be formed, it operated within the Free State and set up a furniture factory in Dublin and a car-park service in Belfast.

Immediately after the war the British government had tried to settle ex-soldiers in smallholdings, but Sinn Féin revived ancient animosities by claiming that the government was settling foreign soldiers in Ireland as Cromwell had centuries before. Even where men were able to get land, they found their homes and allotments attacked and sales of their produce boycotted. After 1920 re-housing was moved to the urban environment, and 3,600 houses were built in Ireland, North and South, within the next fifteen years, often in the form of garden suburbs. In this, and in this only, Irish veterans did better than their British counterparts.

It is hardly surprising, given the attitude of Sinn Féin towards them, that very few veterans joined paramilitary organisations. Thousands, however, re-enlisted in the army and police forces. The Black and Tans and the Auxiliaries both had Irishmen serving in their ranks.[19] Most of those who did join the IRA acted as instructors for the flying columns.

Many ordinary ex-servicemen got into trouble with the IRA; between 1919 and 1924, more than one hundred and twenty civilian veterans were killed. Yet not every ex-soldier supported government policy, and many were openly critical of the policy of reprisals, unofficial or otherwise. Some of these actually killed veterans.

The Civil War offered an opportunity to veterans to participate on behalf of the state and very many joined the National Army, making up nearly half of all recruits. More than six hundred veterans served as officers in the first few years of the new army, including at least one who had served in the American army. In the North, the Special Constabulary was also largely made up of veterans from the Western Front. On all sides ex-comrades were killed, and it took many years before the aftershocks of the Great War gradually faded away.

Chapter 11 ~

THE RESURRECTION OF SINN FÉIN

It was not just the British who thought of Easter 1916 in terms of a Sinn Féin rebellion. The fact that individuals held multiple memberships of Irish cultural and political organisations and moved freely among them made it difficult for the authorities to decide which one had pre-eminence. Sinn Féin had a nice catchy ring to it; the fact that it was in a 'foreign' language meant that it could mean what a person wanted it to mean; finally, it emphasised the separateness of advanced nationalists. The Rising had not been organised by Sinn Féin, although individual members did take part in the fighting. Arthur Griffith had even offered to fight, although he was certain the effort would fail, but he was asked not to get involved, since his great talents in propaganda would be needed in the future.[1] He was, of course, arrested in the sweep of all dissenters after General Maxwell took control, and this was probably good for his image and reputation. He was interned rather than imprisoned and was released towards the end of the year. As soon as he was free, he began publishing attacks on the proposed partition of Ireland and on the threat of conscription in Ireland. He also began to put forward the policy that Ireland should be able to put her case for independence to the Peace Conference that was sure to be held when the war was over.

He was speaking to a much more sympathetic audience than he would have found if he had been writing a year previously. In the words of Yeats, all had changed utterly. The sense of moral shock and revulsion felt by the Irish public after the executions was made worse by the coercive policy enacted under martial law. Dillon warned Lloyd George of this in June, telling him that the temper of the country was bad, but the temper of Dublin was ferocious.[2] There was a growing cult of martyrdom around the dead leaders, helped by repeated commemorative masses being held in the churches of Dublin. As relatives of the dead left these masses, they would be greeted by cheering crowds who would go on to sing provocative songs. Dillon thought that some of the organisers, 'particularly the women', were hoping to provoke an intemperate reaction from the military.[3]

Martial law was another irritant. Even when a new Chief Secretary, H. E. Duke, had been appointed, Maxwell remained the power in the land. Every prospect was vile. The home rule negotiations were a farce. The prosecution of Roger Casement was conducted by his political opponent, Sir Edward Carson, a man who himself had advocated treason to the UVF. The details of the Sheehy Skeffington murder, and the lenient way in which his murderer was treated, contrasted sharply with the sentence of death which Casement, who had killed no one, received. And, as Griffith was warning, there was still the danger of conscription being extended to Ireland.

What the British should have been worried about, but weren't, was the fact that the organisation which had brought the Rising about was still in existence and still active. The Volunteers might have gone, but members of the IRB were meeting within days of the executions. Two new organisations had been added to the fray: the Irish National Aid Association; and the Irish Volunteers' Dependants' Fund. Although started by people who wanted to do something for the families of the dead, the wounded and the prisoners, by their very existence these organisations provided a focus for the bitterness, even hatred, that was growing like some bacterial culture on the psyche of nationalist Ireland.

In retrospect, the way in which this moral force was harnessed seems simple enough. Count Plunkett, the father of the executed leader Joseph Plunkett, stood as an Independent candidate in the North Roscommon by-election of January 1917, opposed by a Parliamentary Party nominee. Sinn Féin gave vigorous support to the Papal Count and he won easily. He chose not to take his seat in Westminster. Redmond was shattered by this proof that the IPP had lost its grip and in particular that the country seemed to be supporting what he saw as men of violence. Dillon took it so seriously that he took personal charge of the next election, South Longford, in May. 'We have the bishop, the great majority of the priests and the mob, and four-fifths of the traders of Longford,' he wrote to Redmond. 'If in the face of that we are beaten, I do not see how we can hold the party in existence.'4 They were beaten, though by a margin of only thirty-seven votes, and were beaten again in July and August.

The fifth by-election of the year, in East Clare, was significant for a number of reasons. In the first place, it had been the constituency of Redmond's very popular brother Willie, and had been caused by Willie's death on the Western Front. Secondly, it marked the emergence on the political stage of the man who would dominate Irish politics for the next half-century. Éamon de Valera's birth was no promise of great things. His mother was Kate Coll of Bruree in County Limerick. She was the eldest of four children whose father died when she was seventeen. She went to America when she was twenty-two and entered domestic service. Two years later she married a Spanish music-teacher, Vivion Juan de Valera. They had a boy, Edward, born on 18 October 1882. It does not seem to have been a happy home, and his father left it in 1884 and died the following year. Kate sent Edward back to Bruree, where he lived with his granny, his Aunt Hannah and his Uncle Patrick. Although Kate married again and had a second son, she left Edward in Ireland. He was expected to work for his living; his Uncle Patrick gave him a beating when, for example, he played hurling rather than working in the fields. The young boy might never have escaped had it not been for the help and support of his parish priest, and for his own hard work at school. He eventually won a scholarship to Blackrock College and from here to University. He became a mathematics teacher and mathematics was to be a life-long love.

A second love was the Irish language and through this he found his way into Irish nationalism as Éamon de Valera. He joined the Volunteers at the start and showed so much promise that he was chosen as a battalion commander, even though he was not at the time a member of the IRB. He was sentenced to death in his court martial after the Rising. His career would have ended there but the American Consul in Dublin intervened, claiming that de Valera was an American citizen, and the death penalty was commuted to life imprisonment. In prison he had set about establishing himself as a leader. Shortly after he had arrived in Dartmoor he became aware that MacNeill had given himself up and had joined the others in jail. On the morning after MacNeill arrived, the prisoners were lined up outside the cells, waiting to be taken out for exercise. When he saw MacNeill, de Valera swung out of line and gave the order, 'Eyes left.' The prisoners obeyed, and de Valera had established three things. He was a leader, and seen as one by his fellow-prisoners. The authorities recognised this immediately; although he was ordered back to his cell he received no punishment. MacNeill also recognised the gesture as one of peace; the prisoners had honoured him, and he would not disown them when he was set free. The first step had been taken to nationalist unity.

Now in East Clare de Valera took as his manifesto the Proclamation of the Republic made on Easter Monday by Pearse and the others. He was careful not to be too prescriptive in his definition of a republic. This is what the leaders had wanted, but he used it as shorthand for an independent government of Ireland. If it turned out that the Irish people wanted another form of government, then so be it, 'as long as it was an Irish government'.[5] All summer, the people had been voting against the Parliamentary Party. Now they had a chance to vote for the leaders of 1916. It was no contest, and de Valera won by 5,000 votes to 2,000. Although the Parliamentary Party still had support, and would still win constituencies, they had lost their greatest strength, the ability to claim that they alone spoke for Irish nationalism.

There were other major developments. America had come into the war in April 1917 and had become involved, said President Wilson, because 'every people has the right to choose the sovereignty under which it shall live'.[6] In addition, America's need to get support for the war from Irish Americans meant that Britain had to stop its policy of coercion in Ireland and try to get some form of satisfactory self-government for the country. Eoin MacNeill, de Valera and twenty-four others had written to President Wilson informing him that the Irish people were intent upon establishing their right to defend themselves against external aggression, interference and control. Lloyd George tried an initiative of his own, setting up a Convention that would allow Irishmen to sort out their future for themselves. It was ignored by Sinn Féin, but John Redmond tried once more. The unionists remained inflexibly opposed to any form of home rule and the effort was a waste of time.[7] It disposed of the myth that there was a chance of a settlement based on a united Ireland, although that is easier seen with hindsight than it was at the time. It is now possible to see that the unionists, however unsure of themselves before the war, were now absolutely certain that they had the clout to refuse home rule.

Of more immediate importance was the fact that, in any future political battle between the rump of the Parliamentary Party—and it was, at least up till the General Election of 1918, a big rump—and Sinn Féin, the odds were heavily weighted on the side of Sinn Féin. For the second time in twelve months, Redmond had committed his full prestige to a gamble that was no more than that. When his policy crashed, it took the party with it. The government persisted in its old policy of ineffective coercion, even though this had the effect of encouraging support for Sinn Féin: they proclaimed meetings illegal, banned uniforms and the carrying of arms, and started to arrest individuals whose opposition to the regime was articulate enough to be dangerous. One of those arrested was Thomas Ashe, a Kerry school-master, who was prominent in the reorganisation of the IRB. He and others were held in Mountjoy Jail, in Dublin. A number of them went on hunger strike and the prison authorities chose to force-feed them. As a result of injuries sustained in this process, Thomas Ashe died in hospital on 25 September.

The funeral arrangements were reminiscent of those made for O'Donovan Rossa, two years previously. The Volunteers marched in uniform, carrying rifles, defying the authorities. There was no oration at the graveside; three volleys were fired over the grave, as if to say that guns might talk in future. A strapping young man stood by the grave and said, 'There is nothing more to be said. The volley which we have just heard is the only speech which it is proper to make above the grave of a dead Fenian.'[8] Few who attended knew his name, though he was to become one of the two great icons of Irish republicanism. His name was Michael Collins.

Collins had a very different background from de Valera. He was born near Clonakilty in Cork, had left school aged sixteen and had emigrated to London, where he got work in the post office and, later, with a firm of bankers. In London he became closely involved in the thriving Irish community. He was noticed in the GAA and Gaelic League, and invited to join the IRB in 1909. He joined a London company of the Volunteers in 1914, but returned to Ireland when conscription was introduced in Great Britain. Once again he was involved with the IRB and Joseph Plunkett chose him as his aide during the week in the GPO. Because he was unknown to the Dublin police he escaped being court-martialled, but was interned for a few months in Frongoch, in North Wales. When he was released he returned to Dublin, when he became an important cog in the fund-raising and reorganisation that was going on. He proved his ability as an organiser and was elected to the Supreme Council, where he worked closely with Ashe. He gained a brash repu- tation and the nickname 'The Big Fellow'; people either loved or detested him. Underneath this he was the most realistic of politicians and was determined that no more lives would be lost for high-blown sentiment or romantic idealism. He believed that Pearse had betrayed the Volunteers, leading them to their deaths as a gesture.

In that autumn of 1917 relations were strained between the IRB and the Volunteers, and between both organisations and Sinn Féin. One reason was that some of those who had fought during Easter Week had seen the scale of the deception that had been used against them and were reluctant to trust themselves to IRB control once more.[9] Cathal Brugha, that indomitable fighting man, believed that there was no longer a need for the IRB, that it had served its purpose. For people like de Valera, who had joined the Brotherhood reluctantly, who were still observing Catholics, it was respect for the Church's ban on such secret organisations that weighed heaviest. He also believed that it was the excessive secrecy of the IRB that had led to the military disaster of Easter Week. It was important that Sinn Féin be recognised for what it was: a non-violent organisation and not the over-arching controller of all advanced nationalism. This was important because of the need not to be disrupted by arrests and deportations. The three main organis- ations and their aims might be summed up as follows. The IRB were committed to the achievement of independence by armed methods when they had the support of the Irish population, as was consistent with their constitution. The Volunteers were committed to the use of force in a defensive capacity; against the imposition of conscription, for example. Sinn Féin was committed to non-violent, constitutional means. The amiable Count Plunkett had already sponsored a con- vention in April 1917, where he hoped some form of unity could be established among these groups. This only brought the problems out into the open, without providing a solution to them. The best that was achieved was the setting up of a National Council so that the different organisations could at least keep in touch.

Another, much more successful, attempt at unity took place in October. This was when Sinn Féin had traditionally held its Ard-Fheis, or annual convention. Before the Ard-Fheis proper was held, a committee met which was charged with drafting a new constitution. This kept the battle between republicans and non-republicans away from the public view. Cathal Brugha was the most outspoken of the republicans, but was faced by Arthur Griffith, who held firmly to the doctrine of non-violence that he had been advocating for ten years. It seemed as if the meeting was going to break up in disarray, just as before. The difference this time was de Valera, empowered by his recent success in East Clare. He suggested a neatly framed compromise:

> Sinn Féin aims at securing the international recognition of Ireland as an independent Irish Republic.
> Having achieved that status the Irish people may by referendum freely choose their own form of government.[10]

The full meeting of the Ard-Fheis, held on 25 October, was attended by over one thousand delegates. It had the potential of being as divisive as any of the meetings before, but it passed in unexpected harmony. This was partly due to the gracious way in which Griffith stood down as President of the organisation he had founded in order to allow de Valera to be elected unopposed. Even this might not have been enough to maintain unity if it had not been for the careful phrasing of de Valera's formula. He had recognised that in America, that greatest republic, the people had established the fact of their independence before deciding on a way to govern themselves. Even among the republican delegates at the Ard-Fheis, there were few who expected another insurrection.[11]

Shortly after becoming President of Sinn Féin, de Valera also became President of the Volunteers. This meant that the majority of individuals pledged to full Irish independence at least had the unity of a single leader. Things did not work out as simply as that. The IRB quickly moved to establish three of their number on the Volunteer executive: Michael Collins became Director of Organisation; Diarmuid Lynch was Director of Communications; and Sean McGarry was appointed General Secretary. Future friction was almost guaranteed when Cathal Brugha, who hated the IRB, was appointed Chief of Staff.

For the time being, advanced nationalism had achieved a shape and, to some extent, a strategy. That was no guarantee of future success, however, and even the series of by-election successes seemed to dry up, when the Parliamentary Party won three in a row. Worse, some of the wilder spirits among the advanced nationalists began to revert to the tactics of the land war, raiding homes for arms and breaking up large ranches in the west and handing them out for tillage to small farmers and labourers. The risk of social revolution could frighten off those who would support political revolution. Sinn Féin was faced with the dilemma of how to deal with it.

In March 1918, there was a development on the Western Front that affected almost every family in Ireland. America had entered the war on the Allied side in 1917, but it would be many months before American troops would be available to fight in Europe. The German staff calculated that the entry of the Americans would tilt the balance inevitably in favour of the Allies and decided on a bold stroke. They would launch a major offensive against the French and the British that would overwhelm them before the Americans could make a difference. This attack, which came to be known as the Kaiser's Battle, was very nearly successful, and swept up several British divisions in its rush towards the sea. The 16th Division and the 36th (Ulster) Division were wiped out, suffering the greatest losses of any divisions in the British army. Those who were not killed or wounded were captured by the advancing Germans. This was only a part of the catastrophe that was looking the government in the face. They needed extra troops, 150,000 of them, and the only part of the United Kingdom where they might be got was Ireland. Conscription in Ireland was on the cards yet again. Since ministers in the Cabinet were contemplating the conscription of men up to the age of fifty, or even fifty-five, in Great Britain, from the British perspective it seemed only right that Ireland should contribute more. It was beyond their comprehension that nationalists in Ireland no longer saw it as their war.

When Lloyd George introduced a Bill in the House of Commons which would allow the government to apply conscription to Ireland by Order in Council, he was warned by Dillon, 'All Ireland will rise against you.'[12] When the bill became law, the nationalist members of Parliament returned to Dublin. As Dillon had warned, all the nationalist organisations in Ireland came together in a show of solidarity that had not been seen since the beginning of the war. Even the Catholic hierarchy showed support, saying that a people had a right to oppose such an unjust law by any means. The fact that they added the qualification 'that are consonant with the laws of God' went largely unnoticed by the laity.[13] Only two days after the bill had passed through Parliament there was a meeting at Dublin's Mansion House under the auspices of the Lord Mayor where all threads of nationalism were brought together. The meeting produced a pledge: 'Denying the right of the British government to enforce compulsory service in this country, we pledge ourselves solemnly to one another to resist conscription by the most effective means at our disposal.' This pledge was signed by thousands outside masses around the country the following Sunday. To add support, the Irish Congress of Trade Unions called a twenty-four-hour general strike which shut down the entire country except for some areas in the north-east.

The truce between the Parliamentary Party and Sinn Féin did not last long. There was a by-election in East Cavan and Arthur Griffith stood against the Parliamentary Party candidate. It might have been an interesting contest, and it might have been a close result, but the government, in its blundering way, managed to intervene in a way that guaranteed a Sinn Féin victory. Firstly, Wimborne was replaced as Viceroy by Lord French, who was given wide powers for containing disorder. On 17 May almost the entire leadership of Sinn Féin and the Volunteers was arrested, although Michael Collins and Cathal Brugha escaped the net. The press was notified that Sinn Féin had been conspiring with the Germans. The evidence was somewhat flimsy. Intelligence reports from America suggested that Devoy had been in contact with the Germans after the Easter Rising; that the possibility of a further arms shipment had been discussed; even that arms had already been sent to Ireland, but had failed to arrive. One concrete piece of information was that a member of Casement's Irish Brigade had landed from a German submarine near Galway, but was arrested. The Germans had sent him on their own initiative to see whether there was any likelihood of another rising. He may have got a message through to the IRB, but there was no reply from Collins, since at that time the priority of the IRB was to conserve itself.[14]

These bits and pieces allowed the government to persuade itself that these dangerous individuals must be taken out of circulation. There is evidence that most of these dangerous individuals knew in advance of the plan to arrest them, but decided to allow themselves to be put in jail because of the effect it would have on public opinion. In this they were correct, and Griffith had the satisfaction of learning, in his prison cell, that he had won the election by over a thousand votes.

The arrests following the German Plot were only a beginning. On 3 July the Volunteers, the Gaelic League and the various manifestations of Sinn Féin were proscribed—made illegal—because of their grave menace to the peace of the country. Over a thousand arrests were made, but the leadership simply went underground. There, unseen, they became a greater menace than ever. The competence of this small group of leaders was such that they not only preserved Sinn Féin but expanded it. It was at this time that Michael Collins became pre-eminent in the struggle for independence. One of his great achievements during the period was to build up an intelligence network from contacts in the post office, the prison service; even in Dublin Castle and among the detectives of G Division in the Dublin Police. While he was doing this, Cathal Brugha and his deputy Richard Mulcahy and Rory O'Connor concentrated on military training, discipline and tactics, while Piaras Béaslaí produced the first issue of *An t-Óglach*, which became the main organ for propaganda against conscription. Harry Boland, a Dublin tailor, concentrated on building up Sinn Féin membership, which grew from 66,000 at the start of 1918 to 112,000 at the end of the year.

It was the cloud of conscription overhanging the country that kept the nationalist effort together. Most of those who joined the Volunteers at this time were opposing conscription, not embracing revolution. Nevertheless, they were made to realise that there was a real possibility that they would have to fight. Both Piaras Béaslaí and Ernest Blythe wrote that the imposing of conscription would be an act of war on the Irish people and had to be met by war. Blythe went further, arguing that anyone who co-operated with conscription in any way was an enemy of the people and should be shot, 'or otherwise destroyed'.[15]

These admonitions were never put to the test, because the Great War was suddenly over and conscription was an irrelevance. Nevertheless, in the cold savagery of Blythe in particular, there was an indication of how far Ireland had come since 1916. The determination, which opponents might call fanaticism, which Sinn Féin had used in opposing conscription was now available for the General Election which was scheduled for December 1918. When the old Parliament was dissolved, the Parliamentary Party held sixty-eight seats, William O'Brien's supporters and a couple of Independents held ten, the Unionists had eighteen, while Sinn Féin had seven. A few weeks later, in a Parliament where the Irish had been allocated two extra seats, the Unionists had increased their representation to twenty-six, O'Brien's supporters, and O'Brien, were no longer represented and the Parliamentary Party had six, of which four were in what would be border constituencies. The other seventy-three seats went to Sinn Féin, although the fact that some Sinn Féin candidates had entered for multiple constituencies meant that the seventy-three seats were held by sixty-nine people. Although Dan Breen called this 'the greatest manifestation of self-determination recorded in history', it is important not to be too simplistic in the interpretation of the results.

Firstly, 31 per cent of the electorate did not vote. Of the votes cast, only 47 per cent were cast for Sinn Féin. On the other, hand, Sinn Féin was unopposed in twenty-six constituencies. The Labour Party had stood back, and they might have taken some seats. There were complaints of electoral fraud, but this could hardly have made a substantial difference to the result.[16] One change that almost certainly had benefited Sinn Féin was the extension of the franchise to younger voters: men over twenty-one and women over thirty could now vote. It was among these two classes of voter that support for the radical politics of Sinn Féin was most secure. As Richard English has noted, it was not the last time that British legislation would benefit anti-British nationalism in Ireland.[17]

It is worth considering what people thought they were voting for. At the centre of the Sinn Féin message was the idea of Ireland achieving self-determination and becoming a sovereign power. This was not necessarily a vote for a war of independence. For the time being, the role of the Volunteers was to defy the authorities.[18]

As for the elected members of Sinn Féin, it was difficult to do anything constructive with their electoral triumph, since many of them were still locked up in prison. Those who were at liberty did what they had promised they would. They turned their backs on the historic legislature on the eastern island and established their own forum for government. After a meeting held on 7 January 1919, Sinn Féin sent out invitations to all those successful candidates who had stood for Irish constituencies to attend the first meeting of the Assembly of Ireland, or Dáil Éireann. These invitations were ignored by all but Sinn Féin, and many of their own successful candidates were still in prison, so it was a group of only twenty-seven who met on that historic day. They kept themselves busy, however. Cathal Brugha was elected presiding officer for the day; the roll was called and absentees noted; and temporary clerks were appointed. The first order of political business was the adoption of a provisional constitution. This called for the election of a Prime Minister, and of four other ministers to be chosen by him to run departments of Finance, Home Affairs, Foreign Affairs and Defence. The Assembly claimed for itself full legislative and financial control. It could also dismiss the government by unanimous vote. The ministers appointed were: Cathal Brugha, Prime Minister; Eoin MacNeill, Minister of Finance; Michael Collins, Minister of Home Affairs; Count Plunkett, Minister for Foreign Affairs; and Richard Mulcahy as Minister of Defence.

Some major statements were then read to and approved by the Dáil. The first was a Declaration of Independence which claimed that the Irish were a free people who had resisted foreign usurpation by word and in arms. The Dáil was the only body which could legislate for Ireland since it was the only body to which the Irish people would give their allegiance. It was presented to the Dáil as a reaffirmation of the Proclamation of the Republic in Easter 1916, and it echoed the wording of the original in places. It also claimed recognition and support from all free nations. To make sure this message was heard, the members appointed de Valera, Arthur Griffith and Count Plunkett as delegates to the Peace Conference.

The next initiative was a Democratic Programme, written by Thomas Johnson, the labour leader, based on premises laid out by Pearse in his pamphlet, *The Sovereign People*, but toned down to meet objections by Michael Collins, who felt that there should be nothing to distract from the struggle to get British soldiers out of Ireland. The Programme as it stood was a form of social contract. In return for willing service, the government would ensure that every citizen had an adequate share of the nation's produce. The first duty of a government, it went on, was to make provision for the physical, mental and spiritual well-being of the children; no child should suffer hunger or cold from lack of food, clothing or shelter. They would be provided with all that was needed for their proper education and training as 'Citizens of a Free and Gaelic Ireland'.[19]

There was a problem in that so much was defined by a Dáil with so few members present. As de Valera put it later, it was as if a strait-jacket was being fashioned which would prevent manoeuvre as the battle for independence went on. De Valera simply ignored the Democratic Programme and it eventually went away. The other initiative, the embassy to the Peace Conference, also descended into unfulfilled aspirations, since Sean T. O'Kelly, the chosen envoy, never got permission to attend the conference in spite of months of trying. President Wilson had become disenchanted with the leaders of Clan na Gael, Devoy and Judge Cohalan, who had allowed their desire for Irish freedom to be expressed too often in pro-German terms. He maintained this opposition even after the House of Representatives had passed a motion calling on the Peace Conference to consider sympathetically Ireland's claim to self-determination. Without pressure from America, there was no hope of an invitation. It was little consolation to Sinn Féin that Wilson became very unpopular in America because of his attitude.

There was an incident which occurred on the very day that the Dáil met for the first time which, while being fairly minor in itself, gave a hint of what was to follow in the coming years. The first shots of the Easter Rising had killed a policeman. On 21 January 1919, the killing of two more policemen signalled the fact that the struggle for independence had once more reached an armed phase. At Soloheadbeg, a dreary back road a few miles north of Tipperary Town, a group of Volunteers intended to capture some explosives from a consignment that was being taken to a quarry. An account of the episode was written by one of the participants, Dan Breen. He had joined the IRB in 1912 and the Volunteers in 1914. His friend Sean Treacy had been arrested in the aftermath of the Easter Rising and spent two years in jail. When Treacy was released in July 1918 the two joined with other interested young nationalists in the area and began to get ready to fight. They set up what they rather grandly called a munitions factory, but they blew up the house in which it was situated. They had episodes almost of farce in their dealings with the police, and it sometimes must have seemed like a game of boyhood cops and robbers.

There was a serious side to it nevertheless, and when Sean Hogan joined Treacy and Breen in their safe house, they were to form the core

of one of the most dangerous groups of gunmen in the whole of
Ireland. They got arms from Dublin; Treacy and Breen rode there by
bike and collected six revolvers and 500 rounds of ammunition. All of
them were enthused by the landslide victory of Sinn Féin in the General
Election of December 1918. They knew that gelignite was to be taken
from Tipperary Town to the quarry at Soloheadbeg where it was to be
used for blasting. There would be a police escort, expected to number
six. An ambush would collect the explosives but would have the added
bonus of guns and ammunition that could be taken from the police
escort.

In his account of the ambush, Breen implies at least that he was
leader of the group, but the organiser was a man called Seamus
Robinson, who had taken part in the Easter Rising, while the logistics
were taken care of by Sean Treacy. The Tipperary Brigade had actually
ordered the attack before Christmas. Dan Breen's brother took a job in
the quarry so that he could provide the conspirators with information.
Eleven men were originally chosen to carry out the raid, but three of
them had to go back to work, after waiting a number of weeks. A total
of eight gunmen confronted the two policemen. Breen implies that
they were given every chance to surrender, 'but they were Irishmen too
and would rather die than surrender'.[20] He says that he would have
preferred them to surrender, but he also said that the action had been
taken deliberately, that they had wanted to start a war and the only way
to do that was to kill a policeman.

Both policemen were very popular in the area, and there was a great
deal of criticism from pulpit and press. There was also criticism from
Volunteer GHQ, where Richard Mulcahy described the incident as tan-
tamount to murder. Both men were quiet, decent and inoffensive, and
one was probably a native speaker of Irish. The gelignite was taken to a
safe place, and Treacy, Breen, Robinson and Hogan went on the run.
Instead of mobilising republican forces in the area, it left them leaderless, and there was a drop in the level of activity which lasted for several
months.

In the immediate aftermath, the government declared South
Tipperary a Special Military area under the Defence of the Realm Act
on 23 January. On the last day of the month *An t-Óglach* claimed that
the formation of Dáil Éireann 'justifies Irish Volunteers in treating the
armed forces of the enemy—whether soldiers or policemen—exactly as

a National Army would treat the members of an invading army'. Although this might have given the impression that the raid had been part of a grand strategy, the fact is that it was done without the know-ledge of the Volunteers or Sinn Féin. It also showed the beginnings of the cycle which would consume Ireland for the next few years: atrocity would be followed by repression; repression would be followed by alienation of the civilian population; alienation would be taken as a justification for another atrocity.

It could hardly be described as a war. The disturbances for most of 1919 would fall comfortably within what another Briton, William Whitelaw, who was Secretary of State for Northern Ireland in 1972, described as 'an acceptable level of violence'. Certainly the British authorities at the time were much more concerned about what to do with respect to this new National Assembly. They considered suppress-ing it, but held their hand. Michael Collins and Harry Boland stirred the pot by organising the escape of de Valera from Lincoln Jail. Another prominent Sinn Féiner, Richard Barton, managed his own escape from Mountjoy Jail in Dublin; shortly afterwards, a further twenty prisoners escaped from Mountjoy by the simple expedient of climbing over the wall in broad daylight. Bowing to the inevitable, the government used the excuse of a flu epidemic in March to release the rest of the prisoners, and de Valera was able to come out of hiding.[21]

There was a much better attendance at the Dáil on its second meeting, held on 1 April, with fifty-two members present. Most of them were young men, with only 25 per cent of them over the age of forty-five. There were only two Protestants: Robert Barton and Ernest Blythe. There was very little connection in most cases between the men and their constituencies compared with what would be normal; less than half of them lived in their constituencies. Only 10 per cent had experience of local government. Many, perhaps most of them, had become Dubliners by adoption. On a more positive note, 60 per cent had a secondary education and more than 25 per cent had been to uni-versity. There were only seven farmers, which is surprising, considering that agriculture was the country's major industry. Most of the rest were representatives of the lower middle classes.

Some changes were made to the constitution. A speaker was chosen, Sean T. O'Kelly, and two deputy speakers nominated, together with clerks of the House. It was decided to have a larger executive. De Valera replaced Cathal Brugha as Prime Minister, although he was more usually termed the President of the Dáil. The following day he submitted his choice of ministers for ratification by the Dáil. The choice was of great significance, because he had already decided that he would be of more use in America, so power was going to be in the hands of the executive for an unspecified time. The chosen members were: Griffith, Home Affairs and deputy to de Valera; Collins, Finance; Brugha, Defence; Plunkett, Foreign Affairs; Countess Markievicz, Labour; Cosgrave, Local Government; Eoin MacNeill (Industry); and Robert Barton (Agriculture). In addition, Lawrence Ginnell was appointed Director of Propaganda. His tenure only lasted until May, when he was arrested. Desmond FitzGerald was appointed in his place and held the position for some eighteen months before he in his turn was arrested. From then until the Truce, the position was held by Erskine Childers.

The ministers, however, remained in post, and it was they who guided the development of an alternative government to Dublin Castle, in the hope that the Irish would naturally turn to it rather than the alien alternative. It was a difficult task. Although the Dáil was not suppressed formally until September 1919, individual members were subject to harassment by the security forces, with some of them actually on the run. Within weeks the institutions were driven underground and by September it was considered necessary for some key individuals to be asked to absent themselves from meetings, for fear they would be arrested. In December, most of the staff of the Dáil were arrested and many documents were seized. They managed to have six meetings of the Dáil in 1919, but this was down to three in 1920 and three again in 1921. Because of this, there was little check kept upon ministers, who were allowed to operate in secret and to improvise solutions where necessary. The result was that a ministry would flourish or fade entirely depending on the character of the minister. Michael Collins managed to raise a loan of nearly £358,000. Robert Barton was able to set up a Land Bank which, in a small way at first, could advance loans to farmers to enable them to buy their land.

A particular success story was the Ministry of Local Government. Here W. T. Cosgrave, with his assistant Kevin O'Higgins, built up contacts with local councils and officials all over the country. Their job was made easier after the local elections of January and June 1920. Out of 127 Corporations and town councils they controlled seventy-two;

they shared authority with other nationalists in a further twenty-six. In the same way they dominated the vast majority of county councils, rural district councils and Poor Law boards. After the June elections, Cosgrave asked the councils to break off their connections with the Local Government Board and, by October, most of those outside the north-east of Ulster had done so. To underline this, in 1921, the Irish Republican Army, as the Volunteers now termed themselves, burned down the Custom House in Dublin, home of the Local Government Board, in an operation that was militarily inept and was an assault on the country's heritage and culture. The original interior was completely destroyed and the dome collapsed. A large number of historical documents were destroyed in the fire. To cap it all, many of the members who took part in the attack were captured as they tried to flee the scene. Although the building was restored, the limestone used to reconstruct the dome is Irish, and is much darker than the Portland stone that was used in the original. The contrast between the dome and the rest of the building is still easily seen.

The results of the local elections were not as straightforward as they might look at first. Sinn Féin was doing best in the countryside. In towns in County Meath Sinn Féin had taken less than 20 per cent of the electorate, far less than Labour candidates. In total, Sinn Féin won 572 seats, as opposed to 872 won by other parties.[22] The popularity of such institutions as the Dáil courts, often presided over by women, helped to reinforce the sense of change in the country. These courts took a very dim view of the traditional tactics of the Land War, cattle driving and the seizure of land. This ensured that respectable farming opinion was not turned against Sinn Féin. This is particularly striking since an analysis of much early IRA activity shows that it was inspired by land hunger or labour agitation, rather than the drive towards a republic. The Dáil was using its court to try to keep its armed supporters under control.[23]

But that is looking far ahead, and such a major undertaking was beyond the small groups of IRA that were operating in 1919. The tactics of the IRA at this time were, quite simply, shoot any policeman you can point a gun at, on or off duty, since the RIC were the embodiment of the alien domination.[24] Twenty policemen were killed in the year, eighteen of them after 1 May, while twelve people were killed by government forces. In addition, some of the more vulnerable police barracks in the south and west were evacuated.[25] The attacks were also designed to discourage membership of the RIC, and many serving policemen resigned. The policy was a deliberate, if uncoordinated, attempt to outflank Sinn Féin's political offensive. It was one of many cases in Irish history when a minority tries to enforce its strategy on the majority. It was making a case for total freedom, far beyond any sort of home rule that the government might be likely to grant. It was for this reason that Collins, who was theoretically a supporter of Sinn Féin policy, wanted to create a state of disorder throughout the country and was prepared to attack—verbally for the time being—the weaklings and cowards who disagreed.

As time went on and the government's response became more heavy-handed, Collins's position became a more tenable one. There were pointless displays of military force and unfortunate activists, seemingly chosen at random, were imprisoned. The key mistake that the government made was to put off proscribing the Dáil for eight months; this gave the time for the Dáil ministries to take root. The Dáil itself was dominated by de Valera, and he would have continued to do so if he had not left for America in June, when he stayed away for ten months. This allowed Collins to build a parallel status within the Dáil, which complemented his position as de-facto commander of the IRA, even though he was not its Chief of Staff. The profile of the IRA was increased when they attempted to assassinate Lord French, the Viceroy, in December. The attack failed, but it was followed by a series of attacks on the G-men of the Dublin Metropolitan Police by Michael Collins's specially picked group of Volunteers, known as the Squad.

In March 1920 there occurred something which changed the intensity of the revolution. Tomás MacCurtain was Lord Mayor of Cork as well as being the Commandant of Cork No. 1 Brigade of the IRA. He was killed in his own house by a gang of masked raiders who were probably policemen; the jury at his inquest returned a verdict of wilful murder against the British government, the Viceroy, District Inspector Swanzy and other individual policemen. Collins certainly believed the evidence, and he ordered that Swanzy be killed. Although the Inspector had been transferred almost immediately to the north of Ireland for his own protection, he was followed there and shot, using MacCurtain's own handgun, a few months later.[26] This led to further attacks on Catholics and many homes were burned.

Collins was also very careful about keeping the Dáil funds secret. Alan Bell, an elderly magistrate, had been given the task of tracing Sinn

Féin funds lodged in various banks under various names. He proved to be very effective at this, and he was taken from a crowded tram in Dublin and shot dead by the roadside.

Reprisals from police barracks began to take on a more savage character. Worse, resignations from the RIC were reaching critical levels. The government wanted to dismiss the IRA claim that it was fighting a war so it wanted the IRA to be fought by the police rather than the military. But by early summer, the authorities had lost effective control of many rural areas. In May, transport workers took industrial action, refusing to transport supplies for the police or for troops. Those who wavered were helped in their resolve when the IRA took to tarring blacklegs. Republican propaganda emphasised that this was done with popular support, but in reality it was simply part of the armed intimidation that almost always accompanies civil resistance.

Lloyd George decided to go ahead with his decision to partition Ireland and introduced the Government of Ireland Bill to Parliament. This was considered unworkable by those nationalist MPs who still attended Westminster and was totally ignored by Sinn Féin. It offered Ireland two Home Rule Parliaments with fairly limited powers and no control of finance. There would also be a Council of Ireland with modest powers of its own. It was envisaged that the partition would be temporary and that there would eventually be a single parliament for the entire country. Since what was being offered was so much less than what was currently being demanded by republicans, it was totally irrelevant to the situation on the ground and had no effect on the struggle in most of the country. In Ulster, however, there was an immediate reaction. Catholics, almost all of them nationalists, constituted roughly half of the population of Ulster as a whole and one-third of the to-be-partitioned counties. One of the main problems of what came to be called Northern Ireland was how to assimilate, or at least control, this huge minority. For many Protestants, it was easier to control Catholics, and a series of sectarian attacks on nationalist communities began in towns across the north, particularly in Derry and Belfast. Long before the Government of Ireland Act came into effect, the riots had produced sixty-two dead and 200 wounded.

The use of troops posed some delicate questions to the administration, as they raised some controversial points of law; Dublin Castle at least was aware of the damage done to their cause by General

Maxwell in 1916. It was only after the attempted assassination of Lord French in 1920 that troops were used in an offensive capacity. The position at this time was uncertain, and they were given duties that were normally carried out by police. The government shrank from putting troops on active service and declaring martial law. It was at this stage that Lloyd George and others started turning a blind eye to 'unauthorised' reprisals carried out by Crown forces. Even when the opportunity arose and the military started patrolling the countryside, the IRA squads preferred to attack police rather than soldiers. By the time of the Truce, 160 soldiers had been killed, compared with 400 policemen.

The government solution was to use rigorous coercion imposed by a reinforced police force. This coercion had three aims: to suppress all illegal organisations; to imprison those convicted, or even suspected, of political crimes; and to stamp out republican propaganda.[27] Not a single one of these aims was achieved. The illegal organisations went underground, anyone arrested was quickly replaced, while propaganda could be as simple a thing as the spoken word or a duplicated sheet. Many liberal English newspapers, including the *Times*, began to be sympathetic to the republican cause. English people became horrified at what was being done in their name.

A major contributor to this was the quality of recruit that was joining the RIC. The first of these arrived in the spring of 1920. Chosen, in the beginning at least, by the same standards as the RIC had always used, these young men were originally noticeable mainly by their makeshift uniforms and webbing, a mixture of army and police issue, which earned them the nickname the Black and Tans. Most of them were men who had difficulty settling down to civilian life after the war. They were paid ten shillings a day with full board, in a society where unemployment was almost the norm and those jobs that were available were poorly paid and dreary. All of them had been brutalised to some extent by the war, but had learnt to survive. In order to survive in their present employment, in a war where the other side did not wear a distinguishing uniform, they found it safest to treat every civilian as hostile, and to expect an attack from anywhere.

Another group of specially recruited men were the Auxiliary Division of the RIC. These were ex-officers who were paid one pound per day; they had their own uniform, topped by a Glengarry cap. Reports on their behaviour vary considerably, but in action they seem to have been a better spoken version of the Black and Tans, and their own brigadier would resign rather than go on leading what he called a drunken and insubordinate body of men.[28]

The build-up of Crown forces was substantial. By the time of the Truce in 1921 there were 1,400 Auxiliaries and up to 7,000 Black and Tans in a total of 14,000 police. In addition to this, the army commander, General Macready, estimated that he had about twenty-five thousand soldiers.[29] Facing this was a total of about fifteen thousand IRA, of whom about five thousand were on active service at any given time. The Black and Tans and the Auxiliaries accepted the control neither of the police nor of the military, acting very much as bands of mercenaries might have during the Thirty Years War. By the autumn, the reprisals were officially condoned.[30] The civilian population was being intimidated by both sides. The IRA was claiming that the killings by the Black and Tans proved that they had been right to attack the police. They were now shooting more than the police, however. They shot people who got in their way, like farmers' sons who refused to dig trenches for them.[31] Boycotts were another important tool, with slightly less permanent results. The IRA reorganised themselves into flying columns, full-time companies which could move quickly around the land and were sheltered and supported by local sympathisers.

In Cork, these columns inflicted such heavy casualties on police and military that the Auxiliaries burned the centre of Cork City in retaliation. As the actions of these para-police forces escalated, so they were given official approval until, by the end of 1920, they had draconian powers of search and arrest but went beyond that to burn villages and towns. Their colonial attitude towards the natives—'I regarded all civilians as Shinners,' said one officer—drove many recruits into the hands of the IRA.[32] The result was that Dublin Castle became an irrelevance, so that any change of personnel there had no credibility. Possibly the worst single day in this atrocity/counter-atrocity sequence was Sunday, 21 November 1920. On that day a group of men, on the orders of Michael Collins, killed eleven unarmed British officers on suspicion that they were working for the Intelligence Services. Later the same day a group of Black and Tans fired into a crowd of football supporters; twelve civilians were killed in the crush.

The Restoration of Order in Ireland Act was a special extension of the Defence of the Realm Act meant to address the problem of collapsing British administration in Ireland. It was forced through Parliament and became law on 13 August 1920. It allowed for the use of courts martial in areas where the IRA was active and it replaced coroners' inquests with military courts of enquiry. Not all its consequences were expected. Although more accused were convicted, many men went on the run. Since these could no longer hold down a job, they were free to enrol in the highly effective flying columns which the IRA was developing.

Martial law was introduced in Munster and later extended to the rest of the country. Even with these powers the military was unhappy, because the government kept a tight political grip on what was allowed, particularly in the case of the arrest of individuals. Even with the government's restrictions, this allowed the IRA to claim that they were fighting a war with the British. Erskine Childers, in his *Irish Bulletin*, was expert at turning any military activity into a notorious looting or burning.[33] Another weapon used was the hunger strike. This evoked great sympathy when Terence MacSwiney, republican Lord Mayor of Cork, died. Though the tactic had earned great sympathy, the IRA called it off immediately after MacSwiney's death.

The key tactic used against the IRA was the seizure of suspects, and this was normally carried out by the Black and Tans or the Auxiliaries. They preferred to work at night and in the cities. Their preferred transport was a converted chassis which had a lorry body fitted, capable of carrying eight or ten fully armed men; these were the Crossley tenders that all Irishmen, nationalist or otherwise, learned to dread. People lay in their beds at night, trying to work out the destination from the roar of the engine in the still streets and dreading the possibility of it stopping outside their house, dreading the knocking on their door and the chaos of a search of room and people.

The Act also sanctioned official reprisals in areas where martial law had been declared. General Macready could identify houses of people known to be involved in IRA or Sinn Féin activity and these could be destroyed. Since the IRA then undertook their own reprisals, often burning two loyalist houses for every one that was lost to a republican, it was not a tactic that was very often used. Instead, unofficial reprisals carried out 'in the heat of the moment' were winked at. These formed an already established pattern even before the Act. Shooting incidents were followed by destruction of property, often by the burning of creameries which had been set up under a government initiative long before 1914. These had already happened in Tuam and Newport and Templemore, but the worst example was at Balbriggan, north of Dublin. Here an RIC officer had been killed by an expanding bullet, known colloquially as dum-dums, and enraged and drunken Black and Tans terrorised the town and destroyed part of it. The fact that the first targets of these raids tended to be the public houses did not go down well with liberal circles in England and increased the pressure on Lloyd George and his government. Kindlier minds might have said that the semi-oblivion of permanent drunkenness was the only way in which the Black and Tans could live their lives.

The IRA continued to attack, nevertheless. In Dublin a party of soldiers was shot by Volunteers in plain clothes. One of the attackers, an eighteen-year-old student called Kevin Barry, was captured, tried and subsequently hanged. The execution was carried out only a week after MacSwiney's death and set the stage for what was probably the deadliest month of the struggle: November 1920. There have been many 'Bloody Sundays' in modern Irish history, but the name was truly earned by Sunday, 21 November 1920. On that morning a group of gunmen, organised by two officers of the IRA's Dublin Brigade, made a concerted attempt to wipe out the intelligence-gathering capabilities of the British. Eleven men were shot dead in their homes or hotels; three more were shot dead either because they intervened or simply by accident. That afternoon, some Black and Tans went to Croke Park, where a match was going on, and shot indiscriminately into the crowd, killing twelve and wounding sixty. That did not end the day's killing. By coincidence, Peader Clancy and Dick McKee, who had organised the morning's shootings with Michael Collins, had been arrested the night before. Now, on Sunday night, they were killed 'while trying to escape' from Dublin Castle.[34]

The final event of the month was possibly the most chilling for the authorities. At Kilmichael, in County Cork, the IRA introduced a new tactic. Their leader was Tom Barry, who had fought as a sergeant in the British army during the war. He was now commandant of Cork No. 3 Brigade and was to become one of the most successful exponents of guerrilla warfare. His flying column consisted of fewer than forty men, but he decided to ambush two lorry-loads of Auxiliaries as they returned towards Macroom. The action took place as dusk fell, and

Barry himself stood on the road wearing what he claimed was a Volunteer tunic, but which the British said was a British uniform. The driver of the lorry, obviously suspicious, stopped thirty-five yards from the spot where Barry was standing. Barry threw a hand-grenade into the open cab and the IRA opened fire. In a savage, close-quarter fight, all nine Auxiliaries in this lorry were killed, some with rifle butts or bayonets. While this was still going on, the second lorry arrived and an exchange of rifle fire began. Once again, all the Auxiliaries were killed, or left for dead. Among the dead was the commander of the Auxiliaries in Macroom. Two IRA men were killed and another mortally wounded.

The government introduced martial law to Cork on 10 December, to which the IRA responded by launching another ambush on the Auxiliaries, this time just outside Cork City. A mixed mob of Auxiliaries and Black and Tans went on the rampage in the city, drinking, looting and burning, and then preventing the fire brigade from dealing with the fires. As a result, a substantial part of Cork's centre was destroyed. The Chief Secretary for Ireland made the ridiculous claim in the House of Commons that Cork had been burned by its own citizens. The military report on the incident turned out to be so damning that the Cabinet did not allow it to be published. The Auxiliaries passed their own comment; many of them dangled burnt corks from their caps as they moved around Dublin.[35]

The military organisation of the IRA was fairly loose; fighters were more concerned about what the local commanders wanted rather than any orders coming from Dublin, and the local commanders had a growing sense of their own independence of action. This was reinforced by the almost romantic sense of continuity that they found in what they were doing. Ernie O'Malley, for example, imagined the different garrisons as the modern equivalent of King John's castles with the IRA continuing the resistance that had gone on since Norman and Tudor times. Most of the action took place in Munster, or around the border counties of Ulster. Membership of the flying columns was made up mostly of young men from small towns, young men of no property. For the first time in Irish history, revolutionary leadership was in the hands of people who had no claims to social distinction.[36]

As the year changed into 1921, the attacks by the flying columns increased. Some of the most intense fighting took place in the first six months and at the same time more and more civilians found themselves caught up like pawns in the struggle. A group at a tennis party in Galway was massacred by the IRA and they shot a seventy-year-old woman who had warned the British of a planned ambush. It was during this period that the attack on the Custom House took place.[37] The only gleam of hope was that de Valera had returned from America at Christmas and he seemed to be the only person who was confident that a political solution could be found to the situation. What seems to have made his mind up was the arrest of Arthur Griffith, who had acted as his deputy, and Griffith's replacement by Michael Collins. Perhaps he felt that too much power was being concentrated in the hands of the physical force men.

The first time he addressed the Dáil after coming back he alarmed many of those present by suggested that the burden that ordinary people had to carry should be lightened by the IRA easing off in their attacks on the enemy.[38] There were also signs that a truce might be on its way. It was politically impossible for Lloyd George to discuss peace terms unless the Irish surrendered their arms, which of course they refused to do. Now that de Valera had returned—someone who had not been involved in this phase of the armed struggle—it might be possible to have discussions without the accusation that the government was negotiating with murderers. Care was taken to make sure that no over-eager agent of the Security Services should arrest de Valera. There were many initiatives, so many that at one time de Valera insisted that he was the only person with whom the government could negotiate. He met with Lord Derby and Sir James Craig, but the results were entirely negative.

Chapter 12

A NORTHERN SOLUTION

In the very act of creating the Ulster Unionist Council in 1905, the Ulster unionists took the first steps towards abandoning their southern counterparts to the home rule wolves. It did give some limited representation to those from the south of Ireland, but it was primarily a tool of the north. There were still links with the southern brethren through the Orange Order, and the splendidly titled Joint Committee for the Unionist Associations of Ireland. Some of the UUC's leading lights, such as Carson and Walter Long, remained bound to the south through family or constituency ties, but they were part of a movement that was northern to the marrow. From now, the only effective roles that southern unionists played were as a part of Ulster unionism. In its very structure, the UUC was a prototype for the Unionist-to-the-Core Parliament that was established in 1921. Southern unionism was a fragile flower; northern unionism was taking the first organisational steps that would allow it to mobilise its members from 1912 onwards. It was as if Ulster unionists had decided that unionism itself no longer had the power to control the island and so they were surveying a laager where they could keep safe all that they held dear.

Not all southern unionists went quietly. In Kingstown, gateway to Wales and England, the local unionist club set up its own paramilitary unit. It went no further than drilling practice, and this group of middle-class men decided that they had too much to lose to stick their heads out too far. In a way this was typical of many southern unionists, who roared their opposition to home rule like Britannia's lions, only for that opposition to collapse at the least pressure.[1] Others believed that a successful opposition to home rule on the part of Ulster would lead to a Union renewed. By 1913, however, there was tension between the two groupings, with Carson complaining that the southerners weren't prepared to take any risk. The decision of the Ulster unionists to situate their laager in the six north-eastern counties established a partition within unionism before ever there was a geographical partition of the island itself.

From the beginning of the war, then, southern unionists had to fend for themselves. They saw a future for a while, in Redmond's support for the British army, though they subsequently sabotaged the discussions with Lloyd George in 1916. By the time they tried once more to broker a deal with the constitutional nationalists in the Irish Convention of July 1917–April 1918, it was too late, and Sinn Féin was unstoppable in its accumulation of support. The southern unionists were now politically dead, unable even in these years of crisis to approach anything like a singleness of purpose. As a group they had seen their income from land dwindle, and witnessed the disasters that followed one upon the other in the Great War and then the War for Independence; they did not even have a forum which could negotiate terms for their people.

Although the Ulster unionists had watched the developments in the rest of Ireland after 1916 with some trepidation, their history from 1912 onwards gave them the self-confidence that they could deal with whatever happened. Sectarian passions that were only just latent came to the fore, especially when they heard of outrages—and these did not lose in the telling—committed against their co-religionists in the south and west. Protestants found it easy to consider that all Catholics were rebels and that the presence of so many rebels within the north was a threat to their well-being. From the summer of 1920 on, rioting became a regular hazard in Belfast and other major towns. Although at times a direct response to an incident, such as when Inspector Swanzy was shot while leaving church, at other times it seems to have been planned in advance. Thousands of families were driven from their homes. The irony is that most of these would have been supporters of the Hibernians and as opposed to the IRA as the Protestants were.[2]

These were not welcome developments to the unionist leaders, who realised that these incidents were doing great damage to their reputation in the eyes of the British public. They could also see that they did not have the same level of support from the British conservatives that they had had before the war. It became obvious to them that they should look for a speedy settlement in case they should lose out completely. When the government offered them the Government of Ireland Act, which was approved by the Cabinet in September 1920 and became law in December, they accepted it as being the best they were likely to get. They complained of course: that unionists in the south had been abandoned; and that there was no longer the full integration into the United Kingdom that had been their goal. Nevertheless, in Alvin Jackson's analysis this had been the compromise for which they had been manoeuvring since 1914, so they knew what they were getting. They had an earldom to play with, where they had a majority that was unlikely ever to be challenged. They also had a constitution, in a sense a contract with the British government, which meant that they could not be dumped into a United Ireland. When the first elections were held, in May 1921, the unionists took forty of the fifty-two seats. Carson was suffering from ill health, so it was Sir James Craig who became the first Prime Minister of Northern Ireland.

In the south, the Government of Ireland Act was not quite ignored. Republicans used the election in May to reinforce their hold over the politics of the country. One hundred and twenty-four seats went to Sinn Féin, the candidates being returned unopposed. Trinity College elected four unionists. They were the only ones to appear when the southern parliament was formally opened in June. They adjourned at once and met no more.

As Alvin Jackson has said, the history of Northern Ireland from 1920 is rather like a *Reader's Digest* version of Irish history in the eighteenth and nineteenth centuries.[3] Certainly it started off with similarities, the ascendancy parliament which managed the country for the elite until 1800 being replaced by a Protestant parliament for a Protestant people in 1921. The new state was formed by act of parliament, but the cement that held it together for half a century was the defeat of the northern IRA. There was no political consensus to use as a foundation, and when the effort was made to find this it was already much too late. Northern Ireland has been described as a lean-to which needed a stable Britain to keep it upright.[4] Britain was not at all sure that she wanted the structure hanging there. The choice offered was not whether Northern Ireland wanted home rule or not, but which of two versions of home rule she was prepared to accept. This was confirmed by the hands-off attitudes of succeeding British administrations until the late 1960s.

The skills which had helped to see off the threat of an all-Ireland home rule parliament sitting in Dublin were not necessarily the skills needed to build a functioning state. Craig had learned the need for unionist unity, and it was this block of granite-hard unity which he imposed which proved to be unmovable by the Free State or by Britain. In this he was helped by his Home Secretary, Richard Dawson Bates, a solicitor who was somewhat limited intellectually, but who was an apparatchik to the core, and who was a seasoned defender of the unionist cause. Confronted by a nationalist electorate that was split between supporters of the Hibernians and supporters of Sinn Féin, Craig was determined that there should be unity in the Protestant vote. He had held ministerial posts at Westminster, and knew many of the top civil servants and senior politicians, and could depend on their advice and cooperation. His experience in the South African and in the Great War had given him a good eye for defence, and it was this he chose as his priority in the first years of Northern Ireland, when he made the state secure against outside threats. The ultimate threat was to come from inside, however, and he did little to unite a divided society or to produce the prosperity that might have given Catholics a stake in Northern Ireland. There was neither the intelligence nor the imagination within the Craig Cabinet to bring this about.

The single tool that Craig found most useful in the defeat of the IRA was the Special Constabulary, a force that was to earn a mixed reputation over the years. Originally in three categories, with A Specials being full-time, B Specials being part-time and C Specials constituting an emergency reserve, only the B Specials survived after the collapse of the Northern IRA in the mid-1920s. As a force it used tactics that were intrusive and repressive. At its mildest, this might be something as simple as holding a neighbour at gunpoint until he identified himself, even though the two people involved might live only a few hundred yards apart. At its worst it was wilful murder. The Specials were probably involved in the murder in Belfast of the MacMahon family. Four family members and an employee were shot in the family home; a young boy was the only male in the house to survive, by crawling under a table. A patrol of Specials certainly killed three Catholic youths in Cushendall.[5]

The Specials were in place before the full-time police force had changed its name from Royal Irish Constabulary to Royal Ulster Constabulary. Under the treaty that had by then been signed between Britain and the Free State, the RIC was disbanded south of the border by March 1922. It soldiered on a little longer in the North and the force that replaced it was built along the same paramilitary lines as the original RIC. This meant that it did not in the least reflect the normal structure of a police service in Great Britain, in rank structure, in organisation, and in the fact that it was armed. One third of its 3,000 members were to be Catholic and it was hoped that these could be recruited from the RIC veterans. It benefited from the fact that its late establishment meant that it was not closely associated with the worst weeks of fighting against the IRA and carried little stigma for most Catholics. Nevertheless, the quota for Catholics was never filled, and the force built up a culture that was largely, if not exclusively, Protestant, a fact that became apparent in crisis situations.

To support this rigorous policing, Craig introduced a set of draconian laws, starting with the Special Powers Act of 1922. This was an adaptation of the Restoration of Order Act (1920) which granted the Minister for Home Affairs power 'to take all such steps and to issue all such orders as may be necessary for preserving the peace and maintaining order'. Implementation of the act was delayed because of a series of talks between Craig and Collins, by this time a member of the Free State Government, with a view to working out a modus vivendi between the two states. In May, however, the Unionist MP W. J. Twaddell was one of fourteen people killed in a single weekend, and the Special Powers Act was brought into effect immediately. The IRA was proscribed and 500 Catholics were interned. There was a country-wide curfew from 11 p.m. to 5 a.m. Flogging was one of the punishments available to and used by the authorities. The effects of this repression were felt almost exclusively by the Catholic population. Although the Unionist government could point out that there was similar legislation in the south, at least there it was not applied on the basis of religion.

The most active IRA commander operating in Northern Ireland outside Belfast was Frank Aiken. He was from the Camlough area of South Armagh and had been operating around there since 1920. His column had forced the RIC out of Newtownhamilton barracks, had captured arms and had burned the building. In retaliation, the Specials burned his home and the homes of ten of his relatives. After that, Aiken's campaign took on a very bitter character. In April 1921 his unit held an entire Protestant congregation hostage in the townland of Creggan, in County Armagh, with the intention of ambushing some police and Specials who were expected to attend the service. One Special was killed. Although none of the civilian congregation was harmed, the incident aroused a great deal of animosity among Protestants in the area, and from the next month the Specials initiated the practice of shooting Catholics in retaliation for IRA attacks. An example of this happened in June, when Aiken's men derailed a troop train carrying a cavalry unit to Belfast. The guard, three troopers and sixty-nine horses were killed. Shortly afterwards, the Specials took four Catholics from their homes in Bessbrook and Altnaveigh and killed them. This was not the last tragedy to visit Altnaveigh. Although Aiken's men were not supposed to be taking part in the IRA assault on the North begun the month before, in June 1922 his men shot seven Protestant civilians in Altnaveigh, allegedly in retaliation for the death of two Catholics and the rape of a woman by Specials the previous day.

A last crisis in the conflict between Craig's government and the IRA occurred on the winding banks of the River Erne. There is a stretch of western Fermanagh that digs deep into County Donegal. This is the Pettigo-Lough Erne-Belleek triangle. Republicans seized this and occupied Belleek; Pettigo was already in County Donegal. It proved impossible for the forces available to Craig to dislodge them, and he had to prevail on Winston Churchill to use the military to retake the area. As a result of this, a force of the British army remained in County Donegal till 1924, over two years later.

Long before this, the Free State had other matters to concern it, as it fought a bitter civil war with a breakaway IRA. This allowed Craig to get on with setting up his Northern Ireland state in a way that would not be dismantled easily. There had been a mini-crisis for unionism when the Northern Ireland Parliament had been opened in June 1921 by King George V; the King called on all Irishmen 'to stretch out the hand of forbearance and to forgive and forget'. This was the gesture towards Sinn Féin which led to the Truce of 1921, but it led to pressure on Craig to try to come to an accommodation with de Valera. Craig did not agree to a meeting unless de Valera would give a written assurance that he accepted the principle of Northern Ireland's independent rights. Back bench pressure in the House of Commons prevented Lloyd George leaning as heavily on Craig as he was to lean later on Collins. Even so, it was not until 5 November 1921 that Lloyd George agreed to hand over executive powers to the Northern Ireland government.[6]

Even then the British Prime Minister kept up the pressure. He tried to persuade Craig to accept subordination to a dominion parliament in

Dublin. Craig replied that he wanted dominion status for Northern Ireland. The fact that Lloyd George was trying to hold together a coalition government meant that he could not try to coerce Craig without the government losing cohesion altogether, and he backed off. On 25 November he assured Craig that there would be no change to Northern Ireland's position without an agreement.

The Treaty that was signed by British and Irish representatives on 6 December 1921 was a cleverly worded document. It recognised Ireland as a unity, but gave the north-eastern counties the right to opt out of that unity. If it did so, however, its territory would be subject to review by a Boundary Commission. Craig claimed to be horrified by this, but it was in fact an idea that he had floated in Parliament in 1919 during discussions of the Government of Ireland Bill. No one thought to remind him of this when the Northern Ireland government rejected the Treaty, claiming that it threatened the borders of the state. Lloyd George tried to defuse the problem by assuring the unionists that there would be no more than a minor boundary revision.[7]

Craig decided that he would have to make assurance doubly sure by coming to some sort of an agreement with Michael Collins, the coming man in the Dublin government. This was the wrong man to deal with because, while he disliked the Boundary Commission as much as Craig, Collins was worried that it would get in the way of more direct action to reclaim the lost counties. They agreed in March that the Commission should be replaced by face-to-face meetings between the two governments. This came to nothing, however, as political realities in both jurisdictions meant that they had other priorities, and Collins's death in a gun battle on 22 August put an end to the possibility of any more discussions. By 1923, the Boundary Commission was back on the agenda.

After the Civil War, the Free State government was less bellicose in its approach to Northern Ireland. A member of the government, Ernest Blythe, himself an Ulster Protestant, argued that the quest for Irish unity should be a gradual and constructive process. This became orthodoxy for the Irish government and it encouraged a vision of the Boundary Commission as a way of addressing the problems of partition in a legal and constitutional way. When the Irish Free State came into existence in December 1922, and Northern Ireland immediately opted out, the Boundary Commission became a legal requirement.

Once again Craig came under pressure to reach an accommodation with the Free State. Once again he side-stepped the issue, and refused to appoint a Northern Ireland representative. The government went ahead and picked one anyway, J. R. Fisher, a barrister and former editor of the *Northern Whig*. The Free State representative was the venerable Eoin MacNeill whose background in Early Irish History was hardly a preparation for legalistic debate. The fact that a member of the South African judiciary, Richard Feetham, was chosen as chairman, meant that MacNeill was in a definite minority, the only one with no legal background. The Commission met for the first time in November 1924 and considered evidence until the following summer. The report was complete by October and leaked in November, when the *Morning Post* published details. The Free State government was not pleased, and the reason was the interpretation that Feetham—or 'cheat 'em' as he became known in Dublin—had interpreted his task in a very conservative way. He had looked at Article 12 of the Government of Ireland Act and read that the boundary should be done in accordance with the wishes of the inhabitants 'in so far as may be compatible with economic and geographic conditions'. MacNeill had neither the training nor the personality to argue against this position, so the economic and geographic concerns were considered as having primacy over cultural and demographic ones. Nationalists and republicans felt that they had been let down twice by MacNeill; once by his countermanding the Easter Rising and now by his handing over thousands of Catholics to Protestant domination. The furore brought about by the *Morning Post* revelations forced MacNeill to resign.

The Commission had recommended some minor changes from which the Free State would have made a net gain of 24,000 citizens and 130,000 acres. But the game wasn't worth the candle and, at a meeting held on 3 December 1925, Cosgrave, Craig and the British Prime Minister, Stanley Baldwin, signed an agreement suppressing the Commission report and reverting to the old boundaries. There were a few financial concessions made to the Free State, while the powers that had been held by the British in trust for the Council of Ireland were delegated to the Belfast administration. As Alvin Jackson has pointed out, if the decisions of the Commission had stood, it would have been a permanent arrangement against which there could be no appeal. What Craig and the others had signed was a settlement, and a settlement can be revisited.[8]

Such a view was not shared by Northern Irish Catholics, who had based their hopes on a wholesale transfer of land, particularly in the border counties, to the Free State. The hopes of Belfast Catholics, who could have had no such expectation, had already been devastated by the crushing of the IRA in the north. Now that the Free State government had recognised the separate jurisdictions, they were condemned to live in a partitioned island. Condemned is almost too appropriate a word. In the civil strife that had taken place in Belfast in the first years of the decade, 58 per cent of the deaths had been of Catholics, although Catholics were only about 33 per cent of the population. Protestant reaction to high-profile IRA assassinations meant that Catholics were no longer able to work in most of the heavy engineering firms in Belfast. Great numbers of houses occupied by Catholics were burned down and families had to flee across the city. Catholics saw this as a pogrom, and the fighting of the IRA as defensive. When the IRA was defeated in Belfast, Catholics saw themselves as powerless.

Their answer seems, in many cases, to have been to close their eyes to reality. Nationalist MPs did not take their seats in Parliament till 1926. The nationalist councils of Tyrone and Fermanagh, which felt most aggrieved by the inaction of the Boundary Commission, refused to recognise the authority of Craig's government. Some nationalist teachers refused to be paid by Belfast and were paid, for a while, by Dublin. There had been efforts to put pressure on the southern government in their negotiations about the border, but after Collins's death, the Free State seemed to lack the will to pursue this. All that Northern Ireland nationalists could hope for from Dublin was tea and sympathy, and they could not be too sure of the tea.

Whereas the south had moved to support Sinn Féin in the political struggle for independence, the northern nationalists showed a determined loyalty to Joe Devlin, whom Belfast Catholics saw as one of their own and who had his core support among the Hibernians. The eastern counties supported Joe and traditional nationalism; the western counties tended to support Sinn Féin. This split meant that the Catholic population of the six partitioned counties wielded even less political power than they might have. Full unity did not return till 1928. A false unity had begun in the election of 1921, but the only thing Catholic representatives had in common was a policy to abstain from attending the Northern Ireland Parliament. This was a disastrous policy, because it meant that there was no one to call Craig's ministers to account, and these ministers had a free hand to put into place a series of institutions that were to dominate the state on behalf of Protestant unionism for half a century.

The weight of establishing Northern Ireland as a functioning entity was borne more by senior civil servants than by politicians. The politicians had limited experience of government at best and none had held a post which required subtlety or imagination. The late 1920s might have provided an opportunity to create institutions that would have lessened sectarian divisions or have given opportunities for economic growth. Instead, Craig moved to increase the unionist grip on the land. Proportional representation was abolished in local elections by 1922. The Leech Commission redrew council boundaries to the advantage of the unionist vote, most notoriously in Derry, where a Unionist minority almost automatically had a majority in Londonderry Corporation. This should have put unionism in a position where it might have been confident enough to make a few concessions to Catholics, but many Protestants still saw Northern Ireland in terms of a zero sum; if the Catholics were to get anything it would be at the expense of the Protestants.9 Craig was intent on maintaining unity among his supporters, and would not take the risk of alienating any of them. Anyway, the Catholics were so cowed that they were not a political threat. In 1929 Unionists abolished proportional representation in elections to the Northern Ireland Parliament.

Problems with the economy were possibly just as important as inter-community relations for the long-term survival of Northern Ireland. Craig may have been in such haste to establish the state as an accomplished fact that he did not negotiate very effectively on Northern Ireland's behalf when it came to matters of detail. The Imperial government had reserved to itself all matters involving trade, commerce and taxation. Belfast could impose new taxes, but the current taxes went to London. The Belfast government had to budget not only for its own operations but for any of the operations of the Imperial government that were carried out in Northern Ireland. Worse, it had to pay a contribution of £7.92 million to the Treasury in London. This contribution was to be the first charge on the revenue of Northern Ireland. The negotiations had taken place at a time that Northern Ireland was going through a period of prosperity brought on by the post-war boom. The prosperity did not last and it looked as if Northern Ireland, having seen off the IRA, might fall victim to the Treasury.

Craig was in a bind. The cost of the social and welfare services, especially as unemployment grew, was beyond the capacity of Belfast to pay. If he lowered welfare payments, the chosen people would become second-class citizens of the United Kingdom and show up the economic failings of the Unionist Party. To raise taxes, at a time when the Free State had a very liberal tax regime, was to imply that the border had been an economic mistake. They had to go to London and ask for relief; they had to do this at least twice more during the decade, as the costs of unemployment increased.

One Unionist fear was that the proletariat, Catholic and Protestant, would unite against them. This nearly happened in late 1932, when there were ferocious riots by the united working class of Belfast. This was a brief aberration, and an incident which occurred in the early summer of the year might be taken as more typical.

In 1932, the Catholic Church organised a Eucharistic Congress in Dublin in order to celebrate the presence of Christ in the Eucharist. The reason that Ireland had been chosen was that that was the year of the 1500th anniversary of the supposed date of St Patrick's arrival in Ireland. The theme of the congress was to be 'The Propagation of the Sacred Eucharist by Ireland's Missionaries'. It took place on five days towards the end of June, and proved to be one of the largest congresses of the twentieth century. So many foreign visitors arrived that seven ocean liners were moored along the quays to act as floating hotels, while another five anchored around Scotsman's Bay, south of Dun Laoghaire. The most spectacular occasion would be on the final day, when the final public mass was to be held in the Phoenix Park, celebrated by the Archbishop of Baltimore in America. Special trains were organised from all over Ireland, and Catholics from every county made their way to Dublin that day.

Among them was a group of Catholics from the overwhelmingly Protestant town of Larne. They were parishioners from the Church of St MacNissi, on the northern edge of the town. As early as February they had begun to collect names of those who would be interested in attending the Phoenix Park mass. Between six and seven hundred parishioners gave their names to the secretary of the committee. It was decided that a special train should be arranged to take the pilgrims from Larne Station. As early as this, however, so many special trains had been arranged that there simply were no more available. The local manager of the LMS Railway suggested that the pilgrims instead should travel on the ferry *Princess Victoria*, which would be idle that day. This was accepted as a good idea by the committee, but they asked that the slightly larger *Princess Margaret* be made available instead. This was agreed on, with a return fare of ten shillings and sixpence (52½p). When news of the arrangement got around the Catholics of County Antrim, applications came in from many surrounding parishes, and about twelve hundred tickets were sold. To reinforce the sense that this was a pilgrimage, and not simply a day excursion, the priests of the parish decided there would be midnight mass, after which those going to Dublin would walk from the chapel to the ship.

The treasurer of the committee was John McKenna, the policeman who had been dubious about the strength of the UVF in County Antrim. He had by now retired from the police and was living in Larne. He collected money and distributed tickets after mass on Sunday mornings, and on Wednesday and Friday evenings in the local primary school. On the Friday before the pilgrimage, the Head Constable from Larne RUC came to see him. The Head Constable wanted McKenna to use his influence with the priests to have them cancel the 'march' to the harbour. The reason he gave was that there might be trouble if the procession went ahead, since there was bad feeling in the town. Since McKenna had served in Larne for six years and lived in it since his retirement, he knew that Saturday nights were normally quiet, with few people on the streets after midnight, let alone at 1:30 a.m., the time when the procession was due to leave the chapel. The Head Constable insisted, on the contrary, that there would be hundreds out at that time. When McKenna reported this conversation to the pilgrimage committee, the idea that the procession would be attacked was treated as a joke.

Midnight mass was packed. Although most of the people from out-lying parishes made their own way to the ship, some of them had squeezed into the chapel, which was full to capacity. Members of the committee did their best to see that most people were seated. At the end of mass the curate spoke to the congregation, asking them to assemble outside the church and warning them to do nothing that would offend anybody. The people formed up and as soon as the priests had changed out of their vestments, they moved off. Buses had been provided for elderly and sick pilgrims and these went first. At their head a crucifix was carried, then came the priests, the women pilgrims, the choir and, bringing up the rear, the men pilgrims.

Although it was now getting on for two o'clock in the morning, there was a crowd of over one hundred waiting for them at Larne's War Memorial. There were also some policemen, and the pilgrims were subjected only to verbal abuse and to the singing of Orange songs. Beyond this, however, there were no more policemen and missiles were thrown from the nearby railway line and several of the pilgrims were cut or hurt. Even as the procession approached the harbour and some policemen could be seen, the hail of missiles continued. At that time it was necessary to board ships through the Harbour Railway Station. When the pilgrims entered this their way was blocked by a crowd of about fifty men, cursing and singing offensive songs. Policemen came forward and forced the demonstrators back, though the mob launched another attack as soon as the male pilgrims appeared. One of these attackers worked for the railway company and was actually on duty that night. He was led away by a policeman, but was neither charged by the police nor disciplined by his employers.

Those who had travelled in the buses fared no better. As these vehicles passed the Olderfleet Hotel, well ahead of the procession, they were surrounded by a hostile crowd of some two hundred. Stones were thrown and many windows on the buses were broken. The report from the RUC's Inspector General claimed that the police could not protect the buses because they had not followed the approved route. It was the view of the pilgrims that the buses were not part of the procession, and so were not limited to any prescribed route. Other vehicles were attacked at the harbour that night, cars that had come to leave pilgrims or to see them off. This was in spite of the fact that the police had urged people to make their own way to the ship.

The *Irish News* maintained that the number of troublemakers was exaggerated by the police as an excuse for their not doing enough to maintain the peace. The newspaper claimed that only 150 had been involved, as opposed to more than 400 as the police claimed. It was the reporter's view that twelve determined policemen could have seen them off.

There was an exchange of letters between the Catholic Bishop of Down and Connor and the Northern Ireland Minister for Home Affairs, Sir Dawson Bates. The latter, who had already gained a reputation for ensuring that Protestants who attacked Catholics were not brought before the courts, claimed that the police had taken no names that night because they had seen no wrongdoing taking place. In fact, the only people known to have broken the law that night were the priests, who had worn their surplices—conduct, he said, likely to lead to a breach of the peace. The parade should not have been permitted to proceed. The police, he maintained, were to be congratulated on a job well done.

Larne was a cold place for Catholics for years to come.

And so was Northern Ireland.

Chapter 13 ~

A SOUTHERN SPLIT

The Truce which came into effect on 11 July 1921 puzzled many of the young men who commanded flying columns in the IRA. Some, including Tom Barry, believed that it was a sure sign of victory and that the IRA had won. Others, such as Ernie O'Malley, were suspicious, wondering why the British were looking for a political solution so soon after declaring that the IRA consisted of a few hundred gunmen who were fighting a little war. A clue may lie in the identity of one of those who helped to draw up the terms of the Truce. This was South African General Jan Smuts. He had fought the British in the long-drawn-out Second Boer War, which the British had won at great expense and by using tactics that were morally repugnant. One of these was a burnt-earth policy which included putting the wives and children of Boers into concentration camps, where a combination of cramped conditions, poor hygiene and malnutrition led to the deaths of thousands. In the actual fighting, any Boer caught wearing or using British uniform or equipment was liable to be shot as a war criminal. There was the probability of a festering relationship that would last for years, but the British had offered such generous terms that the defeated republics had chosen to remain within the Dominion of South Africa; and men who had fought against the British in South Africa had fought with them on the Western Front. The British press saw parallels in Ireland, and it seems likely that the British government thought that a straight debate with nationalists, now that the unionists were out of the frame, could lead to a similar result. Anyway, Ireland was becoming a political embarrassment. However, it was the coercive pressure of the security forces that had maintained solidarity among republicans. An unintended consequence of removing pressure on the Provisional Government was that the British did more to threaten republican unity than anything they had done hitherto.[1]

De Valera himself seemed to be open to compromise. Although he had been elected President of the Irish Republic, he laid no stress on the idea of a republic during the negotiations, nor did he rule out the possibility of some ongoing relationship between Britain and Ireland. Indeed, the formula for negotiations laid stress on this relationship, rather than on republican aspirations. Michael Collins was to claim that the fight for a republic had been lost when the invitation to talks with this formula was accepted. They would meet, the wording ran, 'with a view to ascertaining how the association with Ireland with the community of nations known as the British Empire may be best reconciled to Irish national aspirations'.[2]

The British wanted to put the Sinn Féin delegation at a psycho-logical disadvantage. The talks were held in London, which meant that the Irish delegates were separated from their sources of moral, emotional and intellectual support. De Valera weakened their position even more by refusing to attend himself. Although the Dáil gave the delegates plenipotentiary powers, that is, full powers to come to final terms and sign them on behalf of the Dáil, de Valera muddied the waters by insisting that they consult Dublin before any final agreement. It seems as if the President wanted to have his cake and eat it. The ambiguity of the delegation's position would lead to ultimate tragedy.[3] There were other facts that weakened the delegates' position. The military position was weak, particularly in the logistics of taking the fight to the British. Previous fudges on policy matters which had been made to maintain the unity of Sinn Féin meant that there was no single vision of what the Irish nation should be. De Valera had said himself that the members of the Dáil were not doctrinaire republicans, under-mining much of what the delegation wanted to achieve.[4] Finally, there was the fact that many commanders of flying columns were beyond control, warlords in their own fiefdoms.

The delegation was to consist of five people, led by Arthur Griffith. In fact, as the British realised, the real power lay with Michael Collins, who was also a member. Robert Barton was from a landed Protestant family from Glendalough who had held a commission in the British army, which he resigned in the aftermath of the Easter Rising. He had been arrested twice by the British. On the first occasion he had escaped from Mountjoy Jail; on the second, he was released as part of a general amnesty. He was a convinced republican. Gavan Duffy was an English-born barrister who had been on the defence team at Roger Casement's trial. He came to live permanently in Ireland after that and became involved in Sinn Féin. He was elected MP for South County Dublin in 1918. He had been part of the unsuccessful delegation which had sought Irish recognition at the Versailles peace conference. Eamon Duggan was a solicitor and a veteran of the Easter Rising who had been elected MP for South Meath. The head of the secretariat was Erskine Childers, ex-clerk of the House of Commons, ex-novelist, ex-gunrunner, ex-Royal Naval officer and intense republican. These men would face the Prime Minister, Winston Churchill, Austen Chamberlain, Lord Birkenhead, and others, including the Attorney-General, Sir Gordon Hewart. Only Collins and Griffith had the stature and stamina to stand up to these.

There was another problem at the heart of the delegation. Griffith was convinced, even before he left Dublin, that the team would be unsuccessful in bringing back recognition of a republic, and was dubious about de Valera's formula of external association. That the two most convinced republicans in the Dáil, Brugha and Stack, were not going to be party to the negotiations meant that the extreme republican position was being over-represented in Dublin, in the absence of the pragmatic Griffith and Collins. The already existing animosity between Brugha and Collins meant that there already existed a crack between the two positions. Finally, within the delegation, there was abrasion between Griffith and the almost fanatical Childers, whom Griffith considered to be an Englishman poking his nose into Irish affairs.[5]

The Irish wanted an independent state, loosely bound to the Empire, with the King as head of the Empire. The British were prepared to concede modified dominion status, with an oath of fidelity to the King as head of state, as long as the fact of a partitioned Ireland was recognised. The Irish made an error by seeking to insist on the unity of Ireland. To tell the truth, the delegation had not prepared a stance on the position of unionists, and was forced to follow the same learning curve undertaken by the Redmondites between 1914 and 1916. Confronted by the realities, they fell back on a more defensible position, comforted by the device of the Boundary Commission, one of Lloyd George's more cunning flights of fancy. The commission, Lloyd George hinted to the Irish delegation, would pare off so much of the territory of Northern Ireland that it would no longer be a viable entity, and a future united Ireland would be assured.[6] It is difficult to understand how the delegation could believe that the British would have any more power—or will—to coerce the Ulster Unionists than they had shown in 1914.[7] This compromise destroyed the hand that de Valera had wanted them to play. He had insisted that, if the talks failed, the point of breakdown should be partition. All republicans would unite to oppose that. Now, by throwing away the Orange card, they had thrown away the ace of trumps.[8]

Moving on from this, the talks focused on the relationship between the two islands. Again, the Irish seemed to weaken their position by concentrating on the symbolism of dominion rather than on the practical working out of that domination. They agreed to the British maintaining naval bases without any great reluctance, yet they got hung up on the trappings in which the British wanted to dress up the Treaty. Since the British were conceding most of what the republicans were demanding, accepting a Governor-General and an oath of fidelity to the King might seem a small price. What the Irish failed to recognise was the need that Lloyd George had to offer independence wrapped in imperial trappings. It was the only way he could get it accepted by Tories who had baulked at a much more limited form of home rule in 1912.[9]

Yet this imperial window dressing was the most difficult for the republicans to swallow. Symbols that were being included to ease the pain for the English were proving to be thorns in the flesh of the negotiators. The oath of allegiance to the Crown was the most bitter, yet the one that the British were going to cling to longest. Having former rebels taking the oath could be taken as an indication that the British had achieved some sort of victory in the troubles. At the same time, the oath blocked the way to a true Irish Republic, the thing of the people, where the legitimacy of the ruler derives from the people. For a monarchist institution like the Houses of Parliament, the idea of a republic was anathema to all that was British. For the Irish, however, the ideal of the republic carried an almost sacred aura; foretold by the United Irishmen, proclaimed by Pearse in 1916, the logical next step was its establishment. For them an oath was more than a form of words. Oaths had been used to bind Irish nationalists together in various secret societies over the years, and the members of the Dáil had taken an oath to bear true faith and allegiance to the Irish Republic. If they were now to take an oath to King George with tongue in cheek, it would debase their previous oaths. If they took it seriously, they would perjure and dishonour one another.[10]

It has been suggested that this idea of the sacredness of an oath, of the need to stand by one's word once it is given, apes, consciously or otherwise, the ideal of the English gentleman, an unusual role-model for people who had been at war with just such gentlemen for the previous two years. It may have more to do with the importance that words have in Catholic Canon Law. Priests said that words were weapons that the weak could use against the strong, and to break one's word was not only dishonourable, but threw away the weaks' only weapon.[11] Griffith was later to say, during the Dáil debate on the Treaty, that, in its final wording, the oath was one that could be taken with honour, since it was an oath of loyalty to the Irish Constitution with the addition of a declaration of faithfulness to the head of the British Commonwealth.[12]

De Valera, the wordsmith, offered a compromise whereby the oath-taker would swear allegiance to the Constitution of the Irish State, to the Treaty of Association and to the King as head of the Associated States. This was too mealy-mouthed for the British, who offered wording swearing true faith and allegiance to the Irish constitution, then to the King 'in virtue of the common citizenship of Ireland with Great Britain' and the other members of the Commonwealth. This seemed a distinct concession, since other dominions swore allegiance to the King in his own person. One member of the Irish delegation, Arthur Griffith, was not totally against the idea of self-determination combined with the monarchy. He had argued in the past for a dual monarchy system for Britain and Ireland, such as existed in Austria and Hungary before the Great War. Other members of the delegation saw the reality of independence that the imperial trappings sought to hide and decided that these were a price worth paying. On 6 December, a Treaty was signed which included the oath, partition and various concessions on security. Perhaps the cleverest piece of linguistic management was the name of the new country, the Irish Free State. This echoed the title of the South African Orange Free State, which had fought against the British in the Boer War, while the Irish translation, Saorstát, had the same connotations as Poblacht.

Although the delegation had been given plenipotentiary powers as 'envoys plenipotentiary from the elected Government of the Republic of Ireland', the Treaty had to be ratified by the Dáil.[13] It is worth considering the nature of this second Dáil, so sacred in republican mythology. It was not, for example, a body that had been elected by normal, democratic means. The TDs had been selected by Collins and a few others. The names were chosen from lists sent up by local Sinn Féin clubs, which were often in the control of the local IRA chief. They were almost all returned unopposed in an election held under conditions of guerrilla war. Almost half of them were professionals of one sort or another, though three quarters of these had parents who were farmers or who were engaged in small scale business. In social terms, they were upwardly mobile. Two thirds of the TDs had taken part in the Easter Rising, and three quarters of them had had political experience of some sort, usually in local politics. One quarter had experience only in guerrilla warfare.

Those Cabinet ministers who had remained at home were not pleased. The seven members were all present, as were Gavan Duffy and Childers. The debate was long and bitter and the Irish Cabinet endorsed the Treaty by four votes to three only after Barton, who had changed his mind about the Treaty, felt that he had to vote for it as he had signed it. After the meeting, de Valera still maintained that he could not recommend the Treaty to the Dáil. The vote in the Dáil, which met a week later, and met again on numerous occasions for nearly a month, was also tight, though the Treaty was accepted by the Dáil by sixty-four votes for to fifty-seven against when the count was taken on 7 January. This was a defeat for de Valera, who then asked for a vote of confidence. This was lost by the closest vote of all, sixty to fifty-eight. His place as President of the Dáil was then taken by Arthur Griffith. De Valera and his supporters left the building, albeit temporarily, after the election of Griffith, but it was obvious that the time for debate was over.[14] In a gesture of great symbolism, Dublin Castle was surrendered on 16 January by the British to Michael Collins. It is doubtful how many really understood the magnitude of the Irish achievement; that it was a political revolution that marked the end of Anglo-Ireland.[15] It was Michael Collins who was left to deal with much of the transition, often travelling between Dublin and London arranging the final details of the transfer of power. The soldiers went back to barracks, while the Black and Tans and the Auxiliaries were sent home. A new Civic Guard was formed to replace both the RIC and their republican counterparts.[16]

This last task did not proceed altogether smoothly. At first it was to be a paramilitary force, like the RIC before it, and at first it consisted mostly of Volunteers, many of whom had fought in flying columns. In mid-May, however, there was a mutiny among these ex-Volunteers, who complained that ex-members of the RIC at headquarters and in the officer corps had undue influence. The embryo force was brought from the Curragh to the RIC barracks in the Phoenix Park and disarmed. Eoin O'Duffy, who had been Mulcahy's deputy, was made Chief Commissioner and set about establishing the new service. Recruits had to stand at least five feet nine inches tall and have a thirty-six inch chest. They also had to be literate enough to write a letter or short com-position on a simple subject.[17]

For those who still aspired to a republic, the gap between what they had demanded and what had been accepted on their behalf was too wide to swallow, and could be explained by the Irish delegation giving in too easily, or by the British demonstrating their 'usual' duplicity; the phrase 'perfidious Albion' became popular with nationalists who lived through this time. Since the British were across the Irish Sea, the treaty delegation was easier to attack. Opponents of the Treaty focused on the fact that the Treaty had not been referred back to Dublin before being signed. The fact that this was a request from de Valera rather than the Dáil was quietly ignored, as was the fact that de Valera was at home in Limerick on the night of the signing and could not be reached. It is interesting that TDs who were Protestant and those had been born outside Ireland were most fundamental in their opposition to the Treaty. It was as if they had the enthusiasm of the converted.[18]

Some of the out-and-out republicans, many of whom were leaders of flying columns, believed that, if the Irish delegation had refused to concede an inch, in imitation of the unionists, a republic was there for the taking, even if it meant a return to war. They had had experience of defeating units of the British army, and believed that they could go on doing so. They looked at the way Lloyd George had suddenly dropped all pre-conditions before agreeing to a ceasefire.[19] Collins, on the other hand, was not at all confident about the IRA's prospects. Although they had an influx of recruits during the period of the truce, there was a shortage of ammunition and other supplies, while the extra numbers caused problems of discipline and security.[20] Mulcahy pointed out that the IRA could drive the British out of nothing more substantial than a police barracks, and admitted to the Chief Secretary that the IRA could not have lasted more than another three weeks.[21]

Although it is possible to argue that what was on offer was a *de facto* republic, and that the two sides in the Treaty debate were arguing about very little, the British were also anxious about details. It was obvious that Lloyd George was negotiating with representatives of the Dáil, but the British refused to recognise the Dáil formally, and the Treaty had to be ratified by the MPs elected in May 1921 under the Government of Ireland Act. This meeting took place on 14 January, though it was boycotted by de Valera and his supporters. It was at this meeting that a Provisional Government was set up. The Irish, too, fought against the bit. In the first stamps issued by the new regime, the head of the monarch was obliterated by a franking which read 'Provisional Government of Ireland'. More important, the initial drafts of the Irish constitution laid great emphasis on the freedoms that dominion status conferred, rather than more restrictive, legal definitions. This draft was vetoed by the British.

For the first part of 1922 neither side in the Irish debate did or said anything that might increase the tension. Collins and de Valera agreed that voting on the matter would polarise opinion and no vote was taken at the Ard-Fheis in February. Equally, Collins tried to write the King out of the constitution, but was frustrated by the British. This level of cooperation seemed likely to extend to the elections, due to be held in June, and it seemed that all those serving in the Dáil would be returned unopposed. Once again the British were not pleased, as such a situation would not reflect the pro-Treaty majority in the country. Collins repudiated the pact before the election, and 78 per cent of the electorate voted pro-Treaty.[22]

The real threat was coming from another quarter. As early as 12 January, senior figures in the IRA had written to Richard Mulcahy, the Minister of Defence, demanding that an Army Convention be held. It was being proposed that the army should reconfirm its allegiance to the Republic, but should set up its own executive, which would control it independently of the civil authorities.[23] By this time it was obvious that, although the army was split just as much as the rest of the population, the majority in the rank and file of the IRA were opposed to the Treaty. To buy time, Mulcahy agreed to hold the convention within two months. At the same time he went about setting up a National Army to guard against a republican coup. He was helped in this task by the number of unemployed veterans of the Great War and when time for the Convention arrived, he felt strong enough to do an about-turn so he banned it.

Although Mulcahy claimed the allegiance of the IRA, setting up the National Army was a tortuous business. Most of the staff officers supported the Treaty, but the majority of divisional and brigade commanders were loyal to the Army Council. Mulcahy was lucky in that the three main areas of disaffection were separated by forces loyal to the Provisional Government. In the north, 2nd and 3rd Northern Divisions were anti-Treaty, while 1st and 5th Northern Divisions supported the Provisional Government. In Armagh and South Down, 4th Northern Division declared itself neutral, though it continued to fight its own war against the Northern state. The problem of the 2nd and 3rd Divisions was dealt with by dismissing their commanders. The 4th Division then repudiated the Provisional Government. In fact, most Volunteers repudiated both sides and simply went home.[24] Another area of disaffection was Connacht. There were strong enough pro-Treaty forces in Clare and Longford to contain this threat, so it was in Munster that the main threat lay.

Not enough Volunteers were enlisting in the National Army. A new Volunteer organisation was set up at the start of the Civil War and its members were urged to enlist for a minimum of six months. As noted above, many of these were ex-servicemen who were glad to escape unemployment. Many of them saw enlistment as a way of escaping the unpopularity that most of them had experienced in their communities. Several hundred officers and senior NCOs with war experience were given commissions in the new force. There were tensions in the force between Old IRA and British army veterans that were to erupt in 1924.[25]

The people who supported the Treaty were made up to a large extent of people who would have supported the Parliamentary Party in the past: the urban middle classes; the larger farmers; and the industrialised working class. Most Protestants also supported the Treaty, though some, like Erskine Childers, did not. Bryan Cooper, a Sligo landlord who had been in Gallipoli with 10th (Irish) Division, had been a Unionist MP before the war, stood as an Independent after the Treaty and joined the Free State party, Cumann na nGaedheal, in 1927.

Among the republicans, de Valera struggled for recognition. Here, power lay with military command, who regarded all politicians, even among their own supporters, with contempt. Although the Army Executive appointed de Valera as President and Chief Executive of the Republic in October, it was a decision made without any effort to bring it about in practice. He at first was refused access to an Army Executive meeting in March 1923; when he was admitted, he had no voting rights. If he had not been arrested by the Free State authorities after the Civil War was over, and had to spend a year in jail, it is possible his prestige would never have been regained.

The military leaders of the republicans were confident in their abilities. In their numbers they had the majority of good leaders at the middle level; in a regular army they would have been colonels and brigadiers. In particular, they had the four most successful leaders from Munster: Tom Barry, Dan Breen, Ernie O'Malley and Liam Lynch. Only at the highest levels did the National Army have an equivalent level of ability. But the level of zeal and enthusiasm which the republicans brought to continuing the war was part of what distanced them from the war-weary people, who saw in the Treaty enough to satisfy their ambitions. They also faced an enemy with easy access to weaponry, ammunition and recruits.[26]

Many of the most committed republicans were women. The convention of Cumann na mBan held on 5 February 1922 rejected the Treaty by over four hundred votes to sixty-three. Free State supporters went on to establish their own organisation, Cumann na Saoirse, the Freedom Association. One Free State supporter described republican women as 'implacable and irrational upholders of death and destruction'.[27] Republican women who were not quite so bloodthirsty, such as Hanna Sheehy Skeffington, raised money in the United States to be used for the comforts of republican internees. Among these internees were about four hundred women, who were the most unruly of prisoners; some of those imprisoned in the North Dublin Union rioted in April 1923.

Only a few of the republicans came from the wealthier classes. One of these was Robert Barton, who had reneged on his part in signing the Treaty and was now on the republican side. Although most of the republicans came from the less comfortably off sections of society, they were from the more remote parts of Ireland and they did not succeed in attracting poorer industrial workers to their ranks.[28] These depended too much on trade links with Britain to want a complete break with the other island. Land seems to be the basis of much republican support.

This idea is supported by the fact that the Civil War, the War between Friends, as it was called in Irish, was at its bitterest in some western areas that had been very active during the land wars, but which had been quiet during the fighting against the British of 1919-1921, even when the fighting was going on around them.[29]

The republicans were quite puritanical, a reflection of the austere Catholicism in which many of them had been brought up. The purity of their marriage to the Republic, a relationship which would not tolerate compromise, contrasted with the pragmatism of the Free State government, who were prepared to defer the Republic until the time it could be achieved at a reasonable cost. There was also the contrast between a totalitarian regime implied in the republican decision to continue a fight that was disapproved of by most Irish citizens, and the pro-Treaty idea of a civic state of citizens who were burdened by a minimum of legislation and for whom morality was a private matter. Another way of putting this is to say that it was a war between pro-Treaty administrators and anti-Treaty guerrillas.[30] Seen in this light, the war was central to the definition of what was to be the final goal of the national struggle.

There is something about a civil war which induces ferocity, especially when it is being contested by people who have been members of the same oath-bound society. Having shared the same experiences, they cannot understand why the other side does not agree with their conclusions. There are also questions of loyalty; each side felt betrayed by the other. The pragmatists claimed that the anti-Treaty side was composed of holier-than-thou hypocrites who were indulging their emotions at the expense of the community, disloyal to the ordinary people of Ireland. The republicans in turn accused the pro-Treaty majority of being disloyal to the Republic of 1919 in pursuit of career, power and snobbery. General Macready could not resist stirring the pot. The Treaty offered peace, he said, and this would be a disaster for republicans. In future they would have to work for a living.[31]

As British soldiers evacuated their barracks, the local IRA commanders occupied them. Whether they held them for the Provisional Government or for the Republic depended on circumstances that were beyond the control of Griffith or Collins. In Limerick, for example, two different groups struggled for control of the town. A compromise deal was reached before shooting began. Griffith wanted any trouble to be stamped on right away, but Collins still felt close to the IRA, and still thought of himself as a soldier. He was delighted when Mulcahy said that the Free State forces were not yet strong enough to force the pace.[32] The trouble was that, as Griffith had foreseen, Limerick was just the start of it. It was followed by other worrying incidents. Against this background, Collins worked to demonstrate that he was not in Griffith's pocket, and tried to bring as many of the IRA leaders as he could into the fold. Those who did not succumb to his charm developed their own conspiracy theory. Collins, they said, had been seduced by his treatment in London and had even been offered the opportunity of marrying royalty. Collins's tactics of bullying, bribing and cajoling IRA men and TDS to side with the Free State led men like Ernie O'Malley to feel that Collins and his lieutenants were morally inferior to the leaders of 1916. The purists could feel that, though they were in a minority, it was a spiritually superior minority.[33]

De Valera was not yet out of the picture. In March he announced himself as the head of a new party, Cumann na Poblachta (League of the Republic), which was, of course, made up of his supporters from the rump of the Dáil that opposed the Treaty. He said that the Treaty was a bar to independence and that it was only by civil war that independence could be achieved.[34] On three successive days he said that unless the Treaty was rejected, war was the only way forward, though Irishmen would die on both sides.[35] It was at this stage that Mulcahy banned the Army Convention. His National Army was not yet ready to confront the IRA head on, so he was put in the humiliating position of seeing it go ahead anyway. It was dominated by Rory O'Connor, who was emerging as one of the most intransigent republicans. Under his influence those present confirmed their allegiance to the Republic and elected an executive of sixteen IRA officers. At a press conference O'Connor repudiated the Dáil and said that they were not under the authority of the Provisional Government. When he was asked directly whether what had been established was a military dictatorship, he replied, 'You can take it that way if you like.'[36]

A few weeks after that, the IRA, who were coming to be called irregulars, seized the Four Courts, together with some other positions in Dublin, and began to fortify them. One of these, ironically, was Fowler Hall, headquarters of the Grand Orange Lodge of Ireland before that institution had evacuated to Belfast in January 1922.[37] In taking this action the republicans demonstrated that they had learned nothing from the failure of the Easter Rising or from the success of their own campaign against the British. In 1922, the IRA was taking on a fight with the embryonic National Army that it might possibly win. In the last eighteen months they had demonstrated their ability to fight against superior numbers in open country. Now they were repeating the mistakes of 1916, occupying iconic buildings which were easy to isolate and besiege. Once again the possibility of humiliating the government was more important than the possibility of ultimate victory. Efforts made by Collins to persuade de Valera back into the political process became irrelevant as de Valera himself became more marginalised within the republican front. The Civil War might have begun sooner, but the nationalists of Northern Ireland were going through a purgatory that had little promise of heaven, and both sides looked at ways in which they could intervene to support the beleaguered Northerners. Even Collins was tempted to march on the North, if that would bring about republican unity.

For a while it seemed as if the republicans were trying to administer the death of the thousand cuts to the Provisional Government. They began to build up their funds by launching a series of bank raids. They used their fortresses in Dublin to post snipers who could dominate government buildings and the army headquarters at Beggar's Bush. It was an act of direct defiance. Yet the precipitating factor for fighting was something else entirely. Someone assassinated Sir Henry Wilson, a man who had combined the highest rank in the British Army with support for the Ulster unionists. Although the two assassins were caught and hanged, they did not say who had ordered the attack, so there is no chain of evidence back to either of the two sides in Ireland.[38] The British chose to blame the republicans, or the irregulars, as they were coming to be known. The assassination took place on 22 June, and the following day the British ordered a reprisal in Dublin. General Macready managed to have the plan drawn up, but found excuses not to put it into operation because, he afterwards said, it would only have embroiled Britain in another Irish war against a united Irish front. Instead, pressure was put on the Provisional Government, with the threat that if they did not clear out the irregular strongpoints, the British would come and do it themselves. Such coercion would not look well when reported in Irish newspapers.

The irregulars managed to remove this problem. On 27 June a raiding party of republicans set out from the Four Courts to collect transport from a garage. They were intercepted and arrested by a patrol of the National Army. Ernie O'Malley replied by abducting General Ginger O'Connell, Deputy Chief of Staff of the National Army. Not even Collins could ignore this, and he asked for the use of British field guns while the Irish Cabinet ordered its forces to take action against the republican strongpoints. One of the most memorable photographs of the fighting was of Free State troops using artillery that had probably been used against the rebels of 1916 against their ex-comrades in the Four Courts. The attack began on Wednesday 28 June and lasted until Friday. By that time the building was in flames and the garrison had to surrender. The attack had the effect of uniting opposition to the Treaty. Before long, the old warhorses of the republic, Brugha, Stack, Markievicz and de Valera, all rushed to Dublin, where they met at the headquarters of the irregulars. Even yet they had not learned the lessons of 1916, and they occupied buildings in O'Connell Street. It took the government forces a week to winkle them out of these strongpoints, and the week ended with the death of Cathal Brugha, shot as he emerged, gun in hand, from the ruins of a burning building.[39]

Michael Collins was commander in chief of the government forces. Under his command were men from a variety of backgrounds. There were many who had fought in the War of Independence, including Collins's own Squad, and men who were veterans of the British army and the Great War. A third grouping was younger men from an urban background who would in the past have joined one of the Irish regiments of the British army. The greatest strength that the Free State forces had was the undoubted support of the vast majority of the people. Even the Catholic hierarchy blessed them. Collins's army was supplied by the British, largely through the good efforts of Winston Churchill. They could have had tanks, but they couldn't find qualified tank drivers in Ireland. They did get aeroplanes and boats, armoured cars and field guns, in addition to 11,000 rifles, 1,000 revolvers and eighty machine-guns.[40] This help was crucial to the success of the Free State forces.

In general terms, the fighting in the Civil War took place in Dublin and Munster, where the fighting against the British had also occurred. It differed from the earlier war because this time large forces were involved in large scale operations of a type unknown in the earlier struggle. The Free State forces attacked the irregulars and drove them from town after town. Liam Lynch, commanding the republicans, had wanted to establish a defensive line from Limerick to Waterford, a Munster Republic, but did little to deter the advancing Free Staters. Limerick City was captured on 21 July, and Waterford at about the same time. In August Cork was taken by a ship-borne invasion, with the troops landing in nearby Passage West. This was the end of conventional warfare in the struggle, which now reverted to a guerrilla conflict, fought in the hills and bogs of the south-west. The aim of the irregulars was to avoid captivity, keep their weapons safe, create sufficient havoc to provoke government coercion and arouse popular indignation, thereby destabilising the state. It had worked with the British, but it did not work now. The Irish forces could use a level of ferocity in their actions that the British never could, simply because they were Irish, and had the support of most of the civilian population. The irregulars did not have the same access to a sympathetic people, and were forced to rely on intimidation, the very action that they had tried to provoke in the National Army.

On 12 August, Arthur Griffith died. Although in photographs he looks much older than the young warriors who surrounded him, he was only fifty years old. He had been driven to exhaustion by the struggles and disappointments of more than a decade of endeavour. Only ten days later, Michael Collins was shot in the back of the head, leading a small patrol deep into irregular territory in County Cork, where no commander in chief should have been. Writing to a friend at the time he had signed the Treaty, he said that he had signed his own death warrant. It was as if he had chosen the time and place of his own execution. The place of these two pillars of the Free State was taken by Cosgrave, O'Higgins and Mulcahy. When the third Dáil sat for the first time in September, it confirmed Cosgrave as head of the administration and the task of building up the new state was begun.

De Valera and his supporters stayed away; not only did they refuse to recognise the Dáil's authority, but they joined with the irregulars' Army Executive and set up an alternative government. When this entity threatened to have members of the Dáil and the Seanad shot, the Free State government was forced to react in the same way that the British had. In September it adopted a Special Powers resolution which was a form of martial law, granting wide authority to the military. It also began a series of executions, starting in November. One of the first to face a firing squad was Erskine Childers, who had been Minister for Propaganda on the republican side. He had been captured with a gun that had been given to him by Michael Collins and was deemed to be in arms against the government. He was killed on 24 November. The republicans reacted by killing Sean Hales, a pro-Treaty TD, on 7 December. In a cold-blooded calculation, the government reacted by choosing four leading republicans, one from each province, and having them shot the following morning. One of those shot, Rory O'Connor, had been best man at Kevin O'Higgins's wedding less than a year before. This shooting seems to have had a depressing effect on the morale of the irregulars, but it was not the end. A total of seventy-seven republicans were shot by firing squad.

These were legal killings, but there were others that went on. In Kerry, the occupying Free State forces included members of Collins's old Squad. They were not popular, and there were rumours that they had been mistreating republican prisoners. On 6 March, in what they described as an act of reprisal, the irregulars set a mine which killed five Free State soldiers. The Free State commander, Paddy Daly, ordered that republican prisoners be used to clear republican mines. The actions which followed this order were so controversial that it will probably be impossible to get at the truth of them. On 7 March, the republicans alleged, eight republican prisoners were tied together before a nearby mine was set off by their Free State captors. The following day, four republicans were killed by a mine near Killarney. Four days later another five were blown up at Cahirciveen.

Liam Lynch himself was killed on 10 April, and he was replaced by the more pragmatic Northerner, Frank Aiken. Even before Lynch's death de Valera had called for negotiations but it was Aiken who made the move towards having a ceasefire, which came into force in May. The legion of the rearguard, as de Valera called them, dumped their arms. The killings did not stop immediately. Noel Lemass, whose brother Sean would become Taoiseach, or Prime Minister, was killed in July and his body was dumped in the Wicklow mountains. As late as July 1927, Kevin O'Higgins was killed on his way to mass, an incident that was undoubtedly related to the Civil War. The War between Friends had created some long-lasting enmities. There are few reliable figures for the number of deaths in the war. About eight hundred Free State soldiers died, and probably twice that number of republicans. If you add to this the executions by the state and the probability of collateral damage to civilians, then a figure of around three thousand sounds realistic.[41]

With the death of Collins, the Northern Catholics had lost their best supporter in the Free State government. The same might be said of the republicans, and it is possible that, if he had survived, there would have been an earlier ceasefire. The dead on the republican side included many of their most inspirational leaders. As was the case with Aiken, more pragmatic lieutenants began to see the impossibility of winning an extended fight. It is possible that it was the death of these idealists that allowed the compromises to be made that allowed the state to survive as a settled, democratic institution. The war left a legacy of distrust and alienation, and a bill that was calculated at £17 million, with a further £30 million paid out in compensation, an enormous sum for a country with a low taxation base. Even the embryo state's historic archive was largely destroyed, when the irregulars had set off a bomb as they evacuated the Four Courts. The sense of unity of purpose that had characterised the fight against the British was lost, perhaps never to be regained. It is scarcely surprising that the response of many who suffered the trauma of these years was silence.

Although the war was won by the Free State forces, in the sense that it was the irregulars who called off the struggle in May 1923, victory was paid for in terms of lost leadership, of enmities that were intensified and perpetuated by the tactics used by both sides. Repression by the government continued. Only those who repudiated the Republic were given an amnesty when the government forces rounded up all those suspected of being irregulars. At one time 11,000 republicans were interned, fifteen times the number held in Northern Ireland. Most of them were released over the following year, cowed by state repression. As in Northern Ireland, a large percentage of the population had been alienated by the state.[42]

Coda ⌐

MAKING IT WORK

The Cosgrave government that was charged with making a success of the Irish Free State was still not altogether sure what that state was going to be. It was defined by the Anglo-Irish Treaty, but there were aspects of the Treaty that were in themselves ambiguous. The Crown was still represented in Dublin, albeit by an Irishman. The country was still a member of the British Commonwealth, albeit one with a right to separate representation at the League of Nations. The government took the decision to define itself in contrast to Britain in both cultural and political matters. All other priorities, social and otherwise, were subordinate to these. The Constitution of the Free State played down the colonial and imperial connection and emphasised that legitimate authority lay in popular sovereignty and allegiance to the Treaty. Indeed, when the Dáil was debating the terms of the Constitution, the government was so committed to the Treaty that ministers threatened to resign if key passages supporting it were not accepted.

The new state had defined itself geographically when, appropriately on April Fool's Day, it set up a chain of customs posts along the border with Northern Ireland to support a customs barrier against Northern Ireland and Great Britain despite complaints from Southern producers that they would be the ones harmed. Most people simply ignored it, and border towns like Derry and Enniskillen and Newry still served large hinterlands within the Free State. On the other hand, it gave the Craig government the opportunity to establish the principle of partition as being inviolable. When, in 1927, an attempt was made to coordinate an all-Ireland tourist policy by inviting representatives from Northern Ireland to visit Cork and Kerry as guests of the Irish Tourist Board, the answer from Craig was a single-word telegram: 'Decline.'

While Cosgrave was in office, the Northern Ireland government looked on the Free State as a benign, if alien, entity. In 1924, there was a crisis amounting almost to a mutiny within the Free State army. In the aftermath of the Civil War, the Irish executive had decided that it was possible to reduce army numbers to peacetime standards. This was perfectly satisfactory with the rank and file, who had mostly enlisted for a short time, but it did not go down so well with some of the officers, who had intended making a career of the army. Over two thousand of them were being made redundant. A group of these, led by some of Collins's intelligence squad, decided to resist. It was an awkward situation, but by the end of it, the primacy of the civilian government had been established. Kevin O'Higgins was quick to respond to the challenge and he gave the Garda Commissioner, O'Duffy, special powers over the IRA. He also forced the resignation of General Mulcahy among others. He cleared out the last of the Old IRA and those who were sympathetic to them.[1] In the North, Craig took the fact that some of the officers concerned had gone on the run to mean that there was a continuing threat to Northern Ireland. This gave him the excuse to maintain the high numbers in the Special Constabulary.

In cultural terms, the new state defined itself as being Gaelic. The Irish language was in a weakened state; in 1911 only 17.6 per cent of the people had been able to speak Irish at all, while fewer spoke it regularly.[2] It was made a subject on its own and became a compulsory component of secondary school examinations from 1924. The aim of teaching Irish history was to inculcate national pride and self-respect by showing the important role that the Irish had played in the advance of civilisation. The role of English writers was to be downplayed and education should be structured to revive the ancient life of Ireland as a Gaelic state. It was ambitious, and it did not work. Making Irish compulsory for official positions simply meant discrimination in favour of those from Irish-speaking areas without making Irish the living language of the nation.[3] As Owen Dudley Edwards has noted, even de Valera, when he was speaking to the Dáil about the Treaty, spoke in English, because it was in English that he could best elucidate his concerns.

This could well have been over-compensation in reaction to the accusation that the Treaty had sold the Irish Republic for a mess of pottage. Even more, it was a deliberate policy to emphasise the stability of the state, that it drew its strength from ancient roots. This aspect was helped by the fact that de Valera's party kept away from the Dáil and the other, minor, parties had too few members to matter. It was easy for the government to be authoritarian, and it was in the nature of its members to be so. To many onlookers, Cumann na nGaedheal began to resemble the Irish Parliamentary Party.

There seemed to be no hint that Connolly's social welfare policies had survived in any form. In 1924 the government actually cut the old age pension by a shilling a week. Although this was probably necessary in order to control the economy, since pensions used up over 16 per cent of the nation's budget, it would have been political suicide if there had been an opposition party in place. The characteristic life of rural Ireland, particularly in the west, was one of poverty. There did not seem to be much sympathy for the rural poor in the comment of Patrick McGilligan, a Northerner who served as TD for NUI, when he said, 'People may have to die in the country, and die through starvation.'[4] O'Higgins referred to Pearse's social ideas as 'largely poetry'.[5] There was no labour reaction to the government's policy because there had been a split in the Irish Transport and General Workers' Union in the early 1920s, when the radical James Larkin was marginalised by the conservative William O'Brien. Cosgrave was able to concentrate on managing his 'conservative, rural, strongly *petit bourgeois* state without fear of opposition'.[6]

Although there was a reference made in the Constitution to the state's ownership of natural resources, the only real state intervention in the 1920s was in various forms of energy exploitation under the auspices of the Electricity Supply Board (ESB). The most prestigious of these initiatives was the hydro-electric scheme on the River Shannon, which was built with the help of German—Weimar rather than National Socialist—expertise.

It would have been difficult to introduce radical policies, because the real expertise of government was in the Civil Service. In the earliest days of the Free State, 98 per cent of civil service personnel had worked for the pre-1922 administration. As late as 1934, this proportion was still as high as 45 per cent.[7] At the heart of the Civil Service was the Department of Finance, the influence of which was so great that legislation emanating from other departments was checked by Finance before being presented to the Dáil. Senior personnel were allowed to make decisions in circumstances of autonomy. The department still carried something of the aura of Michael Collins, and its success in floating the first National Loan of 1923 established its reputation.[8]

In view of the success of the Dáil courts, it is perhaps surprising that the legal system owed more to the status quo that had been in place before the troubles. For all the Gaelic culture that was being encouraged by the state, there was no incorporation of the Brehon laws either. In the first case, it may have been a result of the policy of centralisation; too much freedom of judgement to individual magistrates might have undermined this. In the case of the Brehon system, the frequency and ease of divorce in Gaelic Ireland, where marriage was a civil contract between a man and a woman with no church involvement, would not have been tolerated by the Catholic Church. In this and in other social matters, the administration demonstrated its adherence to the ideals of Catholic social theory. With the dominating presence of the increasingly Rome-centred Church, and the proximity of the old colonial power, it was, perhaps, impossible to be completely independent. It was, perhaps, understandable that the Cosgrave government accepted dominion status, but tried to give it a uniquely Irish stamp.

Economically, Ireland was still closely tied to Britain. In 1924, 98 per cent of Irish exports still went to Britain. Particularly favoured was the Irish cattle farmer, bogeyman of the Land Wars, who was a key figure in British markets. This continuing dependency on agricultural exports skewed the employment situation in Ireland, so that more than half the workforce was directly involved in agriculture. Land was still being distributed to the people; the Land Commission distributed nearly half a million acres among 24,000 families in the first ten years of its existence. There was some consolidation of farms, and the emphasis on beef saw a reduction in the amount of tillage, but productivity remained at half the level of Denmark's. Cosgrave saw farmers as the core of his support, and believed that the prosperity of farmers was central to a successful economy. The reason that the establishment of a Free State customs area in 1923 was not followed by a system of tariffs was that the tariffs would increase agricultural labourers' wages, which would not have pleased farmers.[9]

For all the success of Irish agricultural exports, the country was faced with a balance of payments crisis in the late 1920s. The growth of agricultural exports was offset by a decline in industrial exports. The peak year for exports overall was 1929, when they paid for 77 per cent of the country's imports. If it had not been for money sent home by emigrants, the country would have been bankrupt. One of its greatest problems, a leftover from the fighting from 1919 until 1924, was the cost of defence and of paying out compensation. In the early years it took 30 per cent of the nation's budget. By careful management it was down to £1.5 million by 1929. Such good practice impressed the money markets; Ireland did not suffer during the Great Depression from hyper-inflation, and maintained an excellent credit rating. The problem was that such cautious practice meant that there was nothing in Ireland to dissuade young people from emigrating. In fact, the emphasis on traditional farming practice, where extra mouths had traditionally been exported, probably increased emigration. There were no social initiatives to alleviate the condition of the poor. Savings were used to fund tax cuts.

It was not in de Valera's nature to remain outside active politics for long. By 1924 he was manoeuvring to establish a position from which, with honour, he could take up his seat in the Dáil. He reverted to the approach that he had used after the Easter Rising; he worked at persuading the active irregulars that the time had come to return to politics. Not all agreed with him, and a rump of the IRA continued a policy of assassination, of which Kevin O'Higgins was the most prominent victim after Michael Collins. With the majority he was able to form a new political party, which he called Fianna Fáil, or the Warriors of Destiny. This allowed him to contest the 1927 election. Five years of a government which demonstrated no empathy with the ordinary people gave him a good start, and he very nearly took power; the government had a majority of only three. Cumann na nGaedheal had become identified with a Ballsbridge type of upper middle class—smoked salmon the symbol of the risen people, as one disgruntled republican put it—and began to resemble the old IPP, even down to the family names that were coming to the fore.[10] There was, of course, the problem of the Oath of Fidelity, which the government had made a necessity before taking part in constitutional politics at any level after the death of O'Higgins. De Valera managed to turn a climb-down into a declaration of moral superiority. If he had spoken these words outside the Dáil, he said, he would have understood it to be a vow. Here, having being told by the government that it was only a form of words, he would speak these words. After reciting the formula, he lifted the Bible and said again that he regarded it only as a form of words. After five years in opposition, de Valera's party achieved a majority in 1932.

By this time the Irish had achieved a two-party democracy that was a close imitation of the British original, although proportional representation in voting allowed for the existence of many minor parties. These smaller parties tended not to get first preference votes, but picked up transfers. The only distinguishing mark between the two major parties was their attitude to the Treaty. Other than that, it would have been hard to distinguish between them. What Irish politics lacked at this stage, with the towering exception of de Valera, was someone with the personal magnetism of a leader. In the previous decade, anyone else with the qualifications to challenge this pre-eminence had passed on to literal or political afterlives. There was no single individual in either party to challenge him. He was a lion among collie pups.

De Valera's personality moulded the Ireland of the 1930s and beyond. In the beginning, the Free State had been squeezed into a Gaelic mould; the attempt had failed because there were too many aspects of the state that simply could not be fitted into such a constraint. It had been easier to define the state by its religion. Without a doubt it was Catholic. This resulted largely from its demography, and it would be wrong to say that Protestants were made unwelcome. Indeed the religious and educational rights of Southern Protestants were carefully guarded by the state and by statute. Many emigrated, in spite of this, almost 30 per cent of them by the end of the decade. Those who remained were likely to be the better off: large farmers, members of the higher professions and, in particular, bank officials.[11] Cosgrave had used the Church hierarchy to guard his flank while he got on with the job of managing the country. The price to be paid for that was a state based on the social and educational theories of the Catholic Church. Catholic children were to be taught by Catholic teachers in Catholic schools under Catholic control. There was to be no divorce and contraceptive devices were outlawed. The *Ne Temere* decree, by ensuring that the children of mixed marriages would be brought up as Catholics, meant that Protestants would be an ever-diminishing minority.

In this country where there was no political voice that dissented from this view of society—in politics dissent was limited to discussion of the Treaty—the one final area of intellectual freedom was blocked off when the Censorship Board was set up in 1929. The intelligentsia formed the only real opposition to the regime; their works were now banned for the most minor of transgressions.[12] The Cosgrave government, and its successors, legitimised their authority by reference to the years after 1917 and air-brushed the struggle for independence that had happened before that. Gone was the parliamentary struggle for home rule; disappeared utterly were the thousands who had fought in the Great War.

De Valera extended that policy even to the great and the good of republicanism. When, on one occasion, Liam Lynch asked him what Tom Clarke would have done, de Valera answered quite testily, 'Tom Clarke is dead. He has not our responsibilities. No one will ever know what he would do for this situation did not arise for him. But it has arisen for us and we must face it with our intelligence and conscious of our responsibility.'[13] This rejection of the dead was needed to enable him, when Fianna Fáil came to power in 1932, to set about redefining Ireland's relationship with the Commonwealth.

There was also a re-emphasis of Ireland's internal structure, and Fianna Fáil set about protecting this, culturally and economically. The Catholicism of the country was emphasised by the Eucharistic Conference held in Dublin in the year that Fianna Fáil came to power, an event which set the moral tone for the next half-century. Those who felt that the country did not suit them had a history of doing nothing to change the country; they simply left it. The population did not grow for much of this period, though improvements in world transport meant that emigration was a less permanent experience than it had been in the past. A pattern of late marriages in Ireland—in 1929 the average age of marriage was 34.9 for men, 29.1 for women, the highest in the world[14]— together with the fact that 25 per cent of women were still unmarried by their forty-fourth birthday, kept some brake on the growing population, and that growth was neutralised by emigration. Between 1929 and 1946, six in every thousand of the population emigrated; most of the emigrants were single, most were women, and most were country people moving to cities. After the start of America's Great Depression, most of the flow was towards England. In this period, there was another rise in the emigration of Protestants from the Free State.

For those who remained in the country, life tended to be a stoic acceptance of life as it was. Outside the cities, most people lived in single-storey, occasionally even single-roomed cottages. Families were large and conditions basic; tuberculosis was as much a fact of life as emigration. By the 1930s, two-storey, slate-roofed houses were beginning to appear, many of them built by the Land Commission. Even these new houses were basic enough and even by 1946 only 5 per cent of farmhouses had an indoor lavatory, while only another 15 per cent had an outdoor one. For the rest, it was the byre for the womenfolk and the open fields for the men. In cities matters were scarcely better, in spite of urban housing programmes. In Derry 'nightsoil' was collected street by street up till the 1930s. In Dublin, in 1938, 65,000 people lived in tenements and cottages unfit for human habitation.[15]

Although in some of the larger farms tractors began to appear by the end of the 1930s, in most farms agricultural practices were still primitive. Extra mouths, men or women, went to the hiring fairs to be poked and prodded like a domestic animal, to see if it was worth a farmer's while to take one on for a half year's labour. Yet rural life was not a priority for improvement, as far as de Valera was concerned. His ideal countryside was of small agricultural units owned by industrious, Gaelic and anti-material families. He saw such a life as ancient and dignified, and ignored the fact that this literary construct had little to do with the realities of rural life. Indeed, by the late 1930s, there were signs of a growing alienation towards rural norms and the sterility and frustration they produced.

This ideal, Gaelic Ireland had little to do with the metropolitan areas of Dublin and Cork, or even of large towns like Limerick. Here, and in other areas where there had been a strong garrison influence, an anglicised culture was the norm. People read a popular press, much of it printed in England. The well-to-do played golf and went to race meetings; the less-well-off went to local bookmakers and to the cinema. Industrial production, largely helped by electrification under ESB, was on a par with Italy and Portugal, but could not compare with that of England.

De Valera and Fianna Fáil saw no necessity to change the tight economic policies of the previous administration. They cut back on government expenditure by withholding land annuity payments due to the British government. The British countered with economic sanctions, and Ireland imposed her own, making protectionism in Ireland a reality. At the core of Fianna Fáil planning was the setting up of native industries. In a way, this was self-defeating, since the materials required to set up these industries had to be imported. There was not in Ireland's private sector the venture capital needed to fund these developments, so state-sponsored corporations were set up for specific purposes. This was not an indication of a growing socialism in the country, or even of a belief in corporate government. In this area, government policy was somewhere to the right of Catholic social teaching.

In so far as Fianna Fáil was prepared to interfere with agriculture at all, its desire was to see a move from cattle to tillage. Partly this was in response to British sanctions on Irish cattle. It was also believed that tillage would offer more employment for rural workers. Sugar beet was to be grown on a large scale under the auspices of one of the state-sponsored corporations, the Irish Sugar Company. Wheat was to be another large-scale crop. Throughout the 1930s, however, the percentage of males employed in agriculture continued to drop. Payments given to dairy farmers were used by those farmers to subsidise store cattle, helping to compensate for the lower prices they were receiving in the English market. The store cattle industry expanded during this period.

Although there may have been little internal change when de Valera came to power, it was in Ireland's relationship with the outside world, and in particular with Britain, that he established a reputation for statesmanship. In 1932 it was Ireland's turn to take the presidency of the League of Nations, and it was in his opening address to the thirteenth meeting of the League's council, held in Geneva, that he stated his position on the dominance of powerful nations over others. He complained that vital issues were not being discussed because it did not suit one or other of the great powers. Action on the economic sphere was paralysed by the pressure of national interests. Might was proving to be right, and the only way to stop it was to make the League of Nations a covenant, in which no state, great or small, could ignore the will of the League. He said that the primary duty of statesmen, 'national or international', was to plan for the well-being of their fellows, the ordinary human beings of every country.[16]

Even before this, he had taken the role of David to Britain's Goliath. Within a fortnight of taking power he informed the British government that he was abolishing the Oath of Allegiance. At the same time, as noted above, he informed the British that he was no longer passing on the Land Annuities that were being collected from farmers. When the British replied that the Oath and the Annuities were enshrined in the Treaty, de Valera countered that the people of Ireland had only accepted the Treaty because they were coerced by the threat of immediate and terrible war. The argument continued for some time, but after a little while the Oath was no longer mentioned. The Annuities were another matter, as they involved good hard cash, much needed in London. The British tried to get the matter settled by arbitration by an Imperial Board of the Commonwealth. De Valera refused, on the grounds that such a board would imply that Ireland was part of the Commonwealth.

There now followed a period when penal tariffs were imposed on goods traded between the two countries. Although some Irish industries were set up to provide alternatives, most Irish people persisted in buying the imported article, so the cost of living shot up. The members of the government took a cut in pay to show solidarity with the people and the people of Ireland seem to have accepted the inconvenience and privation of the economic war with good humour. Not so the Senate. This chamber of the Irish Parliament had been set up to allow for the representation of minority interests which might not find a voice in the Dáil. It was largely made up of a cross-section of old unionism and it tried to delay the Bill to remove the Oath of Allegiance. De Valera was not pleased.

Having got rid of the Oath and withheld the Annuities—which were still collected but which now went to the Irish Exchequer—de Valera set about diminishing the role of the Governor-General. The post, at the time, was held by James MacNeill, brother of Eoin. When the Governor-General arrived at a reception in the French Legation, two members of de Valera's Cabinet walked out. During the Eucharistic Conference, the Army Band was not allowed to play at a reception where the Governor-General would be present. Finally, just before MacNeill was due to finish his five-year term of office, de Valera dismissed him and replaced him four weeks later with an old friend, Daniel Buckley. Buckley, who owned a spirit grocery and a bicycle shop in Maynooth, had been part of the struggle for independence since 1907, when he had been fined for having his name written in Irish on his grocery cart. The appointment, as *Time* magazine noted at the time, was a step taken with tongue in cheek, a move towards abolishing the post altogether. De Valera installed Buckley in a suburban house, gave him a salary of £2,000, and gave him nothing to do except sign Acts of Parliament on the King's behalf.[17]

Up till now, the Labour Party had held the balance of power in the Dáil, so de Valera decided to capitalise on the popular support he was getting for these anti-imperial measures. His election pledge was that there would be more of the same. Cosgrave, on the other hand, said that he would end the economic war with Britain within three days of coming to power. Although he certainly had the support of most of the electorate, de Valera's overall majority was only one, and he began to doubt the system of proportional representation. Although it helped to guarantee representation for smaller groupings within the population, he claimed that it got in the way of strong government. Nevertheless, a majority of one was enough, and he began to cut away some more of the strands which connected the two islands.

There were a few problems to deal with first. Fascism was becoming a popular political philosophy in the 1930s, spreading from Mussolini's Italy to Germany and on to Spain. Even in countries where there was a strong tradition of democracy, fascist organisations were becoming a vociferous minority. In England there was Oswald Mosley and his Blackshirts. In Ireland there were the Blueshirts. The organisation had been started by Dr T. F. O'Higgins, brother of the murdered Kevin O'Higgins. Its apologists say it was begun to counter the intimidation and interference being carried out by the IRA at election meetings. Its membership was open to anyone who was prepared to intervene to prevent meetings being disrupted. It styled itself the National Guard and, when de Valera dismissed the Garda Commissioner, General O'Duffy, the latter took command of the vigilante group. At this stage, many opposition TDS joined the Blueshirts, including Cosgrave, and they in turn joined the Centre Party, a fringe group in the Dáil, to form the United Ireland Party.

There was little need to fight Communism in Ireland, and most Irishmen saw little that impressed them in grown men playing at soldiers; they had seen the real thing, and the general reaction was one of scorn. The organisation fell apart, though in 1936 O'Duffy led an Irish brigade to support Franco's rebellion in Spain. Franco sent them home. While this confusion was going on among the opposition, de Valera abolished the Senate.[18]

If the Blueshirts were something of a joke, continued activity by the IRA was not. The laws that de Valera passed to curtail the Blueshirts were also used against his erstwhile comrades: military tribunals had been reinstated; uniforms, badges and military titles were banned for political parties; and the carrying of weapons, including sticks, was forbidden. In June 1936, he banned the IRA.

In the English constitutional crisis surrounding the abdication of
Edward VIII, de Valera had a bill passed which became a new External
Relations Act. This removed the Crown from the Constitution. A few
months later he abolished the office of Governor-General. He did not
send an Irish representative to the Coronation of King George V.
Although Britain still had control of three naval bases on Irish soil, the
Irish Free State was effectively independent of the United Kingdom. The
way was open for de Valera's next piece of diplomatic prestidigitation.

In April 1937, he published a revised Constitution. This tackled
head-on the partition of Ireland. He proposed that the title of the Irish
Free State be changed to Éire, and that the term should be taken as
applying to the island as a whole, although he acknowledged that the
Constitution did not yet apply to the six north-eastern counties. Éire
was to be a sovereign, independent and democratic state. There was no
reference to Crown, Commonwealth or Governor-General. Instead
there was to be a President, to be elected for a term of seven years. This
President was to be head of state, signing all acts of the Dáil and
accrediting ambassadors. The leader of the Dáil was now given the Irish
title of Taoiseach, or Leader. There was also to be a new Senate, but with
strictly limited powers. Any law passed by the Dáil could be challenged
in the Dáil and could be declared unconstitutional; any changes to the
Constitution could only be made if approved by both houses and in a
general referendum. Freedom of Conscience and Freedom of Religious
Expression were guaranteed, subject to public order and morality. The
state could not endow any religion; religious discrimination was non-
constitutional. The family was recognised as the basic unit of society,
and there was no provision for divorce. The Constitution stated that it
was the duty of parents to have their children educated. And it allowed
for censorship of books, magazines and films.

The Constitution was supported by a majority in a fairly apathetic
referendum, and by a majority in the Dáil. It became law in December
1937. Britain said she would ignore it; that the status quo prevailed.
De Valera responded by saying that Britain could say what she liked,
but it did not. In January, there was a meeting between the two
countries to settle outstanding issues. De Valera came away with a full
shopping basket, lacking only the end of partition to be considered an
absolute triumph. The Economic War was ended, with a measure of
protection for Irish industries still being permitted while still allowing

British imports to be competitive. Land Annuities were settled for a down-payment of £10 million. The tariffs on Irish cattle were removed, and the British agreed to hand over her three naval bases. While this was happening, Hitler annexed Austria.

The Republic had been achieved in all but name. It was not a final settlement, for Northern Ireland was still territory over which Éire claimed a moral right of government. No rapprochement would—or could—be made between the constituent parts of Ireland while de Valera remained in politics. But Ireland had already moved far beyond what anyone would have believed possible before the turmoil of the Great War. Now another great war was on the horizon, and who knew what changes that might throw up?

NOTES

Chapter 1. To Arms (pp 1–32)
1. O'Casey (1945) p. 21
2. Johnstone (1992) p. 6
3. Taylor (2005) pp 19/20
4. Ibid p. 24

Chapter 2. Rallying Round the Flag (pp 33–47)
1. Catriona Pennell in Horne (ed.) (2008) p. 38
2. Ibid p. 39
3. Ibid p. 39
4. Ibid p. 40
5. Ibid p. 40
6. Ibid p. 45
7. Ibid pp 45–6
8. *Western Nationalist* 15/8/14; quoted in Horne (2008) p. 41
9. Catriona Pennell in Horne (2008) p. 41
10. Ibid pp 42–3
11. Ibid p. 41
12. Ibid pp 43–4
13. Ibid p. 44
14. Ibid p. 44
15. Orr (2006) p. 18
16. Ibid p. 19
17. Simkins (2007) p. 57
18. Philip Orr (2006) p. 19
19. Ibid pp 21–2
20. Orr (1987) pp 38–9
21. Ibid p. 40
22. Ibid pp 41–3
23. Ibid p. 45
24. Ibid pp 46–7
25. Ibid p. 48
26. Ibid p. 49
27. Mitchell (1991) pp 11–13
28. Orr (1987) pp 52–3
29. Gregory & Paseta (2002) p. 6

Chapter 3. The Deadly Peninsula (pp 48–81)

1. Keegan (1999) p. 256
2. Ibid p. 256
3. Ibid p. 257
4. Ibid p. 259
5. Carlyon (2002) p. 103
6. Ibid p. 126
7. Ibid p. 128
8. Cooper (2003) p. 48
9. Ibid p. 51
10. Johnstone (1992) p. 125
11. Cooper (2003) p. 48
12. Ibid p. 80
13. Johnstone (1992) p. 126
14. Orr (2006) p. 81
15. Johnstone (1992) p. 135
16. Ibid p. 138

Chapter 4. Dissenting Voices (pp 82–115)

1. Townshend (2006) p. 88
2. Ibid p. 116
3. Fitzpatrick (1998) pp 45–6
4. Ibid p. 47
5. McKenna (2009) pp 19–21
6. Fitzpatrick (1998) p. 48
7. Ibid p. 48
8. Foy & Barton (2004) p. 9
9. Fitzpatrick (1998) p. 53
10. Foy & Barton (1998) p. 13
11. Townshend (2006) p. 48
12. Foy & Barton (2004) p. 18
13. Townshend (2006) p. 92
14. Ibid p. 93
15. Ibid p. 96
16. Fitzpatrick (1998) p. 50
17. Ibid p. 55
18. Foy & Barton (2004) p. 16
19. Townshend (2006) p. 97
20. Ibid p. 98
21. Ibid p. 99
22. Ibid p. 77
23. Ibid p. 78

24. Ibid p. 85
25. Ibid p. 107
26. Ibid p. 108
27. Ibid p. 117
28. Ibid p. 118

Chapter 5. To the Western Front (pp 116–132)

1. Johnstone (1992) p. 220
2. Ibid p. 219
3. Falls (1996) p. 15
4. Ibid p. 17
5. Johnstone (1992) p. 188
6. Ibid p. 190
7. Denman (2008) p. 54
8. Johnstone (1992) p. 192
9. Denman (2008) p. 55
10. Johnstone (1992) p. 196
11. Denman (2008) p. 40
12. Ibid p. 43
13. Ibid p. 60
14. Ibid p. 61
15. Johnstone (1992) p. 198
16. Ibid p. 200
17. Denman (2008) p. 62
18. Johnston (1992) p. 204
19. Ibid p. 205
20. Denman (2008) pp 64–5
21. Johnstone (1992) p. 208
22. Ibid p. 208
23. Denman (2008) p. 69
24. Ibid p. 69
25. Ibid p. 69

Chapter 6. Dublin Sundered (pp 133–179)

1. Ryan (1957) pp 90–93
2. Ibid p. 94
3. Townshend (2006) p. 136
4. Ryan (1957) pp 94–5
5. Ibid p. 96
6. Townshend (2006) pp 138–9
7. O'Broin (1970) pp 82–4
8. Townshend (2006) p. 140

9. Foy & Barton (2004) p. 84
10. Ibid p. 87
11. Ibid p. 191
12. Ibid p. 171
13. Ibid p. 173
14. Ibid p. 139
15. Ibid p. 150
16. Ibid p. 150
17. O'Broin (1970) p. 91
18. Townshend (2006) p. 160
19. Foy & Barton (2004) p. 153
20. Ibid p. 154
21. Ryan (1957) p. 180
22. Townshend (2006) p. 174
23. Ibid p. 175
24. Foy & Barton p. 115
25. Ibid p. 92
26. Townshend (2006) p. 183
27. Ibid p. 184
28. Ibid p. 187
29. Foy & Barton (2004) p. 98
30. Ibid p. 155
31. Townshend (2006) p. 190
32. Foy & Barton p. 142
33. Ibid p. 174
34. Townshend (2006) p. 192
35. Ibid pp 193–4
36. Ryan (1957) pp 193–4
37. Townshend (2006) pp 204–5
38. Foy & Barton (2004) pp 289–290

Chapter 7. The Big Push (pp 180–197)

1. Orr (1987) p. 147
2. Ibid p. 148
3. Ibid p. 158
4. Ibid p. 161
5. Ibid p. 163
6. Ibid p. 164
7. Ibid p. 170
8. Ibid p. 174
9. Ibid p. 175
10. Ibid p. 178

11. Ibid p. 181
12. Ibid p. 185
13. Ibid p. 186
14. Ibid p. 191
15. Ibid p. 194
16. Ibid p. 197
17. Ibid p. 197

Chapter 9. Nationalist Ireland on the Western Front (pp 217–237)
1. Denman (2008) p. 71
2. Ibid p. 76
3. Ibid p. 75
4. Ibid p. 80
5. Ibid p. 81
6. Ibid p. 83
7. Ibid p. 85
8. Ibid p. 85
9. Ibid p. 95
10. Ibid p. 99
11. Kettle p. 34
12. Denman p. 105
13. Ibid p. 107
14. Ibid p. 110
15. Ibid p. 112
16. Ibid p. 115
17. Ibid p. 115
18. Ibid p. 116
19. Ibid p. 118
20. Ibid p. 119
21. Ibid p. 121
22. Ibid p. 121
23. Ibid p. 123

Chapter 10. Back Home (pp 238–252)
1. David Fitzpatrick in Horne (2008) p. 135
2. Ibid p. 136
3. Niamh Purseil in Horne (2008) p. 184
4. David Fitzpatrick in Horne (2008) p. 137
5. Niamh Purseil in Horne (2008) p. 185
6. Ibid p. 186
7. Ibid p. 187
8. David Fitzpatrick in Horne (2008) p. 139

9. Ibid p. 140
10. Catriona Clear in Horne (2008) p. 163
11. Ibid p. 164
12. Ibid p. 166
13. Ibid p. 167
14. Ibid p. 168
15. Niamh Purseil in Horne (2008) p. 191
16. Jane Leonard in Horne (2008) p. 213
17. Ibid p. 215
18. Ibid p. 216
19. Ibid p. 218

Chapter 11. The Resurrection of Sinn Féin (pp 253–277)
1. Lyons (1971) p. 380
2. Ibid p. 381
3. Ibid p. 381
4. Ibid p. 382
5. Ibid p. 383
6. Ibid p. 384
7. Ibid p. 385
8. Ibid p. 386
9. Ibid p. 388
10. Ibid p. 389
11. Ibid p. 389
12. Ibid p. 391
13. Ibid p. 391
14. Ibid p. 394
15. Ibid p. 395
16. Ibid p. 397
17. English (2007) p. 283
18. Ibid p. 284
19. Lyons (1971) p. 400
20. Breen p. 39
21. Lyons (1971) pp 402–3
22. Foster (1989) p. 497
23. Ibid p. 497
24. Ibid p. 494
25. Lyons (1971) p. 410
26. Ibid p. 411
27. Ibid p. 413
28. Ibid p. 414
29. Ibid p. 415

30. Foster (1989) p. 498
31. Ibid p. 498
32. Ibid p. 499
33. Lyons (1971) p. 417
34. Ibid p. 418
35. Foster (1989) p. 500
36. Lyons (1971) p. 420
37. Ibid p. 421

Chapter 12. A Northern Solution (pp 278–291)

1. Jackson (1999) p. 232
2. Beckett (1966) p. 449
3. Jackson (1999) p. 335
4. Ibid p. 336
5. Ibid p. 337
6. Ibid p. 340
7. Ibid p. 341
8. Ibid p. 343
9. Ibid p. 346

Chapter 13. A Southern Split (pp 292–308)

1. Gray (1966) p. 144
2. Lyons (1971) p. 428
3. Ibid p. 428
4. Ibid p. 427
5. Ibid p. 429
6. Jackson (1999) p. 259
7. Lyons (1971) p. 431
8. Jackson (1999) p. 259
9. Ibid p. 260
10. Ibid p. 261
11. Gray (1966) p. 145
12. Lyons (1971) p. 440
13. Ibid p. 428
14. Ibid p. 448
15. Gray (1966) p. 145
16. Lyons (1971) p. 450
17. Fitzpatrick (1998) p. 127
18. Gray (1966) p. 150
19. Lyons (1971) p. 425
20. Jackson (1999) p. 263
21. Lyons (1971) p. 425

22. Jackson (1999) p. 264
23. Lyons (1971) p. 449
24. Fitzpatrick (1998) p. 128
25. Ibid p. 129
26. Jackson (1999) p. 269
27. Ibid p. 269
28. Gray (1966) p. 145
29. Jackson (1999) p. 270
30. Gray (1966) p. 148
31. Ibid p. 146
32. Lyons (1971) p. 451
33. Gray (1966) p. 147
34. Lyons (1971) p. 452
35. Ibid p. 452
36. Ibid p. 452
37. Fitzpatrick p. 129
38. Lyons p. 456
39. Ibid p. 460
40. Fitzpatrick p. 130
41. Jackson (1999) p. 272
42. Fitzpatrick (1998) p. 136

Coda—Making it Work (pp 309–321)

1. Foster (1989) p. 525
2. Ibid p. 518
3. Ibid p. 519
4. Ibid p. 520
5. Ibid p. 521
6. Ibid p. 521
7. Ibid p. 522
8. Ibid pp 521–2
9. Ibid p. 523
10. Ibid p. 533
11. Ibid p. 534
12. Ibid p. 535
13. Ibid p. 536
14. Ibid p. 539
15. Ibid p. 538
16. Gray (1966) p. 101
17. Ibid p. 101
18. Ibid p. 106

BIBLIOGRAPHY

— Beckett, J. C.: *The Making of Modern Ireland, 1603–1923*; Faber & Faber, London, 1966
— Breen, Dan: *My Fight for Irish Freedom*; Talbot, Dublin, n.d.
— Carlyon, Les: *Gallipoli*; Doubleday, London 2002
— Cooper, Bryan: *The Tenth (Irish) Division at Gallipoli*; Irish Academic Press, Dublin, 2003
— Denman, Terence: *Ireland's Unknown Soldiers*; Irish Academic Press, Dublin, 2008
— Edwards, Owen Dudley: *Eamon de Valera*; GPC Books, Cardiff, 1987
— English, Richard: *Irish Freedom*; Pan Books, London, 2007
— Falls, Cyril: *The History of the 36th (Ulster) Division*; Constable, London, 1996
— Fitzpatrick, David: *The Two Irelands*; OPUS, 1998
— Foster, R. F.: *Modern Ireland, 1600–1972*; Penguin, London, 1989
— Foy, Michael and Barton, Brian: *The Easter Rising*; Sutton, Stroud, 2004
— Gray, Tony: *The Irish Answer*; Heinemann, London, 1966
— Gregory, Adrian & Paseta, Senia (eds): *Ireland and the Great War*; Manchester University Press, 2002
— Horne, John (ed.): *Our War*; Royal Irish Academy, Dublin, 2008
— Jackson, Alvin: *Ireland, 1798–1998*; Blackwell, Oxford, 1999
— Johnstone, Tom: *Orange, Green & Khaki*; Gill & Macmillan, Dublin, 1992
— Keegan, John: *The First World War*; Pimlico, London, 1999
— Lyons, F. S. L.: *Ireland since the Famine*; Weidenfield & Nicolson, London, 1971
— McKenna, John: *A Beleaguered Station*; Ulster Historical Foundation, Belfast, 2009
— Mitchell, Gardiner S.: *Three Cheers for The Derrys!*; Yes! Publications, Derry, 1991
— O'Broin, Leon: *Dublin Castle and the 1916 Rising*; Sidgwick & Jackson, London, 1970
— O'Casey, Sean: *Drums under the Windows*; Macmillan, London, 1945
— Orr, Philip: *The Road to the Somme*; Blackstaff, Belfast, 1987
— Orr, Philip: *Field of Bones*; Lilliput, Dublin, 2006
— Ryan, Desmond: *The Rising*; Golden Eagle Books, Dublin, 1957

— Simkins, Peter: *Kitchener's Army*; Pen & Sword Military, Barnsley, 2007
— Taylor, James W.: *The 2nd Royal Irish Rifles in the Great War*; Four Courts Press, Dublin, 2005
— Townshend, Charles: *Easter 1916*; Penguin Books, London, 2006

INDEX